A·N·N·U·A·L EDITI

The Family

03/04

Twenty-Ninth Edition

EDITOR

Kathleen R. Gilbert

Indiana University

Kathleen Gilbert is an associate professor in the Department of Applied Health Science at Indiana University. She recieved a B.A. in Sociology and an M.S. in Marriage and Family Relations from Northern Illinois University. Her Ph.D. in Family Studies is from Purdue University. Dr. Gilbert's primary areas of interest are loss and grief in a family context, trauma and the family, family process, and minority families. She has published several books and articles in these areas.

McGraw-Hill/Dushkin

530 Old Whitfield Street, Guilford, Connecticut 06437

Visit us on the Internet
http://www.dushkin.com

Credits

1. **Varied Perspectives on the Family**
   Unit photo—© 2003 by Cleo Freelance Photography.
2. **Exploring and Establishing Relationships**
   Unit photo—Courtesy of Marcuss Oslander.
3. **Finding a Balance: Maintaining Relationships**
   Unit photo—© 2003 by PhotoDisc, Inc.
4. **Crises—Challenges and Opportunities**
   Unit photo—© 2003 by Cleo Freelance Photography.
5. **Families, Now and Into the Future**
   Unit photo—© 2003 by PhotoDisc, Inc.

Copyright

Cataloging in Publication Data
Main entry under title: Annual Editions: The Family. 2003/2004.
1. The Family—United States—Periodicals. I. Gilbert, Kathleen, *comp.* II. Title: The Family.
ISBN 0-07-283865-5   658'.05   ISSN 0272-7897

Twenty-Ninth Edition

Cover image © 2003 PhotoDisc, Inc.
Printed in the United States of America   1234567890BAHBAH543   Printed on Recycled Paper

To the Reader

In publishing ANNUAL EDITIONS we recognize the enormous role played by the magazines, newspapers, and journals of the public press in providing current, first-rate educational information in a broad spectrum of interest areas. Many of these articles are appropriate for students, researchers, and professionals seeking accurate, current material to help bridge the gap between principles and theories and the real world. These articles, however, become more useful for study when those of lasting value are carefully collected, organized, indexed, and reproduced in a low-cost format, which provides easy and permanent access when the material is needed. That is the role played by ANNUAL EDITIONS.

The purpose of *Annual Editions: The Family 03/04* is to bring to the reader the latest thoughts and trends in our understanding of the family, to identify current concerns as well as problems and possible solutions, and to present alternative views of family process. The intent of this anthology is to explore intimate relationships as they are played out in marriage and family and, in doing this, to reflect the family's evolving function and importance.

The articles in this volume are taken from professional publications, semiprofessional journals, and popular lay publications aimed at both special populations and a general readership. The selections are carefully reviewed for their currency and accuracy. In some cases, contrasting viewpoints are presented. In others, articles are paired in such a way as to personalize the more impersonal scholarly information. In the current edition, a number of new articles have been added to reflect reviewers' comments. As the reader, you will note the tremendous range in tone and focus of these articles, from first-person accounts to reports of scientific discoveries as well as philosophical and theoretical writings. Some are more practical and applications-oriented, while others are more conceptual and research-oriented.

This anthology is organized to cover many of the important aspects of marriage and family. The first unit looks at varied perspectives on the family. The second unit examines the beginning steps of relationship building as individuals go through the process of exploring and establishing connections. In the third unit, means of finding and maintaining a relationship balance are examined. Unit 4 is concerned with crises and ways in which these can act as challenges and opportunities for families and their members. Finally, unit 5 takes an affirming tone as it looks at families now and into the future.

Instructors can use *Annual Editions: The Family 03/04* as a primary text for lower-level, introductory marriage and family classes, particularly when they tie the content of the readings to basic information on marriage and family. This book can also be used as a supplement to update or emphasize certain aspects of standard marriage and family textbooks. Because of the provocative nature of many of the essays in this anthology, it works well as a basis for class discussion about various aspects of marriage and family relationships.

This edition of *Annual Editions: The Family* contains a *topic guide* to the articles and *World Wide Web* sites that can be used to further explore topics addressed in the articles.

I would like to thank everyone involved in the development of this volume. My appreciation goes to those who sent in *article rating forms* and comments on the previous edition as well as those who suggested articles to consider for inclusion in this edition. To all of the students in my Marriage and Family Interaction class who have contributed critiques of articles, I would like to say thanks.

Anyone interested in providing input for future editions of *Annual Editions: The Family* should complete and return the postage-paid *article rating form* at the end of this book. Your suggestions are much appreciated and contribute to the continuing quality of this anthology.

Kathleen R. Gilbert
Editor

Contents

UNIT 1
Varied Perspectives on the Family

Four articles explore different views on where our images of family come from and how they are influenced by our life experiences as well as societal and cultural constraints.

UNIT 2
Exploring and Establishing Relationships

Eleven articles address factors that influence the formation of close relationships, both romantic and generative.

The concepts in bold italics are developed in the article. For further expansion, please refer to the Topic Guide and the Index.

The concepts in bold italics are developed in the article. For further expansion, please refer to the Topic Guide and the Index.

UNIT 3
Finding a Balance: Maintaining Relationships

Twelve articles consider the complex issues of relating to others. From marriage to parent/child interactions to sibling attachments, maintaining relationships requires thought and commitment from members.

The concepts in bold italics are developed in the article. For further expansion, please refer to the Topic Guide and the Index.

UNIT 4
Crises—Challenges and Opportunities

A wide variety of crises, normative and catastrophic, are detailed in 14 articles. From family violence, stress, and chaos to the intimate crises of infidelity, divorce, caregiving, and death, these articles provide accounts of devastation and hope.

The concepts in bold italics are developed in the article. For further expansion, please refer to the Topic Guide and the Index.

The concepts in bold italics are developed in the article. For further expansion, please refer to the Topic Guide and the Index.

UNIT 5
Families, Now and Into the Future

Seven articles examine ways of establishing and/or maintaining health and healthy relationships within families.

The concepts in bold italics are developed in the article. For further expansion, please refer to the Topic Guide and the Index.

Topic Guide

This topic guide suggests how the selections in this book relate to the subjects covered in your course. You may want to use the topics listed on these pages to search the Web more easily.

On the following pages a number of Web sites have been gathered specifically for this book. They are arranged to reflect the units of this *Annual Edition.* You can link to these sites by going to the DUSHKIN ONLINE support site at *http://www.dushkin.com/online/.*

ALL THE ARTICLES THAT RELATE TO EACH TOPIC ARE LISTED BELOW THE BOLD-FACED TERM.

Abuse
19. New Evidence for the Benefits of Never Spanking

Adoption
25. Adoption by Lesbian Couples

Aging
11. Sex for Grown-Ups
12. Making Time for a Baby
26. Why We Break Up With Our Siblings
29. Sex & Marriage
39. Elder Care: Making the Right Choice
45. What's Ahead for Families: Five Major Forces of Change

Attachment
18. Welcome to the Love Lab
20. Family Matters
22. Father Nature: The Making of a Modern Dad
26. Why We Break Up With Our Siblings
48. Reconnect With Your Family

Beliefs
1. The American Family
2. The Myth of the "Normal" Family
15. Our Babies, Ourselves
43. Generation 9-11
44. Getting the Word
46. Happiness Explained
47. Examining Family Rituals
48. Reconnect With Your Family

Bereavement
40. Still Birth
41. After a Loss, Kids Need to Mourn—and Be Reassured

Biology
5. Sex Differences in the Brain
8. Can Men and Women Be Friends?
13. Too Posh to Push?
14. Shaped by Life in the Womb
22. Father Nature: The Making of a Modern Dad

Child care
15. Our Babies, Ourselves
21. Who's Raising Baby?
22. Father Nature: The Making of a Modern Dad
24. Unmarried, With Children
32. What Kids (Really) Need
41. After a Loss, Kids Need to Mourn—and Be Reassured

Children
3. Weighing the Price of 'Perfect' in Family Life
12. Making Time for a Baby
15. Our Babies, Ourselves
19. New Evidence for the Benefits of Never Spanking
21. Who's Raising Baby?
22. Father Nature: The Making of a Modern Dad
23. What About Black Fathers?

Children and childhood
24. Unmarried, With Children
25. Adoption by Lesbian Couples
32. What Kids (Really) Need
41. After a Loss, Kids Need to Mourn—and Be Reassured

1. The American Family
3. Weighing the Price of 'Perfect' in Family Life
17. No Wedding? No Ring? No Problem
21. Who's Raising Baby?
22. Father Nature: The Making of a Modern Dad
23. What About Black Fathers?

Communication
7. The Feminization of American Culture
8. Can Men and Women Be Friends?
18. Welcome to the Love Lab
26. Why We Break Up With Our Siblings
29. Sex & Marriage
44. Getting the Word

Counseling
9. What's Your Love Story?
10. Love Is Not All You Need
18. Welcome to the Love Lab

Culture
1. The American Family
4. American Families Are Drifting Apart
6. The New Woman: Daring to Be Less Than Perfect
7. The Feminization of American Culture
15. Our Babies, Ourselves
16. The Science of a Good Marriage
20. Family Matters
23. What About Black Fathers?
31. The Politics of Fatigue: The Gender War Has Been Replaced by the Exhaustion of Trying to Do It All
43. Generation 9-11

Dating
8. Can Men and Women Be Friends?
9. What's Your Love Story?

Divorce
16. The Science of a Good Marriage
35. Is Divorce Too Easy?
36. The Happy Divorce: How to Break Up and Make Up
37. Divorced? Don't Even Think of Remarrying Until You Read This
45. What's Ahead for Families: Five Major Forces of Change

Emotions
22. Father Nature: The Making of a Modern Dad
36. The Happy Divorce: How to Break Up and Make Up

Family
21. Who's Raising Baby?
43. Generation 9-11

World Wide Web Sites

The following World Wide Web sites have been carefully researched and selected to support the articles found in this reader. The easiest way to access these selected sites is to go to our DUSHKIN ONLINE support site at *http://www.dushkin.com/online/*.

AE: The Family 03/04

The following sites were available at the time of publication. Visit our Web site—we update DUSHKIN ONLINE regularly to reflect any changes.

General Sources

American Psychological Association
http://www.apa.org/psychnet/
Explore the APA's "Resources for the Public" site to find links to an abundance of articles and other resources related to interpersonal relationships throughout the life span.

Encyclopedia Britannica
http://www.britannica.com
This huge "Britannica Internet Guide" leads to a cornucopia of informational sites and reference sources on such topics as family structure and other social issues.

Penn Library: Sociology
http://www.library.upenn.edu/resources/subject/social/sociology/sociology.html
This site provides a number of indexes of culture and ethnic studies, population and demographics, and statistical sources that are of value in studies of marriage and the family.

Social Science Information Gateway
http://sosig.esrc.bris.ac.uk/
This is an online catalog of Internet resources relevant to social science education and research. Sites are selected and described by a librarian or subject specialist.

UNIT 1: Varied Perspectives on the Family

American Studies Web
http://www.georgetown.edu/crossroads/asw/
This eclectic site provides links to a wealth of resources on the Internet related to American studies, from gender to race and ethnicity to demography and population studies.

Anthropology Resources Page
http://www.usd.edu/anth/
Many cultural topics can be accessed from this site from the University of South Dakota. Click on the links to find comparisons of values and lifestyles among the world's peoples.

Human Rights Report—India
http://www.usis.usemb.se/human/human1998/india.html
Read this U.S. Department of State 1998 report on India's human-rights practices for an understanding into the issues that affect women's mental and physical health and well-being in different parts of the world.

Women's Studies Resources
http://www.inform.umd.edu/EdRes/Topic/WomensStudies/
This site provides a wealth of resources related to women and their concerns. You can find links to such topics as body image, comfort (or discomfort) with sexuality, personal relationships, pornography, and more.

UNIT 2: Exploring and Establishing

Relationships

Ask NOAH About Pregnancy: Fertility & Infertility
http://www.noah-health.org/english/pregnancy/fertility.html
NOAH (New York Online Access to Health) seeks to provide relevant, timely, and unbiased health information for consumers. At this site, the organization presents extensive links to a variety of resources about infertility treatments and issues.

Bonobo Sex and Society
http://songweaver.com/info/bonobos.html
This site, accessed through Carnegie Mellon University, contains an article explaining how a primate's behavior challenges traditional assumptions about male supremacy in human evolution. Guaranteed to generate spirited debate.

Go Ask Alice!
http://www.goaskalice.columbia.edu/index.html
This interactive site of the Columbia University Health Services provides discussion and insight into a number of personal issues of interest to college-age people—and those younger and older.

The Kinsey Institute for Research in Sex, Gender, and Reproduction
http://www.indiana.edu/~kinsey/
The purpose of this Kinsey Institutes Web site is to support interdisciplinary research in the study of human sexuality.

Mysteries of Odor in Human Sexuality
http://www.pheromones.com
This is a commercial site with the goal of selling a book by James Kohl. Look here to find topics of interest to nonscientists about pheromones. Check out the diagram of "Mammalian Olfactory-Genetic-Neuronal-Hormonal-Behavioral Reciprocity and Human Sexuality" for a sense of the myriad biological influences that play a part in sexual behavior.

Planned Parenthood
http://www.plannedparenthood.org
Visit this well-known organization's home page for links to information on the various kinds of contraceptives (including outercourse and abstinence) and to discussions of other topics related to sexual and reproductive health.

The Society for the Scientific Study of Sexuality
http://www.sexscience.org
The Society for the Scientific Study of Sexuality is an international organization dedicated to the advancement of knowledge about sexuality.

Sympatico: HealthyWay: Health Links
http://www1.sympatico.ca/Contents/health/
This Canadian site meant for consumers will lead you to many links related to sexual orientation. It also addresses aspects of human sexuality over the life span as well as reproductive health.

UNIT 3: Finding a Balance: Maintaining

www.dushkin.com/online/

Relationships

Child Welfare League of America
http://www.cwla.org

The CWLA is the largest U.S. organization devoted entirely to the well-being of vulnerable children and their families. This site provides links to information about such issues as teaching morality and values.

Coalition for Marriage, Family, and Couples Education
http://www.smartmarriages.com

CMFCE is dedicated to bringing information about and directories of skill-based marriage education courses to the public. It hopes to lower the rate of family breakdown through couple-empowering preventive education.

The National Academy for Child Development
http://www.nacd.org

The NACD, dedicated to helping children and adults reach their full potential, presents links to various programs, research, and resources into a variety of family topics.

National Council on Family Relations
http://www.ncfr.com

This NCFR home page leads to valuable links to articles, research, and other resources on issues in family relations, such as stepfamilies, couples, and children of divorce.

Positive Parenting
http://www.positiveparenting.com

Positive Parenting is an organization dedicated to providing resources and information to make parenting rewarding, effective, and fun.

SocioSite
http://www.pscw.uva.nl/sociosite/TOPICS/Women.html

Open this site to gain insights into a number of issues that affect family relationships. It provides wide-ranging issues of women and men, of family and children, and more.

UNIT 4: Crises—Challenges and Opportunities

Alzheimer's Association
http://www.alz.org

The Alzheimer's Association, dedicated to the prevention, cure, and treatment of Alzheimer's and related disorders, provides support to afflicted patients and their families.

American Association of Retired Persons
http://www.aarp.org

The AARP, a major advocacy group for older people, includes among its many resources suggested readings and Internet links to organizations that deal with social issues that may affect people and their families as they age.

Caregiver's Handbook
http://www.acsu.buffalo.edu/~drstall/hndbk0.html

This site is an online handbook for caregivers. Topics include medical aspects and liabilities of caregiving.

Children & Divorce
http://www.hec.ohio-state.edu/famlife/divorce/

Open this site to find links to articles and discussions of divorce and its effects on the family. Many bibliographical references are provided by the Ohio State University Department of Human Development & Family Science.

Parenting.com
http://www.parenting.com/parenting/

With numerous articles and advice columns, this Web site offers a wealth of resources for parents.

National Crime Prevention Council
http://www.ncpc.org

NCPC's mission is to enable people to create safer and more caring communities by addressing the causes of crime and violence and reducing the opportunities for crime to occur.

Widow Net
http://www.fortnet.org/WidowNet/

Widow Net is an information and self-help resource for and by widows and widowers. The information is helpful to people of all ages, religious backgrounds, and sexual orientation who have experienced a loss.

UNIT 5: Families, Now and Into the Future

National Institute on Aging
http://www.nih.gov/nia/

The NIA presents this home page that will take you to a variety of resources on health and lifestyle issues that are of interest to people as they grow older.

The North-South Institute
http://www.nsi-ins.ca/ensi/about_nsi/research.html

Searching this site of the North-South Institute—which works to strengthen international development cooperation and enhance gender and social equity—will lead to a variety of issues related to the family and social transitions.

We highly recommend that you review our Web site for expanded information and our other product lines. We are continually updating and adding links to our Web site in order to offer you the most usable and useful information that will support and expand the value of your Annual Editions. You can reach us at: *http://www.dushkin.com/annualeditions/*.

UNIT 1

Varied Perspectives on the Family

Unit Selections

1. **The American Family**, Stephanie Coontz
2. **The Myth of the "Normal" Family**, Louise B. Silverstein and Carl F. Auerbach
3. **Weighing the Price of 'Perfect' in Family Life**, Marilyn Gardner
4. **American Families Are Drifting Apart**, Barbara LeBey

Key Points to Consider

- Why, in the face of strong evidence that the "good old days" weren't all that good, do we cling to the view that life in the past was superior to the present? What are some of the common beliefs about the past in contrast with the present? What is the truth about the quality of life in earlier times?

- What are your expectations for the family as an institution? How do personally held views of family influence policy? What might be the effects of this?

- What are your thoughts on the increasing pressures for parents to push their children into many activities? What is the effect of these pressures on family life? What can be done to find the best balance in children's (and families') lives?

 **Links: www.dushkin.com/online/**
These sites are annotated in the World Wide Web pages.

American Studies Web
http://www.georgetown.edu/crossroads/asw/
Anthropology Resources Page
http://www.usd.edu/anth/
Human Rights Report—India
http://www.usis.usemb.se/human/human1998/india.html
Women's Studies Resources
http://www.inform.umd.edu/EdRes/Topic/WomensStudies/

Our image of what family is and what it should be is a powerful combination of personal experience, family forms we encounter or observe, and attitudes we hold. Once formed, this image informs decision making and interpersonal interaction throughout our lives. It has far-reaching impacts—on an intimate level, it influences individual and family development as well as relationships both inside and outside the family. On a broader level, it affects legislation as well as social policy and programming.

In many ways, this image can be positive. It can act to clarify our thinking and facilitate interaction with like-minded individuals. It can also be negative, because it can narrow our thinking and limit our ability to see that other ways of carrying out the functions of family have value. Their very differentness can make them seem "bad." In this case, interaction with others can be impeded because of contrasting views.

This unit is intended to meet several goals with regard to perspectives on the family: (1) to sensitize the reader to sources of beliefs about the "shoulds" of the family—what the family should be and the ways in which family roles should be carried out, (2) to show how different views of the family can influence attitudes toward community responsibility and family policy, and (3) to show how views that dominate one's culture can influence awareness of ways of structuring family life.

In the first reading, "The American Family," Stephanie Coontz takes a historical perspective to examine the contrast between common beliefs about the past and the reality of that time. "The Myth of the 'Normal' Family," by Louise Silverstein and Carl Auerbach, explores the myths surrounding a variety of family forms and the reality of family life within those family forms. "Weighing the Price of 'Perfect' in Family Life," talks about the pressure that parents and children face to have children participate in activities, often at the expense of family time. "American Families Are Drifting Apart," examines the decline of the American family.

THE AMERICAN FAMILY

New research about an old institution challenges the conventional wisdom that the family today is worse off than in the past. Essay by Stephanie Coontz

As the century comes to an end, many observers fear for the future of America's families. Our divorce rate is the highest in the world, and the percentage of unmarried women is significantly higher than in 1960. Educated women are having fewer babies, while immigrant children flood the schools, demanding to be taught in their native language. Harvard University reports that only 4 percent of its applicants can write a proper sentence.

Things were worse at the turn of the last century than they are today. Most workers labored 10 hours a day, six days a week, leaving little time for family life.

There's an epidemic of sexually transmitted diseases among men. Many streets in urban neighborhoods are littered with cocaine vials. Youths call heroin "happy dust." Even in small towns, people have easy access to addictive drugs, and drug abuse by middle-class wives is skyrocketing. Police see 16-year-old killers, 12-year-old prostitutes, and gang members as young as 11.

America at the end of the 1990s? No, America at the end of the 1890s.

The litany of complaints may sound familiar, but the truth is that many things were worse at the start of this century than they are today. Then, thousands of children worked full-time in mines, mills and sweatshops. Most

workers labored 10 hours a day, often six days a week, which left them little time or energy for family life. Race riots were more frequent and more deadly than those experienced by recent generations. Women couldn't vote, and their wages were so low that many turned to prostitution.

DAHLSTROM COLLECTION/TIME INC.

c. 1890 A couple and their six children sit for a family portrait. With smaller families today, mothers spend twice as much time with each kid.

In 1900 a white child had one chance in three of losing a brother or sister before age 15, and a black child had a fifty-fifty chance of seeing a sibling die. Children's-aid groups reported widespread abuse and neglect by parents. Men who deserted or divorced their wives rarely paid child support. And only 6 percent of the children graduated from high school, compared with 88 percent today.

LEWIS HINE/CULVER PICTURES

1915 An Italian immigrant family gathers around the dinner table in an apartment on the East Side of New York City. Today, most families still eat together—but often out.

Why do so many people think American families are facing worse problems now than in the past? Partly it's because we compare the complex and diverse families of the 1990s with the seemingly more standard-issue ones of the 1950s, a unique decade when every long-term trend of the 20th century was temporarily reversed. In the 1950s, for the first time in 100 years, the divorce rate fell while marriage and fertility rates soared, crating a boom in nuclear-family living. The percentage of foreign-born individuals in the country decreased. And the debates over social and cultural issues that had divided Americans for 150 years were silenced, suggesting a national consensus on family values and norms.

Some nostalgia for the 1950s is understandable: Life looked pretty good in comparison with the hardship of the Great Depression and World War II. The GI Bill gave a generation of young fathers a college education and a subsidized mortgage on a new house. For the first time, a majority of men could support a family and buy a home without pooling their earnings with those of other family members. Many Americans built a stable family life on these foundations.

But much nostalgia for the 1950s is a result of selective amnesia—the same process that makes childhood memories of summer vacations grow sunnier with each passing year. The superficial sameness of 1950s family life was achieved through censorship, coercion and discrimination. People with unconventional beliefs faced governmental investigation and arbitrary firings. African Americans and Mexican Americans were prevented from voting in some states by literacy tests that were not ad-

ministered to whites. Individuals who didn't follow the rigid gender and sexual rules of the day were ostracized.

Leave It to Beaver did not reflect the real-life experience of most American families. While many moved into the middle class during the 1950s, poverty remained more widespread than in the worst of our last three recessions. More children went hungry, and poverty rates for the elderly were more than twice as high as today's.

Even in the white middle class, not every woman was as serenely happy with her lot as June Cleaver was on TV. Housewives of the 1950s may have been less rushed than today's working mothers, but they were more likely to suffer anxiety and depression. In many states, women couldn't serve on juries or get loans or credit cards in their own names.

And not every kid was as wholesome as Beaver Cleaver, whose mischievous antics could be handled by Dad at the dinner table. In 1955 alone, Congress discussed 200 bills aimed at curbing juvenile delinquency. Three years later, LIFE reported that urban teachers were being terrorized by their students. The drugs that were so freely available in 1900 had been outlawed, but many children grew up in families ravaged by alcohol and barbiturate abuse.

Rates of unwed childbearing tripled between 1940 and 1958, but most Americans didn't notice because unwed mothers generally left town, gave their babies up for adoption and returned home as if nothing had happened. Troubled youths were encouraged to drop out of high school. Mentally handicapped children were warehoused in institutions like the Home for Idiotic and Imbecilic Children in Kansas, where a woman whose sister had lived there for most of the 1950s once took me. Wives routinely told pollsters that being disparaged or ignored by their husbands was a normal part of a happier than-average marriage.

Many of our worries today reflect how much better we want to be, not how much better we used to be.

Denial extended to other areas of life as well. In the early 1900s, doctors refused to believe that the cases of gonorrhea and syphilis they saw in young girls could have been caused by sexual abuse. Instead, they reasoned, girls could get these diseases from toilet seats, a myth that terrified generations of mothers and daughters. In the 1950s, psychiatrists dismissed incest reports as Oedipal fantasies on the part of children.

Spousal rape was legal throughout the period and wife beating was not taken seriously by authorities. Much of what we now label child abuse was accepted as a normal part of parental discipline. Physicians saw no reason to question parents who claimed that their child's broken bones had been caused by a fall from a tree.

MARGARET BOURKE-WHITE

1937: The Hahn family sits in the living room of a working-class Muncie home, which rents for $10 a month. Class distinctions have eroded over 60 years.

American Mirror

Muncie, Ind. (pop. 67,476), calls itself America's Hometown. But to generations of sociologists it is better known as America's Middletown—the most studied place in the 20th century American landscape. "Muncie has nothing extraordinary about it," says University of Virginia professor Theodore Caplow, which is why, for the past 75 years, researchers have gone there to observe the typical American family. Muncie's averageness first drew sociologists Robert and Helen Lynd in 1924. They returned in 1935 (their follow-up study was featured in a LIFE photo essay by Margaret Bourke-White). And in 1976, armed with the Lynds' original questionnaires, Caplow launched yet another survey of the town's citizens.

Caplow discovered that family life in Muncie was much healthier in the 1970s than in the 1920s. No only were husbands and wives communicating more, but unlike married couples in the 1920s, they were also shopping, eating out, exercising and going to movies and concerts together. More than 90 percent of Muncie's couples characterized their marriages as "happy" or "very happy." In 1929 the Lynds had described partnerships of a drearier kind, "marked by sober accommodation of each partner to his share in the joint undertaking of children, paying off the mortgage and generally 'getting on.'"

Caplow's five-year study, which inspired a six-part PBS series, found that even though more moms were working outside the home, two thirds of them spent at least two hours a day with their children; in 1924 fewer than half did. In 1924 most children expected their mothers to be good cooks and housekeepers, and wanted their fathers to spend time with them and respect their opinions. Fifty years later, expectations of fathers were unchanged, but children wanted the same—time and respect—from their mothers.

This year, Caplow went back to survey the town again. The results (and another TV documentary) won't be released until December 2000.

—Sora Song

There are plenty of stresses in modern family life, but one reason they seem worse is that we no longer sweep them under the rug. Another is that we have higher expectations of parenting and marriage. That's a good thing. We're right to be concerned about inattentive parents, conflicted marriages, antisocial values, teen violence and child abuse. But we need to realize that many of our worries reflect how much better we *want* to be, not how much better we *used* to be.

Fathers in intact families are spending more time with their children than at any other point in the past 100 years. Although the number of hours the average woman spends at home with her children has declined since the early 1900s, there has been a decrease in the number of children per family and an increase in individual attention to each child. As a result, mothers today, including working moms, spend almost twice as much time with each child as mothers did in the 1920s. People who raised children in the 1940s and 1950s typically report that their own adult children and grandchildren communicate far better with their kids and spend more time helping with homework than they did—even as they complain that other parents today are doing a worse job than in the past.

Despite the rise in youth violence from the 1960s to the early 1990s, America's children are also safer now than they've ever been. An infant was four times more likely to die in the 1950s than today. A parent then was three times more likely than a modern one to preside at the funeral of a child under the age of 15, and 27 percent more likely to lose an older teen to death.

If we look back over the last millennium, we can see that families have always been diverse and in flux. In each period, families have solved one set of problems only to face a new array of challenges. What works for a family in one economic and cultural setting doesn't work for a family in another. What's helpful at one stage of a family's life may be destructive at the next stage. If there is one lesson to be drawn from the last millennium of family history, it's that families are always having to play catch-up with a changing world.

Take the issue of working mothers. Families in which mothers spend as much time earning a living as they do raising children are nothing new. They were the norm throughout most of the last two millennia. In the 19th century, married women in the United States began a withdrawal from the workforce, but for most families this was made possible only by sending their children out to work instead. When child labor was abolished, married women began reentering the workforce in ever large numbers.

For a few decades, the decline in child labor was greater than the growth of women's employment. The result was an aberration: the male-breadwinner family. In the 1920s, for the first time, a bare majority of American children grew up in families where the husband provided all the income, the wife stayed home full-time, and they and their siblings went to school instead of work. During the 1950s, almost two thirds of children grew up in such increase from 1900 to 1950. Today, 40 percent of all marriages will end in divorce before a couple's 40th anniversary. Yet despite this high divorce rate, expanded life expectancies mean that more couples are reaching that anniversary than ever before.

Families and individuals in contemporary America have more life choices than in the past. That makes it easier for some to consider dangerous or unpopular options. But it also makes success easier for many families that never would have had a chance before—interracial, gay or lesbian, and single-mother families, for example. And it expands horizons for most families.

Women's new options are good not just for themselves but for their children. While some people say that women who choose to work are selfish, it turns out that maternal self-sacrifice is not good for children. Kids do better when their mothers are happy with their lives, whether their satisfaction comes from being a full-time homemaker or from having a job.

Largely because of women's new roles at work, men are doing more at home. Although most men still do less housework than their wives, the gap has been halved since the 1960s. Today, 49 percent of couples say they share childcare equally, compared with 25 percent of 1985.

Men's greater involvement at home is good for their relationships with their parents, and also good for their children. Hands-on fathers make better parents than men who let their wives do all the nurturing and childcare: They raise sons who are more expressive and daughters who are more likely to do well in school, especially in math and science.

The biggest problem is not that our families have changed too much but that our institutions have changed too little.

In 1900, life expectancy was 47 years, and only 4 percent of the population was 65 or older. Today, life expectancy is 76 years, and by 2025, about 20 percent of Americans will be 65 or older. For the first time, a generation of adults must plan for the needs of both their parents and their children. Most Americans are responding with remarkable grace. One in four households gives the equivalent of a full day a week or more in unpaid care to an aging relative, and more than half say they expect to do so in the next 10 years. Older people are less likely to be impoverished or incapacitated by illness than in the past, and they have more opportunity to develop a relationship with their grandchildren.

Even some of the choices that worry us the most are turning out to be manageable. Divorce rates are likely to remain high, but more non-custodial parents are staying

MARK KAUFFMAN

1955 A family poses in Seattle. Husbands today are doing more housework.

families, an all-time high. Yet that same decade saw an acceleration of workforce participation by wives and mothers that soon made the dual-earner family the norm, a trend not likely to be reversed in the next century.

What's new is not that women make half their families' living, but that for the first time they have substantial control over their own income, along with the social freedom to remain single or to leave an unsatisfactory marriage. Also new is the declining proportion of their lives that people devote to rearing children, both because they have fewer kids and because they are living longer. Until about 1940, the typical marriage was broken by the death of one partner within a few years after the last child left home. Today, couples can look forward to spending more than two decades together after the children leave.

The growing length of time partners spend with only each other for company has made many individuals less willing to put up with an unhappy marriage, while women's economic independence makes it less essential for them to do so. It is no wonder that divorce has risen steadily since 1900. Disregarding a spurt in 1946, a dip in the 1950s and another peak around 1980, the divorce rate is just where you'd expect to find it, based on the rate of in touch with their children. Child-support receipts are up. And a lower proportion of kids from divorced families are exhibiting problems than in earlier decades. Stepfamilies are learning to maximize children's access to supportive adults rather than cutting them off from one side of the family.

Out-of-wedlock births are also high, however, and this will probably continue because the age of first marriage for women has risen to an all-time high of 25, almost five years above what it was in the 1950s. Women who marry at an older age are less likely to divorce, but they have more years when they are at risk—or at choice—for a nonmarital birth.

Nevertheless, births to teenagers have fallen from 50 percent of all nonmarital births in the late 1970s to just 30 percent today. A growing proportion of women who have a nonmarital birth are in their twenties and thirties and usually have more economic and educational resources than unwed mothers of the past. While two involved parents are generally better than one, a mother's personal maturity, along with her educational and economic status, is a better predictor of how well her child will turn out than her marital status. We should no longer assume that children raised by single parents face debilitating disadvantages.

As we begin to understand the range of sizes, shapes and colors that today's families come in, we find that the differences *within* family types are more important than the differences *between* them. No particular family form guarantees success, and no particular form is doomed to fail. How a family functions on the inside is more important than how it looks from the outside.

The biggest problem facing most families as this century draws to a close is not that our families have changed too much but that our institutions have changed too little. America's work policies are 50 years out of date, designed for a time when most moms weren't in the workforce and most dads didn't understand the joys of being involved in childcare. Our school schedules are 150 years out of date, designed for a time when kids needed to be home to help with the milking and haying. And many political leaders feel they have to decide whether to help parents stay home longer with their kids or invest in better childcare, preschool and afterschool programs, when most industrialized nations have long since learned it's possible to do both.

So America's social institutions have some Y2K bugs to iron out. But for the most part, our families are ready for the next millennium.

LIFE IN AMERICA

The Myth of the
"Normal" Family

"Rather than trying to find the 'one right way,' parents need to be flexible and creative in finding strategies that work for their particular family."

BY LOUISE B. SILVERSTEIN AND CARL F. AUERBACH

OUR CULTURAL MYTHOLOGY about parenting is that there is "one right way" to raise children. Most people believe that the best way to raise children is with both a stay-at-home mother (at least while the kids are young) and a breadwinner father in a long-term marriage that lasts "till death do us part." We have been told that any family that is different from this norm shortchanges youngsters.

This point of view has become known as the family values perspective. However, the majority of families do not fit this model. Most mothers have to, or want to, be part of the paid workforce; about half of all marriages will end in divorce; and many more people than ever before will choose to have children without getting married.

New scientific information has emerged in the last 10 years that contradicts the idea that there is one right way. We now know that children can thrive in many different family forms. The scientific evidence shows conclusively that what is important for them is the quality of the relationships they have with the people who care for them, rather than the number, sex, or marital status of their caregivers.

Nevertheless, perfectly normal families that do not fit into the traditional mold feel abnormal and berate themselves for providing their offspring with an inferior version of family life. For these parents, trying to conform to the Myth of the Normal Family often generates guilt, anxiety, power struggles, and other stress.

The Myth of Father Absence maintains that most social problems—like juvenile violence, crime, and teen pregnancy—are caused by the lack of a father. If every child had a father, these social problems would disappear, argue the advocates of this viewpoint.

Susan and John, a middle-class African-American couple, had two boys aged six and 10 when Susan came into therapy asking for help to work out her marital problems. John attended one or two sessions, but then refused to come to therapy. John was a devoted father in terms of spending time with the boys. The marital problems were caused because he was of-

ten out of work. He had difficulty getting along with bosses and had recently begun to smoke marijuana.

John was a bright man, but always had difficulty in school. He had graduated from high school with a great deal of tutoring and had gone to junior college briefly. From his description of his struggles in school, he probably had an undiagnosed learning disability. Because these problems had not been understood, John had not gotten the help he needed, and he felt stupid. This sense of inadequacy about his intelligence was probably at the root of his difficulty in getting along with superiors and his retreat into drugs.

Susan, in contrast, had always done well in school. She had become a licensed practical nurse and was going to night school to become a registered nurse. She often worked additional hours on the weekends in a nursing home so that the boys could attend parochial school. She was exhausted from this difficult work schedule and the responsibility for all of the cooking and housework. Her stress was exacerbated by the fact that, in the last year, she was frequently the only breadwinner, as John had been fired from several jobs.

Over the next eight years, John's drug problems became much worse. He began using and selling cocaine. When he was using, he often became physically violent with Susan. Although he continued to share responsibility for child care, John was mostly out of work.

Susan stated that she wanted to leave John, but just could not bring herself to do it. She knew that their fights were frightening to the children and that seeing their father in bad shape was not helpful to them. Still, she could not convince herself to separate from her husband. Despite the fact that she was functioning as both caregiver and breadwinner, she believed that her boys needed their father. She worried that leaving John would mean that she was the stereotypical "black matriarch" who emasculated her man. Most important, she feared that, if John left, the boys would become involved with gangs, drop out of school, and generally get into trouble.

Did it make sense for Susan to stay in a marriage that was not working for her, for John, or for her children? If she did decide to raise the boys on her own, would they really be more likely to get into trouble than if she stayed in a marriage with a husband who was abusing her and cocaine?

The Myth of the Male Role Model is based on the premise that boys have a special need for fathers because only a male role model can teach a boy how to become a man.

Sharon is a physician. She is a very bright, no-nonsense kind of woman who feels more comfortable in the operating room than in a dating situation. She has always liked men and gotten along well with them, but had difficulty establishing and maintaining a romantic relationship. She had one very serious boyfriend in medical school, but they broke up after four years because of his drinking. After that, she had brief affairs with several other doctors throughout internship and residency training, but none of those relationships ever developed. The men she was involved with always ended up marrying nurses or secretaries, never a doctor.

In her late 30s, she began a relationship with an investment banker who recently had been divorced. He was determined never to get married again and certainly never to have children. He and Sharon were very compatible. However, she really wanted children. When she celebrated her

40th birthday, she decided that she would have to contemplate having children without a man or lose the opportunity to have kids altogether. She contacted a sperm bank and became pregnant through artificial insemination. Her boyfriend decided he did not want to remain in the relationship. Sharon had a relatively easy pregnancy and delivery, and with her new baby boy, she embarked on the adventure of single motherhood. Sharon has felt a great deal of anxiety that she will not be able to teach her son how to be a man. Although her son is now four years old and doing fine, she still worries constantly that he may be permanently scarred by not having a father.

Myths about Gay Families. A major component of the myth of the idealized father is that he cannot be gay.

Many of the gay fathers in our research study forced themselves to deny the fact that they were gay because they wanted to be fathers. As one of them put it, "Being gay and being a father seemed mutually exclusive." These men desperately wanted to be "normal" which was defined as being married and having children. They tried to fit themselves into the mold of a married man, hoping against hope that getting married would save them from being gay.

Tom is one of these men. He met Sheri, his wife, in college, and she became a good friend. He admired her and liked her a lot. Tom is very religious, so he prayed that marriage would turn friendship into love. "If Christ could raise the dead, I thought that he could surely cure a homosexual," he reasoned.

Although he and Sheri developed a relationship of mutual respect, they were not in love. Yet, when they had children, they were both so pleased with becoming parents that the kids provided a sort of glue that kept the marriage together. Tom recalled that he felt so happy bonding with his offspring that he was able to avoid the loneliness he felt in his relationship with Sheri.

However, when their second child was six years old, the pleasure of being a father was no longer enough to compensate for an empty marriage. Tom remembered "the moment my life fell apart"—the day he no longer could deny his homosexuality to himself. He then spent several years in torment, feeling torn between his desire to live with his children and his desire to be true to himself. When he finally got enough courage to leave his marriage, he still did not feel brave enough to admit his homosexuality to his wife or his children.

He was terrified that he would lose visitation rights with his kids if the court discovered that he was gay.

To his surprise and sorrow, many of his gay friends were not a source of support on this issue. They were interested in living a single gay lifestyle that did not include children. Thus, he could not admit his identity as a gay man to his family, and his gay friends did not support his identity as a father. He expressed his isolation by saying, "I felt I was the only man on the planet who was a father and was gay."

Did Tom have to feel tortured about being a gay father? Can only straight men be good fathers?

In reviewing the scientific research, we found that there is not a single study showing that a male role model is necessary for boys to become well-adjusted men. We now know that both boys and girls use same-sex and opposite-sex role models: parents, grandparents, and other extended family members; teachers; and cultural heroes. In our own research, many of our subjects stated, "My mother taught me how to be a good father."

In terms of "fatherless" families, it is important to point out that the research has been done primarily with poor, ethnic minority families. Because more single-mother families are poor, it is difficult to differentiate the effects of father absence from the effects of poverty. When we look at the research on middle-class lesbian-mother families, we find that the children being raised in these fatherless families are doing just fine.

These youngsters score within the normal range on measures of intelligence, social behavior, and emotional well-being. This finding suggests that the studies focusing on poor, mother-headed families are actually studying the effect of poverty, rather than the absence of a father.

Studies on children being raised by gay fathers have also shown that children raised in these families are growing up healthy. They do not become gay any more frequently than children raised by heterosexual parents.

The people cited above were able to establish a sense of psychological security only after they stopped trying to live up to a family values ideal that simply did not fit their realities. Susan's story is a dramatic example of trying to live up to the cultural mythology about fathers and families, even when it flies in the face of one's better judgment. Susan's decision to stay with John was not helpful to herself, her sons, or John. When she left him, he finally sought help for his drug addiction. He ultimately got and kept a good job, remarried, and became a financially responsible father to his sons and stepdaughter.

Sharon's story is another example of how the family values point of view generates unnecessary stress. Although Sharon worries about raising her son without a father, she is not raising him without a man. In fact, he has close relationships with several men.

Her first cousin is his godfather and spends every Sunday with him. One of his usual babysitters is another cousin of hers, a male student who loves kids and needs spending money. Moreover, Sharon's father comes to stay with her for several weeks three times a year. The presence of men in the life of a single mother is not un-usual. Most women have men in their lives.

Finally, Tom is the same father as an openly gay male that he was as a married man. His relationship with his teenage children did not deteriorate when he told them he was gay; rather, their relationship deepened. The kids' immediate reaction was, "Oh, Dad, we've known that for a long time! Tell us something we don't know." Tom reported that he felt so reassured by their acceptance of him that he has since been able to establish a much deeper sense of closeness with them.

We are not saying that everything will be easy or will work out fine if only people give up the family values perspective. Instead, we are suggesting that there is no general solution to the complex challenges of family life. Trying to conform to a single version of family life is not just doomed to failure, but unnecessary. Intimate relationships and good-enough parenting are always difficult to achieve. However, if people attempt to conform to idealized myths, they are making the difficult challenge of raising healthy children even more difficult. Rather than trying to find the "one right way," parents need to be flexible and creative in seeking strategies that work for their particular family.

Louise B. Silverstein and *Carl F. Auerbach* are associate professors at the Ferkauf Graduate School of Psychology, Yeshiva University, Bronx, N.Y.

Weighing the price of 'perfect' in family life

Parents face pressure to push their children into many activities and to be involved as well.

By Marilyn Gardner
Staff writer of The Christian Science Monitor

When her two children were small, Bugs Peterschmidt made a quiet vow: She would not become "one of those moms whose kids are in a ton of things."

But by the time her son reached sixth grade, he was involved in six activities. No wonder, perhaps, that when soccer sign-up sheets arrived, both of her children said no. They just wanted to stay home that summer. Rather than push, she let them follow their leanings.

"It was a huge success," says Mrs. Peterschmidt, of Plymouth, Minn., describing their summer. "Cousins came to visit, and we'd visit cousins." Instead of spending four eve-nings a week at soccer practice, the family enjoyed leisurely dinners at home.

> Every added activity that a child takes part in exacts a price from the whole family in time spent together.

Yet when acquaintances learn that her children have, for now, dropped all activities except music lessons, they respond with incredulity. In an era characterized by over-committed children, overinvolved parents, and pressure to succeed at an early age, the Peterschmidts' brave approach is hardly the typical American way of parenting.

But here and there, small signs of change are appearing, which sup-port decisions like Peterschmidt's. Several new books warn against ex-cessive pushing and parental overin-volvement. A grassroots group in suburban Minneapolis is also chal-lenging the competitive culture of parenting. Its organizers want to cre-ate a better balance between family life and outside activities.

"We need to have a cultural conversation about what we have wrought," says William Doherty, a professor of family social science at the University of Minnesota and a co-founder of the group Family Life First. He is also the author of a forthcoming book, "Putting Family First," to be published in August.

That cultural conversation begins with a fundamental question: What is a good parent? One who is heavily invested in children's activities, pressing hard to help them build impressive "résumés" of their accomplishments? Or one who guides gently from the sidelines, mindful that every added activity exacts a price from the whole family in lost time together?

Professor Doherty likens parents to recreation directors on a cruise ship. "A lot of this is driven by a sense of anxiety that their children not lose out, not be behind," he says. But pushing sometimes goes beyond simply serving children's best interests. Their achievements, Doherty observes, also reflect on how parents are doing as parents.

Calling pushing a "really big problem that seems to be getting worse, not better," he says, "Now we have 6-month-olds in music classes and swimming classes." Parents fear that if other children are attending these classes, they will be holding their own children back if they do not enroll, too.

What author Elisabeth Guthrie calls "push parenting" begins in the crib and the playpen. Toymakers' promotions for educational toys, for instance, tap into parents' concerns about children getting ahead. But what manufacturers are really promoting, she says, is competition.

That kind of subtle pressure throughout childhood is the subject of Dr. Guthrie's new book, "The Trouble With Perfect: How Parents Can Avoid the Overachievement Trap and Still Raise Successful Children" (Broadway, $22.95). In recent years she has observed a trend toward résumé padding and "résumé

exhibitionism" for both adults and children.

> Taylor also laments the ubiquitous pop-culture messages that emphasize success... Popular culture... offers extremely narrow definitions of success: wealth, fame, power, status, beauty.

"Just about no parent wants to push, but most feel they must," she says. "The great, gnawing fear is that if you don't push, if you relax and let the chips fall where they may, your child will fail, or at least not succeed."

Jim Taylor, whose book, "Positive Pushing," will be published in April, offers several reasons for parents' extreme investment in their children.

Many parents understandably want to ensure that their children will become financially successful. To that end, they push them to earn top grades and high SAT scores so they can get into the best schools.

In addition, the potential rewards of greatness, particularly in sports, have increased dramatically. That encourages some parents to pressure a child to become a professional athlete. As a cautionary tale, Taylor, who works with young achievers and their parents, recommends the movie "Searching for Bobby Fischer." It illustrates, he says, what can happen when parents become overly invested in their child's achievements and activities.

Taylor also laments the ubiquitous pop-culture messages that em-

phasize success and happiness, particularly success. Popular culture, he notes, offers extremely narrow definitions of success: wealth, fame, power, status, beauty. "Very few people can live up to that."

Doherty uses sports as an example of good parental intentions gone awry. When he was growing up in the 1950s, it would have been "mortifying" and "beyond the pale" for parents to attend sports practice sessions.

"We expected our kid world to be a kid world," he recalls. "We had zero expectations for parents to be observers and cheerleaders. A parent too much in evidence would have been embarrassing, as if we needed monitoring. We felt just as much loved as the current generation."

By the late 1970s, parental attendance at games had become mandatory. "It's a sign that you're a good parent if you go to all the games," Doherty says. "The really good parents go to all the practices, too. You have to be there for your kid, cheering your kid, protecting your kid."

Today, Doherty says, a good parent is defined as "somebody who is there for the kid's extracurricular activities, rather than someone who is home cooking a nice meal."

The other extreme, simply taking a laissez-faire approach and letting children do—or refuse to do—whatever they want, is not the answer either, of course.

Taylor emphasizes that parents need to push their children based on what is best for the children, not what is best for themselves. If children understand that an activity is in their best interests, then they will accept it, he finds.

How can families resist excessive pressure? The first step in any change, Guthrie says, is education—getting some insight into what is wrong with the family picture. She urges parents to heed the little voices within that say, "This is crazy. This is too much."

Taylor and other family experts remain pessimistic about the possibilities for widespread societal change. "The force of our popular culture, driven by money and superficial values, cannot be resisted," he says. But change can take place at a "micro-level," in families and schools.

When changes do occur, the rewards can benefit everyone in the family, Peterschmidt and others say. She cites the advantages her family experienced after her children cut back on activities.

"The biggest thing is that since we have done this, we are rested," she says. "Not only are our kids rested, because they're not in a ton of stuff, but my husband and I are rested, because we're not driving them everywhere. We weren't living in the moment when we were always busy. We were living by the schedule. The return on our investment of spending time together has been enormous."

AMERICAN FAMILIES
Are Drifting Apart

The sexual revolution, women's liberation, relaxation of divorce laws, and greater mobility are fracturing the traditional family structure.

BY BARBARA LEBEY

A VARIETY OF REASONS—from petty grievances to deep-seated prejudices, misunderstandings to all-out conflicts, jealousies, sibling rivalry, inheritance feuds, family business disputes, and homosexual outings—are cause for families to grow apart. Family estrangements are becoming more numerous, more intense, and more hurtful. When I speak to groups on the subject, I always ask: Who has or had an estrangement or knows someone who does? Almost every hand in the room goes up. Sisters aren't speaking to each other since one of them took the silver when Mom died. Two brothers rarely visit because their wives don't like each other.

A son alienates himself from his family when he marries a woman who wants to believe that he sprung from the earth. Because Mom is the travel agent for guilt trips, her daughter avoids contact with her. A family banishes a daughter for marrying outside her race or religion. A son eradicates a divorced father when he reveals his homosexuality. And so it goes.

The nation is facing a rapidly changing family relationship landscape. Every assumption made about the family structure has been challenged, from the outer boundaries of single mothers raising out-of-wedlock children to gay couples having or adopting children to grandparents raising their grandchildren. If the so-called traditional family is having trouble maintaining

harmony, imagine what problems can and do arise in less-conventional situations. Fault lines in Americans' family structure were widening throughout the last 40 years of the 20th century. The cracks became evident in the mid 1970s when the divorce rate doubled. According to a 1999 Rutgers University study, divorce has risen 30% since 1970; the marriage rate has fallen faster; and just 38% of Americans consider themselves happy in their married state, a drop from 53% 25 years ago. Today, 51% of all marriages end in divorce.

How Americans managed to alter their concept of marriage and family so profoundly during those four decades is the subject of much scholarly investigation and academic debate. In a May, 2000, *New York Times Magazine* article titled "The Pursuit of Autonomy," the writer maintains that "the family is no longer a haven; all too often a center of dysfunction, it has become one with the heartless world that surrounds it." Unlike the past, the job that fits you in your 20s is not the job or career you'll likely have in your 40s. This is now true of marriage as well—the spouse you had in your 20s may not be the one you will have after you've gone through your midlife crisis.

In the 1960s, four main societal changes occurred that have had an enormous impact on the traditional family structure. The sexual revolution, women's

liberation movement, states' relaxation of divorce laws, and mobility of American families have converged to foster family alienation, exacerbate old family rifts, and create new ones. It must be emphasized, however, that many of these changes had positive outcomes. The nation experienced a strengthened social conscience, women's rights, constraints on going to war, and a growing tolerance for diversity, but society also paid a price.

The 1960s perpetuated the notion that we are first and foremost *entitled* to happiness and fulfillment. It's positively un-American *not* to seek it! This idea goes back to that early period of our history when Thomas Jefferson dropped the final term from British philosopher John Locke's definition of human rights—"life, liberty, and... property"—and replaced it with what would become the slogan of our new nation: "the pursuit of happiness." In the words of author Gail Sheehy, the 1960s generation "expressed their collective personality as idealistic, narcissistic, anti-establishment, hairy, horny and preferably high."

Any relationship that was failing to deliver happiness was being tossed out like an empty beer can, including spousal ones. For at least 20 years, the pharmaceutical industry has learned how to cash in on the American obsession with feeling good by hyping mood drugs to rewire the brain circuitry for happiness through the elimination of sadness and depression.

Young people fled from the confines of family, whose members were frantic, worrying about exactly where their adult children were and what they were doing. There were probably more estrangements between parents and adult children during the 1960s and early 1970s than ever before.

In the wake of the civil rights movement and Pres. Lyndon Johnson's Great Society came the women's liberation movement, and what a flashy role it played in changing perceptions about the family structure. Women who graduated from college in the late 1960s and early 1970s were living in a time when they could establish and assert their independent identities. In Atlanta, Emory Law School's 1968 graduating class had six women in it, the largest number ever to that point, and all six were in the top 10%, including the number-one graduate. In that same period, many all-male colleges opened their doors to women for the first time. No one could doubt the message singer Helen Reddy proclaimed: "I am woman, hear me roar." For all the self-indulgence of the "hippie" generation, there was an intense awakening in young people of a recognition that civil rights must mean equal rights for everyone in our society, and that has to include women.

Full equality was the battle cry of every minority, a status that women claimed despite their majority position. As they had once marched for the right to vote, women began marching for sexual equality and the same broad range of career and job opportunities that were always available to men. Financial independence gave women the freedom to walk away from unhappy marriages. This was a dramatic departure from the puritanical sense of duty that had been woven into the American fabric since the birth of this nation.

For all the good that came out of this movement, though, it also changed forever traditional notions of marriage, motherhood, and family unity, as well as that overwhelming sense of children first. Even in the most-conservative young families, wives were letting their husbands know that they were going back to work or back to school. Many women had to return to work either because there was a need for two incomes to maintain a moderate standard of living or because they were divorced and forced to support their offspring on their own. "Don't ask, don't tell" day-care centers proliferated where overworked, undertrained staff, and two-

income yuppie parents, ignored the children's emotional needs—all in the name of equality and to enable women to reclaim their identifies. Some might say these were the parents who ran away from home.

Many states began to approve legislation that allowed no-fault divorce, eliminating the need to lay blame on spouses or stage adulterous scenes in sleazy motels to provide evidence for states that demanded such evidence for divorces. The legal system established procedures for easily dissolving marriages, dividing property, and sharing responsibility for the children. There were even do-it-yourself divorce manuals on bookstore shelves. Marriage had become a choice rather than a necessity, a one-dimensional status sustained almost exclusively by emotional satisfaction and not worth maintaining in its absence. Attitudes about divorce were becoming more lenient, so much so that the nation finally elected its first divorced president in 1980—Ronald Reagan.

With divorced fathers always running the risk of estrangement from their children, this growing divorce statistic has had the predictable impact of increasing the number of those estrangements. Grandparents also experienced undeserved fallout from divorce, since, almost invariably, they are alienated from their grandchildren.

The fourth change, and certainly one of the most pivotal, was the increased mobility of families that occurred during those four decades. Family members were no longer living in close proximity to one another. The organization man moved to wherever he could advance more quickly up the corporate ladder. College graduates took the best job offer, even if it was 3,000 miles away from where they grew up and where their family still lived.

Some were getting out of small towns for new vistas, new adventures, and new job opportunities. Others were fleeing the overcrowded dirty cities in search of cleaner air, a more reasonable cost of living, and retirement communities in snow-free, warmer, more-scenic locations. Moving from company to company had begun, reaching what is now a crescendo of job-hopping. Many young people chose to marry someone who lived in a different location, so family ties were geographically severed for indeterminate periods of time, sometimes forever.

According to Lynn H. Dennis' *Corporate Relocation Takes Its Toll on Society*, during the 10 years from 1989 to 1999, more than 5,000,000 families were relocated one or more times by their employ-

ers. In addition to employer-directed moves, one out of five Americans relocated at least once, not for exciting adventure, but for economic advancement and/or a safer place to raise children. From March, 1996, to March, 1997, 42,000,000 Americans, or 16% of the population, packed up and moved from where they were living to another location. That is a striking statistic. Six million of these people moved from one region of the country to another, and young adults aged 20 to 29 were the most mobile, making up 32% of the moves during that year. This disbursement of nuclear families throughout the country disconnected them from parents, brothers, sisters, grandparents, aunts, uncles, and cousins—the extended family and all its adhesive qualities.

Today, with cell phones, computers, faxes, and the Internet, the office can be anywhere, including in the home. Therefore, we can *live* anywhere we want to. If that is the case, why aren't more people choosing to live in the cities or towns where they grew up? There's no definitive answer. Except for the praise heaped on "family values," staying close to family no longer plays a meaningful role in choosing where we reside.

These relocations require individuals to invest an enormous amount of time to reestablish their lives without help from family or old friends. Although nothing can compare to the experience of immigrants who left their countries knowing they probably would never see their families again, the phenomenon of Americans continually relocating makes family relationships difficult to sustain.

Our culture tends to focus on the individual, or, at most, on the nuclear family, downplaying the benefits of extended families, though their role is vital in shaping our lives. The notion of "moving on" whenever problems arise has been a time-honored American concept. Too many people would rather cast aside some family member than iron out the situation and keep the relationship alive. If we don't get along with our father or if our mother doesn't like our choice of mate or our way of life, we just move away and see the family once or twice a year. After we're married, with children in school, and with both parents working, visits become even more difficult. If the family visits are that infrequent, why bother at all? Some children grow up barely knowing any of their relatives. Contact ceases; rifts don't resolve; and divisiveness often germinates into a full-blown estrangement.

In an odd sort of way, the more financially independent people become, the more families scatter and grow apart. It's not a cause, but it is a facilitator. Tolerance levels decrease as financial means increase. Just think how much more we tolerate from our families when they are providing financial support. Look at the divorced wife who depends on her family for money to supplement alimony and child support, the student whose parents are paying all college expenses, or the brother who borrows family money to save his business.

Recently, a well-known actress being interviewed in a popular magazine was asked, if there was one thing she could change in her family, what would it be? Her answer was simple: "That we could all live in the same city." She understood the importance of being near loved ones and how, even in a harmonious family, geographical distance often leads to emotional disconnectedness. When relatives are regularly in each other's company, they will usually make a greater effort to get along. Even when there is dissension among family members, they are more likely to work it out, either on their own or because another relative has intervened to calm the troubled waters. When rifts occur, relatives often need a real jolt to perform an act of forgiveness. Forgiving a family member can be the hardest thing to do, probably because the emotional bonds are so much deeper and usually go all the way back to childhood. Could it be that blood is a thicker medium in which to hold a grudge?

With today's families scattered all over the country, the matriarch or patriarch of the extended family is far less able to keep his or her kin united, caring, and supportive of one another. In these disconnected nuclear families, certain trends—workaholism, alcoholism, depression, severe stress, isolation, escapism, and a push toward continuous supervised activity for children—are routinely observed. What happened to that family day of rest and togetherness? We should mourn its absence.

For the widely dispersed baby boomers with more financial means than any prior generation, commitment, intimacy, and family togetherness have never been high on their list of priorities. How many times have you heard of family members trying to maintain a relationship with a relative via e-mail and answering machines? One young man now sends his Mother's Day greeting by leaving a message for his mom on *his* answering machine. When she calls to scold him for forgetting to call her, she'll get a few sweet words wishing her a happy Mother's Day and his apology for being too busy to call or send a card! His sister can expect the same kind of greeting for her birthday, but only if she bothers to call to find out why her brother hadn't contacted her.

Right now, and probably for the foreseeable future, we will be searching for answers to the burgeoning problems we unwittingly created by these societal changes, but don't be unduly pessimistic. Those who have studied and understood the American psyche are far more optimistic. The 19th-century French historian and philosopher Alexis de Tocqueville once said of Americans, "No natural boundary seems to be set to the effort of Americans, and in their eyes what is not yet done, is only what they have not yet attempted to do." Some day, I hope this mindset will apply not to political rhetoric on family values, but to bringing families back together again.

Barbara LeBey, *an Atlanta, Ga.-based attorney and former judge, is the author of* Family Estrangements—How They Begin, How to Mend Them, How to Cope with Them.

UNIT 2
Exploring and Establishing Relationships

Unit Selections

Key Points to Consider

- What is your view of the basis for gendered behavior? Is it nature or is it nurture? What are the special issues related to rearing girls and boys? What is the role of culture in determining appropriate behavior for men and women?

- Is it possible for men and women to be friends without their relationship becoming a sexual one? Defend your answer.

- What do you look for in a mate? Would you be willing to settle for less? Why or why not?

- What, in addition to love, is needed for a relationship to be a success? Why is love not enough?

- At what age should one stop considering having a child? What should be the determining factor?

- What are your attitudes and beliefs about parenthood?

 **Links: www.dushkin.com/online/**
These sites are annotated in the World Wide Web pages.

Ask NOAH About Pregnancy: Fertility & Infertility
http://www.noah-health.org/english/pregnancy/fertility.html
Bonobo Sex and Society
http://songweaver.com/info/bonobos.html
Go Ask Alice!
http://www.goaskalice.columbia.edu/index.html
The Kinsey Institute for Research in Sex, Gender, and Reproduction
http://www.indiana.edu/~kinsey/
Mysteries of Odor in Human Sexuality
http://www.pheromones.com
Planned Parenthood
http://www.plannedparenthood.org
The Society for the Scientific Study of Sexuality
http://www.sexscience.org
Sympatico: HealthyWay: Health Links
http://www1.sympatico.ca/Contents/health/

By and large, humans are social animals, and as such, we seek out meaningful connections with other humans. John Bowlby, Mary Ainsworth, and others have proposed that this drive toward connection is biologically based and is at the core of what it means to be human. However it plays out in childhood and adulthood, the need for connection, to love and be loved, is a powerful force moving us to establish and maintain close relationships. At the same time, our biology influences the way in which we relate to each other and the way in which we create and maintain relationships.

As we explore various possibilities, we engage in the complex business of relationship building. In this business, many processes occur simultaneously—messages are sent and received; differences are negotiated; assumptions and expectations are or are not met. The ultimate goals are closeness and continuity.

How we feel about others and what we see as essential to these relationships play an important role in our establishing and maintaining relationships. In this unit, we look at factors that underlie the establishment of relationships as well as their beginning stages.

The first subsection explores gender differences and their influences in relationships and on how we relate to the world. The first article, "Sex Differences in the Brain" addresses the biological differences between male and female brains and their impact on relationship building and maintenance. The second article, "The New Woman: Daring to Be Less Than Perfect," takes a different approach, looking at gender through a cultural lens. Lastly, "The Feminization of American Culture" explores the reversal of gender stereotypes.

The second subsection takes a broad look at factors that influence the building of meaningful relationships and at the beginning stages of adult relationships. The first essay, "Can Men and Women Be Friends?" explores the nature of male–female friendship relationships and questions the assumption that these relationships are inherently sexualized. We form relationships in the context of stories, and in "What's Your Love Story?" Robert Sternberg describes 12 stories he has identified that act as guides for the formation, maintenance, and end of love relationships. For all its power, love is not the only requirement for a satisfying, long-lasting relationship. The final article in this section, "Love Is Not All You Need," describes six additional components of a successful relationship.

In the third subsection, important aspects of adult relationships are explored: sexuality and pregnancy. "Sex Is for Grown-Ups" proposes that one's sex life improves with age and long-term relationships contribute to the improvement. "Making Time for a Baby" presents a controversial position that waiting to have children puts women at risk of never being able to have a child. The third article in this section, "Too Posh to Push," addresses recent dramatic increases in caesarean section deliveries in the United States and questions whether this is progress in childbirth or if it is merely being done out of convenience. In the fourth subsection, two articles focus on the idea of the next generation. "Shaped by Life in the Womb" discusses the long-term effects of prenatal health. Finally, cross-cultural variations in maternal attitudes and beliefs are presented in "Our Babies, Ourselves."

Sex Differences in the Brain

Men and women display patterns of behavioral and cognitive differences
that reflect varying hormonal influences on brain development

by Doreen Kimura

Men and women differ not only in their physical attributes and reproductive function but also in many other characteristics, including the way they solve intellectual problems. For the past few decades, it has been ideologically fashionable to insist that these behavioral differences are minimal and are the consequence of variations in experience during development before and after adolescence. Evidence accumulated more recently, however, suggests that the effects of sex hormones on brain organization occur so early in life that from the start the environment is acting on differently wired brains in boys and girls. Such effects make evaluating the role of experience, independent of physiological predisposition, a difficult if not dubious task. The biological bases of sex differences in brain and behavior have become much better known through increasing numbers of behavioral, neurological and endoctinological studies.

We know, for instance, from observations of both humans and nonhumans that males are more aggressive than females, that young males engage in more rough-and-tumble play than females and that females are more nurturing. We also know that in general males are better at a variety of spatial or navigational tasks. How do these and other sex differences come about? Much of our information and many of our ideas about how sexual differentiation takes place derive from research on animals. From such investigations, it appears that perhaps the most important factor in the differentiation of males and females is the level of exposure to various sex hormones early in life.

In most mammals, including humans, the developing organism has the potential to be male or female. Producing a male, however, is a complex process. When a Y chromosome is present, testes, or male gonads, form. This development is the critical first step toward becoming a male. When no Y chromosome is present, ovaries form.

Testes produce male hormones, or androgens (testosterone chief among them), which are responsible not only for transformation of the genitals into male organs but also for organization of corresponding male behaviors early in life. As with genital formation, the intrinsic tendency that occurs in the absence of masculinizing hormonal influence, according to seminal studies by Robert W. Goy of the University of Wisconsin, is to develop female genital structures and behavior. Female anatomy and probably most behavior associated with females are thus the default modes in the absence of androgens.

If a rodent with functional male genitals is deprived of androgens immediately after birth (either by castration or by the administration of a compound that blocks androgens), male sexual behavior, such as mounting, will be reduced, and more female sexual behavior, such as lordosis (arching of the back when receptive to coitus), will be expressed. Similarly, if androgens are administered to a female directly after birth, she will display more male sexual behavior and less female behavior in adulthood. These lifelong effects of early exposure to sex hormones are characterized as "organizational" because they appear to alter brain function permanently during a critical period in prenatal or early postnatal development. Administering the same sex hormones at later stages or in the adult has no such effect.

Not all the behaviors that categorize males are organized at the same time, however. Organization by androgens of the male-typical behaviors of mounting and of rough-and-tumble play, for example, occur at different times prenatally in rhesus monkeys.

The area in the brain that regulates female and male reproductive behavior is the hypothalamus. This tiny structure at the base of the brain connects to the pituitary, the master endocrine gland. It has been shown that a region of the hypothalamus is visibly larger in male rats than in females and that this size difference is under hormonal control. Scientists have also found parallel sex differences in a clump of nerve cells in the human brain—parts of the interstitial nucleus of the anterior hypothalamus—that is larger in men than in women. Even sexual orientation and gender identity have been related to anatomical variation in the hypothalamus. In 1991, while at the Salk Institute for Biological Studies in San Diego, Simon Levay reported that one of the interstitial nuclei of the anterior hypothalamus that is usually larger in human males than in females is smaller in homosexual than in heterosexual men. Other researchers, Jiang-Ning Zhou of the Netherlands Institute of Brain Research and his colleagues there and at Free University in Amsterdam, observed another part of the hypothalamus to be smaller in male-to-female transsexuals than in a male control group. These findings are consistent with suggestions that sexual orientation and gender identity have a significant biological component.

Hormones and Intellect

What of differences in intellectual function between men and women? Major sex differences in function seem to lie in patterns of ability rather than in overall level of intelligence (measured as IQ), although some researchers, such as Richard Lynn of the University of Ulster in Northern Ireland, have argued that there exists a small IQ difference favoring human males. Differences in intellectual pattern refer to the fact that people have different intellectual strengths. For example, some people are especially good at using words, whereas others are better at dealing with external stimuli, such as identifying an object in a different orientation. Individuals may have the same overall intelligence but differing abilities.

Sex differences in problem solving have been systematically studied in adults in laboratory situations. On average, men perform better than women at certain spatial tasks. In particular, men seem to have an advantage in tests that require the subject to imagine rotating an object or manipulating it in some other way. They also outperform women in mathematical reasoning tests and in navigating their way through a route. Further, men exhibit more accuracy in tests of target-directed motor skills—that is, in guiding or intercepting projectiles.

Women, on average, excel on tests that measure recall of words and on tests that challenge the person to find words that begin with a specific letter or fulfill some other constraint. They also tend to be better than men at rapidly identifying matching items and performing certain precision manual tasks, such as placing pegs in designated holes on a board.

In examining the nature of sex differences in navigating routes, one study found that men completed a computer simulation of a maze or labyrinth task more quickly and with fewer errors than women did. Another study by different researchers used a path on a tabletop map to measure route learning. Their results showed that although men learned the route in fewer trials and with fewer errors, women remembered more of the landmarks, such as pictures of different types of buildings, than men did. These results and others suggest that women tend to use landmarks as a strategy to orient themselves in everyday life more than men do.

Other findings seemed also to point to female superiority in landmark memory. Researchers tested the ability of individuals to recall objects and their locations within a confined space—such as in a room or on a tabletop. In these studies, women were better able to remember whether items had changed places or not. Other investigators found that women were superior at a memory task where they had to remember the locations of pictures on cards that were turned over in pairs. At this kind of object location, in contrast to other spatial tasks, women appeared to have the advantage.

It is important to keep in mind that some of the average sex differences in cognition vary from slight to quite large and that men and women overlap enormously on many cognitive tests that show average differences. For example, whereas women perform better than men in both verbal memory (recalling words from lists or paragraphs) and verbal fluency (finding words that begin with a specific letter), there was a large difference in memory ability but only a small disparity for the fluency tasks. On the whole, variation between men and women tends to be smaller than deviations within each sex, but very large differences between the groups do exist —in men's high level of visual-spatial targeting ability, for one.

Although it used to be thought that sex differences in problem solving did not appear until puberty, the accumulated evidence now suggests that some cognitive and skill differences are present much earlier. For example, researchers have found that three- and four-year-old boys were better at targeting and mentally rotating figures within a clock face than girls of the same age were. Prepubescent girls, however, excelled at recalling lists of words.

Male and female rodents have also been found to solve problems differently. Christina L. Williams of Duke University has shown that female rats have a greater tendency to use landmarks in spatial learning tasks, as it appears women do. In Williams's experiment, female rats used landmark cues, such as pictures on the wall, in preference to geometric cues: angles and the shape of the room, for instance. If no landmarks were available, however, females used the geometric cues. In contrast, males did not use landmarks at all, preferring geometric cues almost exclusively.

Williams also found that hormonal manipulation during the critical period could alter these behaviors. Depriving newborn males of sex hormones by castrating them or administering hormones to newborn females resulted in a complete reversal of sex-typed behaviors in the adult

Problem-Solving Tasks Favoring
Men

Men tend to perform better than women on certain spatial tasks. They do well on tests that involve mentally rotating an object or manipulating it in some fashion, such as imagining turning this three-dimensional object

or determining where the holes punched in a folded piece of paper will fall when the paper is unfolded:

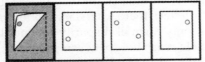

Men also are more accurate than women at target-directed motor skills, such as guiding or intercepting projectiles:

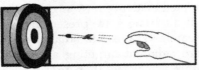

They do better at matching lines with identical slopes:

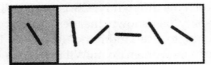

And men tend to do better than women on tests of mathematical reasoning:

| 1,100 | If only 60 percent of seedlings will survive, how many must be planted to obtain 660 trees? |

Problem-Solving Tasks Favoring
Women

Women tend to perform better than men on tests of perceptual speed in which subjects must rapidly identify matching items—for example, pairing the house on the far left with its twin:

In addition, women remember whether an object, or a series of objects, has been displaced:

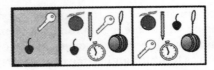

When read a story, paragraph or a list of unrelated words, women demonstrate better recall:

Dog, shadow, hamburger, cloud, flower, eyelash, pencil, paper, water, light, fork, road, building....

Women do better on precision manual tasks—that is, those involving fine-motor coordination—such as placing the pegs in holes on a board:

And women do better than men on mathematical calculation tests:

| 77 | $14 \times 3 - 17 + 52$ |
| 43 | $2(15 + 3) + 12 - \frac{15}{3}$ |

DOREEN KIMURA AND JOHN MENGEL

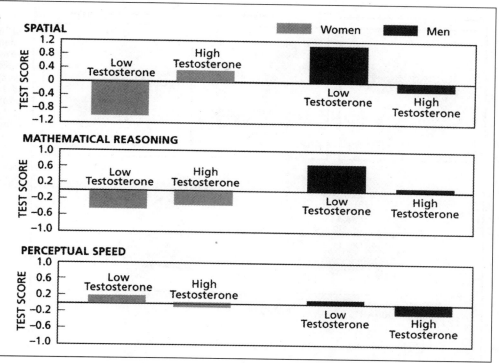

TESTOSTERONE LEVELS can affect performance on some tests (see boxes for example of tests). Women with high levels of testosterone perform better on spatial tasks (top) than women with low levels do, but men with low levels outperform men with high levels. One a mathematical reasoning test (middle), low testosterone corresponds to better performance in men; in women there is no such relation. On a test of perceptual speed in which women usually excel (bottom), no relation is found between testosterone and performance.

DOREEN KIMURA

animals. Treated males behaved like females and treated females like males.

Structural differences may parallel behavioral ones. Lucia F. Jacobs, then at the University of Pittsburgh, discovered that the hippocampus—a region thought to be involved in spatial learning in both birds and mammals–is larger in several male species of rodents than in females. At present, there are insufficient data on possible sex differences in hippocampal size in human subjects.

One of the most compelling areas of evidence for hormonally influenced sex differences in humans comes from studies of girls exposed to excess androgens in the prenatal or neonatal stage. The production of abnormally large quantities of adrenal androgens can occur because of a genetic defect in a condition called congenital adrenal hyperplasia (CAH). Before the 1970s a similar condition also unexpectedly appeared in the offspring of pregnant women who took various synthetic steroids. Although the consequent masculinization of the genitals can be corrected by surgery and drug therapy can stop the overproduction of androgens, the effects of prenatal exposure on the brain cannot be reversed.

Sheri A. Berenbaum of Southern Illinois University at Carbondale and Melissa Hines of the University of California at Los Angeles observed the play behavior of CAH girls and compared it with that of their male and female siblings. Given a choice of transportation and construction toys, dolls and kitchen supplies, or books and board games, the CAH girls preferred the more typically masculine toys—for example, they played with cars for the same amount of time that boys did. Both the CAH girls and the boys differed from unaffected girls in their pat-

terns of choice. Berenbaum also found that CAH girls had greater interest in male-typical activities and careers. Because there is every reason to think parents would be at least as likely to encourage feminine preferences in their CAH daughters as in their unaffected daughters, these findings suggest that these preferences were actually altered in some way by the early hormonal environment.

Other researchers also found that spatial abilities that are typically better in males are enhanced in CAH girls. But the reverse was reported in one study of CAH-affected boys–they performed worse than unaffected boys on the spatial tests males usually excel at.

Such studies suggest that although levels of androgen relate to spatial ability, it is not simply the case that the higher the levels, the better the spatial scores. Rather studies point to some optimal level of androgen (in the low male range) for maximal spatial ability. This finding may also be true with men and mathematical reasoning; low-androgen men tested higher. There was no obvious correlation between hormone levels and women's math scores, however.

These findings are relevant to the suggestion by Camilla P. Benbow of Iowa State University that high mathematical ability has a significant biological determinant. Benbow and her colleagues have reported consistent sex differences in mathematical reasoning ability that favor males. In mathematically talented youth, the differences were especially sharp at the upper end of the distribution, where males outnumbered females 13 to one. Benbow argues that these differences are not readily explained by socialization.

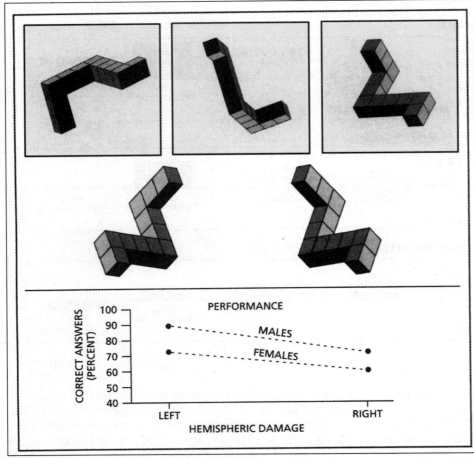

RIGHT HEMISPHERIC DAMAGE *affects spatial ability to the same degree in both sexes (graph at bottom), suggesting that women and men rely equally on that hemisphere for certain spatial tasks. In one test of spatial-rotation performance, photographs of a three-dimensional object must be matched to one of two mirror images of the same object.*

DOREEN KIMURA

It is important to keep in mind that the relation between natural hormone levels and problem solving is based on correlational data. Although some form of connection between the two measures exists, we do not necessarily know how the association is determined nor what its causal basis is. We also know little at present about the relation between adult levels of hormones and those in early life, when abilities appear to become organized in the nervous system.

Hormonal Highs and Lows

One of the most intriguing findings in adults is that cognitive patterns may remain sensitive to hormonal fluctuations throughout life. Elizabeth Hampson of the University of Western Ontario showed that women's performances at certain tasks changed throughout the menstrual cycle as levels of estrogen varied. High levels of the hormone were associated not only with relatively depressed spatial ability but also with enhanced speech and manual skill tasks. In addition, I have observed seasonal fluctuations in spatial ability in men: their performance improves in the spring, when testosterone levels are lower. Whether these hormonally linked fluctuations in intellectual ability represent useful evolutionary adapta-

tions or merely highs and lows of an average test level remains to be seen through further research endeavors.

A long history of studying people with damage to one half of their brain indicates that in most people the left hemisphere of the brain is critical for speech and the right for certain perceptual and spatial functions. Researchers studying sex differences have widely assumed that the right and left hemispheres of the brain are more asymmetrically organized for speech and spatial functions in men than in women.

This belief rests on several lines of research. Parts of the corpus callosum, a major neural system connecting the two hemispheres, as well as another connector, the anterior commissure, appear to be larger in women, which may permit better communication between hemispheres. Perceptual techniques that measure brain asymmetry in normal-functioning people sometimes show smaller asymmetries in women than in men, and damage to one brain hemisphere sometimes has a lesser effect in women than the comparable injury in men does. My own data on patients with damage to one hemisphere of the brain suggest that for functions such as basic speech and spatial ability, there are no major sex differences in hemispheric asymmetry, although there may be such disparities in certain more abstract abilities, such as defining words.

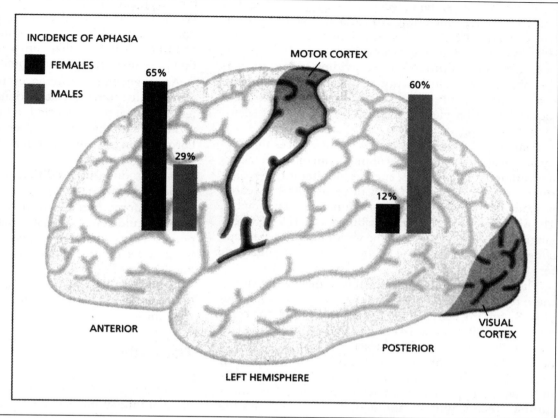

APHASIA, or speech disorders, occur most often in women when damage is sustained in the anterior of the brain. In men, they occur more frequently when damage is in the posterior region. The data presented at the right derive from one set of patients.

INCIDENCE OF APHASIA

■ FEMALES
▨ MALES

65%
29%
60%
12%

MOTOR CORTEX
VISUAL CORTEX
ANTERIOR
POSTERIOR
LEFT HEMISPHERE

JARED SCHNEIDMAN

If the known overall differences between men and women in spatial ability were related to differing dependence on the right brain hemisphere for such functions, then damage to that hemisphere might be expected to have a more devastating effect on spatial performance in men. My laboratory has studied the ability of patients with damage to one hemisphere of the brain to visualize the rotation of certain objects. As expected, for both sexes, those with damage to the right hemisphere got lower scores on these tests than those with damage to the left hemisphere did. Also, as anticipated, women did less well than men on this test. Damage to the right hemisphere, however, had no greater effect on men than on women.

The results of this study and others suggest that the normal differences between men and women on rotational and line orientation tasks need not be the result of different degrees of dependence on the right hemisphere. Some other brain systems may be mediating the higher performance by men.

Another brain difference between the sexes has been shown for speech and certain manual functions. Women incur aphasia (impairment of the power to produce and understand speech) more often after anterior damage than after posterior damage to the brain. In men, posterior damage more often affects speech. A similar pattern is seen in apraxia, difficulty in selecting appropriate hand movements, such as showing how to manipulate a particular object or copying the movements of the experimenter. Women seldom experience apraxia after left posterior damage, whereas men often do.

Men also incur aphasia from left hemisphere damage more often than women do. One explanation suggests that restricted damage within a hemisphere after a stroke more often affects the posterior region of the left hemisphere. Because men rely more on this region for speech than women do, they are more likely to be affected. We do not yet understand the effects on cognitive differences of such divergent patterns of speech and manual functions.

Although my laboratory has not found evidence of sex differences in functional brain asymmetry with regard to basic speech, movement or spatial-rotation abilities, we have found slight differences in some verbal skills. Scores on a vocabulary test and on a verbal fluency test, for instance, were slightly affected by damage to either hemisphere in women, but such scores were affected only by left hemisphere damage in men. These findings suggest that when using some more abstract verbal skills, women do use their hemispheres more equally than men do. But we have not found this to be true for all word-related tasks; for example, verbal memory appears to depend just as much on the left hemisphere in women as in men.

In recent years, new techniques for assessing the brain's activity—including functional magnetic resonance imaging (fMRI) and positron emission tomography (PET), when used during various problem-solving activities—have shown promise for providing more information about how brain function may vary among normal, healthy individuals. The research using these two techniques has so far yielded interesting, yet at times seemingly conflicting, results.

Some research has shown greater differences in activity between the hemispheres of men than of women during certain language tasks, such as judging if two words rhyme and creating past tenses of verbs. Other research has failed to find sex differences in functional asymmetry. The different results may be attributed in part to different language tasks being used in the various studies, perhaps showing that the sexes may differ in brain organization for some language tasks but not for others.

The varying results may also reflect the complexity of these techniques. The brain is always active to some degree. So for any activity, such as reading aloud, the comparison activity—here, reading silently—is intended to be very similar. We then "subtract" the brain pattern that occurs during silent reading to find the brain pattern present while reading aloud. Yet such methods require dubious assumptions about what the subject is doing during either activity. In addition, the more complex the activity, the more difficult it is to know what is actually being measured after subtracting the comparison activity.

Looking Back

To understand human behavior—how men and women differ from one another, for instance—we must look beyond the demands of modern life. Our brains are essentially like those of our ancestors of 50,000 and more years ago, and we can gain some insight into sex differences by studying the differing roles men and women have played in evolutionary history. Men were responsible for hunting and scavenging, defending the group against preda-

tors and enemies, and shaping and using weapons. Women gathered food near the home base, tended the home, prepared food and clothing, and cared for small children. Such specialization would put different selection pressures on men and women.

Any behavioral differences between individuals or groups must somehow be mediated by the brain. Sex differences have been reported in brain structure and organization, and studies have been done on the role of sex hormones in influencing human behavior. But questions remain regarding how hormones act on human brain systems to produce the sex differences we described, such as in play behavior or in cognitive patterns.

The information we have from laboratory animals helps to guide our explanations, but ultimately these hypotheses must be tested on people. Refinements in brain-imaging techniques, when used in conjunction with our knowledge of hormonal influences and with continuing studies on the behavioral deficits after damage to various brain regions, should provide insight into some of these questions.

The Author

DOREEN KIMURA studies the neural and hormonal basis of human intellectual functions. She is professor of psychology at Simon Fraser University. Until recently, she was professor of psychology and honorary lecturer in the department of clinical neurological sciences at the University of Western Ontario. Kimura is a fellow of the Royal Society of Canada.

Further Reading

SEX ON THE BRAIN; THE BIOLOGICAL DIFFERENCES BETWEEN MEN AND WOMEN. Deborah Blum. Viking Press, 1997.
THE TROUBLE WITH TESTOSTERONE; AND OTHER ESSAYS ON THE BIOLOGY OF THE HUMAN PREDICAMENT. Robert M. Sapolsky. Scribner, 1997.
SEX AND COGNITION. Doreen Kimura. MIT Press, 1999.

The New Woman:
Daring to Be Less than Perfect

Over these past few years there has been much talk about the "new good man." But, in contrast, there's been little discussion of a corresponding "new good woman." Indeed, many modern women aspire to, or at least talk about, "the beautiful bad girl." What's going on? Does being a "good woman" mean that one must be traditional, self-sacrificing, and unhappy? Is it so difficult to be the perfect "new good woman"—combining traditional homemaker with modern career woman—that no one is interested in pursuing that "honored" status? Is there a type of new woman who is autonomous, happy, and confident about herself, her family, and her job? Is there a secret to being a "new woman"?

Yes
We have been unable to escape the net of marriage
After numerous rounds of negotiations
We are leaving out the "till death do us part" stuff
We seek independent equality
We will treasure the time that we spend together
And give each other personal space
Old wine in new bottles
The new era of legal cohabitation has arrived!
October 20, at the Yellow Peacock Restaurant
You are welcome to attend
Chuang Hsueh-hua
Liu Han-chin

This is the wedding invitation given out by Chuang Hsueh-hua, an English teacher in the city of Kaohsiung. Talk about this manifesto of the "new era of legal cohabitation" spread like wildfire among her friends and co-workers. The teachers of Kaohsiung, who are relatively conservative, saw this challenge to the entrenched marriage system as being rather bizarre.

The controversy even carried over to the wedding banquet.

At one table, a guest—a teacher named Wu—says: "You'd never expect that a woman like Hsueh-hua would choose marriage. But she may change. After marriage comes taking care of all the routine daily tasks, and the pre-marriage atmosphere is worn away."

A Dr. Chang declares: "You don't know what kind of person the mother-in-law's going to be. This kind of 'equality of the sexes' manifesto might be fine with the husband, but that doesn't mean it's going to go over very well with the mother-in-law."

Finally, a business owner named Lin warns, in a tone of voice rich with implication, "The bride is very lucky to have found a 'new man.' The thing is, whatever may be said before the marriage, men only really show their true character after they get married."

The groom, Liu Han-chin, says that he is very willing to accept a marriage which is really more closely akin to cohabitation, in which his wife does not have to bear any of the traditional responsibilities of a marriage. He is doing it because the woman he loves is an advocate of equality between the sexes. Even if his wife's friends like to poke fun at him by calling him "Mr. Chuang," he doesn't really care.

The so-called good woman

"In fact our married life is really more like students living together. Hsueh-hua doesn't have to wait on me hand and foot, but we support each other spiritually and emotionally, and greatly appreciate the fact that we can rely on and learn from each other. As for the details of housework, whoever thinks that something needs to be done goes ahead and takes care of it. Of course," Liu laughs, "I'm more meticulous about cleanliness, so I take care of most of the housework."

In Liu's eyes, a "good woman" is intelligent and independent. But he is unusual. At present, most of the men in Taiwan do not feel this way about gender roles; many still have traditional views. Huang Li-chang, who runs an auto repair shop in Yungho, is a case in point.

He says that he only made one requirement of his wife: "I am responsible for outside the house [earning money], she is responsible for inside." The most important thing for him is that she take good care of his parents and children. He only married his wife after she was "run by" his mom, and his mom declared herself very satisfied.

"Even though now my wife helps out sometimes in the shop—because the economy is not so good and the pressures of being responsible for an extended family are great, I had to lay off some workers—still her main responsibility is the family. Jeez! What kind of a man would I be if I couldn't support my own family?" says Huang.

However, the overall economic structure of society is changing. Psychiatrist Wang Hao-wei notes that the costs of daily life in Taiwan are rising, and it is no longer so easy for a man to support a household relying simply on his own economic productivity. For example, the average salary of a university graduate fresh in the job market, about NT$30,000, is only enough for about 1.5 persons. It has been necessary for women to enter the workforce, and inevitably, there have been adjustments in relations between the sexes.

Luo Hsiao-hsin, who works in an engineering consulting firm, says he urged his wife to pursue the career she wanted, and not stay home lagging behind the times. As for the housework, this is divided up according to the basic natures of men and women. For example, bathing children and cooking are things women are good at, so his wife does them. Meanwhile, he takes care of moving heavy objects or picking the children up from the babysitter's. He doesn't want his wife to be economically dependent, but he still wants her to put him at the center of her life. For example, if they go out or return to his parents' home, he hopes his wife will "pretend" awhile and make it look like he's in charge and she follows.

The new double standard

Faced with these conflicting demands from men, Sony Hu of the Millennium Cultural and Educational Foundation states: Though many men in two-income households know that they cannot do without their wife's salaries, in conversation they treat their wife's work as supplementary, and do not credit them with any autonomy. This is because most Taiwan men, as always, think that it is good for society if women follow the traditional "three obediences and four virtues."

"In terms of social life, although most men believe that their wives can have their own friends, they do not think women should be out socializing at business-related functions the way men do," says Sony Hu. From this you can see that men have contradictory and selective views towards the status of women.

Women's career experiences and economic contributions are causing the self-sacrificing and obedient traditional type to disappear, and women now know how to fight for their rights. But there is still a double standard, even for men who accept equality in principle.

Chen Cheng-hsien, an engineer, says that he is proud of his wife, who is a high-level manager in her firm. However, he doesn't take much to the idea that a wife should be equal in everything. For example, when they return to his parents' home, it is hard to have male-female equality.

"My family is a traditional Taiwanese family. Although we don't live with my parents, sometimes we go back. My parents still expect their son to be filial and their daughter-in-law to be 'virtuous.' At these times, I ask my wife to be as traditional as she can, such as getting up early, making formal greetings to my parents, and doing housework. In our own home, we usually share the housework, but in front of the parents a woman should play the role of the traditional wife," he says. His parents are old, he says, and unlikely to change their attitudes. At times like these people have to be understanding, and make adjustments.

Super woman

Chen Cheng-hsien says that the social structure is beginning to change, but traditional values persist. Under the circumstances, the two sexes are still learning how to get along with each other. As his wife Chen Ya-li says, men want their wives to be independent and to perform competitively in the workplace, but at home they want them to be genteel and lady-like. In their own nuclear families, they divide up the housework, but when returning to the extended family, they expect women to put up with doing all the housework by themselves. Men have different standards for different circumstances, and women find it hard to know what to do.

Not only are individual men like this, but society as a whole has a double standard for women, which puts women in a difficult position. Wang Wen-fang, a founder of Awakening Kaohsiung, is a case in point.

Wang comes from Taichung, but very early on she married into a family in Kaohsiung. Her mother-in-law was very pleased, saying "she has the face of someone who will make a good helpmate" for her husband. Because of her hard work and her character she was able to do many things for her family: Besides taking care of every detail in the home, she also ran a second-hand car dealership. Her income was much greater than her husband's, and she became the main economic pillar of the family. Fearing that her husband was under too much pressure, she even opened a supermarket for him to manage.

Wang's mother-in-law was very proud of herself for being right on target in her early judgment of her daughter-in-law, and everybody was always giving Wang's husband the big thumbs up. But early this year came the news that Wang was going to be divorced. The reason was like something out of a soap opera: Her husband was unable to deal with the pressure of his wife being so successful, had an affair, and insisted on divorce. Suddenly, the praise that had long surrounded Wang turned to criticism that she was unable to keep her family harmonious. It was said that she was too dominating, "no wonder the guy couldn't stand it anymore."

Sadly, she herself felt ashamed on this point. "Although my husband was wrong to have an affair, a woman still must bear most of the responsibility for the failure to manage the family well," she says.

New Women in the public sphere

Shane Wang, as associate professor in the Department of Social Work at Soochow University, states that although many women have more influence at home than their husbands, they are still accustomed to giving the man pride of place. Indeed, they acquire power under the very rubric of "being a good helpmate." Under the circumstances, the man is like a king who reigns but does not rule. However, Wang explains, this situation by no means suggests that women and men are on an equal footing, because in most cases women still believe that it is "more clever" to pretend to observe traditional virtues. Accumulating power in that way does not challenge entrenched views, and is less likely to be suppressed.

In the public sphere, however, women cannot use this method to achieve a quiet revolution.

In recent years, with advocacy by women's groups and changing social and economic relations, the social participation and status of Taiwan women has begun to change. The legislature has passed a number of measures to make men and women more equal. However, Tang Wen-hui, an assistant professor in the graduate institute of political economy at National Chengkung University, believes that the public role of women in Taiwan is still limited by traditional family values, and that there has not been as much change as many might think.

"According to statistics I've compiled, over half of women in politics in Taiwan are single. This indicates that women actually have greater room to show their skills if they are unmarried," says Tang. Gender attitudes in Taiwan's political scene are still extremely conservative. It is taken for granted that a wife should help her husband's political career. But if the shoe is on the other foot, a man would find it difficult to accept the way the outside world looks at him if his wife is more successful. As a result, women in politics have difficulty finding an ideal marriage partner and often remain single.

Wake up, sister!

The modern man's idea of what constitutes a "new good woman" is one who observes traditional virtues at home but is economically productive in the workplace. The problem is: Who can pull that off?

Su Chien-ling, owner of Fembooks, says that most married working women in Taiwan are "two-career women." That is, besides having a full-time job, upon returning home they must play the role of the traditional homemaker.

Su makes an interesting point with regard to the standard of a good woman: the current unequal distribution of labor in society can be illustrated by setting men and women at two extremes on a continuum, with men (who do less) at point zero and women (who do more) at 100, with 50 each being a perfect balance of labor. The man only needs to do a little and he "gets points," whereas if the woman seeks equality then she is considered to "lose points." Men are praised for any change (thus the appearance of the "new good man"), while women are blamed for the same thing (thus no talk of a "new good woman").

Cultural critic Ping Lu suggests another reason why there has been little discussion of the "new woman." For a long time, women have been seen as the "long suffering" side of the gender relationship; they do not have some negative image they need to overturn.

Of course this does not mean that women should not demand that men change. "Males were the beneficiaries of the patriarchal structure, so it would be impossible to expect men to wake up to

its inequalities first. Equality between the sexes has to begin with women's consciousness, and women then demand that men change," says Ping Lu.

She says that women do not have to try to be "100% new women" incorporating the expectations of traditional as well as modern society. A real new woman should set her own standards.

In fact, many women would prefer not to be considered "good" if that means bearing too many burdens. Some have deliberately gone in the other direction, and discussion of "bad" women has been increasing. About ten years ago, Shih Chi-ching, director of the Warm Life Association for Women, hoping to encourage abused wives to dare to leave their marriages and to be independent self-confident women, raised the slogan of the "beautiful bad woman." And five years ago, Ho Chun-jui, an associate professor of Anglo-American literature at National Central University, challenged the "good girl" mold by raising high the banner of sexual liberation under the slogan "orgasms, not sexual harassment" (the terms rhyme in Chinese).

Why Marriage? Why children?

Ho says that, whereas the new man is getting all the media attention, in fact the sexually liberated woman represents a much more fundamental gender reconstruction.

She says that sexual liberation is beginning to undermine gender attitudes in Taiwan. Traditionally a "good woman" was expected to be "lady-like" in behavior, speech, appearance and skills (especially embroidery). Social expectations were internalized in women as repression and limitation of their own sexual activities. But now women are aware that they should have autonomy over their own bodies.

Examples can be seen in both the public and private spheres. In shops are clothes that show off women's shoulders or midriffs, and young women are increasingly unafraid to display their bodies. In the public sphere, women politicians like Sisy Chen have gotten a lot of attention and even envy for their casual, natural look—like wearing open-toed shoes. Explicitly or implicitly, popular culture has begun to challenge traditional gender viewpoints.

Ho Chun-jui continues: "There are other aspects as well, such as smashing 'the virgin complex,' resisting domestic

violence, and gay activism. Everywhere you can see that gender self-awareness doesn't have to be taught, that it is flowing through society. A future in which everyone is conscious of gender issues is not only inevitable, it is to be looked forward to."

There is one interesting point in which Taiwan differs from the West. In the early years of feminism in the West, many women deliberately promoted loosening the bonds of "beauty"—for instance, by removing their bras—and pursuing a gender-neutral look. This has not occurred in Taiwan. Ping Lu says that this is because feminism was already mature by the time it arrived in Taiwan. Taiwan has not experienced any of the step-by-step process of advancement or a backlash from men. Be that as it may, many people still equate the feminist movement with the stereotype of "no make-up, no marriage, no children."

Chuang Hsueh-hua rejects this stereotype: "In fact what we really care most about is: Why make up? Who are we getting married for? Why should we have children? We ask: Facing the major events of human life, do you as a woman have the right to make your own choices? If you decide to wear make-up, it should be because you want to, not because it pleases your male boss. If you choose marriage, it should be because you know that if things don't work out, you are clear-headed enough and have the ability to leave and still be a complete person. If you have children, it should be because you have the maturity to raise and educate the next generation."

Chuang emphasizes that every woman must make the key that unlocks her own life, and opens her own door of hope. A woman cannot sit passively waiting and checking her horoscope or reading the tea leaves, waiting for her future to appear by magic.

To rebel is justified

Currently women in different parts of Taiwan face dissimilar circumstances and levels of resistance.

Chou Fen-tzu, director of Awakening Kaohsiung, states that because of the greater financial pressures of living in urban areas, women have to work more, and this creates a situation in which men cannot but make concessions. Moreover, in cities, interpersonal relations are often fluid and remote, and an untraditional woman is not likely to meet as much outside pressure.

However, on the margins of the city or in the countryside, because interpersonal relations are so close, the conservativeness of couples, in-laws, neighbors, and colleagues creates a dense net. There will be tremendous resistance to any change in a marital relationship. Women in rural areas need to resolve these issues. That is why Awakening Kaohsiung has constantly worked with local governments to hold seminars or activities on gender topics. One example is the "women's study group," co-sponsored with the Kaohsiung Municipal Government, which is in its sixth session this year. It has gotten an excellent response to its promotion of gender equality. The class being held on January 15 at the Nantzu Youth Welfare Services Center was the last one of the most recent session.

Tables in the lecture hall are arranged in a semi-circle. The students have prepared snacks and placed them on the tables for all to share. Because this is the last class, everyone is anxious to talk about what they've gotten out of the course.

"My husband thinks that I'm coming every week to some 'mama's class' like cooking or flower arranging. If he knew I was coming to this place to 'rebel,' he would go nuts," says Mrs. Lin, who can't hold back a smile, adding that she will still come to the next session.

Chou Fen-tzu, who participated in the course design, says that attendance at class definitely plants the seed of self-awareness in those who come, but it is just a seed. She frankly admits that the woman must put in a great deal of effort to face up to the tests of interaction with

her husband and various other problems after this seed sprouts and blooms.

Su Chien-ling states that even she herself a practitioner of feminism—much less women who have just had an initial sprouting of self-awareness—faces a continuous series of challenges in life, such as family responsibilities, and children's education.

She wrote a book called *My Maternal Duties* in which she notes that the greatest gap between the feminist ideal and reality is the fear that most career women have about "not being model mothers." Her solution has been to rethink the terms of the problem: Why does "not model" have to mean "selfish"? Why is it that if a woman wishes to loosen the restraints of her maternal duties, then her children must automatically be "abandoned"? Are there no other possibilities?

Her thinking runs along these lines: When children still cannot fend for themselves, it is absolutely the responsibility of adults to care for them. But "adults" does not mean only the mother, but can also include the father, relatives, and friends. Most importantly, it may include social resources such as better neighborhood planning or child day-care centers.

Therefore, she feels that there is no harm at this stage in mothers investing 50% of their energy in the children, 30% in educating the father to do his share, and the other 20% in supporting women's organizations in their proposals for day-care and other services in the workplace and community. As the children get bigger, the mother should allow them to take care of themselves. This will save the mother from exhaustion with the added bonus of teaching the children to be more independent. One day when the children say to you, "don't help me, I can

do it myself," then you'll know what it means to say "it was worth it."

Su says that of course implementation is always very difficult. But in any case rational thinking should replace complaining; this is the best psychological "vitamin."

Future trends in the lives of women

Recently the international women's magazine *Elle* published the results of a survey conducted last May and June in 30 countries on global trends in women's lives. The expectations that young single working women in Taiwan have for themselves are already very different from the past. Most of the 3,600 respondents from Taiwan were young single women with middle- to high-level jobs. Asked to list their most important concerns, 45% said work, followed by "themselves" (31%), children (14%), and love (10%). Women in Taiwan showed less concern about love than women in other countries. Also, 54% said that they were unwilling to sacrifice for their partner, while 72% said that they felt divorce was the best solution for problem marriages.

As Ping Lu says, Taiwan is at the intersection of old and new value systems: The old traditions have not yet completely disappeared, but the new trends have become clear. Movement toward equality between the sexes is inevitable. Men cannot always stay at point zero, and women cannot always stay at 100. The new woman is beginning to dare to put herself first, and to receive a less-than-perfect grade.

(Eric Lin/tr. by Phil Newell)

From *Sinorama*, April 1999, pp. 22–31. © 1999 by Kwang Hwa Publishing. Reprinted by permission.

THE FEMINIZATION OF AMERICAN CULTURE

How Modern Chemicals May Be Changing Human Biology

Leonard Sax, M.D.

In ancient times—by which I mean, before 1950—most scholars agreed that women were, as a rule, not quite equal to men. Women were charming but mildly defective. Many (male) writers viewed women as perpetual teenagers, stuck in an awkward place between childhood and adulthood. German philosopher Arthur Schopenhauer, for example, wrote that women are "childish, silly and short-sighted, really nothing more than overgrown children, all their life long. Women are a kind of intermediate stage between the child and the man."[1]

Psychologists in that bygone era devoted considerable time and energy to the question of why women couldn't outgrow their childish ways. The Freudians said it was because they were trapped in the pre-Oedipal stage, tortured by penis envy. Followers of Abraham Maslow claimed that women were fearful of self-actualization. Jungians insisted that women were born with a deficiency of imprinted archetypes.

A mature adult nowadays is someone who is comfortable talking about her inner conflicts, someone who values personal relationships above abstract goals, someone who isn't afraid to cry. In other words: a mature adult is a woman.

Back then, of course, almost all the psychologists were men.

Things are different now. Male psychologists today are so rare that Ilene Philipson—author of *On the Shoulders of Women: The Feminization of Psychotherapy*—speaks of "the vanishing male therapist" as a species soon to be extinct.[2] As the gender of the modal psychotherapist has changed from male to female, the standard of mental health has changed along with it. Today, Dr. Philipson observes, the badge of emotional maturity is no longer the ability to control or sublimate your feelings but rather the ability to *express* them. A mature adult nowadays is someone who is comfortable talking about her inner conflicts, someone who values personal relationships above abstract goals, someone who isn't afraid to cry. In other words: a mature adult is a woman.

It is now the men who are thought to be stuck halfway between childhood and adulthood, incapable of articulating their inner selves. Whereas psychologists fifty years ago amused themselves by cataloging women's (supposed) deficiencies, psychologists today devote themselves to demonstrating "the natural superiority of women."[3] Psychologists report that women are better able to understand nonverbal communication and are more expressive of emotion.[4] Quantitative personality inventories reveal that the average woman is more trusting, nurturing, and outgoing than the average man.[5] The average eighth-grade girl has a command of language and writing skills equal to that of the average eleventh-grade boy.[6]

As the influence of the new psychology permeates our culture, women have understandably begun to wonder whether men are really, well, human. "What if these women are right?" wonders one writer in an article for *Marie Claire*, a national woman's magazine. "What if it's true that some men don't possess, or at least can't express, nuanced emotions?"[7] More than a few contemporary psychologists have come to regard the male of our species as a coarsened, more violent edition of the normal, female, human. Not surprisingly, they have begun to question whether having a man in the house is desirable or even safe.

Eleven years ago, scholar Sara Ruddick expressed her concern about "the extent and variety of the psychological, sexual, and physical battery suffered by women and children of all classes and social groups… at the hands of fathers, their mothers' male lovers, or male relatives. If putative fathers are absent or perpetually disappearing and actual fathers are controlling or abusive, *who needs a father*? What mother would want to live with one or wish one on her children?"[8] Nancy Polikoff, former counsel to the Women's Legal Defense Fund, said that "it is no tragedy, either on a national scale or in an individual family, for children to be raised without fathers."[9]

The feminization of psychology manifests itself in myriad ways. Consider child discipline. Seventy years ago, doctors agreed that the best way to discipline your child was to punish the little criminal. ("Spare the rod, spoil the child.") Today, spanking is considered child abuse.[10] You're supposed to *talk* with your kid. Spanking sends all the wrong messages, we are told, and may have stupendously horrible consequences. Psychoanalyst Alice Miller confidently informed us, in her book *For Your Own Good*, that Adolf Hitler's evil can be traced to the spankings his father inflicted on him in childhood.[11]

THE NEW MEN'S MAGAZINES

It isn't only psychology that has undergone a process of feminization over the past fifty years, and it isn't only women whose attitudes have changed. Take a stroll to your neighborhood bookstore or newsstand. You'll find magazines such as *Men's Health, MH-18, Men's Fitness, Gear*, and others devoted to men's pursuit of a better body, a better self-image. None of them existed fifteen years ago. The paid circulation of *Men's Health* has risen from 250,000 to more than 1.5 million in less than ten years.[12] Many of the articles in these magazines are reminiscent of those to be found in women's magazines such as *Glamour, Mademoiselle*, and *Cosmopolitan*: "The Ten Secrets of Better Sex," "The New Diet Pills—Can They Work For You?" or "Bigger Biceps in Five Minutes a Day." (The women's magazine equivalent might be something like "slimmer thighs in five minutes a day.")

Today, the best qualification for leadership may be the ability to listen. The feminine way of seeing the world and its problems is, arguably, becoming the mainstream way.

Men didn't use to care so much about their appearance. Psychiatrists Harrison Pope and Katharine Phillips report that in American culture today, "Men of all ages, in unprecedented numbers, are preoccupied with the appearance of their bodies."[13] They document that "men's dissatisfaction with body appearance has nearly tripled in less than thirty years—from 15 percent in 1972, to 34 percent in 1985, to 43 percent in 1997."[14] Cosmetic plastic surgery, once marketed exclusively to women, has found a rapidly growing male clientele. The number of men undergoing liposuction, for instance, quadrupled between 1990 and 2000.[15]

THE FEMINIZATION OF ENTERTAINMENT AND POLITICS

This process of femininization manifests itself, though somewhat differently, when you turn on the TV or watch a movie. Throughout the mid-twentieth century, leading men were, as a rule, infallible: think of Clark Gable in *Gone With the Wind*, Cary Grant in *North by Northwest*, or Fred McMurray in *My Three Sons*. But no longer. In family comedy, the father figure has metamorphosed from the all-knowing, all-wise Robert Young of *Father Knows Best* to the occasional bumbling of Bill Cosby and the consistent stupidity of Homer Simpson. Commercially successful movies now often feature women who are physically aggressive, who dominate or at least upstage the men. This description applies to movies as diverse as *Charlie's Angels* and *Crouching Tiger, Hidden Dragon*. In today's cinema, to paraphrase Garrison Keillor, all the leading women are strong and all the leading men are good-looking.

A transformation of comparable magnitude seems to be under way in the political arena. Military command used to be considered the best qualification for leadership—as it was with Ulysses Grant, Theodore Roosevelt, Charles de Gaulle, and Dwight Eisenhower, to name only a few. Today, the best qualification for leadership may be the ability to listen. The feminine way of seeing the world and its problems is, arguably, becoming the mainstream way.

In 1992, Bill Clinton ran against George Bush *père* for the presidency. Clinton was an acknowledged draft evader. Bush, the incumbent, was a World War II hero who had just led the United States to military success in Operation Desert Storm. Clinton won. In 1996, Clinton was challenged by Bob Dole, another decorated World War II veteran. Once again, the man who had evaded military service defeated the combat veteran. In 2000, Gov. George W. Bush and Sen. John McCain competed for the Republican presidential nomination. McCain was a genuine war hero whose courageous actions as a prisoner of war in Vietnam had won him well-deserved honors and praise. Bush, on the other hand, was alleged to have used family influence to obtain a position in the Texas National Guard, in order to avoid service in Vietnam. Once again, the man who had never experienced combat defeated the military veteran. Moral of the story: It's all very well to be a war hero, but in our modern, feminized society, being a war hero won't get you elected president. Conversely, being a draft dodger isn't as bad as it used to be.

A number of authors have recognized the increasing feminization of American society. With few exceptions, most of those acknowledging this process have welcomed it.[16] As Elinor Lenz and Barbara Myerhoff wrote in their 1985 book *The Feminization of America*, "The feminizing influence is moving [American society] away from many archaic ways of thinking and behaving, toward the promise of a saner and more humanistic future.... Feminine culture, with its commitment to creating and protecting life, is our best and brightest hope for overcoming the destructive, life-threatening forces of the nuclear age."[17]

The question is, what's causing this shift? Some might argue that the changes I've described are simply a matter of better education, progressive laws, and two generations of consciousness-raising.

I think we can all agree on one point: there have been fundamental changes in American culture over the past fifty years, changes that indicate a shift from a male-dominated culture to a feminine or at least an androgynous society. The question is, what's causing this shift? Some might argue that the changes I've described are simply a matter of better education, progressive laws, and two generations of consciousness-raising: an evolution from a patriarchal Dark Ages to a unisex, or feminine, Enlightenment. I'm willing to consider that hypothesis. But before we accept that conclusion, we should ask whether there are any other possibilities.

FEMINIZED WILDLIFE

We have to make a big jump now, a journey that will begin at the Columbia River in Washington, near the Oregon border. James Nagler, assistant professor of zoology at the University of Idaho, recently noticed something funny about the salmon he observed in the Columbia. Almost all of them were—or appeared to be—female. But when he caught a few and analyzed their DNA, he found that many of the "female" fish actually were male: their chromosomes were XY instead of XX.[18]

Many of these chemicals, it turns out, mimic the action of female sex hormones called estrogens.

Nagler's findings echo a recent report from England, where government scientists have found some pretty bizarre fish. In two polluted rivers, half the fish are female,

and the other half are... something else. Not female but not male either. The English scientists call these bizarre fish "intersex": their gonads are not quite ovaries, not quite testicles, but some weird thing in between, making neither eggs nor sperm. In both rivers, the intersex fish are found downstream of sites where treated sewage is discharged into the river. Upstream from the sewer effluent, the incidence of intersex is dramatically lower. The relationship between the concentration of sewer effluent and the incidence of intersex is so close that "the proportion of intersex fish in any sample of fish could perhaps be predicted, using a linear equation, from the average concentration of effluent constituents in the river."[19]

It's something in the water. Something in the water is causing feminization of male fish.

And it's not just fish. In Lake Apopka, in central Florida, Dr. Louis Guillette and his associates have found male alligators with abnormally small penises; in the blood of these alligators, female hormone levels are abnormally high and male hormone levels abnormally low.[20] Male Florida panthers have become infertile; the levels of male sex hormones in their blood are much lower (and the levels of female hormones higher) than those found in panthers in less-polluted environments.[21]

What's going on?

Our modern society generates a number of chemicals that never existed before about fifty years ago. Many of these chemicals, it turns out, mimic the action of female sex hormones called estrogens. Plastics—including a plasticizer called phthalate, used in making flexible plastic for bottles of Coke, Pepsi, Sprite, Evian water, and so forth—are known to have estrogenic effects.[22] Many commonly used pesticides have estrogenlike actions on human cells.[23] Estrogenic chemicals ooze out of the synthetic lacquer that lines the inside of soup cans.[24] These chemicals and others find their way into sewage and enter the rivers and lakes. Hence the effects on fish, alligators, and other wildlife.

EFFECTS ON HUMANS?

Modern chemicals may have a feminizing effect on wildlife. That's certainly cause for concern in its own right. But is there any evidence that a similar process of feminization is occurring in humans?

Answer: there may be. Just like the Florida panther, human males are experiencing a rapid decline in fertility and sperm count. The sperm count of the average American or European man has declined continuously over the past four decades, to the point where today it is less than 50 percent of what it was forty years ago.[25] This downward trend is seen only in industrialized regions of North America and western Europe. Lower sperm counts are being reported in urban Denmark but not in rural Finland, for example.[26] Of course, that's precisely the pattern one would expect, if the lower sperm counts are an effect of "modern" materials such as plastic water bottles.

Male infertility, one result of that lower count, is now the single most common cause of infertility in our species.[27] The rate of infertility itself has quadrupled in the past forty years, from 4 percent in 1965 to 10 percent in 1982 to at least 16 percent today.[28]

WHAT ABOUT GIRLS?

So far we've talked mainly about the effect of environmental estrogens on males. What about girls and women? What physiological effects might excess environmental estrogens have on them? Giving estrogens to young girls would, in theory, trigger the onset of puberty at an earlier than expected age. In fact, in the past few years doctors have noticed that girls *are* beginning puberty earlier than ever before. Just as the environmental-estrogen hypothesis would predict, this phenomenon is seen only in girls, not in boys. Dr. Marcia Herman-Giddens, studying over seventeen thousand American girls, found that this trend to earlier puberty is widespread. "Girls across the United States are developing pubertal characteristics at younger ages than currently used norms," she concluded.[29]

Rather than labeling all these pubescent eight-year-olds as "abnormal," Dr. Paul Kaplowitz and his associates recently recommended that the earliest age for "normal" onset of puberty simply be redefined as age seven in Caucasian girls and age six in African-American girls.[30] Dr. Kaplowitz is trying, valiantly, to define this problem out of existence. If you insist that normal puberty begins at age six or age seven, then all these eight-year-old girls with well-filled bras suddenly become "normal."

But saying so doesn't make it so. Last year, doctors in Puerto Rico reported that most young girls with premature breast development have toxic levels of phthalates in their blood; those phthalates appear to have seeped out of plastic food and beverage containers. The authors noted that Puerto Rico is a warm island. Plastic containers that become warm are more likely to ooze phthalate molecules into the food or beverages they contain.[31] These authors, led by Dr. Ivelisse Colón, reported their findings in *Environmental Health Perspectives*, the official journal of the National Institute of Environmental Health Sciences (a branch of the National Institutes of Health). On the cover of the issue in which the report appeared, the editors chose to feature the picture of a young woman drinking water from a plastic bottle.

Premature puberty in girls has become so widespread that it has begun to attract the attention of major media. This topic made the cover of *Time* magazine on October 30, 2000. Unfortunately, few of these high-profile articles show any understanding of the possible role of environmental estrogens. The *Time* article barely mentioned the *Environmental Health Perspectives* study, nor did it link the phenomenon of early puberty in girls with declining sperm counts, intersex fish, or tiny penises in alligators. Instead, it featured a picture of a short boy staring at a taller girl's breasts.

What effect might extra estrogen have on adult women? Many scientists have expressed concern that exposure to excessive environmental estrogens may lead to breast cancer. The rate of breast cancer has risen dramatically over the past fifty years. Today, one in every nine American women can expect to develop breast cancer at some point in her life. But this increase is seen only in industrialized countries,[32] where plastics and other products of modern chemistry are widely used. Women born in Third World countries are at substantially lower risk. When they move from a Third World country to the United States, their risk soon increases to that seen in other women living here, clearly demonstrating that the increased risk is an environmental, not a genetic, factor.[33]

CONNECTION?

At this point, you may feel that you've been reading two completely disconnected essays: one about the feminization of American culture, and the second about the effects of environmental estrogens. Could there be any connection between the two?

If human physiology and endocrinology are being affected by environmental estrogens then there is no reason in principle why human psychology and sexuality should be exempt.

There may be. If human physiology and endocrinology are being affected by environmental estrogens—as suggested by lower sperm counts, increasing infertility, earlier onset of puberty in girls, and rising rates of breast cancer—then there is no reason in principle why human psychology and sexuality should be exempt. If we accept the possibility that environmental estrogens are affecting human physiology and endocrinology, then we must also consider the possibility that the feminization of American culture may, conceivably, reflect the influence of environmental estrogens.

The phenomena we have considered show a remarkable synchrony. Many of the cultural trends discussed in the first half of the article began to take shape in the 1950s and '60s, just as plastics and other modern chemicals began to be widely introduced into American life. There are, of course, many difficulties in attempting to measure any correlation between an endocrine variable—such as a decline in sperm counts—and a cultural variable, such as cultural feminization. One of many problems is that no single quantitative variable accurately and reliably measures the degree to which a culture is becoming feminized. However, we can get some feeling for the synchrony of the cultural process with the endocrine process by considering the correlation of the decline in sperm counts with the decline in male college enrollment.

We've already mentioned how sperm counts have declined steadily and continuously in industrialized areas of North America and western Europe since about 1950. Let's use that decline as our endocrine variable. As the cultural variable, let's look at college graduation rates. Since 1950, the proportion of men among college graduates has been steadily declining. In 1950, 70 percent of college graduates were men; today, that number is about 43 percent and falling. Judy Mohraz, president of Goucher College, warned not long ago that if present trends continue, "the last man to graduate from college will receive his baccalaureate in the year 2067.... Daughters not only have leveled the playing field in most college classrooms, but they are exceeding their brothers in school success across the board."[34]

Plot these two phenomena on the same graph. Use no statistical tricks, no manipulation of the data—simply use best-fit trend lines, plotted on linear coordinates—and the two lines practically coincide. The graph of declining sperm density perfectly parallels the decline in male college graduation rates.

Of course, the correlation between these phenomena—one endocrine, one cultural—doesn't prove that they must derive from the same underlying source. But such a strong correlation certainly provides some evidence that the endocrine phenomenon of declining sperm counts may derive from the same source as the cultural phenomenon of declining male college enrollment (as a percentage of total enrollment).

If this hypothesis is ultimately shown to be at least partly correct, it would not be the first time that items of daily household life contributed to the transformation of a mighty civilization.

THE DECLINE AND FALL OF THE MALE AMERICAN EMPIRE?

I have suggested that the feminization of American culture and endocrine phenomena such as declining sperm counts are both manifestations of the effects of environmental estrogens. To the best of my knowledge, no other author has yet made such a suggestion. If this hypothesis is ultimately shown to be at least partly correct, it would not be the first time that items of daily household life con-

tributed to the transformation of a mighty civilization. A number of scientists, most notably toxicologist Jerome Nriagu, have suggested that one factor leading to the decline and fall of the Roman Empire was the lead glaze popular among the Roman aristocracy after about A.D. 100.[35] Bowls and dishes were glazed with lead, which was also widely used in household plumbing. (Our word *plumbing* comes from the Latin *plumbum*, which means lead.) The neurological symptoms of lead toxicity—mania, difficulty concentrating, and mood swings—were not recognized as manifestations of poisoning. No Roman scientist conducted the necessary controlled experiment: a comparison of families that used lead-glazed pottery with families that did not. The scientific worldview necessary for such an experiment did not exist at the time. It is thought-provoking to consider that something as insignificant as pottery glazing may have brought down the Roman Empire.

Could anything of comparable magnitude be happening right now, in our own culture? Testing the hypothesis I have proposed will be difficult. It is probably not possible to randomize humans to a "modern, plasticized" environment versus a "primitive, no-plastics, no-cans, no-pesticide" environment—and even it were possible, it would not be ethical to do so. (It should be noted, however, that one careful study has already been published demonstrating that men who consumed only organic produce had higher sperm counts than men eating regular, pesticide-treated produce.[36]) Measures of the degree to which a culture is "feminized" would be controversial, and only seldom would such measures be objectively quantifiable.

Nevertheless, the world around us is changing in ways that have never occurred in the history of our species. It is possible that some of these changes in our culture may reflect the influence of environmental estrogens, an influence whose effects are subtle and incremental. To the extent that human dignity means being in control of one's destiny, we should explore the possibility that our minds and bodies are being affected by environmental estrogens in ways that we do not, as yet, fully understand.

NOTES

1. "Dass sie selbst kindisch, läppisch und kurzsichtig, mit einem Worte: zeitlebens grosse Kinder sind—eine Art Mittelstufe zwischen dem Kinde und dem Manne." Arthur Schopenhauer, *Parerga und Paralipomena*, §364 (1851).

2. Ilene Philipson, *On the Shoulders of Women: The Feminization of Psychotherapy* (New York: Guilford Press, 1993), 145.

3. *The Natural Superiority of Women* is of course the title of one of Ashley Montagu's most famous books, initially published in 1953. Montagu issued a final revised edition in 1998, in which he eagerly documented the published research that supported what had been mere conjecture forty years before.

4. Judith Hall, *Nonverbal Sex Differences: Accuracy of Communication and Expressive Style* (Baltimore: Johns Hopkins Univ. Press, 1990). See also: Ann Kring and Albert Gordon, "Sex Differences in Emotion: Expression, Experience, and Physiology," *Journal of Personality and Social Psychology* 74 (1998): 686–703.

5. Alan Feingold, "Gender Differences in Personality: a Meta-Analysis," *Psychological Bulletin* 116, no. 3 (1994): 429–556.

6. U.S. Department of Education, *Educational Equity for Girls and Women* (Washington: U.S. Government Printing Office, 2000), 4. The report can be read online at nces.ed.gov/spider/webspider/2000030.html.

7. Marilyn Berlin Snell, "Wisdom of the Ages," *Marie Claire*, September 1999, 123.

8. Ruddick 1990, cited in Philipson, *On the Shoulders of Women*, 142–43. Emphasis added.

9. Quoted in Cathy Young, *Ceasefire!* (New York: Free Press, 1999), 60.

10. According to both the American Academy of Pediatrics and the American Academy of Family Physicians, there is no situation in which spanking is appropriate. Spanking is always child abuse. You can read the AAFP's statement at www.aafp.org/afp/990315ap/1577.html and the AAP's position at www.aap.org/advocacy/archives/aprspr2.html.

11. Alice Miller, *For Your Own Good: Hidden Cruelty in Child-Rearing and the Roots of Violence* (Noonday Press, 1990).

12. Harrison Pope, Katharine Phillips, and Roberto Olivardia, *The Adonis Complex: The Secret Crisis of Male Body Obsession* (New York: Free Press, 2000), 56.

13. Pope, Phillips, and Olivardia, *The Adonis Complex*, xiii.

14. Pope, Phillips, and Olivardia, *The Adonis Complex*, 27.

15. Pope, Phillips, and Olivardia, *The Adonis Complex*, 31.

16. One notable exception is Rich Zubaty's misogynistic diatribe, *Surviving the Feminization of America* (Tinley Park, Ill.: Panther Press, 1993).

17. Elinor Lenz and Barbara Myerhoff, *The Feminization of America: How Women's Values Are Changing Our Public and Private Lives* (New York: St. Martin's Press, 1985), 2.

18. James Nagler et al., "High Incidence of a Male-Specific Genetic Marker in Phenotypic Female Chinook Salmon From the Columbia River," *Environmental Health Perspectives* 109 (2001): 67–69.

19. Susan Jobling et al., "Widespread Sexual Disruption in Wild Fish," *Environmental Science and Technology* 32, no. 17 (1998): 2498–2506.

20. Louis Guillette et al., "Developmental Abnormalities of the Gonad and Abnormal Sex Hormone Concentrations in Juvenile Alligators from Contaminated and Control Lakes in Florida," *Environmental Health Perspectives* 102 (1994): 680–88.

21. C.F. Facemire et al., "Reproductive Impairment in the Florida Panther," *Environmental Health Perspectives* 103, supplement 4 (1995): 79–86.

22. Susan Jobling et al., "A Variety of Environmentally Persistent Chemicals, Including Some Phthalate Plasticizers, Are Weakly Estrogenic," *Environmental Health Perspectives* 103 (1995): 582–87.

23. Ana Soto, Kerrie Chung, and Carlos Sonnenschein, "The Pesticides Endosulfan, Toxaphene, and Dieldrin Have Estrogenic Effects on Human Estrogen-Sensitive Cells," *Environmental Health Perspectives* 102, no. 4 (1994): 380–83.

24. José Brotons et al., "Xenoestrogens Released From Lacquer Coatings in Food Cans," *Environmental Health Perspectives* 103, no. 6 (1995): 608–12.

25. Shanna Swan, Eric Elkin, and Laura Fenster, "The Question of Declining Sperm Density Revisited: Analysis of 101 Studies Published 1934–1996," *Environmental Health Perspectives* 108 (2000): 961–66.

26. Tina Jensen et al., "Semen Quality Among Danish and Finnish Men Attempting to Conceive," *European Journal of Endocrinology* 142 (2000): 47–52.

27. D. Stewart Irvine, "Epidemiology and Aetiology of Male Infertility," *Human Reproduction* 13 (1998): 33–44.

28. Schmidt, Münster, and Helm (*British Journal of Obstetrics and Gynaecology* 102 (December 1995): 978–84, found that 26.2 percent of couples attempting to have a child have experienced infertility. Most authorities regard this figure as too high, however. The rule of thumb currently popular among infertility specialists is "one couple in six" (i.e., a rate of 16.6 percent).

29. Marcia Herman-Giddens et al., "Secondary Sexual Characteristics and Menses in Young Girls Seen in Office Practice," *Pediatrics* 99, no. 4 (1997): 505–12.

30. Paul Kaplowitz et al., "Re-examination of the Age Limit for Defining When Puberty Is Precocious in Girls in the United States: Implications for Evaluation and Treatment," *Pediatrics* 104, no. 4 (1999): 936–41.

31. Ivelisse Colón et al., "Identification of Phthalate Esters in the Serum of Young Puerto Rican Girls with Premature Breast Development," *Environmental Health Perspectives* 108, no. 9 (2000): 895–900.

32. Pisani, Parkin, and Feraly, "Estimates of the Worldwide Mortality From Eighteen Major Cancers in 1985," *International Journal of Cancer* 55, no. 6 (1993): 891–903.

33. J.L. Standford et al., "Breast Cancer Incidence in Asian Migrants to the United States and Their Descendants," *Epidemiology* 6, no. 2 (1995): 181–83.

34. Judy Mohraz, "Missing Men on Campus," *Washington Post*, 16 January 2000.

35. See Jerome Nriagu's book, *Lead and Lead Poisoning in Antiquity* (Baltimore: Johns Hopkins University Press, 1983). See also Lionel and Diane Needleman, "Lead Poisoning and the Decline of the Roman Aristocracy," *Classical Views* 4, no. 1 (1985): 63–94.

36. T.K. Jensen et al., "Semen Quality Among Members of Organic Food Associations in Zealand, Denmark," *Lancet* 347 (1996): 1844.

Leonard Sax, M.D., Ph.D., is a physician and psychologist practicing in Montgomery County, Maryland.

From *The World & I*, October 2001, pp. 263–275. © 2001 by The World & I, a publication of The Washington Times Corporation. Reprinted by permission.

OVERCOMING SEX

CAN MEN AND WOMEN BE FRIENDS?

By Camille Chatterjee

If men are from Mars and women are from Venus, it may explain at least one of their shared beliefs: Men and women can't be real friends. Blame the sexual tension that almost inevitably exists between any red-blooded, heterosexual man and woman. Point to the jealousy that plagues many rational people when a significant other befriends someone of the opposite sex. Boil it down to the inherent differences between the sexes. It just can't be done. Right?

WRONG, SAY RELATIONSHIP EXPERTS. "THE BELIEF that men and women can't be friends comes from another era in which women were at home and men were in the workplace, and the only way they could get together was for romance," explains Linda Sapadin, Ph.D., a psychologist in private practice in Valley Stream, New York. "Now they work together and have sports interests together and socialize together." This cultural shift is encouraging psychologists, sociologists and communications experts to put forth a new message: Though it may be tricky, men and women can successfully become close friends. What's more, there are good reasons for them to do so.

Society has long singled out romance as the prototypical male-female relationship because it spawns babies and keeps the life cycle going; cross-sex friendship, as researchers call it, has been either ignored or trivialized. We have rules for how to act in romantic relationships (flirt, date, get married, have kids) and even same-sex friendships (boys relate by doing activities together, girls by talking and sharing). But there are so few platonic male-female friendships on display in our culture that we're at a loss to even define these relationships.

Peggy and Phil

Is there sexual tension between you?

Phil: No, but there are times that I swear she is jealous of my girlfriends. It could just be my head.

Peggy: No, not really. But at times I feel weird about bringing my boyfriends around; I don't want Phil to get jealous.

Do you fight?

Phil: We only argue when we disagree about which rides to go on at Coney Island.

Peggy: There were actually a few times we got into arguements that ended in physical fights. But no one got hurt.

How is your friendship rewarding?

Phil: We could see each other naked and talk dirty without having to worry about sleeping over or whether or not our breath stinks.

Peggy: We just have so much fun together. I feel like I can tell him anything. There is no pressure.

Part of this confusion stems from the media. A certain 1989 film starring Meg Ryan and Billy Crystal convinced a nation of moviegoers that sex always comes between men and women, making true friendship impossible. "*When Harry Met Sally* set the potential for male-female friendship back about 25 years," says Michael Monsour, Ph.D., assistant professor of communications at the University of Colorado at Denver and author of *Women and Men as Friends: Relationships Across the Life Span in the 21st Century* (Lawrence Erldbaum, 2001). Television hasn't helped either. "Almost every time you see a male-female friendship, it winds up turning into romance," Monsour notes. Think Sam and Diane or Chandler and Monica. These cultural images are hard to overcome, he says. It's no wonder that we expect that men and women are always on the road to romance.

Jenni and Mike

Is there any sexual tension between you?

Jenni: No, I have never experienced any sexual tension between us. We only recently renewed our friendship after many years of living in separate countries, and our focus is on building up a friendship. I trust Mike a lot and could call him in the middle of the night if I needed him—but not to relieve any sexual tension, of course.

Mike: No. None at all. We grew up in Scotland together. I've known her since she was eight years old. I used to babysit her, and that's not really grounds for good sexual tension.

Do you ever fight?

Jenni: No, we don't fight. I don't tend to fight with friends. I wouldn't let it get that far. I am pretty outspoken, and so is Mike. We always find more constructive ways of communicating our differences than by fighting. We both rely on humor too much to move too far into the dark side of friendship.

How is your friendship rewarding?

Jenni: Mike has amazing energy and a positive outlook, and I always get a good vibe when I hang out with him. We share similar passions, such as dance, theatre, cycling and human rights and so we will always find it easy to do stuff together. However, it is just as easy to sit in a cafe with him and laugh, tell stories and chat for hours. I am excited at the prospect of deepening our friendship even further and amazed at the ease with which our lives have connected in New York in such a short time. It is a rare and special thing to click with someone in that way.

Mike: We have a lot of common interests and mutual concerns. We're from the same place. She works for the UN—it's rewarding to hear about the things she does with her life. She's inspiring.

But that's only one of the major barriers. In 1989, Don O'Meara, Ph.D., a sociology professor at the University of Cincinnati-Raymond Walters College, published a landmark study in the journal *Sex Roles* on the top impediments to cross-sex friendship. "I started my research because one of my best friends is a woman," says O'Meara. "She said, 'Do you think anyone else has the incredible friendship we do?'" He decided to find out, and

after reviewing the scant existing research dating back to only 1974, O'Meara identified the following four challenges to male-female friendship: defining it, dealing with sexual attraction, seeing each other as equals and facing people's responses to the relationship. A few years later, he added a fifth: meeting in the first place.

CHALLENGE #1
Defining the relationship: Friends or lovers?

Platonic, friendly love does exist, O'Meara asserts, and a study of 20 pairs of friends published last year in the *Journal of Social and Personal Relationships* lends credence to the notion. In it, Heidi Reeder, Ph.D., an assistant professor in Boise State University's communication department, confirms that "friendship attraction" or a connection devoid of lust or longing, is a bona fide type of bond that people experience. Distinguishing between romantic, sexual and friendly feelings, however, can be exceedingly difficult.

"People don't know what feelings are appropriate toward the opposite sex, unless they're what our culture defines as appropriate," says O'Meara. "You know you love someone and enjoy them as a person, but not enough to date or marry them. What does this mean?"

CHALLENGE #2
Overcoming Attraction: Let's talk about sex

The reality that sexual attraction could suddenly enter the equation of a cross-sex friendship uninvited is always lurking in the background. A simple, platonic hug could instantaneously take on a more amorous meaning. "You're trying to do a friend-friend thing," says O'Meara, "but the male-female parts of you get in the way." Unwelcome or not, the attraction is difficult to ignore.

In a major 1988 study published in the *Journal of Social and Personal Relationships*, Sapadin asked over 150 professional men and women what they liked and disliked about their cross-sex friendships. Topping women's list of dislikes: sexual tension. Men, on the other hand, more frequently replied that sexual attraction was a prime reason for initiating a friendship, and that it could even deepen a friendship. Either way, 62% of all subjects reported that sexual tension was present in their cross-sex friendships.

CHALLENGE #3
Establishing Equality: The Power Play

Friendship should be a pairing of equals. But, O'Meara says, "in a culture where men have always been more equal than women, male dominance, prestige and power is baggage that both men and women are likely to bring to a relationship." Women are at risk of subconsciously adopting a more submissive role in cross-sex friendships, he says, although that is slowly changing as society begins to treat both genders more equally.

CHALLENGE #4
The Public Eye: Dealing with doubters

Society may not be entirely ready for friendships between men and women that have no sexual subtext. People with close friends of the opposite sex are often barraged with nudging, winking and skepticism: "Are you really *just* friends?" This is especially true, says O'Meara, of older adults, who grew up when men and women were off-limits to each other until marriage.

Philou and Patou

Do you ever fight?
Patou: Yes, we do have arguments. Generally our favorite topic relates to our own sexual experiences. He likes to push his frustrations, I think, to reevaluate the intimacy of female and male mysteries. I adore these hot moments, because we always challenge our emotions and mutual fantasies. Overall, I think that a man and woman, lovers or friends, is the best duet.
Philou: I don't really think we fight. We argue, yes. We often meet for dinner and engage in passionate discussions. But I feel we view life in the same way and that's why we are friends. Sometimes she gets mad at my jokes, sometimes I joke at her madness.

CHALLENGE #5
The Meeting Place: Finding friends

As the workplace and other social arenas become increasingly open to women, the sexes are mingling more and more. Still, men and women continue to have surprisingly few opportunities to interact.

"Boys and girls form their own gender groups in elementary school," explains Monsour. "They learn their own ways of relating to each other. So when they do get together, inspired by puberty, they see each other as dating partners because they've never really known each other as friends." A surprisingly major factor in this phenomenon is the kids' own innate interest in children who act like they do. Called "voluntary gender segregation," it continues into adulthood. "You see it at cocktail parties," says Monsour. "Men go off to one corner, and women go to another."

These obstacles may seem numerous and formidable, but male-female friendship is becoming not only a possibility, but also a necessity. If men and women are to work, play and co-exist in modern society, researchers believe they must learn to understand and communicate with each other. To that end, social scientists like Monsour, Sapadin and O'Meara have begun studying how to do just that. The field of research is still in its infancy, but they are now beginning to understand some basic truths about male-female friendship:

TRUTH #1
Friendship is not equal opportunity

Not until high school does puberty really draw boys and girls together, which then continues into college. But as people develop serious romantic relationships or get married, making and maintaining cross-sex friendships becomes harder. "Even the most secure people in a strong marriage probably don't want a spouse to be establishing a new friendship, especially with someone who's very attractive," says Monsour.

Luis and Tiffany

Any sexual tension?
Luis: No, not at all. I'm gay.
Do you fight?
Luis: We don't usually fight because we are mature enough to talk things over. However, when we do, it is usually due to miscommunication.
Tiffany: We have only had one or two arguements, both while working together in very stressful situations. I hate to fight and try to resolve things very quickly. We usually laugh about it afterward.
Rewarding aspects?
Luis: We laugh a lot when we are together.
Tiffany: He makes me smile and we are always laughing together. Luis was also really supportive when I moved from London to Manhattan; he is a friend I will always remember.

The number of cross-sex friendships continues to decline with age—not surprising, since most older adults grew up in an age where consorting with the opposite sex outside of wedlock was taboo. According to Rosemary Blieszner, Ph.D., a family studies professor at Virginia Tech and author of *Adult Friendship* (Sage, 1993), elderly people rarely form new friendships with members of the opposite sex. Her research shows that only about 2% of the friendships elderly women have are with men.

TRUTH #2
Men get more out of cross-sex friendship than women

There are proven—and apparent—distinct differences between female friendship and male friendship. Women spend the majority of their time together discussing their thoughts and feelings, while men tend to be far more group-oriented. Males gather to play sports or travel or talk stock quotes; rarely do they share feelings or personal

Zucco and Deborah

Any sexual tension?
   Zucco: Sometimes, without falling in love with Deborah, I wish to be part of eternity with her. Imagining our two bodies connected to each other and becoming one, it's calling me.
Do you fight?
   Zucco: Yes, if Deborah's crossing the line, I'll be here to remind her of reality. Isn't that what friends are for? Rewarding aspects?
   Zucco: It's like having a wife without the inconvenience.

reflections. This may explain why they seem to get far more out of cross-sex friendship than their female counterparts.

In Sapadin's study, men rated cross-sex friendships as being much higher in overall quality, enjoyment and nurturance than their same-sex friendships. What they reported liking most was talking and relating to women—something they can't do with their buddies. Meanwhile, women rated their same-sex friendships higher on all these counts. They expect more emotional rewards from friendship than men do, explains Sapadin, so they're easily disappointed when they don't receive them. "Women confide in women," notes Blieszner. "Men confide in women."

Eric and Pam

Any sexual tension?
   Pam: We've known each other for nearly 15 years. For the first few years we were very flirtatious, but we've moved past that.
   Eric: No. We're both involved with people we love, and it's just not an issue.
Do you fight?
   Pam: We used to have some ridiculous fights, but that was when we were young. "Did you tell so and so that I said such and such?" Very juvenile. I can't imagine what we would fight about now.

TRUTH #3
...but women benefit too

All that sharing and discussing in female-female friendship can become exhausting, as any woman who's stayed up all night comforting a brokenhearted girlfriend can attest. With men, women can joke and banter without any emotional baggage. "Friendships with men are lighter, more fun," says Sapadin. "Men aren't so sensitive about things." Some women in his study also liked the protec-

tive, familial and casual warmth they got from men, viewing them as surrogate big brothers. What they liked most of all, however, was getting some insight into what guys really think.

TRUTH #4
Cross-sex friendships are emotionally rewarding

Although women dig men's lighthearted attitude, most male-female friendships resemble women's emotionally-involving friendships more than they do men's activity-oriented relationships, according to Kathy Werking, Ph.D., an assistant professor of communications at Eastern Kentucky University and author of *We're Just Good Friends* (Guilford, 1997). Her work has shown that the number one thing male and female friends do together is talk one-on-one. Other activities they prefer—like dining out and going for drives—simply facilitate that communication. In fact, Werking found, close male-female friends are extremely emotionally supportive if they continuously examine their feelings, opinions and ideas. "Males appreciate this because it tends not to be a part of their same-sex friendships," she says. "Females appreciate garnering the male perspective on their lives."

TRUTH #5
It's not all about sex

"In reality, sex isn't always on the agenda," says Werking. "That could be due to sexual orientation, lack of physical attraction or involvement in another romantic relationship." After all, even friends who are attracted to each other may also recognize that qualities they tolerate in a friendship wouldn't necessarily work in a serious romantic relationship. And after years of considering someone as a friend, it often becomes difficult to see a cross-sex pal as a romantic possibility.

Of pairs that do face the question of lust, those that decide early on to bypass an uncertain romantic relationship are more likely to have an enduring friendship, says Werking. One study published last year in the *Journal of Social and Personal Relationships* by Walid Afifi, Ph.D., of Penn State University, showed that of over 300 college students surveyed, 67% reported having had sex with a friend. Interestingly, 56% of those subjects did not transition the friendship into a romantic relationship, suggesting that they preferred friendship over sex.

TRUTH #6
Male-female friendships are political

Men and women have increasingly similar rights, opportunities and interests, which can make cross-sex friendship very political, notes Werking. "It upsets the agreed-upon social order," she explains. "Women and men

Lea and Jean-Christian

Any sexual tension?

Lea: Yes, maybe when I was single. But for as long as we've known each other, he's been a married man.

Jean-Christian: All the time. But she is also my friend's girlfriend, and he would kill me—or go after my wife.

Rewarding aspects?

Lea: I always seem to discover something new about myself, something male and creative that he brings out in me, that I would not otherwise think about. He taught me how to play the harmonica the way an old black man plays the blues.

Jean-Christian: Each time I see her it's like the first time. I always discover new and surprising aspects of her personality.

engage in an equal relationship, or they aren't friends." For one thing, new generations of kids grow up believing that boys can play with dolls and girls can take kickboxing, and they're crossing paths more as a result.

Men and women are also becoming more androgynous as their societal roles become more similar. "Men are more willing to have feminine characteristics, and women are a lot more willing to admit to traditionally masculine characteristics, like assertiveness," says Monsour. His dissertation showed that women and men categorized as androgynous had twice the number of cross-sex friends.

Whatever the challenges of male-female friendship, researchers agree that to succeed as friends, both genders have to openly and honestly negotiate exactly what their relationship will mean-whether sexual attraction is a factor and how they'll deal with it-and establish boundaries. In Afifi's and Reeder's studies, the friendships that survived-and even thrived-after sex or attraction came into play were those in which the friends extensively discussed the meaning of the sexual activity and felt confident and positive about each other's feelings. Once they got past that, they were home free.

"If sex is part of the dynamic, addressing it explicitly is the best strategy" for making sure the friendship survives, says Werking. "The issue will fester if friends try to ignore it." So in the end, male-female friendship does have something in common with romantic relationships: To work, communication is key.

RESEARCHERS tell us that men and women can be friends. But do we really believe them? A survey of more than 1,450 members of the match.com dating site revealed that we're an optimistic bunch:

1. Do you believe men and women can be platonic friends?

Yes: 83%
No: 11%
Unsure: 6%

2. Have you had a platonic friendship that crossed the line and became romantic or sexual?

Yes: 62%
No: 36%
Unsure: 2%

3. Who is more likely to misinterpret the intimacy of friendship for sexual desire?

Men: 64%
Women: 25%
Unsure: 11%

4. It is possible to fall in love with someone who first enters your life as a friend?

Yes: 94%
No: 4%
Unsure: 2%

5. Do you hope that when you do fall in love, your partner will have started out as your friend?

Yes: 71%
No: 9%
Unsure 20%

6. Who is better at keeping sex out of a platonic relationship?

Men: 13%
Women: 67%
Unsure: 20%

READ MORE ABOUT IT:

Men and Women as Friends, Michael Monsour, Ph.D. *(Lawrence Erlbaum, 2001)*

Adult Friendship, Rosemary Blieszner *(Sage, 1993)*

Camille Chatterjee is an associate editor at More *magazine.*

What's Your Love Story?

In your relationship, are you a cop, a comedian, a prince or a martyr? *Robert J. Sternberg*, Ph.D., reveals how you can use your "love story" to find your perfect match.

Relationships can be as unpredictable as the most suspense-filled mystery novel. Why do some couples live happily ever after, while others are as star-crossed as Romeo and Juliet? Why do we often seem destined to relive the same romantic mistakes over and over, following the same script with different people in different places, as if the fate of our relationships, from courtship to demise, were written at birth?

Perhaps because, in essence, it is. As much as psychologists have attempted to explain the mysteries of love through scientific laws and theories, it turns out that the best mirrors of the romantic experience may be *Wuthering Heights, Casablanca* and *General Hospital*. At some level, lay people recognize what many psychologists don't: that the love between two people follows a story. If we want to understand love, we have to understand the stories that dictate our beliefs and expectations of love. These stories, which we start to write as children, predict the patterns of our romantic experiences time and time again. Luckily, we can learn to rewrite them.

I came up with the theory of love as a story because I was dissatisfied—not only with other people's work on love, but also with my own. I had initially proposed a triangular theory of love, suggesting that it comprises three elements: intimacy, passion and commitment. Different loving relationships have different combinations of these elements. Complete love requires all three elements. But the theory leaves an important question unanswered: what makes a person the kind of lover they are? And what attracts them to other lovers? I had to dig deeper to understand the love's origins. I found them in stories.

My research, which incorporates studies performed over the past decade with hundreds of couples in Connecticut, as well as ongoing studies, has shown that people describe love in many ways. This description reveals their love story. For example, someone who strongly agrees with the statement "I believe close relationships are like good partnerships" tells a business story; someone who says they end up with partners who scare them—or that they like intimidating their partner—enacts a horror story.

Couples usually start out being physically attracted and having similar interests and values. But eventually, they may notice something missing in the relationship. That something is usually story compatibility. A couple whose stories don't match is like two characters on one stage acting out different plays—they may look right at first glance, but there is an underlying lack of coordination to their interaction.

This is why couples that seem likely to thrive often do not, and couples that seem unlikely to survive sometimes do. Two people may have similar outlooks, but if one longs to be rescued like Julia Roberts in *Pretty Woman* and the other wants a partnership like the lawyers on the television show *The Practice*, the relationship may not go very far. In contrast, two people with a war story like the bickering spouses in *Who's Afraid of Virginia Woolf* may seem wildly incompatible to their friends, but their shared need for combat may be what keeps their love alive.

More than anything, the key to compatibility with a romantic partner is whether our stories match. To change the pattern of our relationships, we must become conscious of our love stories, seek people with compatible tales, and replot conclusions that aren't working for us.

The Beginning of the Story

We start forming our ideas about love soon after birth, based on our inborn personality, our early experiences and our observations of our parents' relationships, as well as depictions of romance in movies, television and books. We then seek to live out these conceptions of love ourselves.

Based on interviews I conducted in the 1990s, asking college students to write about their romantic ideals and expectations, I have identified at least 25 common stories which people use to describe love. (There are probably many more.)

Some stories are far more popular than others. In 1995, one of my students, Laurie Lynch, and I identified some of the most common tales by asking people to rate, on a scale of one to seven, the extent to which a group of statements characterized their relationships. Their highest-ranked statements indicated their personal love story. Among the most popular were the travel story ("I believe that beginning a relationship is like starting a new journey that promises to be both exciting and challenging"), the gardening story ("I believe any relationship that is left unattended will not survive") and the humor story ("I think taking a relationship too seriously can spoil it"). Among the least popular were the horror story ("I find it exciting when I feel my partner is somewhat frightened of me," or "I tend to end up with people who frighten me"), the collectibles story ("I like dating different partners simultaneously; each partner should fit a particular need") and the autocratic government story ("I think it is more efficient if one person takes control of the important decisions in a relationship").

Another study of 43 couples, conducted with Mahzad Hojji, Ph.D., in 1996, showed that women prefer the travel story more than men, who prefer the art ("Physical attractiveness is the most essential characteristic I look for in a partner"), collectibles and pornography ("It is very important to be able to gratify all my partner's sexual desires and whims," or "I can never be happy with a partner who is not very adventurous in his or her sex life") stories. Men also prefer the sacrifice

story ("I believe sacrifice is a key part of true love"). Originally, we had expected the opposite. Then we realized that the men reported sacrificing things that women did consider significant offerings.

No one story guarantees success, our study showed. But some stories seem to predict doom more than others: the business, collectibles, government, horror, mystery, police ("I believe it is necessary to watch your partner's every move" or "My partner often calls me several times a day to ask what I am doing"), recovery ("I often find myself helping people get their life back in order" or "I need someone to help me recover from my painful past"), science fiction ("I often find myself attracted to individuals who have unusual and strange characteristics") and theater stories ("I think my relationships are like plays" or "I often find myself attracted to partners who play different roles").

How Stories Spin Our Relationships

When you talk to two people who have just split up, their breakup stories often sound like depictions of two completely different relationships. In a sense they are. Each partner has his or her own story to tell.

Most important to a healthy, happy relationship is that both partners have compatible stories—that is, compatible expectations. Indeed, a 1998 study conducted with Mahzad Hojjat, Ph.D., and Michael Barnes, Ph.D., indicated that the more similar couples' stories were, the happier they were together.

Stories tend to be compatible if they are complementary roles in a single story, such as prince and princess, or if the stories are similar enough that they can be merged into a new and unified story. For example, a fantasy story can merge with a gardening story because one can nourish, or garden, a relationship while dreaming of being rescued by a knight on a white steed. A fantasy and a business story are unlikely to

blend, however, because they represent such different ideals—fate-bound princes and princesses don't work at romance!

Of course, story compatibility isn't the only ingredient in a successful relationship. Sometimes, our favorite story can be hazardous to our well-being. People often try to make dangerous or unsatisfying stories come true. Thus, someone who has, say, a horror or recovery story may try to turn a healthy relationship into a Nightmare on Elm Street. People complain that they keep ending up with the same kind of bad partner, that they are unlucky in love. In reality, luck has nothing to do with it: They are subconsciously finding people to play out their love stories, or foisting their stories on the people they meet.

Making Happy Endings

Treating problems in relationships by changing our behaviors and habits ultimately won't work because crisis comes from the story we're playing out. Unless we change our stories, we're treating symptoms rather than causes. If we're dissatisfied with our partner, we should look not at his or her faults, but at how he or she fits into our expectations.

To figure out what we want, we need to consider all of our past relationships, and we should ask ourselves what attributes characterized the people to whom we felt most attracted, and what attributes characterized the people in whom we eventually lost interest. We also need to see which romantic tale we aim to tell—and whether or not it has the potential to lead to a "happily ever after" scenario (see, "Find Your Love Story").

Once we understand the ideas and beliefs behind the stories we accept as our own, we can do some replotting. We can ask ourselves what we like and don't like about our current story, what hasn't been working in our relationships, and how we would like to change it. How can we rewrite the scenario? This may involve changing stories, or transforming an existing story to make it more practical. For example, horror stories may be fantasized during sexual or other activity, rather than actually physically played out.

We can change our story by experimenting with new and different plots. Sometimes, psychotherapy can help us to move from perilous stories (such as a horror story) to more promising ones (such as a travel story). Once we've recognized our story—or learned to live a healthy one of our choosing—we can begin to recognize elements of that story in potential mates. Love mirrors stories because it is a story itself. The difference is that we are the authors, and can write ourselves a happy ending.

READ MORE ABOUT IT

Love Is a Story, Robert J. Sternberg, Ph.D. (Oxford University Press, 1998)

A Natural History of Love, Diane Ackerman (Random House, 1994)

Robert J. Sternberg is IBM Professor of Psychology and Education in the department of psychology at Yale University.

Find Your Love Story

Adapted from *Love Is a Story* by Robert J. Sternberg, Ph.D.

Rate each statement on a scale from 1 to 9, 1 meaning that it doesn't characterize your romantic relationships at all, 9 meaning that it describes them extremely well. Then average your scores for each story. In general, averaged scores of 7 to 9 are high, indicating a strong attraction to a story, and 1 to 3 are low, indicating little or no interest in the story. Moderate scores of 4 to 6 indicate some interest, but probably not enough to generate or keep a romantic interest. Next, evaluate your own love story. (There are 12 listed here; see the book for more.)

STORY #1

1. I enjoy making sacrifices for the sake of my partner.
2. I believe sacrifice is a key part of true love.
3. I often compromise my own comfort to satisfy my partner's needs.
Score:__

The **sacrifice story** can lead to happy relationships when both partners are content in the roles they are playing, particularly when they both make sacrifices. It is likely to cause friction when partners feel compelled to make sacrifices. Research suggests that relationships of all kinds are happiest when they are roughly equitable. The greatest risk in a sacrifice story is that the give-and-take will become too out of balance, with one partner always being the giver or receiver.

STORY #2

Officer:
1. I believe that you need to keep a close eye on your partner.
2. I believe it is foolish to trust your partner completely.
3. I would never trust my partner to work closely with a person of the opposite sex.
Score:__

Suspect:
1. My partner often calls me several times a day to ask exactly what I am doing.
2. My partner needs to know everything that I do.
3. My partner gets very upset if I don't let him or her know exactly where I have been. **Score:__**

Police stories do not have very favorable prognoses because they can completely detach from reality. The police story may offer some people the feeling of being cared for. People who are very insecure relish the attention that they get as a "suspect," that they are unable to receive in any other way. But they can end up paying a steep price. As the plot thickens, the suspect first begins to lose freedom, then dignity, and then any kind of self-respect. Eventually, the person's mental and even physical well-being may be threatened.

STORY #3

1. I believe that, in a good relationship, partners change and grow together.

2. I believe love is a constant process of discovery and growth.

3. I believe that beginning a relationship is like starting a new journey that promises to be both exciting and challenging.
Score:__

Travel stories that last beyond a very short period of time generally have a favorable prognosis, because if the travelers can agree on a destination and path, they are already a long way toward success. If they can't, they often find out quite quickly that they want different things from the relationship and split up. Travel relationships tend to be dynamic and focus on the future. The greatest risk is that over time one or both partners will change the destination or path they desire. When people speak of growing apart, they often mean that the paths they wish to take are no longer the same. In such cases, the relationship is likely to become increasingly unhappy, or even dissolve completely.

STORY #4

Object:
1. The truth is that I don't mind being treated as a sex toy by my partner.

2. It is very important to me to gratify my partner's sexual desires and whims, even if people might view them as debasing.

3. I like it when my partner wants me to try new and unusual, and even painful, sexual techniques. **Score:__**

Subject:

1. The most important thing to me in my relationship is for my partner to be an excellent sex toy, doing anything I desire.

2. I can never be happy with a partner who is not very adventurous in sex.

3. The truth is that I like a partner who feels like a sex object. **Score:__**

There are no obvious advantages to the **pornography** story. The disadvantages are quite clear, however. First, the excitement people attain is through degradation of themselves and others. Second, the need to debase and be debased is likely to keep escalating. Third, once one adopts the story, it may be difficult to adopt another story. Fourth, the story can become physically as well as psychologically dangerous. And finally, no matter how one tries, it is difficult to turn the story into one that's good for psychological or physical well-being.

STORY #5

Terrorizer:

1. I often make sure that my partner knows that I am in charge, even if it makes him or her scared of me.

2. I actually find it exciting when I feel my partner is somewhat frightened of me.

3. I sometimes do things that scare my partner, because I think it is actually good for a relationship to have one partner slightly frightened of the other. **Score:__**

Victim:

1. I believe it is somewhat exciting to be slightly scared of your partner.

2. I find it arousing when my partner creates a sense of fear in me.

3. I tend to end up with people who sometimes frighten me. **Score:__**

The **horror story** probably is the least advantageous of the stories. To some, it may be exciting. But the forms of terror needed to sustain the excitement tend to get out of control and to put their participants, and even sometimes those around them, at both psychological and physical risk. Those who discover that they have this story or are in a relationship that is enacting it would be well-advised to seek counseling, and perhaps even police protection.

STORY #6

Co-dependent:

1. I often end up with people who are facing a specific problem, and I find myself helping them get their life back in order.

2. I enjoy being involved in relationships in which my partner needs my help to get over some problem.

3. I often find myself with partners who need my help to recover from their past. **Score:__**

Person in recovery:

1. I need someone who will help me recover from my painful past.

2. I need help getting over my past. **Score:__**

The main advantage to the **recovery story** is that the co-dependent may really help the other partner to recover, so long as the other partner has genuinely made the decision to recover. Many of us know individuals who sought to reform their partners, only to experience total frustration when their partners made little or no effort to reform. At the same time, the co-dependent is someone who needs to feel he or she is helping someone, and gains this feeling of making a difference to someone through the relationship. The problem: Others can assist in recovery, but the decision to recover can only be made by the person in need of recovery. As a result, recovery stories can assist in, but not produce, actual recovery.

STORY #7

1. I believe a good relationship is attainable only if you spend time and energy to care for it, just as you tend a garden.

2. I believe relationships need to be nourished constantly to help weather the ups and downs of life.

3. I believe the secret to a successful relationship is the care that partners take of each other and of their love. **Score:__**

The biggest advantage of a **garden story** is its recognition of the importance of nurture. No other story involves this amount of care and attention. The biggest potential disadvantage is that a lack of spontaneity or boredom may develop. People in garden stories are not immune to the lure of extramarital relationships, for example, and may get involved in them to generate excitement, even if they still highly value their primary relationship. In getting involved in other relationships, however, they are putting the

primary relationship at risk. Another potential disadvantage is that of smothering—that the attention becomes too much. Just as one can overwater a flower, one can overattend a relationship. Sometimes it's best to let things be and allow nature to take its course.

STORY #8

1. I believe that close relationships are partnerships.

2. I believe that in a romantic relationship, just as in a job, both partners should perform their duties and responsibilities according to their "job description."

3. Whenever I consider having a relationship with someone, I always consider the financial implications of the relationship as well. **Score:__**

A **business story** has several potential advantages, not the least of which is that the bills are more likely to get paid than in other types of relationships. That's because someone is always minding the store. Another potential advantage is that the roles tend to be more clearly defined than in other relationships. The partners are also in a good position to "get ahead" in terms of whatever it is that they want. One potential disadvantage occurs if only one of the two partners sees their relationship as a business story. The other partner may quickly become bored and look for interest and excitement outside the marriage. The story can also turn sour if the distribution of authority does not satisfy one or both partners. If the partners cannot work out mutually compatible roles, they may find themselves spending a lot of time fighting for position. It is important to maintain the option of flexibility.

STORY #9

1. I think fairy tales about relationships can come true.

2. I do believe that there is someone out there for me who is my perfect match.

3. I like my relationships to be ones in which I view my partner as something like a prince or princess in days of yore. **Score:__**

The **fantasy story** can be a powerful one. The individual may feel swept up in the emotion of the search for the perfect partner or of developing the perfect relationship with an existing partner. It is probably no coincidence that in literature most fantasy stories take place before or outside of marriage: Fantasies are hard to maintain when one has to pay the bills, pack the children off to school and resolve marital fights. To maintain the happy feeling of the fantasy, therefore, one has to ignore, to some extent, the mundane aspects of life. The potential disadvantages of the fantasy relationship are quite plain. The greatest is the possibility for disillusionment when one partner discovers that no one could fulfill the fantastic expectations that have been created. This can lead partners to feel dissatisfied with relationships that most others would view as quite successful. If a couple can create a fantasy story based on realistic rather than idealistic ideals, they have the potential for success; if they want to be characters in a myth, chances are that's exactly what they'll get: a myth.

STORY #10

1. I think it is more interesting to argue than to compromise.
2. I think frequent arguments help bring conflictive issues into the open and keep the relationship healthy.
3. I actually like to fight with my partner. **Score:__**

The **war story** is advantageous in a relationship only when both partners clearly share it and want the same thing. In these cases, threats of divorce and worse may be common, but neither partner would seriously dream of leaving: They're both having too much fun, in their own way. The major disadvantage, of course, is that the story often isn't shared, leading to intense and sustained conflict that can leave the partner without the war story feeling devastated much of the time. People can find themselves in a warring rela-

tionship without either of them having war as a preferred story. In such cases, the constant fighting may make both partners miserable. If the war continues in such a context, there is no joy in it for either partner.

STORY #11

Audience:

1. I like a partner who is willing to think about the funny side of our conflicts.
2. I think taking a relationship too seriously can spoil it; that's why I like partners who have a sense of humor.
3. I like a partner who makes me laugh whenever we are facing a tense situation in our relationship. **Score:__**

Comedian:

1. I admit that I sometimes try to use humor to avoid facing a problem in my relationship.
2. I like to use humor when I have a conflict with my partner because I believe there is a humorous side to any conflict.
3. When I disagree with my partner, I often try to make a joke out of it. **Score:__**

The **humor story** can have one enormous advantage: Most situations do have a lighter side, and people with this story are likely to see it. When things in a relationship become tense, sometimes nothing works better than a little humor, especially if it comes from within the relationship. Humor stories also allow relationships to be creative and dynamic. But the humor story also has some potential disadvantages. Probably the greatest one is the risk of using humor to deflect important issues: A serious conversation that needs to take place keeps getting put off with jokes. Humor can also be used to be cruel in a passive-aggressive way. When humor is used as a means of demeaning a person to pro-

tect the comedian from responsibility ("I was only joking"), a relationship is bound to be imperiled. Thus, moderate amounts are good for a relationship, but excessive amounts can be deleterious.

STORY #12

1. I think it is okay to have multiple partners who fulfill my different needs.
2. I sometimes like to think about how many people I could potentially date all at the same time.
3. I tend and like to have multiple intimate partners at once, each fulfilling somewhat different roles. **Score:__**

There are a few advantages to a **collection** story. For one thing, the collector generally cares about the collectible's physical well-being, as appearance is much of what makes a collection shine. The collector also finds a way of meeting multiple needs. Usually those needs will be met in parallel—by having several intimate relationships at the same time—but a collector may also enter into serial monogamous relationships, where each successive relationship meets needs that the last relationship did not meet. In a society that values monogamy, collection stories work best if they do not become serious or if individuals in the collection are each viewed in different lights, such as friendship or intellectual stimulation. The disadvantages of this story become most obvious when people are trying to form serious relationships. The collector may find it difficult to establish intimacy, or anything approaching a complete relationship and commitment toward a single individual. Collections can also become expensive, time-consuming, and in some cases illegal (as when an individual enters into multiple marriages simultaneously).

Reprinted with permission from *Psychology Today*, July/August 2000, pp. 52–59. © 2000 by Sussex Publishers, Inc.

Love is *not* all you need

By Pepper Schwartz, Ph.D.

The experience of love is unique for every person, and using that feeling to measure the potential success of a relationship is even more subjective. Nonetheless, at some point most of us face the timeless question of what makes a relationship work. Though we can't quantify love, we can look at variables that help us choose the right partner. Research shows that a few crucial compatibilities make the difference between making up and breaking up.

WE ARE A LOVE CULTURE. UNLIKE SOME SOCIETIES that think of passionate love as a nuisance that can undermine sound reasoning about whom and when to marry, we think passion is our truest guide. When we say, "He did it all for love," we mean it as a compliment. In many cultures it would be said with pity or contempt. But not us—we sigh with happiness when witnessing lovers who barely know each other connect as powerfully as lightning striking the Earth.

This approach is romantic, but it's also a little daft. Sure, being passionately attracted to someone is a great elixir, but making a commitment based on hormone-addled logic is a recipe for disappointment, if not disaster. We shouldn't be misled by fleeting moments of bliss. Love is not all you need, and you will not know—across a crowded room or even on a first date—that this person absolutely is the One. While some hunches work out (and, of course, those are the Cinderella stories), most do not. There is a real danger when you think that fate has delivered the One: You may stop looking for disconfirming evidence, even if there are big problems (like his tendency to drink too much or her occasional disappearances).

Theories about love that are based on fate are not only untrue, they aren't even in the best interest of love. Of course, Cupid forbid, if the One does not work out, you might think you've lost your true love and forego giving other people a chance. Choosing the right partner is arguably the most important decision you will make. In the last 10 years, a multitude of studies have shown how bad relationships can negatively affect job performance, physical and mental health, financial security and even life span. Certainly, such an important decision requires more than the adrenaline rush of infatuation.

When considering what it takes to make love work, it is useful to look at those who have tried and succeeded as well as those who have tried and failed. Besides observations from my own work, I have included data from The Enrich Couple Inventory, 195 questions developed by David Olson, Ph.D., David Fournier, Ph.D., and Joan Druckman, Ph.D., that were administered to 21,501 couples throughout the country. The researchers compared the answers of the happiest couples to those of the most unhappy and found that the differences between their answers to a few key questions tell a lot about what makes love work. If we are willing to be rational about love, we can learn from others' experiences—and perhaps find and maintain a true love even after the initial chemistry fades.

"I DIDN'T KNOW YOU FELT THAT WAY...."
My partner is a very good listener

Percentage of unhappy couples who agree:	**18%**
Percentage of happy couples who agree:	**83%**

My partner does not understand how I feel

Unhappy couples:	**79%**
Happy couples:	**13%**

If you want to feel alone in a relationship, be with someone who hasn't a clue about what you are going through. Or worse, someone who does have a clue but cannot understand why your pain is a big deal. The two of you can be totally different people

On Flexibility
Joel and Gaby
Married four years

Joel, 34, composer: "A lot of people imagine that when you're in a relationship you're facing opposite your partner. I like to think of a relationship as your partner standing next to you, and you're both facing the same direction, which means that the relationship doesn't block your view of the world. And your partner is actually and metaphorically by and on your side. That's going to demand some flexibility, because at times, you're going to have to go against yourself to be on your partner's side."

Gaby, 36, administrative assistant: "It doesn't work if things are too patterned and strict; every day is different. If you are flexible, then surprises don't catch you off guard and it's easier to get along."

On Empathy
Zucco and Barbara
Together one year

Zucco, 48, bartender: "Empathy is very important. Our relationship is based on mutual understanding. It permits us to progress together toward a better life. Barbara moved from France to the U.S. to be with me, and I know it's not easy for her—she's learning a new language and hasn't made many friends yet. I feel for her, and sometimes I embrace her tightly to give her my energy and receive hers. Couples who don't see each other's point of view are destined to fail. When two beings get together, there is some kind of electric reaction. First there is passion, then in the aftermath they feel for each other, protect one another, respect the other's mind. then finally—through understanding, learning from each other, apologizing, laughing, crying, talking, experiencing day-to-day reality—they become a couple, whereas before they were just lovers."

On Communication
Brisco and Ann
Together one year, one month

Brisco, 34, photographer: "If there's a problem, you should speak up immediately so the other person will know where you are coming from, instead of not communicating or waiting until the last minute to reveal your feelings. When you first start dating, you don't voice everything you feel out of fear of what the other person might think. But after a certain period of time, the communication comes. Trust and communication go hand in hand; you become comfortable enough to trust that you're not going to be judged. Right now we live in different cities, and I think good communication is even more important if you are in a long-distance relationship. We talk every day on the phone, if only for a short time. The communication we have is good enough that we don't have to see each other to reinforce the comfort level or security. I am sure that when we are living in the same place we will have to continue to let each other know when we need space."

On Sexual Compatibility
Kiera and Matt
Together one year, three months

Kiera, 28, marketing consultant: "It doesn't determine the success of a relationship, but it is important. Everyone is looking for something different—if we weren't, we'd all want to date the same person and be in the same relationship. However, if there's no sexual compatibility, there would be very little distinguishing this person from any other close friend."

Matt, 27, art director: "It is an important piece, but only one of many that make up a relationship. Just because you have sexual compatibility does not mean you have a relationship. At least not one that is going to last."

On Intelligence
Melissa and Will
Together one year, six months

Melissa, 20, college student: "I think it's good if you challenge your partner intellectually, because otherwise there's not enough substance to the relationship. If you can't do it on the same abstract level—if you can't sit down to dinner and have a conversation about what's going on in the world—then there's a lot missing. You need someone who can push you and make you think in a different way. It's good to have similar interests, but I think it's also good to have different points of view and be able to talk candidly about things, just so you grow as people. If you're too similar, it's no fun."

On Time Together
Pat and George
Together 10 years

George, 52, salesman: "I rate spending time together as the most important thing in a relationship. You always need some time alone, but time with the other person is more fun. They become your partner, your soul mate, your best friend, the person you confide in. Spending time with that person is sheer pleasure. We like to go out to dinner and then dancing, but just sitting and talking is probably the most meaningful thing we spend time doing. From that we get support, companionship, friendship, love and obviously, passion."

in a number of ways, but if a partner is sensitive to how you see the world and experience life, then those differences are unimportant.

Ruth, who has been married to Alex for 31 years, puts it this way, "When we got married, nobody thought it would last because we are so different. Alex is from a working-class family;

I am Jewish, he is Lutheran—everyone thought it was a non-starter from the wedding day on. But what they didn't know, and what has been the most important thing in our relationship, is that Alex knows how to listen. Really listen. No matter what, he can see how I'm feeling and he can feel for me. Trust me, that solves a lot of problems."

"WE NEVER SEE EACH OTHER ANYMORE...."
We have a good balance of leisure time spent together and separately

Unhappy couples:	**17%**
Happy couples:	**71%**

We find it easy to think of things to do together

Unhappy couples:	**28%**
Happy couples:	**86%**

Although it sometimes works if people have different priorities, most often, being out of sync is damaging in the long run. Allotting time in your day, your week and your life for your partner is an important ingredient in a relationship. If one person wants to spend every Saturday and Sunday relaxing in front of the television when the other wants to hike, bike and explore, both will feel deprived. This may not show up in the busy early years of child raising, but over time it can become a real problem. As Marty, an executive for a shipping company, says, "The best thing my second wife and I do together is hang out, just be friends sharing the same space. My first marriage was all about seeing things, doing things, as if just being together wasn't enough. Well, maybe it wasn't with her, but it is one of the greatest joys I have with Ellen."

"DO YOU SEE WHAT I'M SAYING?"
I am very satisfied with how we talk to each other

Unhappy couples:	**15%**
Happy couples:	**90%**

We are creative in how we handle our differences

Unhappy couples:	**15%**
Happy couples:	**78%**

Marriage exists in a constantly changing world. Couples need to be able to talk about these changes, how they feel about them and what they want to do in response. They need to have a sense of teamwork, one arrived at by discussion and joint action. If one person refuses to discuss things, one or both persons will feel the relationship is not intimate and perhaps unfair. And if no one's talking, there is no way to fix a problem and keep it from getting worse. Life is not static, it's messy, and it requires communication.

"WHY ARE YOU SO AMBITIOUS?"
Making financial decisions is not difficult

Unhappy couples:	**32%**
Happy couples:	**80%**

If one person is ambitious, and the other person wants a lifestyle that doesn't support that ambition, there will be growing resentment. Lisa, a young woman who has a small home-based mail-order business, became increasingly unhappy with her husband, Rob. Both wanted a higher standard of living, but he had also promised that he would be "a good father to our children." In-stead, he was around less and less as he became more and more entangled in his work. He wanted to spend more time making money; she wanted him to be home more often. Neither she nor Rob had given serious thought to how incompatible their personalities might be. As life went on, she felt more deprived, and he felt more resentful. Ultimately, they separated.

"SINCE WE'RE ALONE...."
Our sexual relationship is satisfying and fulfilling

Unhappy couples:	**29%**
Happy couples:	**85%**

Sexual incompatibilities can be fixed, right? And sexual disappointment isn't the worst problem when so much else is good about the relationship, right? Wrong and double wrong. First, while it is true that sex therapy can help many problems (especially mechanical ones such as erectile failure or pain during intercourse), it has a woeful track record when it comes to creating or resurrecting sexual desire. Second, while therapists can improve a lover's skill, either you have compatibility in bed or you don't. You can put someone on skates and they can learn to make it around the rink, but triple lutzes? No. Sex isn't important if it isn't important to both of you. But, if one partner is interested and the other is not, the interested party will rarely be content to just forget about it.

"IF IT MAKES YOU HAPPY...."
We are both equally willing to make adjustments in the relationship

Unhappy couples:	**46%**
Happy couples:	**87%**

I can share feelings and ideas with my partner during disagreements

Unhappy couples	**22%**
Happy couples	**85%**

Although it may be mistaken for strength, rigidity is not a good personal or marital quality. If someone doesn't like to admit they are wrong or show some flexibility in how they view problems, the partnership will be either fragile or full of anger and loneliness. Rachel, a woman who describes herself as a "giver," believed she could change her husband's inflexibility. "I thought I could bring him out, make him less rigid by doing so much for him, by always being ready to see his point of view. But he just took and took. When I backed down, he would see it as weakness, not flexibility. Finally, I just couldn't take being so unloved, so I left." There is no marriage in which the ability to apologize and be flexible isn't necessary.

"YOU JUST DON'T GET IT"
My partner understands my opinions and ideas

Unhappy couples:	**19%**
Happy couples:	**87%**

READ MORE ABOUT IT:

Everything You Know About Love and Sex Is Wrong by Pepper Schwartz, Ph.D. (G.P. Putnam's Sons, 2000)

Empowering Couples, Building on Your Strengths by David Olson, Ph.D., and Amy Olson, Ph.D. (Life Innovations, 2000)

Schopenhauer's Porcupines: Intimacy and Its Dilemmas by Deborah Anna Luepnitz, Ph.D. (Basic Books, 2001)

Loving Him Without Losing You: Seven Empowering Strategies for Better Relationships by Beverly Engel, M.S. (John Wiley & Sons, 2000)

In the beginning of a relationship, conversation is mostly self-revelation, which is interesting at first. But over time there are many circumstances that allow you to see the quality of a person's mind. It's OK to be awed by your partner's intelligence, but beware if you think she is less than overwhelmed by the way you solve problems, come to conclusions and think about life. The bedrock of mutual respect is comfort and admiration for each other's opinions. If that isn't present, contempt is just around the corner.

Pepper Schwartz, Ph.D., is professor of sociology at the University of Washington and author of 14 books, including Ten Talks Parents Must Have With Children About Sex and Character (Hyperion, 2000) *and* The Great Sex Weekend (Putnam, 1998).

SEX for Grown-ups

Sorry, all you teenage heartthrobs. Some things get better with age, and making love is one of them

By Carol Lynn Mithers

If you look at advertising, go to movies or watch TV, you're forgiven for thinking that passion is the sole province of the young, the thin and the single. In love scenes, there's nary a sag, wrinkle or wedding ring in sight. The message: Sexually speaking, grown-up means washed up. Right?

Wrong. Here's the startling discovery that a lot of us mature married folks have made: Not only are we having nearly as much sex as the kids, we're—how to put this politely?—having more fun.

And it's probably no coincidence that a growing number of researchers, psychologists and sex therapists are beginning to look at what really happens to hot young lovers after a decade or more of sharing a bed, a mortgage and a couple of kids. It turns out that the old advertising slogan had it right: "You're not getting older, you're getting better." Here's why:

Biology is on our side. Studies over the years—not to mention anecdotes from our friends—have demonstrated again and again that women become more sexually responsive with time, until we reach a peak in our thirties or forties. (After that, we plateau.)

An important confirmation came in 1992, when social scientists Robert T. Michael, John H. Gagnon, Edward O. Laumann and Gina Kolata, working through the National Opinion Research Center at the University of Chicago, embarked on a landmark survey of America's sex life. Among their results, catalogued in the book *Sex in America: A Definitive Survey* (Warner Books, 1995): While 61 percent of women between ages eighteen and twenty-four said that they always or usually reached orgasm with their primary partner, by age forty it was a whopping 78 percent.

No one has definitively proved that a particular physiological change in women's bodies makes them more orgasmic. However, some researchers, notably Helen E. Fisher, Ph.D., the author of *Anatomy of Love* (Fawcett, 1995), and Theresa L. Crenshaw, M.D., a San Diego-based sex therapist and author of *The Alchemy of Love and Lust* (Pocket Books, 1997), speculate that the gradual dropping of our estrogen levels allows the small amount of testosterone in our bodies to exert more influence.

Researchers do agree, though, that men's testosterone levels fall during these same years, causing their sex drives to quiet down. Their lovemaking becomes much more leisurely and touch-oriented, and that translates into more pleasure for their wives.

Terry, forty, married for sixteen years, agrees: "When we were first married, Jack specialized in quickies. These days, he likes to take his time. He says his greatest pleasure is in driving me wild."

Nature also seems to help bind us to those we know best, says Fisher. She points out that levels of oxytocin, a hormone secreted by the hypo- thalamus gland and associated with mother-infant (and in some cases, male-female) attachment in animals, rise each time we climax. (In men, orgasm stimulates a spike in a similar hormone, vasopressin.)

"I don't think it's much of a leap to say that the feeling of deep attachment that comes after orgasm is associated with those hormone levels," Fisher, who originated this theory, asserts. "And that the more you have orgasms with someone, the more attached you feel. We get addicted to those we love."

Practice makes perfect. Regardless of the role physiology plays, the experience grown-ups bring to their sexual encounters is even more important. "By the time they're in their twenties, most men have had much more sex—most of it through masturbation—than women have," notes James W. Maddock, Ph.D., professor of family social science at the University of Minnesota, St. Paul. At that age, however, sex may be less than mind-blowing for women, who are still learning what pleases them and their partners.

By the time we reach our thirties, though, most of us have honed our skills. "I hate to sound clinical," says Judith, thirty-eight, married for eight years, "but only seventeen years of having sex could have taught me how men like to be touched, how I like it, what positions work."

Experience that teaches what women like—especially when combined with the physical slowdown that comes naturally over the years—makes men better lovers, too. "With time, men learn a greater appreciation of activities like kissing, petting and hugging—things that women have wanted all along," says Alvin Baraff, Ph.D., a therapist and director of Men Center Counseling in Washington, D.C., who has treated and surveyed hundreds of men.

Love me, love my body. One of the great ironies of female aging is that even as we grow more genuinely sexual, society tells us that we're less physically desirable. Happily, grown-up women today are far more likely to tell society to go stuff it.

Pepper Schwartz, Ph.D., professor of sociology at the University of Washington, in Seattle, and co-author of *The Great Sex Weekend* (Putnam, 1998), observes, "With time, you realize that it's not having perfect legs or breasts that makes you attractive. It's all of you—your experience, your mind, your personality, your sense of humor. And you learn to say, 'This body may not look like Cindy Crawford's, but I like it.'"

"I can't tell you how many hours I used to spend in front of the mirror hating my big butt and thighs," says Anne, forty-two. "I finally realized that they have nothing to do with the things that are important to me—being a good mother, a good worker, a good wife."

Anne gets no complaints from her husband of eighteen years. "It's clear that he wants me as much as he ever has," she says.

That's the other good news: When it comes to accepting physical imperfections, men are forgiving. In 1996, when Baraff surveyed one hundred men about what they most longed for in marriage, they never mentioned specifics about their spouses' appearance. And the National Opinion Research Center survey found that 67 percent of men over forty-five said they still got great enjoyment from watching their mates undress.

Love can set you free. The sensuality, experience and confidence that define the sexual grown-up would be striking in any intimate relationship, but they reach full flower in a long, happy marriage. Evidence suggests that long-married couples do have sex less often than new lovers, but we also seem to get more out of the encounters we have. The National Opinion Research Center survey found married couples to be the most physically satisfied with their sex lives, while single people—especially those who had more than one partner—were the least satisfied.

These findings are no fluke, asserts Maddock. "The trend is clear: The longer, more steady in all respects of the relationship, the more likely the incidence and consistency of orgasm."

A happy marriage isn't magic; it just makes good sex easier. When lovemaking isn't about proving anything, when it's part of a larger, shared life, it's "less fraught with anxiety," says Amanda, forty, married twelve years. "If sex one night isn't so great, you have faith that tomorrow it will be."

Feeling safe in a relationship also gives us the confidence to make our needs known—or to know what we don't want. Even the most liberated young woman can get hung up by worry "about how her partner perceives her," says Shirley Glass, Ph.D., a psychologist and marital therapist in private practice in Owings Mills, Maryland. "A history of emotional intimacy, vulnerability and acceptance lets a woman expose herself without fear of judgment."

Says Katie, thirty-nine, married for fifteen years, "Because I know my husband does respect me and takes me seriously, I've felt free to do things I never would have dared before. I recently bought my first vibrator—not for me, for us."

Intimacy is the best aphrodisiac. The kids would have us think that nothing is duller than making love to the same person year in and year out. Guess again. A long-term relationship, where you've weathered storms together, laughed at the same jokes—in short, have a history—fosters a kind of intimacy that gives lovemaking an intensity, complexity and richness that isn't available to us earlier in our lives.

In fact, peak sexual experiences are available *only* to grown-ups, suggests David Schnarch, Ph.D., director of the Marriage and Family Health Center in Evergreen, Colorado, and author of *Passionate Marriage* (W. W. Norton & Co., 1997). Why? Because the ability to be intimate—to reveal who we are and what turns us on—is what really makes sex great. And that requires a strong sense of identity and security.

When a couple makes the leap from hormone-driven passion to desire specifically for each other, their sexual connection can really bloom. "It's the difference," Schnarch says, "between having sex like kids and having sex like a woman and a man."

"If you had told me at twenty that my sex life would get better the older I got, I never would have believed you," says Mary, forty-two, married for seventeen years. "But that's exactly what's happened. Maybe it's because my husband and I have gone through so much together, and I feel connected to him in a really deep way. Maybe it's all these things. But something happened just before I turned forty: I fell more deeply in love with him than ever. And I started feeling explosively feminine, explosively sexual. After all these years together, we're having the time of our lives."

Carol Lynn Mithers is a contributing editor to Ladies' Home Journal.

MAKING TIME FOR A BABY

For years, women have been told they could wait until 40 or later to have babies. But a new book argues that's way too late

By NANCY GIBBS

LISTEN TO A SUCCESSFUL WOMAN DISCUSS HER FAILURE TO bear a child, and the grief comes in layers of bitterness and regret. This was supposed to be the easy part, right? Not like getting into Harvard. Not like making partner. The baby was to be Mother Nature's gift. Anyone can do it; high school dropouts stroll through the mall with their babies in a Snugli. What can be so hard, especially for a Mistress of the Universe, with modern medical science devoted to resetting the biological clock? "I remember sitting in the clinic waiting room," recalls a woman who ran the infertility marathon, "and a woman—she was in her mid-40s and had tried everything to get pregnant—told me that one of the doctors had glanced at her chart and said, 'What are you doing here? You are wasting your time.' It was so cruel. She was holding out for that one last glimpse of hope. How horrible was it to shoot that hope down?"

The manner was cold, but the message was clear—and devastating. "Those women who are at the top of their game could have had it all, children and career, if they wanted it," suggests Pamela Madsen, executive director of the American Infertility Association (A.I.A.). "The problem was, nobody told them the truth about their bodies." And the truth is that even the very best fertility experts have found that the hands of the clock will not be moved. Baby specialists can do a lot to help a 29-year-old whose tubes are blocked or a 32-year-old whose husband has a low sperm count. But for all the headlines about 45-year-old actresses giving birth, the fact is that "there's no promising therapy for age-related infertility," says Dr. Michael Soules, a professor at the University of Washington School of Medicine and past president of the Ameri-

can Society for Reproductive Medicine (ASRM). "There's certainly nothing on the horizon."

This means, argues economist Sylvia Ann Hewlett in her new book, *Creating a Life: Professional Women and the Quest for Children* (Talk Miramax Books), that many ambitious young women who also hope to have kids are heading down a bad piece of road if they think they can spend a decade establishing their careers and wait until 35 or beyond to establish their families. Even as more couples than ever seek infertility treatment—the number of procedures performed jumped 27% between 1996 and 1998—doctors are learning that the most effective treatment may be prevention, which in this case means knowledge. "But the fact that the biological clock is real is unwelcome news to my 24-year-old daughter," Hewlett observes, "and she's pretty typical."

27 IS THE AGE AT WHICH A WOMAN'S CHANCE OF GETTING PREGNANT BEGINS TO DECLINE

At 20, the risk of miscarriage is about 9%; it doubles by 35, then doubles again by the time a woman reaches her early 40s

At 42, 90% of a woman's eggs are abnormal; she has only a 7.8% chance of having a baby without using donor eggs

The Limits Of Science

ASSISTED REPRODUCTIVE TECHNOLOGY IS ONE OF THE great medical success stories of the late 20th century. Thanks to fertility drugs, in-vitro fertilization (IVF) and a growing list of even more sophisticated techniques, tens of thousands of healthy babies are born each year that otherwise might never have been conceived. But the process is neither foolproof nor risk free. There are limits to what science can do for infertile couples, and the more doctors have to intervene with drugs, needles and surgery to get sperm to meet egg, the greater the chance that something will go wrong. Among the pitfalls:

OVARIAN HYPERSTIMULATION The first step in most assisted-fertilization techniques is to trick the ovaries into producing a lot of eggs at once. But the hormones doctors use to do this are powerful drugs and in rare cases can cause serious complications, including blood clots and kidney damage.

MULTIPLE GESTATION Not being able to have a baby can be heartbreaking. But having too many at once can be even worse. About 20% to 35% of IVF pregnancies produce multiple fetuses, usually twins. Having more than two or three babies at once is often a medical disaster. Babies that develop in a crowded uterus or are born too early are at risk for a lifetime of developmental problems, including mental retardation, paralysis and blindness. Trying to reduce the number of fetuses through selective abortion has its own problems, not the least of which is an increased chance of miscarriage.

LOW BIRTH WEIGHT Twins and triplets (not to mention septuplets) often weigh less than normal at birth. But a recent study from the U.S. Centers for Disease Control suggests that even single babies conceived through IVF are more likely to be born underweight. Whether that also puts them at greater risk of developmental problems is uncertain.

BIRTH DEFECTS An Australian study published in March reported that IVF children are twice as likely to suffer birth defects—such as cleft palate, a hole in the heart or kidney problems—as children conceived the usual way. Several earlier studies have shown no difference between the two kinds of babies, so further research is needed. Even if the apparent increase is real, it might not be clear whether the birth defects are caused by the artificial reproductive technology or by whatever underlying problem caused the infertility in the first place.

Even the most powerful techniques can turn back a woman's biological clock only so far. Women in their early 30s who want to use their own eggs have a better than 30% chance of delivering a live baby by artificial means. After age 43, the success rate drops to a forbidding 3%.

—*By Christine Gorman*

THE DANGERS OF WAITING

Older women have a harder time getting pregnant and face greater risks when they do

Pregnancy Odds each month

Normal cycle or artificial insemination, based on data from Reproductive Medicine Associates of New Jersey

Age: 15 20 25 30 35 40 45 50

Miscarriage

Risk by age

20-24 25-29 30-34 35-39 40-44 45-50

Ectopic pregnancy

Risk by age

12-19 20-24 25-29 30-34 35-39 40-44 45 and over

Chromosomal abnormality

Fetal risk by maternal age

20 25 30 35 40 45

Sources: American Society for Reproductive Medicine; National Center for Health. Statistics; CDC; *British Medical Journal*; Mayo Clinic. TIME Graphic by Lon Tweeten and Ed Gabel; text by Laura Bradford

THREE WAYS TO GIVE NATURE A HELPING HAND

Sometimes hormone therapy does the trick, but many infertile couples require more sophisticated manipulation of sperm and eggs. Among the techniques that offer the greatest hope for success:

In vitro fertilization

HOW THEY DO IT A woman's eggs are extracted and mixed with her partner's sperm in a Petri dish. The resulting embryo is transferred to her uterus through the cervix
POPULARITY At least 60,000 IVF procedures are performed in the U.S. annually, with an average birthrate of 25%

ICSI (intracytoplasmic sperm injection)

HOW THEY DO IT To counteract problems with sperm count, quality or mobility, doctors inject a single sperm directly into a mature egg to increase the chance of fertilization
POPULARITY ICSI accounts for approximately 24,000 IVF procedures annually. Average birthrate: 30%

Egg donation

HOW THEY DO IT When the problem is aging eggs, a young woman may donate her eggs to the couple. Fertilized with the man's sperm, the resulting embryo is implanted in the older woman's womb
POPULARITY More than 5,000 eggs are donated yearly. After the eggs are fertilized, the birthrate is approximately 40%

Sources: American Society for Reproductive Medicine; National Center for Health Statistics; CDC; *British Medical Journal*; Mayo Clinic; text by Laura Bradford.

"dangerous" and "retrofeminist" because they could give corporations an excuse to derail women's careers. Slow down to start a family, the skeptics warned, and you run the risk that you will never catch up.

And so, argues Hewlett, many women embraced a "male model" of single-minded career focus, and the result is "an epidemic of childlessness" among professional women. She conducted a national survey of 1,647 "high-achieving women," including 1,168 who earn in the top 10% of income of their age group or hold degrees in law or medicine, and another 479 who are highly educated but are no longer in the work force. What she learned shocked her: she found that 42% of high-achieving women in corporate America (defined as companies with 5,000 or more employees) were still childless after age 40. That figure rose to 49% for women who earn $100,000 or more. Many other women were able to have only one child because they started their families too late. "They've been making a lot of money," says Dr. David Adamson, a leading fertility specialist at Stanford University, "but it won't buy back the time."

Recent Census data support Hewlett's research: childlessness has doubled in the past 20 years, so that 1 in 5 women between ages 40 and 44 is childless. For women that age and younger with graduate and professional degrees, the figure is 47%. This group certainly includes women for whom having children was never a priority: for them, the opening of the work force offered many new opportunities, including the chance to define success in realms other than motherhood. But Hewlett argues that many other women did not actually choose to be childless. When she asked women to recall their intentions at the time they were finishing college, Hewlett found that only 14% said that they definitely did not want to have children.

For most women Hewlett interviewed, childlessness was more like what one called a "creeping nonchoice." Time passes, work is relentless. The travel, the hours—relationships are hard to sustain. By the time a woman is married and settled enough in her career to think of starting a family, it is all too often too late. "They go to a doctor, take a blood test and are told the game is over before it even begins," says A.I.A.'s Madsen. "They are shocked, devastated and angry." Women generally know their fertility declines with age; they just don't realize how much and how fast. According to the Centers for Disease Control, once a woman celebrates her 42nd birthday, the chances of her having a baby using her own eggs, even with advanced medical help, are less than 10%. At age 40, half of her eggs are chromosomally abnormal; by 42, that figure is 90%. "I go through Kleenex in my office like it's going out of style," says reproductive endocrinologist Michael Slowey in Englewood, N.J.

Hewlett and her allies say they are just trying to correct the record in the face of widespread false optimism. Her survey found that nearly 9 out of 10 young women were confident of their ability to get pregnant into their 40s.

Women have been debating for a generation how best to balance work and home life, but somehow each new chapter starts a new fight, and Hewlett's book is no exception. Back in 1989, when Felice Schwartz discussed in the *Harvard Business Review* how to create more flexibility for career women with children (she never used the phrase Mommy Track herself), her proposals were called

Last fall the A.I.A. conducted a fertility-awareness survey on the women's website iVillage.com. Out of the 12,524 respondents, only one answered all 15 questions correctly. Asked when fertility begins to decline, only 13% got it right (age 27); 39% thought it began to drop at 40. Asked how long couples should try to conceive on their own before seeking help, fully 42% answered 30 months. That is a dangerous combination: a couple that imagines fertility is no problem until age 40 and tries to get pregnant for 30 months before seeing a doctor is facing very long odds of ever becoming parents.

In one sense, the confusion is understandable: it is only in the past 10 years that doctors themselves have discovered the limitations. "I remember being told by a number of doctors, 'Oh, you have plenty of time,' even when I was 38," says Claudia Morehead, 47, a California insurance lawyer who is finally pregnant, using donor eggs. Even among fertility specialists, "it was shocking to us that IVF didn't work so well after age 42," admits Dr. Sarah Berga, a reproductive endocrinologist at the University of Pittsburgh School of Medicine. "The early '90s, to my mind, was all about how shocked we were that we couldn't get past this barrier." But even as doctors began to try to get the word out, they ran into resistance of all kinds.

One is simply how information is shared. Childlessness is a private sorrow; the miracle baby is an inevitable headline. "When you see these media stories hyping women in their late 40s having babies, it's with donor eggs," insists Stanford's Adamson, "but that is conveniently left out of the stories." The more aggressive infertility clinics have a financial incentive to hype the good news and bury the facts: a 45-year-old woman who has gone through seven cycles of IVF can easily spend $100,000 on treatment. But even at the best fertility clinics in the country, her chance of taking a baby home is in the single digits.

In hopes of raising women's awareness, ASRM launched a modest $60,000 ad campaign last fall, with posters and brochures warning that factors like smoking, weight problems and sexually transmitted infections can all harm fertility. But the furor came with the fourth warning, a picture of a baby bottle shaped like an hourglass: "Advancing age decreases your ability to have children." The physicians viewed this as a public service, given the evidence of widespread confusion about the facts, but the group has come under fire for scaring women with an oversimplified message on a complex subject.

"The implication is, 'I have to hurry up and have kids now or give up on ever having them,'" says Kim Gandy, president of the National Organization for Women. "And that is not true for the vast majority of women." Gandy, 48, had her first child at 39. "It was a choice on my part, but in most ways it really wasn't. It's not like you can create out of whole cloth a partner you want to have a family with and the economic and emotional circumstances that allow you to be a good parent. So to put pressure on

young women to hurry up and have kids when they don't have those other factors in place really does a disservice to them and to their kids."

To emphasize a woman's age above all other factors can be just one more piece of misleading information, Gandy suggests. "There are two people involved [in babymaking], and yet we're putting all the responsibility on women and implying that women are being selfish if they don't choose to have children early." She shares the concern that women will hear the research and see the ads and end up feeling it is so hard to strike a balance that it's futile to even try. "There is an antifeminist agenda that says we should go back to the 1950s," says Caryl Rivers, a journalism professor at Boston University. "The subliminal message is, 'Don't get too educated; don't get too successful or too ambitious.'"

Allison Rosen, a clinical psychologist in New York City who has made it her mission to make sure her female patients know the fertility odds, disagrees. "This is not a case of male doctors' wanting to keep women barefoot and pregnant," she says. "You lay out the facts, and any particular individual woman can then make her choices." Madsen of A.I.A. argues that the biological imperative is there whether women know it or not. "I cringe when feminists say giving women reproductive knowledge is pressuring them to have a child," she says. "That's simply not true. Reproductive freedom is not just the ability not to have a child through birth control. It's the ability to have one if and when you want one."

YOU CAN TRACE THE STRUGGLE BETWEEN HOPE AND BIOLOGY back to *Genesis*, when Abraham and Sarah gave thanks for the miracle that brought them their son in old age. "She was the first infertile woman," notes Zev Rosenwaks, the director of New York Presbyterian Hospital's infertility program. "It was so improbable that an allegedly menopausal woman could have a baby that her firstborn was named Isaac, which means 'to laugh.'" The miracle stories have fed the hope ever since, but so does wishful thinking. "It's tremendously comforting for a 34- or 36-year-old professional woman to imagine that she has time on her side," says Hewlett, which can make for resistance to hearing the truth.

"In just 30 years we've gone from fearing our fertility to squandering it— and very unwittingly."

This is the heart of Hewlett's crusade: that it is essential for women to plan where they want to be at 45 and work backward, armed with the knowledge that the window for having children is narrower than they have been led to believe and that once it begins to swing shut, science can do little to pry it open. And Hewlett argues as well that employers and policymakers need to do more to help families make the balancing act work. "The greatest choice facing modern women is to freely choose to have both, a job and a family, and be supported and admired for it, not be seen as some overweening yuppie."

As it happens, Hewlett knows from personal experience. She says she didn't set out to write about how hard it is for professional women to be moms. She planned to do a book celebrating women turning 50 at the millennium and to look at what forces had shaped their lives. Then she discovered, in interview after interview with college deans and opera divas, a cross section of successful women in various fields, that none of them had children—and few of them had chosen to be childless. Many blamed themselves for working too hard and waiting too long—and waking up to the truth too late. "When I talked to these women," she recalls, "their sense of loss was palpable."

Hewlett had spent most of her professional life writing and lecturing on the need for business and government to develop more family-friendly workplaces; she has a Ph.D. in economics from Harvard. And she has had children and lost them and fought to have more. As a young Barnard professor with a toddler at home, she lost twins six months into her pregnancy: If only, she thought, I had taken time off from work, taken it easier. A year and a half later, she writes, she was turned down for tenure by an appointments committee that believed, in the words of one member, that she had "allowed childbearing to dilute my focus." Hewlett was lucky: she went on to have three more children, including Emma, to whom she gave birth at 51 using her own egg and infertility treatments. Hewlett says she understands "baby hunger."

At least she understands it for women. Men, she argues, have an unfair advantage. "Nowadays," she says, "the rule of thumb seems to be that the more successful the woman, the less likely it is she will find a husband or bear a child. For men, the reverse is true. I found that only one-quarter of high-achieving men end up without kids. Men generally find that if they are successful, everything else follows naturally." But that view of men doesn't quite do justice to the challenges they face as well. Men too are working harder than ever; at the very moment that society sends the message to be more involved as fathers, the economy makes it harder—and Hewlett's prescription that women need to think about having their children younger leaves more men as primary breadwinners. They would be fathers as far as biology goes, but they wouldn't get much chance to be parents. "A lot of my friends who are men and have had families are now divorced," Stanford's Adamson admits. "When you ask them what happened, the vast majority will say, 'Well, I was never home. I was working all the time. I didn't pay enough attention to my family. I wish I had, but it's too late now.'"

Hewlett still insists that men don't face the same "cruel choices" that women confront. "Men who find that they have no relationship with their adult kids at least have a second chance as grandfathers," she argues. "For women, childlessness represents a rolling loss into the future. It means having no children *and* no grandchildren." While her earlier books are full of policy prescriptions, this one is more personal. She salts the book with cautionary tales: women who were too threatening to the men they dated, too successful and preoccupied, too "predatory" to suit men who were looking for "nurturers." The voices are authentic but selective; taken together, it is easy to read certain passages and think she is calling for a retreat to home and hearth, where motherhood comes before every other role.

Hewlett replies that she is simply trying to help women make wise choices based on good information. She is not proposing a return to the '50s, she says, or suggesting that women should head off to college to get their MRS. and then try to have children soon after graduation. "Late 20s is probably more realistic, because men are not ready to commit earlier than that. And the 20s still needs to be a decade of great personal growth." She recommends that women get their degrees, work hard at their first jobs—but then be prepared to plateau for a while and redirect their energy into their personal lives, with the intention of catching up professionally later. "You will make some compromises in your career. But you will catch up, reinvent yourself, when the time is right."

100% RISE IN PAST 20 YEARS OF CHILDLESS WOMEN AGES 40 TO 44

Only 0.1% of babies in the U.S. are born to women age 45 or older

The problem is that Hewlett's own research argues otherwise: in her book all of the examples of successful women who also have families gave birth in their 20s. These women may escape the fate of would-be mothers who waited too long, but they encounter a whole different set of obstacles when it comes to balancing work and family. Biology may be unforgiving, but so is corporate culture: those who voluntarily leave their career to raise children often find that the way back in is extremely difficult. Many in her survey said they felt forced out by inflexible bosses; two-thirds say they wish they could return to the work force.

Much would have to change in the typical workplace for parents to be able to downshift temporarily and then resume their pace as their children grew older. Hewlett hopes that the war for talent will inspire corporations to adopt more family-friendly policies in order to attract and maintain the most talented parents, whether male or female. Many of her policy recommendations, however, are unlikely to be enacted anytime soon: mandatory paid parental leave; official "career breaks" like the generous policy at IBM that grants workers up to three years' leave with the guarantee of return to the same or a similar job; a new Fair Labor Standards Act that would discourage 80-hour workweeks by making all but the very top executives eligible for overtime pay.

Hewlett calls herself a feminist, but she has often crossed swords with feminists who, she charges, are so concerned with reproductive choice that they neglect the needs of women who choose to be mothers. In the history of the family, she notes, it is a very recent development for women to have control over childbearing, thanks to better health care and birth control. But there's an ironic twist now. "In just 30 years, we've gone from fearing our fertility to squandering it—and very unwittingly." The decision of whether to have a child will always be one of the most important anyone makes; the challenge is not allowing time and biology to make it for them.

—Reported by Janice M. Horowitz,
Julie Rawe and Sora Song/New York

TOO POSH TO PUSH?

Cesarean sections have spiked dramatically. Progress or convenience?

BY SUSAN BRINK

The fact is indisputable: The number of babies being delivered by cesarean section is rising sharply. But beyond that fact are vast uncertainties, including the cause of the increase and even whether it's a good or bad thing. Some blame a generation of new mothers unwilling to endure the pain and inconvenience of having a baby the old-fashioned way. Accustomed to controlling every detail of their lives, these women are too impatient for the uncertain timing of labor and too pampered for hours of contractions. They are, in short, too posh to push.

But not everyone is ready to blame the mothers. Others say it's doctors who are cloaking their own preference for C-sections in "women's choice" rhetoric. Worried about malpractice suits and protective of their own free time, OB-GYNs are telling prospective mothers that cesarean sections today are safe—or at least safer than vaginal deliveries. Indeed, some may be using the pain of contractions as a tool to coerce women into surgery, critics say. "You can take almost any laboring patient and talk her into a C-section," says Green Bay, Wis., obstetrician Robert DeMott. "That's part of the reason why we have a tremendous variation in C-section rates in the country."

Trend spotting. Whatever the reason, the U.S. rate of cesarean section spiked in 2001, up 7 percent since 2000 to the highest rate since the government began keeping tabs. Today, 1 in 4 babies in the United States is delivered by cesarean section. The rate of first-time C-sections, at 16.9 percent, is also the highest ever reported, up from a low of 14.6 percent in 1996 and 1997. Adding to the trend is a drop in the rate of vaginal births after a previous cesarean, which fell from 20.6 percent in 2000 to 16.5 percent in 2001.

Certainly, there are good reasons for a C-section, and the availability of the surgery has saved countless lives. A rise in the rate of herpes and in the number of first-time mothers at risk because they are older could account for some of the rise. But not all, and that's why experts are focusing on legal concerns and our culture of convenience and control. The debate among women can be as heated as among doctors. "This is a horrible trend that is in total opposition to natural law," says Anita Woods, vice president of the International Cesarean Awareness Network.

Moya Cook of Marion, Ill., has a rebuttal: "I'm a nurse, and I've seen a lot of complications such as prolapsed uterus, prolapsed bladders. When I found out that I was having twins, I up front told them I wanted a C-section." Cook did indeed have the C-section she wanted.

In her case, the twins presented breech—feet first, a difficult vaginal delivery. Fortunately for Cook, this is a medical indication for the procedure that satisfied insurers. Without a medical reason, physicians cannot ethically perform a cesarean section simply because a woman wants it, says David Walters, Cook's obstetrician and author of *Just Take It Out!: The Ethics and Economics of Cesarean Section and Hysterectomy.* But that doesn't necessarily stop a doctor, Walters notes: "What people do is they'll make up some kind of bogus reason, like 'the umbilical cord is in front of the head.'"

Side effects. There are some shreds of medical evidence on long-term risks of vaginal delivery—damage to the pelvic floor, for example. But they are now just shreds of evidence, nothing strong enough to settle the matter. There is solid science linking vaginal delivery to what are often called "female problems" later in life—the largely unmentionable issues of incontinence and prolapse, or sagging pelvic organs. But no one knows just who may suffer decades later. "C-section has been vilified," says Walters. "But go talk to women who are peeing in their pants 20 years later."

That's what Joseph Schaffer has done. He is director of uro-gynecology and reconstructive pelvic surgery at the University of Texas Southwestern, and he sees women largely for problems of pelvic floor damage, including incontinence and prolapse. An estimated 11 percent of women will undergo surgery in their lifetime for incontinence or prolapse. Two of the biggest known risk factors for pelvic floor damage are forceps delivery and episiotomy, a surgical cut to allow more room for the baby. Both procedures are less common today.

While no one can predict which new mothers will have future medical problems, women who have had incontinence or prolapse following an earlier vaginal delivery, even if the condition got better shortly after delivery, are likely at increased risk for future

problems. They might do better with cesarean deliveries. "That's not a big group," said Schaffer. "We don't have the answer about who is at risk, other than forceps and episiotomy are probably not good."

Cesarean deliveries, while safe for the vast majority of mothers and babies, are major surgery. They carry risks to the mother such as potentially life-threatening blood clots, infection from surgery, longer recovery time, and a risk of placenta accreta, in which the placenta attaches to the incision in a subsequent pregnancy. While most elective surgery is a one-time event, cesarean section often means additional surgery for each pregnancy that follows.

The primary risk to the baby, deprived of that long, hard trip through the birth canal, is lung problems. "Vaginal birth gives the baby a massage, squeezing out the lungs and stimulating the heart," says Robbie Davis-Floyd, author of *Birth as an American Rite of Passage.* Premature birth is also a risk with a C-section because, without the natural trigger of labor, no one really knows when it is time for a baby to be born. And some cesarean-delivered babies have problems feeding at first.

The World Health Organization has recommended a cesarean rate of 10 percent to 15 percent, says Marsden Wagner, a perinatologist who has worked on the WHO studies. The U.S. Department of Health and Human Services would also like the C-section rate in American hospitals to be no more than 15 percent. But if society begins talking about surgical delivery as a woman's right, a choice equal to requesting a face-lift or a tummy tuck, obstetricians trying to keep their C-section rates down will have a harder time. "Doctors will use the rationale that if women can come to me for an elective C-section, why should I work hard to keep the rate down?" says Richard Waldman, an obstetrician in Syracuse, N.Y.

Women have fought for three decades to demedicalize childbirth without sacrificing safety, says Jan Christilaw, an obstetrician from White Rock, British Columbia. She predicts a backlash against the growing C-section rate: "This is a way of remedicalizing birth. I think birth is such an important cultural process that to divorce ourselves from its natural course is horrific."

SHAPED BY LIFE IN THE
WOMB

Scientists used to think that adult illnesses like diabetes, obesity,
cardiovascular disease and breast cancer were the
result of either unhealthy living or bad genes. No longer. Startling new research
suggests that these conditions may have their roots before birth.

BY SHARON BEGLEY

When John Carter was born, 73 years ago, the doctor in the town of Ware just north of London wasn't sure if the little guy would make it: he weighed a mere 3.4 pounds. "They laid me on a hot-water bottle, wrapped me in cotton soaked in cod-liver oil and gave me brandy through the nib of a fountain pen," Carter says. "Surviving was rather a miracle." But the little boy grew to manhood, landing a job as a warehouseman and enjoying normal health—until his early 50s. That's when a physical discovered that Carter had sky-high blood pressure. Another test found that he had adult-onset diabetes.

Carter had no reason to suspect it, but his illnesses may not stem from the usual culprits: genetic defects, unhealthy living or environmental toxins. Cutting-edge research suggests instead that the roots of both his high blood pressure and his diabetes stretch back decades—to his life in the womb. Scientists now think that conditions during gestation, ranging from the torrent of hormones that flow from Mom to how well the placenta delivers nutrients

to the tiny limbs and organs, shape the health of the adult that fetus becomes."Recent research" says Dr. Peter Nathanaielsz of Cornell University, whose new book "Life in the Womb" explores this science, "provides compelling proof that the health we enjoy throughout our lives is determined to a large extent by the conditions in which we developed, [conditions that] can program how our liver, heart, kidneys and especially our brain function." It is no exaggeration to call these findings a revolution in the making. The discovery of how conditions in the womb influence the risk of adult disease casts doubt on how much genes contribute to disease (because what scientists classify as a genetic influence may instead reflect gestational conditions) and suggests that adult illnesses long blamed on years of living dangerously (like dining on pizza and cupcakes) instead reflect "fetal programming." "Two years ago no one was even thinking about this," says Dr. Matthew Gillman of Harvard Medical School. "But now what we are seeing is

nothing short of a new paradigm in public health."

What is so startling is that the findings go far beyond the widespread recognition that conditions during gestation shape the health of the newborn. We've known for a while that alcohol reaching the fetus can lead to mental retardation and heart defects and that the stew of toxins in tobacco can cause upper-respiratory-tract and ear infections. But these compounds work by more or less poisoning the baby. The result is often a child who, at birth or soon after, has detectable problems. The new findings are dramatically different. First of all, the gestational conditions scientists are talking about fall far short of toxic. They are, instead, paragons of subtlety. They are conditions that reprogram the fetus's physiology so that, for instance, the child's (and eventually the adult's) metabolism turns just about everything she eats into body fat. This is the woman who needn't bother actually eating the french fries; she might as well just insert them directly into her hips. Second, unlike the toxic influences

A Tragic But Telling Legacy

Doctors are using a horror of war to learn more about the long-term effects of nutrition on fetal development

YOU COULDN'T DESIGN a grimmer experiment. A Nazi blockade of the western Netherlands in September 1944 and an early winter triggered a famine that lasted until the spring of 1945. By January, daily rations in the cities were down to 750 calories, half of what they had been earlier in the war; they would eventually fall below 500 calories. City dwellers were forced into the country to scavenge for food, including tulip bulbs. The "Hunger Winter" had killed 20,000 people by Liberation Day on May 5, 1945, scarring an entire populace—including, scientists later found, generations yet unborn. In the 1960s, husband-and-wife researchers Zena Stein and Mervyn Susser realized that, horrific as it was, the Dutch Hunger Winter offered unprecedented clues to the effects of prenatal nutrition.

Stein and Susser discovered that fetuses exposed to the famine early in gestation, when organs form, had an increased risk of central-nervous-system defects like spina bifida, in which the brain or spine is not fully developed. Other scientists found that a fetus starved early in development during the famine was at high risk for adult obesity. Two decades later, Stein and Susser's son, Ezra Susser, went further. Now a pioneering epidemiologist at Columbia University, Susser examined psychiatric evaluations of adults who were Hunger Winter babies to study the theory that schizophrenia was the result of a defect in neural development. Susser and Hans Hoek in the Netherlands discovered that fetuses who received poor nutrition early in gestation were twice as likely to develop schizophrenia in adulthood as fetuses whose mothers had an adequate diet. Susser is now looking for links between prenatal nutrition and other mental illnesses. It's a sad but revealing legacy of that season of devastation.

JOHN DAVENPORT

Tragic Echoes: *Children relied on relief programs; infants suffered later in life*

whose effects on a fetus are apparent immediately, the effects of fetal programming often show up only decades later. The nine-pound bouncing girl will be perfectly healthy for decades. But the same influences that gave her layers of baby fat— "growth factors" like estrogen's crossing the placenta from Mom—prime her mammary tissue so that exposure to estrogen after puberty gives her breast cancer at 46.

There is one thing the findings do not mean. While they may tempt you to blame Mom for even more of your ills, or make you feel powerless against a fate that was set before you cried your first cry, forget it: how you live your life outside the womb still matters. Since the conditions in which the fetus develops influence adult health, learning what those conditions are (through measurements of length, weight, girth and head size at birth) tells you what extra risks you carry with you into the world. And that suggests ways to keep these risks from becoming reality. If as a newborn your abdomen was unusually small, for instance, then your liver may be too small to clear cholesterol from your bloodstream as well as it should, and you may have an extra risk of elevated cholesterol at the age of 50. So scrutinize those baby pictures: if your tummy was scrawny compared with the rest of chubby-cheeked you, be careful about controlling your cholesterol levels.

The discovery of fetal programming might never have happened if Dr. David Barker of England's University of Southampton had not noticed, in 1984, some maps that did not seem to make sense. They displayed measures of health throughout England and Wales. Barker saw that neonatal mortality in the early 1900s was high in the same regions where deaths from heart disease were high. That was odd. In general, infant mortality rises in pockets of poverty; heart disease is supposedly a disease of affluence (butter, meat and all that). They shouldn't go together. Barker wondered whether the search for the cause of heart disease should begin in the womb. To embark on his quest, he needed birth records, and lots of them, going back decades, to link conditions at the beginning of life with the health of the adults he would study. Lending a hand, Britain's Medical Research Council hired an Oxford University historian to scour the country for such records. During a two-year hunt, the historian found records in archives, lofts, sheds, garages, boiler rooms and even flooded basements—but the best records were in Hertfordshire. There, the "lady inspector of midwives" had recorded the weight of every baby born in the shire (including John Carter) from 1911 to 1945. Barker had his data.

Ominous signs:
Michels's study of thousands of American women finds a link between a girl's birth weight and her risk of breast cancer at a relatively young age

---

Soon Barker and his colleagues had their "Aha!" moment. Studying 13,249

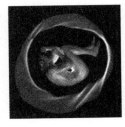

EARLY WIRING: the growth factors that give a newborn fat may prime her mammary tissue, making her more susceptible to breast cancer in her 40s.

The Roots of Health

Disorders such as heart disease and diabetes are not only the result of unhealthy habits or bad genes. The new science of "fetal programming" suggests that as pregnancy progresses, each month in the womb shapes your health for life.

Stress 1

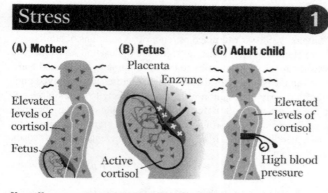

(A) Mother

(B) Fetus — Placenta, Enzyme

(C) Adult child

Elevated levels of cortisol

Fetus

Active cortisol

Elevated levels of cortisol

High blood pressure

Usually, an enzyme in the placenta deactivates cortisol, a stress hormone. But if the mother does not get proper nutrition, the enzyme fails. Cortisol reaches the fetal brain, increasing susceptibility to stress in adulthood. Cortisol can also raise blood pressure.

Obesity 2

Undernutrition during the fetus's first trimester makes obesity more likely in adulthood, perhaps because the appetite-control center in the brain is programmed to overeat.

Diabetes 3

If a mother-to-be is diabetic, she may expose her fetus to high levels of glucose. This can stress the fetal pancreas, producing diabetes in adulthood. If weight is controlled, however, the risk of adult-onset diabetes decreases.

SECOND MONTH

FIFTH MONTH

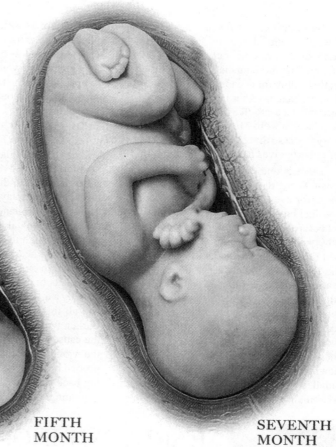

SEVENTH MONTH

Graphic continued on next page.

men born in Hertfordshire and Sheffield, Barker found that a man who weighed less than 5.5 pounds at birth has a 50 percent greater chance of dying of heart disease than a man with a higher birth weight, even accounting for socioeconomic differences and other heart risks. "Death rates from both stroke and coronary heart disease tended to be highest in men whose birth weight had been low," says Barker, especially when it was low compared with their length or head size (an indication that

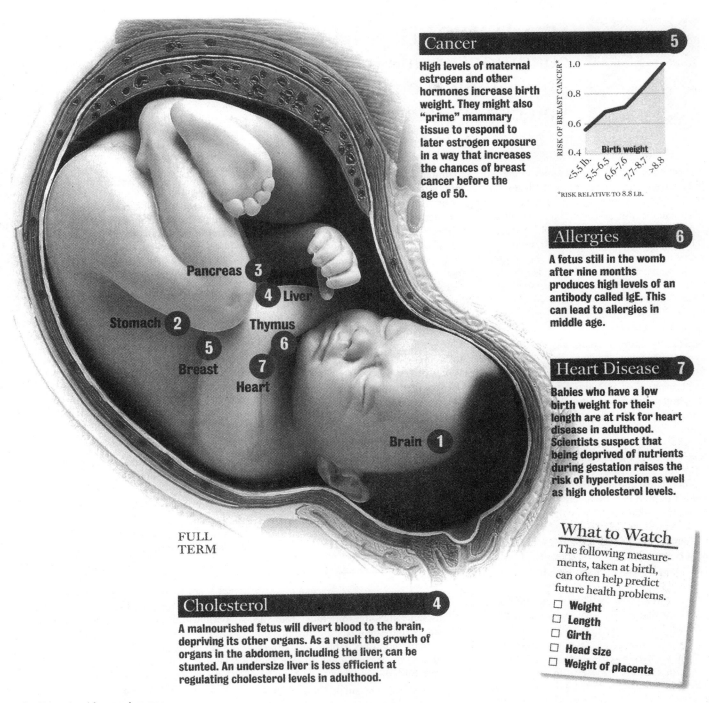

Cancer 5

High levels of maternal estrogen and other hormones increase birth weight. They might also "prime" mammary tissue to respond to later estrogen exposure in a way that increases the chances of breast cancer before the age of 50.

RISK OF BREAST CANCER*

Birth weight

<5.5 lb. 5.5-6.5 6.6-7.6 7.7-8.7 >8.8

*RISK RELATIVE TO 8.8 LB.

Allergies 6

A fetus still in the womb after nine months produces high levels of an antibody called IgE. This can lead to allergies in middle age.

Heart Disease 7

Babies who have a low birth weight for their length are at risk for heart disease in adulthood. Scientists suspect that being deprived of nutrients during gestation raises the risk of hypertension as well as high cholesterol levels.

Pancreas 3
4 Liver
Stomach 2
Thymus
5 6
Breast 7
Heart
Brain 1

FULL
TERM

What to Watch

The following measurements, taken at birth, can often help predict future health problems.

☐ **Weight**
☐ **Length**
☐ **Girth**
☐ **Head size**
☐ **Weight of placenta**

Cholesterol 4

A malnourished fetus will divert blood to the brain, depriving its other organs. As a result the growth of organs in the abdomen, including the liver, can be stunted. An undersize liver is less efficient at regulating cholesterol levels in adulthood.

Graphic continued from previous page.

the baby's growth was stunted). Using other birth records from India, Barker found the same link in a 1996 study. Again, low birth weight predicted coronary heart disease, especially in the middle-aged: 11 percent of 42- to 62-year-olds who weighed 5.5 pounds or less at birth got it, compared with 3 percent of those born chubbier. The link between low birth weight and cardiovascular disease is now one of the strongest in the whole field of fetal programming, holding across continents as well as genders. Researchers led by Dr. Janet Rich-Edwards of Harvard reported, in 1997, that of 70,297 American women studied, those born weighing less than 5.5 pounds had a 23 percent higher risk of cardiovascular disease than women born heftier.

But it is not smallness per se that causes heart disease decades later. Instead, what seems to happen is that the same suboptimal conditions in the womb that stunt a baby's growth also saddle it with risk factors that lead to heart disease. "Birth weight is a proxy for something," says Rich-Edwards. "It's a marker for a complex set of factors that influence both growth in the womb and susceptibility to disease later on." Scientists have some suspects. Nathanielsz suggests it may be as simple as having undersized kidneys: these organs help regulate blood pressure, but if they are not up to the task, the result can be hypertension, a leading cause of heart disease. Or, animal studies have shown that if

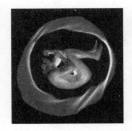

HARD WIRED: A fetus's response to conditions inside the uterus produces permanent physiological changes. But there's still plenty you can fix later.

a fetus does not receive adequate protein, then an enzyme in the placenta loses its punch and can no longer disarm harmful hormones trying to sneak into the fetus. One such hormone is cortisol. Cortisol raises blood pressure, as you are reminded every time stress makes your veins bulge. In the fetus, cortisol seems to raise the set point for blood pressure—irreversibly. "You are talking about hard-wiring the system," says Jonathan Seckl of the University of Edinburgh.

The discoveries are drawing throngs of excited scientists. A year ago the Society for Epidemiologic Research half-filled a small room at its annual meeting for a session on fetal programming. This spring the same subject packed a whole lecture hall. "This whole topic is just now catching fire," says Rich-Edwards. The surge in interest reflects the lengthening list of diseases that scientists are tracing back to the womb. The National Institutes of Health held a conference in January on the link between conditions in the womb and breast cancer; in September, another NIH confab examined the link to cardiovascular disease, kidney disease and other ills. A conference at Harvard will explore the topic in November.

The breast-cancer link is one of the most surprising. The very existence of the disease is bad enough. What terrifies women is that it strikes so many who have no known risk factors—such as age, close relatives with the disease or not bearing a child before 30. Dr. Karin Michels of the Harvard School of Public Health has identified one overlooked cause. After collecting health data from tens of thousands of nurses, Michels and colleagues reported in 1997 that women who had weighed about 5.5 pounds at birth had half the risk of breast cancer compared with women who had weighed about 9 pounds at birth. That was especially true of breast cancers in women 50 or younger. "There is increasing evidence," says Michels, "that breast cancer may originate before birth."

A very high birth weight may be a marker for uterine influences that "prime"

mammary tissue for cancer. Growth factors, living up to their name, make a fetus larger. Such factors include insulin, leptin and estrogen. If the mother has high levels of these substances (being obese raises levels of estrogen, for instance), and if they reach her fetus, the hormones may do more than act like Miracle-Gro on backyard tomatoes: they may alter nascent mammary tissue in such a way that it responds to estrogen during puberty by becoming malignant. This is no reason to starve your girl fetus—stunted fetal growth leads to other problems. But it does suggest that if you were a pudgy newborn you might want to be extra vigilant about breast exams.

Heart of the matter:
Barker's discovery that birth weight is linked to cardiovascular disease in adulthood has launched a revolution in public health

---

The same message emerges from the other links that scientists are turning up. Weight and other traits at birth may offer a map of where your personal disease land mines are buried:

• Cholesterol: The smaller the abdomen at birth, the higher the cholesterol level in adulthood. What may happen is that if the mother is poorly nourished or if a problem with the placenta keeps the fetus from receiving adequate nutrition, then the fetus switches into emergency mode: it shunts blood to the brain, the most vital organ, at the expense of organs in the abdomen. That includes the liver, which plays a key role in regulating cholesterol levels. A smaller liver can't clear cholesterol as well as a hefty one. This suggests an answer to the longstanding puzzle of how some people can eat high-fat and cholesterol-laden

diets with impunity: these lucky folks were programmed as fetuses to process fat and cholesterol as efficiently as a sewage-treatment plant. The others have defective treatment plants. "When a fetus adapts to conditions in the womb," says Southampton's Barker, "that adaptation tends to be permanent."

• Obesity: This was the first trait suspected of reflecting life in the womb. In World War II, the Nazis tried to starve the population of western Holland from September 1944 until the following May (sidebar). Men who were fetuses during all or part of the period showed a telling pattern. If their mothers were starving during the first trimester—from March to May 1945—but got adequate food later, the men were born heavier, longer and with larger heads than babies in normal periods. As adults, they were more likely to be obese. If their mothers went hungry only in the final trimester—if the boys were born in November 1944, say—the men usually stayed svelte. What may happen is this: if food is scarce during the first trimester, the fetus develops a so-called thrifty phenotype. Its metabolism is set so that every available calorie sticks. Or, the availability or scarcity of food may affect the appetite centers in the fetal brain. In that case, undernutrition early in fetal life could dial up the appetite controls to the setting "eat whatever's around: you never know when famine will hit." An abundance of food early keeps the dial at "no need to pig out." Fetuses undernourished later in gestation may develop fewer fat cells (it is in the later months that most cells are added). That makes it harder to become fat after birth.

• Diabetes: Being skinny at birth puts an individual at high risk for diabetes in middle age, finds David Leon of the London School of Hygiene and Tropical Medicine. The effect is powerful: diabetes is three times more common in 60-year-old men who, as newborns, were in the bottom fifth on a scale of plumpness (technically, it's birth weight divided by length cubed) than in more rotund babies. "One explanation is that inadequate nutrition programs the fe-

What Moms Can Do Now

If you're pregnant, take advantage of the latest research to give your babies the best start.
They'll thank you later.

OF COURSE THOSE nine months matter. Doctors now say that from the moment the sperm and egg fuse, conditions in your body determine how healthy your baby will be as an adult. Pediatricians can estimate risk for diseases by measuring length, weight, girth and head size at birth. Visit an obstetrician who's up on the latest research before you get pregnant and follow these guidelines:

Preconception care: A doctor can help you avoid medicines that harm embryos. Tell your obstetrician about any diseases or conditions you have that might complicate the pregnancy. If you're diabetic, make sure to take your insulin. To prevent neural-tube defects such as spina bifida, get at least 400 micrograms of folic acid a day from foods like leafy green vegetables and orange juice.

Meal plan: Eat about 300 extra calories a day during pregnancy. Snack or eat small meals throughout the day if you can't take large amounts of food. Your baby needs nutrients to grow normally, and you can't make up for lost calories by eating more later on.

The right stuff: Eat lots of carbohydrates, but don't skimp on fruits, vegetables, low-fat dairy products and lean meats. These foods contain protein, vitamins and minerals that build your baby's blood, bones and muscles.

Weight gain: Try to put on about 25 to 35 pounds if your weight is normal (more if you're on the thin side and less if you're fat). Focus on gaining weight, not watching calories. Your baby needs the extra nutrition to develop properly.

Drugs: Ask your doctor about any medications you take. Anticonvulsants and the acne drug Accutane can cause birth defects. Some antidepressants and painkillers may affect the baby, but don't stop taking them without consulting a doctor. Cocaine can kill a fetus,

and babies born addicted to narcotics will suffer withdrawal after birth.

Caffeine: Your blood volume doubles during pregnancy, so a java overdose will dehydrate you when you need water most. Some research has linked excessive doses of caffeine to low birth weight, so limit yourself to a couple of cups a day.

Exercise: Staying in shape may ease labor and speed recovery after delivery. But don't exercise to exhaustion, and stay away from sports that expose your belly to trauma. Swimming and walking should be high on your list.

Stress: Reduce it. Both chronic and sudden, intense stress may increase the risk of premature labor by raising your levels of cortisol, a stress hormone. Try cutting back on work hours or joining a yoga class. And remember to get enough sleep.

Seat belts: Use them; your uterus and amniotic fluid prevent seat belts from injuring the fetus. Wear the lap belt below your belly, and adjust the shoulder strap so it rests between your breasts.

Alcohol: Doctors urge temperance during pregnancy. Excessive alcohol causes facial and heart defects, mental retardation and behavioral problems.

Smoking: Kick the habit now. Smoking contributes to 25 percent of cases of low birth weight and can cause miscarriage and premature birth.

STDs: Get tested. Untreated chlamydia, HIV, gonorrhea, syphilis and herpes cause a wide range of complications during pregnancy and childbirth.

ERIKA CHECK

tus to develop a thrifty metabolism," says Leon. "That includes insulin resistance, so the body saves and marshals existing glucose stores." When this metabolism meets junk food, the body is flooded with glucose and becomes diabetic. But diabetes is a prime example of how life in the womb is not an immutable sentence. Although thinness at birth raises the risk of developing diabetes in middle age, finds Leon, that risk is much reduced if you stay thin.

• Brain: Research on how life in the womb influences the brain is only beginning. But already there are hints, from both animal and human research, that something is going on. In a 1997 paper, biologists reported on a study of people with asymmetries in traits like feet, fingers, ears and elbows. IQs were lower in asymmetric people by about as much (percentagewise) as their measurements deviate from perfect symmetry. Some sort of stress during fetal development probably causes asymmetries, suggests Randy Thornhill of

the University of New Mexico. The same stress may cause imperfections in the developing nervous system, leading to less efficient neurons for sensing, remembering and thinking. Here, too, asymmetry is a marker for something going wrong in the womb. Thornhill estimates that between 17 and 50 percent of IQ differences reflect in utero causes.

The new science of fetal programming suggests that we may have gone overboard in ascribing traits to genes. "Programming," concludes Nathanielsz, "is equally if not more important than our genes in determining how we perform mentally and physically." Consider one of the standard ways that scientists assess how much of a trait reflects genetic influences and how much reflects environment: they compare twins. If identical twins share a trait more than other siblings do, the trait is deemed to be largely under genetic control. But twins share something besides genes: a womb. Some of the concordance attributed

to shared genes might instead reflect a shared uterine environment. The womb may have another effect. Merely *having* a gene is not enough to express the associated trait. The genes must be turned on to exert an effect, otherwise they are silent— just as having a collection of CDs doesn't mean that your home is filled with music unless you play them. In the womb, a flood of stress hormones may actually turn off genes associated with the stress response; the response becomes less effective, which is another way of saying this child is at risk of growing into an adult who can't handle stress. "The script written on the genes is altered by... the environment in the womb," says Nathanielsz.

As fetal programming becomes better understood, it may even resurrect the long-discredited theory known as Lamarckism. This idea holds that traits acquired by an organism during its lifetime can be passed on to children—that if a woman spends the 10 years before pregnancy whipping herself into a bodybuilder physique, her baby will emerge ready to pump iron. Modern genetics showed that inheritance does not work that way. But according to fetal programming, some traits a mother acquires can indeed be visited on her child. If she becomes diabetic, then she floods her fetus with glucose; waves of glucose may overwhelm the developing pancreas so that fetal cells that secrete insulin become exhausted. As a result, the child, too, becomes diabetic in adulthood. When this child becomes pregnant, she too, floods her fetus with glucose, stressing its pancreas and priming it for adult-onset diabetes. This baby will develop diabetes because of something that happened two generations before—a kind of grandmother effect.

In "Brave New World," Aldous Huxley describes how workers at the Central London Hatchery, where fetuses grow in special broths, adjust the ingredients of the amniotic soup depending on which kind of child they need. Children destined to work in chemical factories are treated so they can tolerate lead and cadmium; those destined to pilot rockets are constantly rotated so that they learn to enjoy being upside-down. The quest for the secrets of fetal programming won't yield up such simple recipes. But it is already showing that the seeds of health are planted even before you draw your first breath, and that the nine short months of life in the womb shape your health as long as you live.

With WILLIAM UNDERHILL *in London*

Our Babies, Ourselves

By Meredith F. Small

During one of his many trips to Gusii-land in southwestern Kenya, anthropologist Robert LeVine tried an experiment: he showed a group of Gusii mothers a videotape of middle-class American women tending their babies. The Gusii mothers were appalled. Why does that mother ignore the cries of her unhappy baby during a simple diaper change? And how come that grandmother does nothing to soothe the screaming baby in her lap? These American women, the Gusii concluded, are clearly incompetent

mothers. In response, the same charge might be leveled at the Gusii by American mothers. What mother hands over her tiny infant to a six-year-old sister and expects the older child to provide adequate care? And why don't those Gusii women spend more time talking to their babies, so that they will grow up smart?

Both culture—the traditional way of doing things in a particular society—and individual experience guide parents in their tasks. When a father chooses to pick up his newborn and not let it cry,

when a mother decides to bottle-feed on a schedule rather than breast-feed on demand, when a couple bring the newborn into their bed at night, they are prompted by what they believe to be the best methods of caregiving.

For decades, anthropologists have been recording how children are raised in different societies. At first, the major goals were to describe parental roles and understand how child-rearing practices and rituals helped to generate adult per-

Gusii Survival Skills

By Robert A. LeVine

Farming peoples of subSaharan Africa have long faced the grim reality that many babies fail to survive, often succumbing to gastrointestinal diseases, malaria, or other infections. In the 1970s, when I lived among the Gusii in a small town in southwestern Kenya, infant mortality in that nation was on the decline but was still high—about eighty deaths per thousand live births during the first years, compared with about ten in the United States at that time and six to eight in Western Europe.

The Gusii grew corn, millet, and cash crops such as coffee and tea. Women handled the more routine tasks of cultivation, food processing, and trading, while men were supervisors or entrepreneurs. Many men worked at jobs outside the village, in urban centers or on plantations. The society was

polygamous, with perhaps 10 percent of the men having two or more wives. A woman was expected to give birth every two years, from marriage to menopause, and the average married women bore about ten live children—one of the highest fertility rates in the world.

Nursing mothers slept alone with a new infant for fifteen months to insure its health. For the first three to six months, the Gusii mothers were especially vigilant for signs of ill health or slow growth, and they were quick to nurture unusually small or sick infants by feeding and holding them more often. Mothers whose newborns were deemed particularly at risk—including twins and those born prematurely—entered a ritual seclusion for several weeks, staying with their infants in a hut with a constant fire.

Mothers kept infants from crying in the early months by holding them constantly and being quick to comfort them. After three to six months—if the baby was growing normally—mothers began to entrust the baby to the care of other children (usually six to twelve years old) in order to pursue tasks that helped support the family. Fathers did not take care of infants, for this was not a traditional male activity.

Because they were so worried about their children's survival, Gusii parents did not explicitly strive to foster cognitive, social, and emotional development. These needs were not neglected, however, because from birth Gusii babies entered an active and responsive interpersonal environment, first with their mothers and young caregivers, and later as part of a group of children.

An Infant's Three Rs

By Sara Harkness and Charles M. Super

You are an American visitor spending a morning in a pleasant middle-class Dutch home to observe the normal routine of a mother and her six-month-old baby. The mother made sure you got there by 8:30 to witness the morning bath, an opportunity for playful interaction with the baby. The baby was then dressed in cozy warm clothes, her hair brushed and styled with a tiny curlicue atop her head. The mother gave her the midmorning bottle, then sang to her and played patty-cake for a few minutes before placing her in the playpen to entertain herself with a mobile while the mother attended to other things nearby. Now, about half an hour later, the baby is beginning to get fussy.

The mother watches for a minute, then offers a toy and turns away. The baby again begins to fuss. "Seems bored and in need of attention," you think. But the mother looks at the baby sympathetically and in a soothing voice says, "Oh, are you tired?" Without further ado she picks up the baby, carries her upstairs, tucks her into her crib, and pulls down the shades. To your surprise, the baby fusses for only a few more moments, then is quiet. The mother returns looking serene. "She needs plenty of sleep in order to grow," she explains. "When she doesn't have her nap or go to bed on time, we can always tell the difference—she's not so happy and playful."

Different patterns in infant sleep can be found in Western societies that seem quite similar to those of the United States. We discovered the "three R's" of Dutch child rearing—*rust* (rest), *regelmaat* (regularity) and *reinheid* (cleanliness)—while doing research on a sample of sixty families with infants or young children in a middle-class community near Leiden and Amsterdam, the sort of community typical of Dutch life styles in all but the big cities nowadays. At six months, the Dutch babies were sleeping more than a comparison group of American babies—a total of fifteen hours per day compared with thirteen hours for the Americans. While awake at home, the Dutch babies were more often left to play quietly in their playpens or infant seats. A daily ride in the baby carriage provided time for the baby to look around at the passing scene or to doze peacefully. If the mother needed to go out for a while without the baby, she could leave it alone in bed for a short period or time her outing with the baby's nap time and ask a neighbor to monitor with a "baby phone."

To understand how Dutch families manage to establish such a restful routine by the time their babies are six months old, we made a second research visit to the same community. We found that by two weeks of age, the Dutch babies were already sleeping more than same-age American babies. In fact, a dilemma for some Dutch parents was whether to wake the baby after eight hours, as instructed by the local health care providers, or let them sleep longer. The main method for establishing and maintaining this pattern was to create a calm, regular, and restful environment for the infant throughout the day.

Far from worrying about providing "adequate stimulation," these mothers were conscientious about avoiding overstimulation in the form of late family outings, disruptions in the regularity of eating and sleeping, or too many things to look at or listen to. Few parents were troubled by their babies' nighttime sleep routines. Babies's feeding schedules were structured following the guidelines of the local baby clinic (a national service). If a baby continued to wake up at night when feeding was no longer considered necessary, the mother (or father) would most commonly give it a pacifier and a little back rub to help it get back to sleep. Only in rare instances did parents find themselves forced to choose between letting the baby scream and allowing too much night waking.

Many aspects of Dutch society support the three Rs throughout infancy and childhood—for example, shopping is close to home, and families usually have neighbors and relatives nearby who are available to help out with child care. The small scale of neighborhoods and a network of bicycle paths provide local play sites and a safe way for children to get around easily on their own (no "soccer moms" are needed for daily transportation!). Work sites for both fathers and mothers are also generally close to home, and there are many flexible or part-time job arrangements.

National policies for health and other social benefits insure universal coverage regardless of one's employment status, and the principle of the "family wage" has prevailed in labor relations so that mothers of infants and young children rarely work more than part-time, if at all. In many ways, the three Rs of Dutch child rearing are just one aspect of a calm and unhurried life style for the whole family.

sonality. In the 1950s, for example, John and Beatrice Whiting, and their colleagues at Harvard, Yale, and Cornell Universities, launched a major comparative study of childhood, looking at six varied communities in different regions: Okinawa, the Philippines, northern India, Kenya, Mexico, and New England. They showed that communal expectations play a major role in setting parenting styles, which in turn play a part in shaping children to become accepted adults.

More recent work by anthropologists and child-development researchers has shown that parents readily accept their society's prevailing ideology on how babies should be treated, usually because it makes sense in their environmental or social circumstances. In the United States, for example, where individualism is valued, parents do not hold babies as much as in other cultures, and they place them in rooms of their own to

Doctor's Orders

By Edward Z. Tronick

In Boston, a pediatric resident is experiencing a vague sense of disquiet as she interviews a Puerto Rican mother who has brought her baby in for a checkup. When she is at work, the mother explains, the two older children, ages six and nine, take care of the two younger ones, a two-year-old and the three-month-old baby. Warning bells go off for the resident: young children cannot possibly be sensitive to the needs of babies and toddlers. And yet the baby is thriving; he is well over the ninetieth percentile in weight and height and is full of smiles.

The resident questions the mother in detail: How is the baby fed? Is the apartment safe for a two-year-old? The responses are all reassuring, but the resident nonetheless launches into a lecture on the importance of the mother to normal infant development. The mother falls silent, and the resident is now convinced that something is seriously wrong. And something is—the resident's model of child care.

The resident subscribes to what I call the "continuous care and contact" model of parenting, which demands a high level of contact, frequent feeding, and constant supervision, with almost all care provided by the mother. According to this model, a mother should

also enhance cognitive development with play and verbal engagement. The pediatric resident is comfortable with this formula—she is not even conscious of it—because she was raised this way and treats her own child in the same manner. But at the Child Development Unit of Children's Hospital in Boston, which I direct, I want residents to abandon the idea that there is only one way to raise a child. Not to do so may interfere with patient care.

Many models of parenting are valid. Among Efe foragers of Congo's Ituri Forest, for example, a newborn is routinely cared for by several people. Babies are even nursed by many women. But few individuals ever play with the infant; as far as the Efe are concerned, the baby's job is to sleep.

In Peru, the Quechua swaddle their infants in a pouch of blankets that the mother, or a child caretaker, carries on her back. Inside the pouch, the infant cannot move, and its eyes are covered. Quechua babies are nursed in a perfunctory fashion, with three or four hours between feedings.

As I explain to novice pediatricians, such practices do not fit the continuous care and contact model; yet these babies grow up just fine. But my residents see these cultures as exotic,

not relevant to the industrialized world. And so I follow up with examples closer to home: Dutch parents who leave an infant alone in order to go shopping, sometimes pinning the child's shirt to the bed to keep the baby on its back; or Japanese mothers who periodically wake a sleeping infant to teach the child who is in charge. The questions soon follow. "How could a mother leave her infant alone?" "Why would a parent ever want to wake up a sleeping baby?"

The data from cross-cultural studies indicate that child-care practices vary, and that these styles aim to make the child into a culturally appropriate adult. The Efe make future Efe. The resident makes future residents. A doctor who has a vague sense that something is wrong with how someone cares for a baby may first need to explore his or her own assumptions, the hidden "shoulds" that are based solely on tradition. Of course, pediatric residents must make sure children are cared for responsibly. I know I have helped residents broaden their views when their lectures on good mothering are replaced by such comments as "What a gorgeous baby! I can't imagine how you manage both work and three others at home!"

sleep. Pediatricians and parents alike often say this fosters independence and self-reliance. Japanese parents, in contrast, believe that individuals should be well integrated into society, and so they "indulge" their babies: Japanese infants are held more often, not left to cry, and sleep with their parents. Efe parents in Congo believe even more in a communal life, and their infants are regularly nursed, held, and comforted by any number of group members, not just parents. Whether such practices

help form the anticipated adult personality traits remains to be shown, however.

Recently, a group of anthropologists, child-development experts, and pediatricians have taken the cross-cultural approach in a new direction by investigating how differing parenting styles affect infant health and growth. Instead of emphasizing the development of adult personality, these researchers, who call themselves ethnopediatricians, focus on the child as an organism. Ethnopediatricians see the human infant as a product of evolution,

geared to enter a particular environment of care. What an infant actually gets is a compromise, as parents are pulled by their offspring's needs and pushed by social and personal expectations.

Compared with offspring of many other mammals, primate infants are dependent and vulnerable. Baby monkeys and apes stay close to the mother's body, clinging to her stomach or riding on her back, and nursing at will. They are protected in this way for many months, until they develop enough motor and cogni-

The Crying Game

By Ronald G. Barr

All normal human infants cry, although they vary a great deal in how much. A mysterious and still unexplained phenomenon is that crying tends to increase in the first few weeks of life, peaks in the second or third month, and then decreases. Some babies in the United States cry so much during the peak period—often in excess of three hours a day—and seem so difficult to soothe that parents come to doubt their nurturing skills or begin to fear that their offspring is suffering from a painful disease. Some mothers discontinue nursing and switch to bottle-feeding because they believe their breast milk is insufficiently nutritious and that their infants are always hungry. In extreme cases, the crying may provoke physical abuse, sometimes even precipitating the infant's death.

A look at another culture, the !Kung San hunter-gatherers of southern Africa, provides us with an opportunity to see whether caregiving strategies have any effect on infant crying. Both the !Kung San and Western infants escalate their crying during the early weeks of life, with a similar peak at two or three months. A comparison of Dutch, American, and !Kung San infants shows that the number of individual crying episodes are virtually identical. What differs is their length: !Kung San infants cry about half as long as Western babies. This implies that caregiving can influence only some aspects of crying, such as duration.

What is particularly striking about child-rearing among the !Kung San is that infants are in constant contact with a caregiver; they are carried or held most of the time, are usually in an upright position, and are breast-fed about four times an hour for one to two minutes at a time. Furthermore, the mother almost always responds to the smallest cry or fret within ten seconds.

I believe that crying was adaptive for our ancestors. As seen in the contemporary !Kung San, crying probably elicited a quick response, and thus consisted of frequent but relatively short episodes. This pattern helped keep an adult close by to provide adequate nutrition as well as protection from predators. I have also argued that crying helped an infant forge a strong attachment with the mother and—because new pregnancies are delayed by the prolongation of frequent nursing—secure more of her caregiving resources.

In the United States, where the threat of predation has receded and adequate nutrition is usually available even without breast-feeding, crying may be less adaptive. In any case, caregiving in the United States may be viewed as a cultural experiment in which the infant is relatively more separated—and separable—from the mother, both in terms of frequency of contact and actual distance.

The Western strategy is advantageous when the mother's employment outside of the home and away from the baby is necessary to sustain family resources. But the trade-off seems to be an increase in the length of crying bouts.

tive skills to move about. Human infants are at the extreme: virtually helpless as newborns, they need twelve months just to learn to walk and years of social learning before they can function on their own.

Dependence during infancy is the price we pay for being hominids, members of the group of upright-walking primates that includes humans and their extinct relatives. Four million years ago, when our ancestors became bipedal, the hominid pelvis underwent a necessary renovation. At first, this new pelvic architecture presented no problem during birth because the early hominids, known as australopithecines, still had rather small brains, one-third the present size. But starting about 1.5 million years ago, human brain size ballooned. Hominid babies now had to twist and bend to pass through the birth canal, and more impor-

tant, birth had to be triggered before the skull grew too big.

As a result, the human infant is born neurologically unfinished and unable to coordinate muscle movement. Natural selection has compensated for this by favoring a close adult-infant tie that lasts years and goes beyond meeting the needs of food and shelter. In a sense, the human baby is not isolated but is part of a physiologically and emotionally entwined dyad of infant and caregiver. The adult might be male or female, a birth or adoptive parent, as long as at least one person is attuned to the infant's needs.

The signs of this interrelationship are many. Through conditioning, a mother's breast milk often begins to flow at the sound of her own infant's cries, even before the nipple is stimulated. New mothers also easily recognize the cries (and smells) of their infants over those of

other babies. For their part, newborns recognize their own mother's voice and prefer it over others. One experiment showed that a baby's heart rate quickly synchronizes with Mom's or Dad's, but not with that of a friendly stranger. Babies are also predisposed to be socially engaged with caregivers. From birth, infants move their bodies in synchrony with adult speech and the general nature of language. Babies quickly recognize the arrangement of a human face—two eyes, a nose, and a mouth in the right place—over other more Picasso-like rearrangements. And mothers and infants will position themselves face-to-face when they lie down to sleep.

Babies and mothers seem to follow a typical pattern of play, a coordinated waltz that moves from attention to inattention and back again. This innate social connection was tested experimentally by

When to Wean

By Katherine A. Dettwyler

Breast-feeding in humans is a biological process grounded in our mammalian ancestry. It is also an activity modified by social and cultural constraints, including a mother's everyday work schedule and a variety of beliefs about personal autonomy, the proper relationship between mother and child (or between mother and father), and infant health and nutrition. The same may be said of the termination of breast-feeding, or weaning.

In the United States, children are commonly bottle-fed from birth or weaned within a few months. But in some societies, children as old as four or five years may still be nursed. The American Academy of Pediatrics currently advises breast-feeding for a minimum of one year (this may be revised upward), and the World Health Organization recommends two years or more. Amid conflicting advice, many wonder how long breast-feeding should last to provide an infant with optimal nutrition and health.

Nonhuman primates and other mammals give us some clues as to what the "natural" age of weaning would be if humans were less bound by cultural norms. Compared with most other orders of placental mammals, primates (including humans) have longer life spans and spend more time at each life stage, such as gestation, infant dependency, and puberty. Within the primate order itself, the trend in longevity increases from smaller-bodied, smaller-brained, often solitary prosimians through the larger-bodied, larger-brained, and usually social apes and humans. Gestation, for instance, is eighteen weeks in lemurs, twenty-four weeks in macaques, thirty-three weeks in chimpanzees, and thirty-eight weeks in humans.

Studies of nonhuman primates offer a number of different means of estimating the natural time for human weaning. First, large-bodied primates wean their offspring some months after the young have quadrupled their birth weight. In modern humans, this weight milestone is passed at about two and a half to three years of age. Second, like many other mammals, primate offspring tend to be weaned when they have attained about one third of their adult weight; humans reach this level between four and seven years of age. Third, in all species studied so far, primates also wean their offspring at the time the first permanent molars erupt; this occurs at five and a half to six years in modern humans. Fourth, in chimpanzees and gorillas, breast-feeding usually lasts about six times the duration of gestation. On this basis, a human breast-feeding would be projected to continue for four and a half years.

Taken together, these and other projections suggest that somewhat more than two and a half years is the natural minimum age of weaning for humans and seven years the maximum age, well into childhood. The high end of this range, six to seven years, closely matches both the completion of human brain growth and the maturation of the child's immune system.

In many non-Western cultures, children are routinely nursed for three to five years. Incidentally, this practice inhibits ovulation in the mother, providing a natural mechanism of family planning. Even in the United States, a significant number of children are breast-fed beyond three years of age. While not all women are able or willing to nurse each of their children for many years, those who do should be encouraged and supported. Health care professionals, family, friends, and nosy neighbors should be reassured that "extended" breast-feeding, for as long as seven years, appears physiologically normal and natural.

Substantial evidence is already available to suggest that curtailing the duration of breast-feeding far below two and a half years—when the human child has evolved to expect more—can be deleterious. Every study that includes the duration of breast-feeding as a variable shows that, on average, the longer a baby is nursed, the better its health and cognitive development. For example, breast-fed children have fewer allergies, fewer ear infections, and less diarrhea, and their risk for sudden infant death syndrome (a rare but devastating occurrence) is lower. Breast-fed children also have higher cognitive test scores and lower incidence of attention deficit hyperactivity disorder.

In many cases, specific biochemical constituents of breast milk have been identified that either protect directly against disease or help the child's body develop its own defense system. For example, in the case of many viral diseases, the baby brings the virus to the mother, and her gut-wall cells manufacture specific antibodies against the virus, which then travel to the mammary glands and go back to the baby. The docosahesanoic acid in breast milk may be responsible for improved cognitive and attention functions. And the infant's exposure to the hormones and cholesterol in the milk appears to condition the body, reducing the risk of heart disease and breast cancer in later years. These and other discoveries show that breast-feeding serves functions for which no simple substitute is available.

Jeffrey Cohn and Edward Tronick in a series of three-minute laboratory experiments at the University of Massachu- setts, in which they asked mothers to act depressed and not respond to baby's cues. When faced with a suddenly unre- sponsive mother, a baby repeatedly reaches out and flaps around, trying to catch her eye. When this tactic does not

Bedtime Story

By James J. McKenna

For as far back as you care to go, mothers have followed the protective and convenient practice of sleeping with their infants. Even now, for the vast majority of people across the globe, "co-sleeping" and nighttime breast-feeding remain inseparable practices. Only in the past 200 years, and mostly in Western industrialized societies, have parents considered it normal and biologically appropriate for a mother and infant to sleep apart.

In the sleep laboratory at the University of California's Irvine School of Medicine, my colleagues and I observed mother-infant pairs as they slept both apart and together over three consecutive nights. Using a polygraph, we recorded the mother's and infant's heart rates, brain waves (EEGs), breathing, body temperature, and episodes of nursing. Infrared video photography simultaneously monitored their behavior.

We found that bed-sharing infants face their mothers for most of the night and that both mother and infants are highly responsive to each other's movements, wake more frequently, and spend more time in lighter stages of sleep than they do while sleeping alone. Bed-sharing infants nurse almost twice as often, and three times as long per bout, than they do when sleeping alone. But they rarely cry. Mothers who routinely sleep with their infants get at least as much sleep as mothers who sleep without them.

In addition to providing more nighttime nourishment and greater protection, sleeping with the mother supplies the infant with a steady stream of sensations of the mother's presence, including touch, smell, movement, and warmth. These stimuli can perhaps even compensate for the human infant's extreme neurological immaturity at birth.

Cosleeping might also turn out to give some babies protection from sudden infant death syndrome (SIDS), a heartbreaking and enigmatic killer. Cosleeping infants nurse more often, sleep more lightly, and have practice responding to maternal arousals. Arousal deficiencies are suspected in some SIDS deaths, and long periods in deep sleep may exacerbate this problem. Perhaps the physiological changes induced by cosleeping, especially when combined with nighttime breast-feeding, can benefit some infants by helping them sleep more lightly. At the same time, cosleeping makes it easier for a mother to detect and respond to an infant in crisis. Rethinking another sleeping practice has already shown a dramatic effect: In the United States, SIDS rates fell at least 30 percent after 1992, when the American Academy of Pediatrics recommended placing sleeping babies on their backs, rather than face down.

The effect of cosleeping on SIDS remains to be proved, so it would be premature to recommend it as the best arrangement for all families. The possible hazards of cosleeping must also be assessed. Is the environment otherwise safe, with appropriate bedding materials? Do the parents smoke? Do they use drugs or alcohol? (These appear to be the main factors in those rare cases in which a mother inadvertently smothers her child.) Since cosleeping was the ancestral condition, the future for our infants may well entail a borrowing back from ancient ways.

work, the baby gives up, turning away and going limp. And when the mother begins to respond again, it takes thirty seconds for the baby to reengage.

Given that human infants arrive in a state of dependency, ethnopediatricians have sought to define the care required to meet their physical, cognitive, and emotional needs. They assume there must be ways to treat babies that have proved adaptive over time and are therefore likely to be most appropriate. Surveys of parenting in different societies reveal broad patterns. In almost all cultures, infants sleep with their parents in the same room and most often in the same bed. At all other times, infants are usually carried. Caregivers also usually respond quickly to infant cries; mothers most often by offering the breast. Since most hunter-gatherer groups also follow this overall style, this is probably the ancestral pattern. If there is an exception to these generalizations, it is the industrialized West.

Nuances of caretaking, however, do vary with particular social situations. !Kung San mothers of Botswana usually carry their infants on gathering expeditions, while the forest-living Ache of Paraguay, also hunters and gatherers, usually leave infants in camp while they gather. Gusii mothers working in garden plots leave their babies in the care of older children, while working mothers in the West may turn to unrelated adults. Such choices have physiological or behavioral consequences for the infant. As parents navigate between infant needs and the constraints of making a life, they may face a series of trade-offs that set the caregiver-infant dyad at odds. The areas of greatest controversy are breast-feeding, crying, and sleep—the major preoccupations of babies and their parents.

Strapped to their mothers' sides or backs in traditional fashion, human infants have quick access to the breast. Easy access makes sense because of the nature of human milk. Compared with that of other mammals, primate milk is relatively low in fat and protein but high in carbohydrates. Such milk is biologically suitable if the infant can nurse on a frequent basis. Most Western babies are fed in a somewhat different way. At least half are bottle-fed from birth, while others are weaned from breast to bottle after only a few months. And most—whether nursed or bottle-fed—are fed at scheduled times, waiting hours between feedings. Long intervals in nursing disrupt the manufacture of breast milk, making it still lower in fat and thus less satisfying the next time the nipple is offered. And so crying over food and even the struggles of weaning result from the infant's unfulfilled expectations.

Sleep is also a major issue for new parents. In the West, babies are encouraged to sleep all through the night as soon as possible. And when infants do not do so, they merit the label "sleep problem" from both parents and pediatricians. But infants seem predisposed to sleep rather lightly, waking many times during the night. And while sleeping close to an adult allows infants to nurse more often and may have other beneficial effects, Westerners usually expect babies to sleep alone. This practice has roots in ecclesiastical laws enacted to protect against the smothering of infants by "lying over"—often a thinly disguised cover for infanticide—which was a concern in Europe beginning in the Middle Ages. Solitary sleep is reinforced by the rather recent notion of parental privacy. Western parents are also often convinced that solitary sleep will mold strong character.

Infants' care is shaped by tradition, fads, science, and folk wisdom. Cross-cultural and evolutionary studies provide a useful perspective for parents and pediatricians as they sift through the alternatives. Where these insights fail to guide us, however, important clues are provided by the floppy but interactive babies themselves. Grinning when we talk to them, crying in distress when left alone, sleeping best when close at heart, they teach us that growth is a cooperative venture.

RECOMMENDED READING

Parents' Cultural Belief Systems: Their Origins, Expressions, and Consequences, by Sara Harkness and Charles M. Super (Guilford Press, 1996)

Child Care and Culture: Lessons from Africa, by Robert A. LeVine et al. (Cambridge University Press, 1994)

Our Babies, Ourselves, by Meredith F. Small (Anchor Books/Doubleday, 1998)

Breastfeeding: Biocultural Perspectives, edited by Patricia Stuart-Macadam and Katherine A. Dettwyler (Aldine de Gruyler, 1995)

The Family Bed: An Age Old Concept in Childrearing, by Tine Thevenin (Avery Publishing Group, 1987)

Human Birth: An Evolutionary Perspective, by Wenda R. Trevathan (Aldine de Gruyter, 1987)

Six Cultures: Studies of Child Rearing, edited by Beatrice B. Whiting (John Wiley, 1963)

A professor of anthropology at Cornell University, **Meredith F. Small** became interested in "ethnopediatrics" in 1995, after interviewing anthropologist James J. McKenna on the subject of infant sleep. Trained as a primate behaviorist, Small has observed female mating behavior in three species of macaque monkeys. She now writes about science for a general audience; her book *Our Babies, Ourselves* is published by Anchor Books/Doubleday (1998). Her previous contributions to *Natural History* include "These Animals Think, Therefore…" (August 1996) and "Read in the Bone" (June 1997).

UNIT 3

Finding a Balance: Maintaining Relationships

Unit Selections

Key Points to Consider

- Is marriage necessary for a happy, fulfilling life? Why or why not? How is your experience of committed relationships influenced by those you saw while growing up?

- What are your views on spanking? Why is it seen as an ineffective parenting tool? What are other alternatives?

- What are ways in which fathers' involvement in their children's lives can be encouraged and nurtured? What sorts of special stressors do African American fathers face? How can they be encouraged to be more involved in their children's lives? How, if at all, do children reared in lesbian households differ from those reared in heterosexual households?

- How important are your siblings in your life? What are the particular challenges faced by aging siblings who would like to repair a damaged sibling relationship after years of conflict?

 **Links: www.dushkin.com/online/**
These sites are annotated in the World Wide Web pages.

Child Welfare League of America
http://www.cwla.org
Coalition for Marriage, Family, and Couples Education
http://www.smartmarriages.com
The National Academy for Child Development
http://www.nacd.org
National Council on Family Relations
http://www.ncfr.com
Positive Parenting
http://www.positiveparenting.com
SocioSite
http://www.pscw.uva.nl/sociosite/TOPICS/Women.html

And they lived happily ever after.... The romantic image conjured up by this well-known final line from fairy tales is not reflective of the reality of family life and relationship maintenance. The belief that somehow love alone should carry us through is pervasive. In reality, maintaining a relationship takes dedication, hard work, and commitment.

We come into relationships, regardless of their nature, with fantasies about how things ought to be. Whether partners, spouses, parents, children, or siblings—all family members have at least some unrealistic expectations about each other. It is through the negotiation of their lives together that they come to work through these expectations and replace them with other, it is hoped, more realistic ones. By recognizing and acting on their own contribution to the family, members can set and attain realistic family goals. Tolerance and acceptance of differences can facilitate this

process as can competent communication skills. Along the way, family members need to learn new skills and develop new habits of relating to each other. This will not be easy, and, try as they may, not everything will be controllable. Factors both inside and outside the family may impede their progress.

Even before one enters a marriage or other committed relationship, attitudes, standards, and beliefs influence our choices. Increasingly, choices include whether or not we should commit to such a relationship. From the start of a committed relationship, the expectations both partners have of their relationship have an impact, and the need to negotiate differences is a constant factor. Adding a child to the family affects the lives of parents in ways that they could previously only imagine. Feeling under siege, many parents struggle to know the right way to rear their children. These factors can all combine to make child rearing more difficult than it might otherwise have been. Other family relationships also evolve, and in our nuclear family–focused culture, it is possible to forget that family relationships extend beyond those between spouses and parents and children.

The first subsection presents a number of aspects regarding marital and other committed relationships, decisions about entering such a relationship, and ways of balancing multiple and often competing roles played by today's couples who hope to fulfill individual as well as couple needs. It is a difficult balancing act to cope with the expectations and pressures of work, home, children, and relational intimacy. In "The Science of a Good Marriage," the work done by John Gottman on what makes a good marriage is detailed. What is presented may surprise the reader, as some forms of good marriages contradict previously held ideas. Then, "No Wedding? No Ring? No Problem," depicts current trends in the United States toward more and more couples choosing cohabitation as an alternative to marriage. Finally,

"Welcome to the Love Lab" demonstrates how to detect troubled relationships.

The next subsection examines the parent/child relationship. In the first article, "New Evidence for the Benefits of Never Spanking," Murray Straus presents a detailed argument against parents' using corporal punishment as a means of child discipline. The next reading, "Family Matters," presents a supportive view of parental influence on the mental health of children, using data from a 13-year study conducted in Santa Domingo. Then, in "Who's Raising Baby?" Anne Pierce says that parenting and infancy should be more about love of learning than about competition. "Father Nature: The Making of a Modern Dad" details ways in which men are changed, at a fundamental, hormonal level by an active involvement in their children's lives. "What About Black Fathers?" proposes that the involvement of low-income African American fathers in their children's lives is best facilitated through support of existing family forms. "Unmarried, With Children" focuses on single-parent households and their effects on children. The final article in this section, "Adoption by Lesbian Couples," is a detailed analysis of existing literature on children raised in lesbian households and shows that these children are not significantly different from those raised in heterosexual households.

The third and final subsection looks at other family relationships. Sibling relationships and the emotional baggage associated with them, are often assumed to improve with age. "Why We Break Up With Our Siblings" questions this assumption. Then, intergenerational relationships between lesbian daughters and their parents, often initially strained, can sometimes be healed through the intervention of the daughter's partner, according to "The Importance of Partners to Lesbians' Intergenerational Relationships."

The Science of a Good Marriage

Psychology is unlocking the secrets of happy couples.

BY BARBARA KANTROWITZ AND PAT WINGERT

THE MYTH OF MARRIAGE GOES LIKE this: somewhere out there is the perfect soul mate, the yin that meshes easily and effortlessly with your yang. And then there is the reality of marriage, which, as any spouse knows, is not unlike what Thomas Edison once said about genius: 1 percent inspiration and 99 percent perspiration. That sweaty part, the hard work of keeping a marriage healthy and strong, fascinates John Gottman. He's a psychologist at the University of Washington, and he has spent more than two decades trying to unravel the bewildering complex of emotions that binds two humans together for a year, a decade or even (if you're lucky) a lifetime.

Gottman, 56, comes to this endeavor with the best of qualifications: he's got the spirit of a scientist and the soul of a romantic. A survivor of one divorce, he's now happily married to fellow psychologist Julie Schwartz Gottman (they run couples workshops together). His daunting task is to quantify such intangibles as joy, contempt and tension. Ground zero for this research is the Family Research Laboratory on the Seattle campus (nicknamed the Love Lab). It consists of a series of nondescript offices equipped with video cameras and pulse, sweat and movement monitors to read the hearts and minds of hundreds of couples who have volunteered to be guinea pigs in longitudinal studies of the marital relationship. These volunteers have

opened up their lives to the researchers, dissecting everything from the frequency of sex to who takes out the garbage. The results form the basis of Gottman's new book, "The Seven Principles for Making Marriage Work," which he hopes will give spouses a scientific road map to happiness.

Among his unexpected conclusions: anger is not the most destructive emotion in a marriage, since both happy and miserable couples fight. Many popular therapies aim at defusing anger between spouses, but Gottman found that the real demons (he calls them "the Four Horsemen of the Apocalypse") are criticism, contempt, defensiveness and stonewalling. His research shows that the best way to keep these demons at bay is for couples to develop a "love map" of their spouse's dreams and fears. The happy couples all had such a deep understanding of their partner's psyche that they could navigate roadblocks without creating emotional gridlock.

Gottman's research also contradicts the Mars-Venus school of relationships, which holds that men and women come from two very different emotional worlds. According to his studies, gender differences may contribute to marital problems, but they don't cause them. Equal percentages of both men and women he interviewed said that the quality of the spousal friendship is the most important factor in marital satisfaction.

Gottman says he can predict, with more than 90 percent accuracy, which couples

are likely to end up in divorce court. The first seven years are especially precarious; the average time for a divorce in this group is 5.2 years. The next danger point comes around 16 to 20 years into the marriage, with an average of 16.4 years. He describes one couple he first met as newlyweds: even then they began every discussion of their problems with sarcasm or criticism, what Gottman calls a "harsh start-up." Although they professed to be in love and committed to the relationship, Gottman correctly predicted that they were in trouble. Four years later they were headed for divorce, he says.

An unequal balance of power is also deadly to a marriage. Gottman found that a husband who doesn't share power with his wife has a much higher risk of damaging the relationship. Why are men singled out? Gottman says his data show that most wives, even those in unstable marriages, are likely to accept their husband's influence. It's the men who need to shape up, he says. The changes can be simple, like turning off the football game when she needs to talk. Gottman says the gesture proves he values "us" over "me."

Gottman's research is built on the work of many other scientists who have focused on emotion and human interaction. Early studies of marriage relied heavily on questionnaires filled out by couples, but these were often inaccurate. In the 1970s several psychology labs began using direct observation of couples to study marriage. A big

Know Your Spouse

Test the strength of your marriage in this relationship quiz prepared especially for NEWSWEEK by John Gottman.

		TRUE / FALSE
1	I can name my partner's best friends	/
2	I can tell you what stresses my partner is currently facing	/
3	I know the names of some of the people who have been irritating my partner lately	/
4	I can tell you some of my partner's life dreams	/
5	I can tell you about my partner's basic philosophy of life	/
6	I can list the relatives my partner likes the least	/
7	I feel that my partner knows me pretty well	/
8	When we are apart, I often think fondly of my partner	/
9	I often touch or kiss my partner affectionately	/
10	My partner really respects me	/
11	There is fire and passion in this relationship	/
12	Romance is definitely still a part of our relationship	/
13	My partner appreciates the things I do in this relationship	/
14	My partner generally likes my personality	/
15	Our sex life is mostly satisfying	/
16	At the end of the day my partner is glad to see me	/
17	My partner is one of my best friends	/
18	We just love talking to each other	/
19	There is lots of give and take (both people have influence) in our discussions	/
20	My partner listens respectfully, even when we disagree	/
21	My partner is usually a great help as a problem solver	/
22	We generally mesh well on basic values and goals in life	/

Scoring: GIVE YOURSELF ONE POINT FOR EACH "TRUE" ANSWER. ABOVE 12: YOU HAVE A LOT OF STRENGTH IN YOUR RELATIONSHIP. CONGRATULATIONS. BELOW 12: YOUR RELATIONSHIP COULD STAND SOME IMPROVEMENT AND COULD PROBABLY BENEFIT FROM SOME WORK ON THE BASICS, SUCH AS IMPROVING COMMUNICATION.

boon was a relatively new tool for psychologists: videotape. Having a visual record that could be endlessly replayed made it much easier to study the emotional flow between spouses. In 1978 researchers Paul Ekman and Wallace Freisen devised a coding system for the human face (see, "Facing Your Problems") that eventually provided another way to measure interchange between spouses.

Although early studies focused on couples in trouble, Gottman thought it was also important to study couples whose marriages work; he thinks they're the real

experts. The Love Lab volunteers are interviewed about the history of their marriage. They then talk in front of the cameras about subjects that cause conflict between them. One couple Gottman describes in the book, Tim and Kara, argued constantly about his friend Buddy, who often wound up spending the night on Tim and Kara's couch. The researchers take scenes like this and break down every second of interaction to create a statistical pattern of good and bad moments. How many times did she roll her eyes (a sign of contempt) when he spoke? How often did he fidget (indicat-

ing tension or stress)? The frequency of negative and positive expressions, combined with the data collected by the heart, sweat and other monitors, provides a multidimensional view of the relationship. (Tim and Kara ultimately decided Buddy could stay, only not as often.)

Gottman and other researchers see their work as a matter of public health. The average couple who seek help have been having problems for six years—long enough to have done serious damage to their relationship. That delay, Gottman says, is as dangerous as putting off regular

Facing Your Problems

IN THE LAB, THE WAY A MARRIED COUPLE FIGHTS CAN often tell psychologists more than *what* they fight about. The expressions and underlying emotions displayed during a conflict may reveal the strength or weakness of the marriage. During a couple's 15-minute conversation—on a topic known to be a sore point—researchers at the University of Washington measure physiological responses (below) and facial expressions, which can reveal true feelings even when words don't. Videotapes also show how long the partners' emotional responses last—even the happiest of couples has fleeting moments of bad feeling, but if the negative indicators tend to endure, it can signal a marriage in trouble.

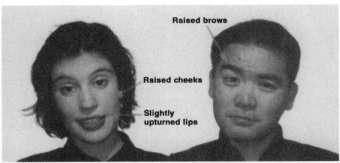

Interest: A calm voice and positive body language—leaning forward, for example—signal the genuine article. It's a real desire to hear a partner's opinion, not an attempt to influence.

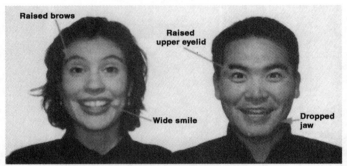

Surprise: A big smile, with popping eyes, indicates a positive surprise. Something unexpected but unpleasant yields the eye-pop only. Either way, a short-lived state.

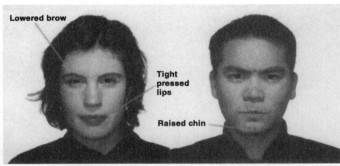

Anger: The tone is cold or loud, the wording staccato. But honest anger, an internal state, is different from contempt, directed at the spouse. A fake smile, without raised cheeks, may mask anger.

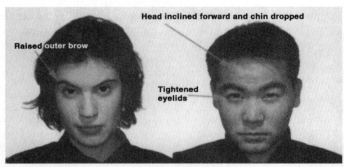

Domineering: A "low and slow" voice often signals that one partner is trying to force the other to his or her view. Ranges from lawyerly cross-examination to blatant threats.

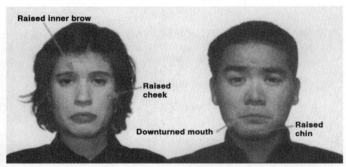

Sadness: Passivity and sulking can look like stonewalling or idsengaging from a fight, but sad people maintain more eye contact that stonewallers.

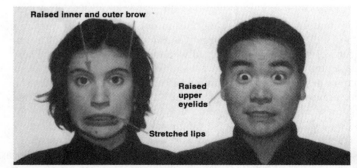

Fear: Outright fear is rare; a lower-grade version—tension— is more common. And a wife's tension, if pronounced, can be a predictor for divorce down the road.

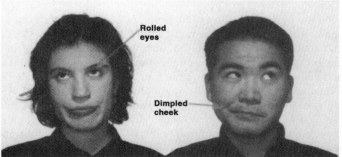

Contempt: If prolonged, this expression is a red alert. Especially when accompanied by sarcasm and insults, it suggests a marriage in serious trouble.

76

mammograms. The United States has one of the highest divorce rates in the industrialized world, and studies have shown a direct correlation between marriage and well-being. Happily married people are healthier; even their immune systems work better than those of people who are unhappily married or divorced. Kids suffer as well; if their parents split, they're more likely to have emotional or school problems.

But going to a marriage counselor won't necessarily help. "Therapy is at an impasse," Gottman says, "because it is not based on solid empirical knowledge of what real couples do to keep their marriages happy and stable." In a 1995 Consumer Reports survey, marriage therapy ranked at the bottom of a poll of patient satisfaction with various psychotherapies. The magazine said part of the problem was that "almost anyone can hang out a shingle as a marriage counselor." Even credentialed therapists may use approaches that have no basis in research. Several recent studies have shown that many current treatments produce few long-term benefits for couples who seek help.

One example: the process called "active listening." It was originally used by therapists to objectively summarize the complaints of a patient and validate the way the patient is feeling. ("So, I'm hearing that you think your father always liked your sister better and you're hurt by that.") In recent years this technique has been modified for marital therapy—ineffectively, Gottman says. Even highly trained therapists would have a hard time stepping back in the middle of a fight and saying, "So, I'm hearing that you think I'm a fat, lazy slob."

Happily married couples have a very different way of relating to each other during disputes, Gottman found. The partners make frequent "repair attempts," reaching out to each other in an effort to prevent negativity from getting out of control in the midst of conflict. Humor is often part of a successful repair attempt. In his book, Gottman describes one couple arguing about the kind of car to buy (she favors a minivan; he wants a snazzier Jeep). In the midst of yelling, the wife suddenly puts her hand on her hip and sticks out her tongue—mimicking their 4-year-old son.

They both start laughing, and the tension is defused.

In happy unions, couples build what Gottman calls a "sound marital house" by working together and appreciating the best in each other. They learn to cope with the two kinds of problems that are part of every marriage: solvable conflicts and perpetual problems that may represent underlying conflicts and that can lead to emotional gridlock. Gottman says 69 percent of marital conflicts fall into the latter category. Happy spouses deal with these issues in a way that strengthens the marriage. One couple Gottman studied argued constantly about order in their household (she demanded neatness, and he couldn't care less). Over the years they managed to accommodate their differences, acknowledging that their affection for each other was more important than newspapers piled up in the corner of the living room.

Inside the Love Lab

In the laboratory, video cameras record facial expressions. Motion-sensing jiggleometers register fidgeting, and a cluster of sensors reads physiological data.

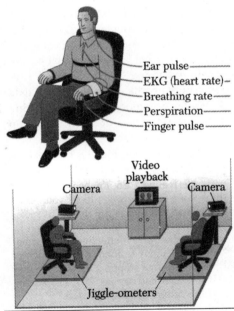

- Ear pulse
- EKG (heart rate)
- Breathing rate
- Perspiration
- Finger pulse

Video playback

Camera   Camera

Jiggle-ometers

DIAGRAM BY CHRISTOPH BLUMRICH—NEWSWEEK

As psychologists learn more about marriage, they have begun devising new approaches to therapy. Philip Cowan and Carolyn Pape-Cowan, a husband-and-wife team (married for 41 years) at the University of California, Berkeley, are looking at one of the most critical periods in a marriage: the birth of a first child. (Two thirds of couples experience a "precipitous drop" in marital satisfaction at this point, researchers say.) "Trying to take two people's dreams of a perfect family and make them one is quite a trick," Pape-Cowan says. The happiest couples were those who looked on their spouses as partners with whom they shared household and child-care duties. The Cowans say one way to help spouses get through the transition to parenting would be ongoing group sessions with other young families to provide the kind of support people used to get from their communities and extended families.

Two other researchers—Neil Jacobson at the University of Washington and Andrew Christensen at UCLA—have developed what they call "acceptance therapy" after studying the interactions of couples in conflict. The goal of their therapy is to help people learn to live with aspects of their spouse's characters that simply can't be changed. "People can love each other not just for what they have in common but for things that make them complementary," says Jacobson. "When we looked at a clinical sample of what predicted failure in traditional behavior therapy, what we came upon again and again was an inability to accept differences."

Despite all these advances in marital therapy, researchers still say they can't save all marriages—and in fact there are some that *shouldn't* be saved. Patterns of physical abuse, for example, are extremely difficult to alter, Gottman says. And there are cases where the differences between the spouses are so profound and longstanding that even the best therapy is futile. Gottman says one quick way to test whether a couple still has a chance is to ask what initially attracted them to each other. If they can recall those magic first moments (and smile when they talk about them), all is not lost. "We can still fan the embers," says Gottman. For all the rest of us, there's hope.

No wedding? No ring? No problem

More and more Americans opt for cohabitation

BY JAY TOLSON

Before 1970, it was called "living in sin" or "shacking up," and it was illegal in every state of the union. Why then, many social scientists are beginning to ask, has America's 30-year rise in unmarried cohabitation remained a shadow issue in the family-values debate? "Unlike divorce or unwed childbearing, the trend toward cohabitation has inspired virtually no public comment or criticism," note David Popenoe and Barbara Dafoe Whitehead, co-directors of Rutgers University's National Marriage Project. University of Michigan sociologist Pamela J. Smock, whose survey of recent research will appear in the *Annual Review of Sociology* to be published this summer, finds that most Americans are still unaware of the extent or significance of cohabitation, even though more than half of today's newlyweds live together before tying the knot, compared with about 10 percent in 1965.

Scholars are quick to point out that the United States is still a long way from Sweden, where unmarried couples—who have all the rights, benefits, and obligations of married partners—make up about 30 percent of couples sharing households. In America, by contrast, cohabiting couples make up only about 7 percent of the total. And for most of those 4 million couples, living together is a transitory business: 55 percent marry and 40 percent end the relationship within five years. "In this country," says University of Chicago sociologist Linda J. Waite, coauthor of the forthcoming *Case for Marriage*, "it's still mostly up or out."

What Smock has found is that the proportion for whom it's "out" of the union is on the rise. In addition, more and more unmarried women who become pregnant choose to cohabit rather than marry, which means that living together is increasingly a substitute for marriage, particularly, notes Smock, among African-Americans.

One of the biggest revelations of the new research is how many cohabiting arrangements involve children. "About one half of previously married cohabitors and 35 percent of never-married cohabitors have children in the household," Smock reports. She adds that almost 40 percent of all supposedly single-parent families are really two-parent cohabiting families. Unfortunately, that doesn't mean that kids in these households fare as well as kids with two married parents. "The nonparent partner... has no explicit legal, financial, supervisory, or custodial rights or responsiblities regarding the child of his partner," notes Linda Waite in the winter issue of *The Responsive Community*. Studies cited by Popenoe and Whitehead suggest there is also a greater risk of physical or sexual abuse in those situations.

Few romantic notions about cohabitational bliss withstand close scrutiny. While there is a little more sex between unmarried cohabitors than between married couples (one more act per month), there's also more cheating by both partners. Then, too, there's more domestic violence and a higher incidence of depression.

But since living together is still mainly a stage in courtship for the majority of marriagebound Americans, the critical question is how the experience affects the subsequent union. Here the evidence is slightly mixed. According to most research, couples who live together—with the possible exception of those who move in already planning to wed—tend to have rockier marriages and a greater risk of divorce. Why this is so is hard to say. It could be that people who cohabit are less traditional in their ideas and less reluctant to divorce. But it's also possible that the experience itself has an effect. "We need to do more qualitative research," says Smock, "and talk to people in their 20s… to find out why they are doing what they are doing."

Old rules. Some of the scholars who are studying the phenomenon—including Popenoe and Whitehead—are also taking sides, urging young adults to reject the argument that cohabitation is good preparation for marriage. Other researchers are taking aim at the economic disincentives to marriage, including the marriage penalty in the tax code and restrictions on Medicaid, both of which often discourage less affluent cohabitors from tying the knot. There is even a movement to bring back an older form of courtship. Leon and Amy Kass co-teach a course at the University of Chicago described by the former as "a higher kind of sex education." Using their own recently published anthology, *Wing to Wing, Oar to Oar: Readings on Courting and Marrying*, they attempt " to train the hearts and minds by means of noble examples for romance leading to loving marriage."

Can such a quaint notion win over minds hardened by the "divorce revolution" of their parents' generation? Steven L. Nock, a University of Virginia researcher, is guardedly optimistic that durable marriages will make a comeback (and in fact, since 1990, have been doing so), whether or not old courtship styles are restored. "My generation," says the 49-year-old sociologist, "was the first to confront equality of the sexes. As a result, many reacted to the changed rules by fleeing from marriage. I suspect that our children, who've grown up with gender equality as a given, will be less likely to flee marriage." That might not be the "horse and carriage" argument, but it makes some sense.

Welcome to the Love Lab

Words can heal an ailing relationship—or seal its negative fate.

By John Gottman, Ph.D. and Sybil Carrere, Ph.D.

The way a couple argues can tell you a lot about the future of their relationship. In fact, just three minutes of fighting can indicate whether the pair will flourish with time or end in ruin.

The 10-year study that led to this discovery was one of many we've conducted over the years. John Gottman began his groundbreaking research on married couples 28 years ago. Since then, his University of Washington laboratory—dubbed the "Love Lab"—has focused on determining exactly what makes marriages thrive or fail. With the help of a remarkable team and hundreds of couples, we can now predict a relationship's outcome with 88% to 94% accuracy.

To do this, we watch couples during spats and analyze partners' communication patterns and physiology, as well as their oral descriptions of their relationship histories. We then follow the pairs over time to see whether their patterns and descriptions lead to happy outcomes or breakups. We have learned that some negative emotions used in arguments are more toxic than others: Criticism, contempt, defensiveness and stonewalling (withdrawing from a discussion, most frequently seen among men) are all particularly corrosive. On the other hand, we have repeatedly found that happy couples use five times more positive behaviors in their arguments than negative behaviors. One way they do this is by using humor to break the tension in an argument. This is a kind of a "repair" effort to mend conflict. We find that happy couples also use expressions of affection for their partner and acknowledge their partner's point of view ("I'm sorry I hurt your feelings") in order to keep quarrels from getting too heated.

We have learned much from our couples over the last 11 years that we try to bring to our own marriages. Two things: One is the importance of building and maintaining a friendship in your marriage so that you give your partner the benefit of the doubt when times are tough. This takes constant work. The second thing is that you have a choice every time you say something to your partner. You can say something that will either nurture the relationship or tear it down. You may win a particular fight with your spouse, but you could lose the marriage in the long run.

In this article, we show just how we diagnose the health of a marriage. Using three examples of dialogue from real couples discussing their problems, we will illustrate how reading between the lines of people's arguments can predict where some marriages have gone wrong—and why others have stayed strong. Welcome to the "Love Lab!"

Susan, 45, and Bob, 47, have been married for 23 years.

Bob: Um, communication. The question is...

Susan: How we disagree.

B: On communication?

S: You don't see a need for it.

B: Oh yeah.

S: You just said you kept to yourself.

B: Well, yeah, I just.... I dunno. Idle chitchat, I guess.

Defensiveness; Tension

S: You what?

B: Idle chitchat, I guess, if that is what you refer to as communication.

S: What do you mean, chitchat?

B: General run-of-the-mill bull.

S: There's nonverbal communication if you're tuned in.

B: (Nods head)

S: Like that man said in that canoeing class, as they went over the rapids, that they were still communicating.

B: That's true. What do you think we need to talk about more then? Huh?

S: Well, I think when there's a problem, or I'm trying to tell you something, sometimes I shouldn't have to say anything. You can know when I'm in a hurry or tired.

B: I just take communication as being, uh, should we sit down and discuss things more fully.

S: We don't sit down and discuss anything unless it's a problem, or if somebody gets mad. You know lots of families have what they call, which is kinda silly, but a weekly meeting or some time when they just sit down and talk about everything that has been going on there all week, what they like and don't like.

B: We used to have those at home.

S: That's a little far-fetched, maybe, but I'm just saying.

B: I know. I just…

S: It makes sense.

B: …you know what major problem we have at work is communication.

S: It's a problem everywhere.

B: Yeah. Yeah.

S: People don't say what they mean.

B: Or assume that people know what they mean or want.

S: Well, how many times have I asked you what's wrong, and you say nothing. And then a month later you say what was wrong and I couldn't have guessed it in a million years.

B: I don't know why that is. Why, you know, you can ask almost anybody at work what's bothering them.

S: But you never ask me what's wrong.

B: Maybe I know.

Expressing Hidden Life Dream: Wants Husband to take Active Interest

S: No, I don't think you do.

B: Maybe I just enjoy the quietness of it. I don't know.

S: Well, seriously, I think that as long as we've been married that you don't know very much about me at all.

B: No, I think it's true, about both of us maybe.

GOTTMAN SAYS: This couple rates quite low in marital satisfaction. They are also emotionally disengaged, with high depression in addition to marital distress. The marriage has generally low conflict, but also low positivity (shared romance, humor, affection)—the best marker of emotional disengagement. Our findings suggest that, in general, emotionally disengaged couples divorce later in life than those who have a "hotter," more explosive pattern of unhappiness, although this couple did not break up.

This couple is also in a state of gridlocked conflict. Susan and Bob keep coming close to resolving their issue, which is that Bob would rather keep to himself than communicate. But they don't—they keep recycling it over and over again. Emotional disengagement is often a later stage of continued gridlock. After a while, a "hot" couple begins polarizing their positions, digging in and becoming more stubborn, vilifying one another, then trying to isolate the problem. Unfortunately, most gridlocked conflict cannot be permanently enclaved, and negotiations to fix a problem reach a stalemate.

The reason gridlocked conflicts don't get resolved is because there is an underlying life dream within each person that isn't being fulfilled. Susan's dream is expressed when she says, "You never ask me what's wrong." Bob responds that "maybe I just enjoy the quietness"—that he prefers emotional distance to fighting—but she sadly replies that he doesn't know her at all. They are lacking in what we call "love maps," which spouses construct by being interested in each other and tracking each other's stresses, hopes, dreams, concerns, etc. Her latent wish for love maps keeps them from agreeing to the weekly meeting plan.

This couple is still married, but unhappily so.

Valerie, 24, and Mark, 25, have a young baby. They have recently moved, and both have new jobs.

Valerie: (Laughter) We don't go that long without talking.

Mark: I know, I just start going stir-crazy.

V: The problem…

M: Huh?

Despite Initial Humor, The Problem Surfaces

V: …is, you told me that when you took the job as manager at Commonwealth that you'd come home in the afternoons and spend some time with us.

M: That's right, but I did not say that it would start in the first week when I'm trying to do two different jobs. I gotta get myself replaced. Right now, I'm not just a manager.

V: It's been three weeks.

M: Well, I just don't go out on the street and say "Hey you. Want to sell insurance?" It's not that easy. There's two people in the program. One of them is probably gonna be hired within the next couple weeks. But in the meantime it's tough. It's just the way it's gotta be.

V: I realize that.

M: Okay.

V: But.

M: At midnight when you get off work and you're all keyed up, I'm all worn out. I haven't been stimulated for two hours.

V: I realize that. That doesn't bother me that much, you going to sleep at night.

M: I'll just be starting to go to sleep and you'll go "Are you listening to me?" I'll be trying to stay awake…

V: I'm laughing about it usually. I'm not upset about it.

M: I don't know by then. I'm half out.

V: But now with me having a car, you'll be able to go to sleep early and get up with Stephanie a little bit. That's one of my big problems. I'm not getting any sleep. I don't get to sleep until two.

M: I've been getting up with her.

V: You've been real good about that.

M: Okay.

V: I guess I just wish that you didn't have to go in early.

M: Yeah, we don't get a whole lot of time together.

V: When I have the car, I can get out and get stuff then. I feel like I'm stuck at home and here you are…

M: I'll be able to meet you for lunch and stuff. I guess that wasn't any big problem.

V: It is a problem. It seems like we talk about it every day.

M: Yeah, we do.

V: That's about the only thing we really complain about.

M: Yeah. The last couple nights I tried to take you out to the lake and look at the stars and stuff, so…

V: I know.

M: We just need to get used to our schedules.

V: That first week I was so, I was real upset cause it seemed like all I did was stay home with Stephanie all morning till three and just work all evening. I wasn't doing anything. It didn't seem like we had family gatherings every weekend. We never had time to go out, just the two of us.

M: I got a little surprise for ya next weekend.

Criticism; Conflict Renewed

V: Yeah, it's always next weekend. It's never this weekend.

M: Eight weekends in a row.

V: I just went from not working at all and being home. We've both been through major job changes and all.

M: And I can't breathe.

V: But we're getting used to it and I feel so much better about going to work at three

(o'clock), three-thirty now than I did that first week.

M: Um.

V: I just wish I had more time to do what I wanted to do. I, it's just being…

M: I'll, I'll be able to stay…

V: …a wife and mother.

M: …to stay at home during the days a little bit more or I'll have to go in early but then I can take a couple of hours off in the afternoons.

Retaliation with Anger

V: Do you have to go in early every day?

M: I'm going to go in early every day.

V: Why?

M: 'Cause there are things I need to do every morning.

V: I think you just like going in to your office.

M: You don't know a thing about it then. Randy was in there early every day, tell me why?

V: Yeah, but he was home at a decent hour too.

M: He stays out late.

V: Eight to eight or eight to nine every day.

M: Every day.

V: Now, then, I don't want you taking that job. You forget it.

M: No.

GOTTMAN SAYS: This couple also has low levels of marital satisfaction. Unlike the previous couple, they have the "hot," corrosive kind of marital conflict characterized by what I call the "Four Horsemen of the Apocalypse": criticism, contempt, defensiveness and stonewalling. This type of conflict tends to lead to early divorce.

However, also unlike the previous couple, there is still a lot of strength in their relationship. Their friendship is intact. There is humor and affection, and they are confident that they can resolve their conflict.

Though the couple begins their discussion very well, by laughing, Valerie soon expresses anger because Mark's new job is demanding so much of his time. She then repairs this with humor and more affection. This shows that there is still quite a bit of strength in this marriage. The respite is only temporary; Valerie raises the family issue again. But Mark agrees affectionately, showing another strength: He makes her problems "their" problems.

They are doing very well discussing the problem until Valerie's angry line about going in early every day. This leads to a pattern of her anger and his defensiveness in response. So there is still a lot of strength in their interaction, but something is keeping him from fully understanding how hard it is for her to have him gone so much. Something is deteriorating in this relationship and it's exemplified by her ultimatums and his resistance.

When we were doing this research, we didn't intervene to help couples, and this one, unfortunately, divorced after seven years of marriage. Now I think we can prevent this type of marital meltdown. The secrets are in keeping fathers involved with their babies so they make the same kind of philosophical transformation in meaning that their wives are probably making; in teaching couples what to expect during this transition to parenthood; and in helping them with the inevitable marital conflict, sleepless irritability and depression that often follow a new baby.

Wilma, 31, and Harris, 35, have been married 11 years.

Wilma: The communication problem. Tell me your feelings. (Both laughing)

Harris: A lot of times I don't know. I've always been quiet.

W: Is it just because you have nothing to talk about, or is it because you don't want to talk about it?

H: A lot of times I don't know.

W: Okay. Example: when we went to Lake Bariessa. I mean, I can understand that you couldn't find your way around and everything, that was fine. But it still doesn't hurt to open your lips, you know?

H: I was kind of burned out that day...

W: Well, you suggested we go...

H: I was trying to take you out somewhere, then I was trying to figure out my money in the bank and I end up coming short...

W: You did all that driving up there...

H: Yeah. And I was trying to figure out my bank account and how I was going to, you know, have the gas money for the week.

W: But, like, when we got there, you didn't want to talk. We got off the truck, we got set up and you ate your sandwich. Your little bologna sandwich. (Both laughing)

H: Yeah. I was starving. (Laughing)

W: I didn't know you were. And then it was like, you still didn't want to talk, so Dominique and me started playing tennis.

H: It was almost time to go then and I had to drive back. I didn't want to check it out.

W: Yeah. I thought it was such a nice drive.

H: I didn't know it was going to be that far.

W: And I really appreciate that.

H: Thank you very much.

Playful Acceptance of Differences

W: You're welcome. I don't mind you talking about bills all the time, but we can only pay what we can pay, so why worry?

H: 'Cause that's how I am.

W: You shouldn't do that.

H: Well, I can't help it. I'm always trying to be preventive.

W: Okay, "Preventive." (Laughter)

H: I can't help it. I have learned from my mistakes. Have you ever heard of people worried about bills?

W: I've heard of those people. I'm one of those people.

H: And I'm one of those people, whether you know it or not.

W: The thing is, I just pay what I can. You can't give everybody money at the same time when you don't have it to give.

H: The only thing I can do is have life insurance for me and you. I paid the kids'. Now I can't pay ours.

W: So you haven't paid the insurance in a month and a half?

H: I paid the kids, but I haven't been able to pay ours.

W: You see, you don't say anything, so I've been thinking that everything is okay.

H: Yeah, I gathered that. (Laughter)

W: (Laughter) Honestly. We need to figure out how we can pay that before it's due. I mean, the same thing with the phone bill.

H: But you haven't been trying to keep that down. Yappity yappity yap!

W: Well, we'll try to figure it out. We'll both of us try to take something out.

H: Right. That's what I'd like.

W: All right. Work with me baby. And now maybe you'll start talking more. See, now you're sitting up here talking about this. And like that day at the park. We could have talked about that. It was a nice relaxing moment to discuss things.

H: I don't know what happened then. When I got there, I was blown out.

W: If you sit and talk with me like this...

H: When do we have a chance to sit down?

W: On weekends.

H: I don't think we have enough time on weekends to sit down.

W: See, that's why I said we need to take a day for ourselves. Momma would keep Dominique for a day. We've got to start focusing on ourselves more.

H: Mmm-hmm.

W: Just every now and then so we can do something for ourselves, even if it isn't anything more than taking in a movie.

H: Yeah.

W: Or go have dinner. When was the last time we had dinner in a restaurant?

H: That would be nice. Or go to a movie. How do you do it? First you go have dinner, then you go to a movie. (Laughter)

W: Or if you go to a movie early enough, you can go have dinner afterwards.

H: Right.

W: Right.

GOTTMAN SAYS: Wilma and Harris have a long-term, stable and happy marriage. They easily discuss two long-standing marital issues: the fact that he doesn't talk very much and she wants him to, and their financial differences. These issues are never going to change fundamentally. Our research has revealed that 69% of couples experience "perpetual problems"—issues with no resolution that couples struggle with for many years. Our data now lead us to believe that whenever you marry someone, your personality differences ensure that you and your partner will grapple with these issues forever. Marriages are only successful to the degree that the problems you have are ones you can cope with.

For most perpetual conflicts in marriages, what matters is not conflict resolution, but the attitudes that surround discussion of the conflict. Wilma and Harris both basically accept that there will always be differences between them, and they essentially accept one another as they are. Still, it is their ability to exchange viewpoints, making each other feel comfortable and supported all the while, that keeps them from getting gridlocked.

This couple, which is typical of our long-term couples, are real pros at being married and at using positive affect—like humor and gentle teasing—to de-escalate conflict. This is likely a sign that they are keeping their arousal levels low. Notice the wide array of strategies used to alleviate potential tension, such as expressing appreciation, softening complaints, responding nondefensively, backing down and using humor. The two of them do this together.

What these middle-aged spouses do is exactly what newlyweds who wind up stable and happy do, and this process moves them toward some semblance of problem-solving. What this master couple has effectively accomplished is to actualize the great marital paradox: that people can only change if they don't feel they have to.

Harris and Wilma make it look easy, just like a high-wire act makes it look easy. They are "athletes" at marriage, and that is one reason we study long-term marriages. There is a marital magic in what they do. The only function of my research is to make this marital magic clear so therapists can teach it to other couples.

READ MORE ABOUT IT

The Seven Principles for Making Marriage Work, John Gottman, Ph.D. (Crown, 1999)
The Marriage Clinic, John Gottman, Ph.D. (W. W. Norton, 1999)

John Gottman, Ph.D., is William Mifflin Professor of Psychology at the University of Washington in Seattle. Sybil Carrere, Ph.D., is a research scientist at the University of Washington in Seattle.

Article 19

Social Science and Public Policy

NEW EVIDENCE FOR THE BENEFITS OF NEVER SPANKING

Murray A. Straus

Virtually a revolution has occurred in the last four years in the state of scientific knowledge about the long-term effects of corporal punishment. This article summarizes the results of that research and explains why the new research shows, more clearly than ever before, the benefits of avoiding corporal punishment.

Somewhat ironically, at the same time as these new studies were appearing, voices arose in state legislatures, the mass media, and in social science journals to defend corporal punishment. Consequently, a second purpose is to put these recent defenses of corporal punishment in perspective.

This is followed by a section explaining a paradox concerning trends in corporal punishment. Public belief in the necessity of corporal punishment and the percentage of parents who hit teenagers is about half of what it was only 30 years ago. Despite these dramatic changes, 94 percent of parents of toddlers in a recent national survey reported spanking, which is about the same as it was in 1975 (Straus and Stewart, 1999).

The article concludes with an estimate of the benefits to children, to parents, and to society as a whole that could occur if corporal punishment were to cease.

Defenders of corporal punishment say or imply that no-corporal punishment is the same as no-discipline or "permissiveness." Consequently, before discussing the new research, it is important to emphasize that no-corporal punishment does not mean no-discipline. Writers and organizations leading the movement away from corporal

punishment believe that rules and discipline are necessary, but that they will be *more* effective without corporal punishment. Their goal is to inform parents about these more effective disciplinary strategies, as exemplified in the very name of one such organization—the Center for Effective Discipline (see their web site: *http://www.stophitting.com;* see also the web site of Positive Parenting program *http://parenting.umn.edu*).

Previous Research on Corporal Punishment

In order to grasp the importance of the new research, the limitations of the previous 45 years of research need to be understood. These 45 years saw the publication of more than 80 studies linking corporal punishment to child behavior problems such as physical violence. A meta-analysis of these studies by Gershoff (in press) found that almost all showed that the more corporal punishment a child had experienced, the worse the behavior of the child. Gershoff's review reveals a consistency of findings that is rare in social science research. Thompson concluded that "Although... corporal punishment does secure children's immediate compliance, it also increases the likelihood of eleven [types of] negative outcomes [such as increased physical aggression by the child and depression later in life]. Moreover, even studies conducted by defenders of corporal punishment show that, even when the criterion is immediate compliance, noncorporal discipline strategies work just as well as corporal punishment.

The studies in my book *Beating the Devil Out of Them* are examples of the type of negative outcome reviewed by Thompson. For example, the more corporal punishment experienced, the greater the probability of hitting a wife or husband later in life. Another study of kindergarten children used data on corporal punishment obtained by interviews with the mothers of the children. Six months later the children were observed in school. Instances of physical aggression were tallied for each child. The children of mothers who used corporal punishment attacked other children twice as often as the children whose mothers did not. The children of mothers who went beyond ordinary corporal punishment had four times the rate of attacking other children. This illustrates another principle: that the psychologically harmful effects of corporal punishment are parallel to the harmful effects of physical abuse, except that the magnitude of the effect is less.

Despite the unusually high constancy in the findings of research on corporal punishment, there is a serious problem with all the previous research, these studies do not indicate which is cause and which is effect. That is, they do not take into account the fact that aggression and other behavior problems of the child lead parents to spank. Consequently, although there is clear evidence that the more corporal punishment, the greater the probability of hitting a spouse later in life, that finding could simply indicate that the parents were responding to a high level of aggression by the child at Time 1. For example, they might have spanked because the child repeatedly grabbed toys from or hit a brother or sister. Since aggression is a relatively stable trait, it is not surprising that the most aggressive children at Time 1 are still the most aggressive at Time 2 and are now hitting their wives or husbands. To deal with that problem, the research needs to take into account the child's aggression or other antisocial behavior at Time 1 (the time of the spanking). Studies using that design can examine whether, in the months or years following, the behavior of children who were spanked improves (as most people in the USA think will be the case) or gets worse. There are finally new studies that use this design and provide information on long term change in the child's behavior.

Five New Landmark Studies

In the three-year period 1997–1999 five studies became available that can be considered "landmark" studies because they overcame this serious defect in 45 years of previous research on the long-term effects of corporal punishment. All five of the new studies took into account the child's behavior at Time 1, and all five were based on large and nationally representative samples of American children. None of them depended on adults recalling what happened when they were children.

Study 1: Corporal Punishment and Subsequent Antisocial Behavior

This research studied over 3,000 children in the National Longitudinal Survey of Youth (Straus, et al., 1997). The children were in three age groups: 3–5, 6–9, and 10–14. The mothers of all three groups of children were interviewed at the start of the study in 1988, and then again in 1990 and 1992. The findings were very similar for all three age groups and for change after two years and four years. To avoid excess detail only the results for the 6–9 year old children and for the change in antisocial behavior two years after the first interview will be described here.

Measure of corporal punishment. To measure corporal punishment, the mothers were told "Sometimes kids mind pretty well and sometimes they don't," and asked "About how many times, if any, have you had to spank your child in the past week?"

Measure of Antisocial Behavior. To measure Antisocial Behavior the mothers were asked whether, in the past three months, the child frequently "cheats or tells lies," "bullies or is cruel/mean to others," "does not feel sorry after misbehaving," "breaks things deliberately," "is disobedient at school," "has trouble getting along with teachers." This was used to create a measure of the number of antisocial behaviors frequently engaged in by the child.

Other Variables. We also took into account several other variables that could affect antisocial behavior by the child. These include the sex of child, cognitive stimulation provided by the parents, emotional support by the mother, ethnic group of the mother, and socioeconomic status of the family.

Findings. The more corporal punishment used during the first year of the study, the greater the tendency for Antisocial Behavior to *increase* subsequent to the corporal punishment. It also shows that this effect applied to both Euro American children and children of other ethnic groups. Of course, other things also influence Antisocial Behavior. For example, girls have lower rates of Antisocial Behavior than boys, and children whose mothers are warm and supportive are less likely to behave in antisocial ways. Although these other variables do lessen the effect of corporal punishment, we found that the tendency for corporal punishment to make things worse over the long run applies regardless of race, socioeconomic status, gender of the child, and regardless of the extent to which the mother provides cognitive stimulation and emotional support.

Study 2: A Second Study of Corporal Punishment and Antisocial Behavior

Sample and Measures. Gunnoe and Mariner (1997) analyzed data from another large and representative sample of American children—the National Survey of Families and Households. They studied 1,112 children in two age groups: 4–7 and 8–11. In half of the cases the mother was interviewed and in the other half the father provided the information. The parents were first interviewed in 1987–88, and then five years later. Gunnoe and Mariner's measure of corporal punishment was the same as in the Straus et al. study just described; that is, how often the parent spanked in the previous week.

Gunnoe and Mariner examined the effect of corporal punishment on two aspects of the child's behavior: fighting at school and antisocial behavior. Their Antisocial Behavior measure was also the same as in the Straus et al. study.

Findings on Fighting. Gunnoe and Mariner found that the more corporal punishment in 1987–88, the greater the amount of fighting at school five years later. This is consistent with the theory that in the long run corporal punishment is counter-productive. However, for toddlers and for African-American children, they found the opposite, i.e. that corporal punishment is associated with *less* fighting 5 years later. Gunnoe and Mariner suggest that this occurs because younger children and African-American children tend to regard corporal punishment as a legitimate parental behavior rather than as an aggressive act. However, corporal punishment by parents of young children and by African-American parents is so nearly universal (for example, 94 percent of parents of toddlers) that it suggests an alternative explanation: that no-corporal punishment means no-discipline. If that is the case, it is no wonder that children whose parents exercise no-discipline are less well behaved. Corporal punishment may not be good for children, but failure to properly supervise and control is even worse.

Findings on Antisocial Behavior. The findings on the relation of corporal punishment to Antisocial Behavior show that the more corporal punishment experienced by the children in Year 1, the *higher* the level of Antisocial Behavior five years later. Moreover, they found that the harmful effect of corporal punishment applies to all the categories of children they studied—that is, to children in each age group, to all races, and to both boys and girls. Thus, both of these major long-term prospective studies resulted in evidence that, although corporal punishment may work in the short run, in the long run it tends to boomerang and make things worse.

An important sidelight of the Gunnoe and Mariner study is that it illustrates the way inconvenient findings can be ignored to give a desired "spin." The findings section includes one brief sentence acknowledging that their study "replicates the Straus et al. findings." This crucial finding is never again mentioned. The extensive discussion and conclusion sections omit mentioning the results showing that corporal punishment at Time 1 was associated with more antisocial behavior subsequently for children of all ages and all ethnic groups. Marjorie Gunnoe told me that she is opposed to spanking and has never spanked her own children. So the spin she put on the findings is not a reflection of personal values or behavior.

Perhaps it reflects teaching at a college affiliated with a church which teaches that God expects parents to spank.

Study 3: Corporal Punishment and Child-to-Parent Violence

Timothy Brezina (1999) analyzed data on a nationally representative sample of 1,519 adolescent boys who participated in the Youth in Transition study. This is a three-wave panel study that was begun in 1966. Although the data refer to a previous generation of high school students, there is no reason to think that the relationship between corporal punishment and children hitting parents is different now that it was then, except that the rate may have decreased because fewer parents now slap teen-agers.

Measure of Corporal Punishment. Corporal punishment was measured by asking the boys "How often do your parents actually slap you?" The response categories ranged from 1 (never) to 5 (always). Twenty eight percent of the boys reported being slapped by their parents during the year of the first wave of the study when their average age was 15, and 19 percent were slapped during the wave 2 year (a year and half later).

Measure of Child Aggression. The boys were asked similar questions about how often they hit their father and their mother. Eleven percent reported hitting a parent the first year, and 7 percent reported hitting a parent at Time 2 of the study.

Findings. Brezina found that corporal punishment at Time 1 was associated with an *increased* probability of a child assaulting the parent a year and a half later. Thus, while it is true that corporal punishment teaches the child a lesson, it is certainly not the lesson intended by the parents.

As with the other four studies, the data analysis took into account some of the many other factors that affect the probability of child-to-parent violence. These include the socioeconomic status and race of the family, the age of the parents, the child's attachment to the parent, child's attitude toward aggression, and child's physical size.

Study 4: Corporal Punishment and Dating Violence

Simons, Lin, and Gordon (1998) tested the theory that corporal punishment by the parents increases the probability of later hitting a partner in a dating relationship. They studied 113 boys in a rural area of the state of Iowa, beginning when they were in the 7th grade or about age 13.

Measure of Corporal Punishment. The mothers and the fathers of these boys were asked how often they spanked or slapped the child when he did something wrong, and how often they used a belt or paddle for corporal punishment. These questions were repeated in waves 2 and 3 of this 5-year study. The scores for the mother and the father for each of the three years were combined to create an overall measure of corporal punishment. More than half of the boys experienced corporal punishment during those years. Consequently, the findings about corporal punishment apply to the majority of boys in that community, not just to the children of a small group of violent parents.

Measure of Dating Violence. The information on dating violence came from the boys, so it is not influenced by whether the parents viewed the boy as aggressive. The boys were asked whether, in the last year, "When you had a disagreement with your girlfriend, how often did you hit, push, shove her?"

Measure of Delinquency at Time 1. As explained earlier, it is critical to take into account the misbehavior that leads parents to use corporal punishment. In this study, that was done by asking the boys at Time 1 how often they had engaged in each of 24 delinquent acts such as skipping school, stealing, and physically attacking someone with a weapon; and also how often they had used drugs and alcohol.

Parental involvement and support. Finally the study also took into account the extent to which the parents showed warmth and affection, were consistent in their discipline, monitored and supervised the child, and explained rules and expectations. In addition, it also controlled for witnessing parental violence.

Findings. Simons and his colleagues found that the more corporal punishment experienced by these boys, the greater the probability of their physically assaulting a girlfriend. Moreover, like the other prospective studies, the analysis took into account the misbehavior that led parents to use corporal punishment, and also the quality of parenting. This means that the relation of corporal punishment to violence against a girlfriend is very unlikely to be due to poor parenting. Rather, it is another study showing that the long run effect of corporal punishment is to engender more rather than less misbehavior. In short, spanking boomerangs.

Study 5: Corporal Punishment and Child's Cognitive Development

The last of these five studies (Straus and Paschall, 1999) was prompted by studies showing that talking to children (including pre-speech infants) is associated with an increase in neural connections in the brain and in cognitive performance. Those findings led us to theorize that if parents avoid corporal punishment, they are more likely to engage in verbal methods of behavior control such as explaining to the child, and that the increased verbal interaction with the child will in turn enhance the child's cognitive ability.

This theory was tested on 806 children of mothers in the National Longitudinal Study of Youth who were age 2 to 4 in the first year of our analysis, and the tests were repeated for an additional 704 children who were age 5 to 9 in the first year. Corporal punishment was measured by whether the mother was observed hitting the child during the interview and by a question on frequency of spanking in the past week. A corporal punishment scale was created by adding the number of times the parent spanked in two sample weeks. Cognitive ability was measured in Year 1 and two years later by tests appropriate for the age of the child at the time of testing such as the Peabody Picture Vocabulary Test.

The study took into account the mother's age and education, whether the father was present in the household, number of children in the family, mother's supportiveness and cognitive stimulation, ethnic group, and the child's age, gender, and child's birth weight.

The less corporal punishment parents use on toddlers, the greater the probability that the child will have an above average cognitive growth. The greater benefit of avoiding corporal punishment for the younger children is consistent with the research showing the most rapid growth of neural connections in the brain of early ages. It is also consistent with the theory that what the child learns as an infant and toddler is crucial because it provides the necessary basis for subsequent cognitive development. The greater adverse effect on cognitive development for toddlers has an extremely important practical implication because the defenders of corporal punishment have now retreated to limiting their advocacy to toddlers. Their recommendation is not based on empirical evidence. The evidence from this study suggests that, at least in so far as cognitive development is concerned, supporters of corporal punishment have unwittingly advised parents to use corporal punishment at the ages when it will have the most adverse effect.

The Message Of The Five Studies: "Don't Spank"

Each of the five studies I briefly summarized is far from perfect. They can be picked apart one by one, as can just about every epidemiological study. This is what the tobacco industry did for many years. The Surgeon General's committee on smoking did the opposite. Their review of the research acknowledged the limitations of the studies when taken one-by-one. But they concluded that despite the defects of the individual studies, the cumulative evidence indicated that smoking does cause lung cancer and other diseases, and they called for an end to smoking. With respect to spanking, I believe that the cumulative weight of the evidence, and especially the five prospective studies provides sufficient evidence for a new Surgeon General's warning. A start in that direction was made by the American Academy of Pediatrics, which in 1998 published "Guidelines for Effective Discipline" (*Pediatrics* 101: 723–728) that advises parents to avoid spanking.

Is There a Backlash?

It is ironic that during the same period as the new and more definitive research was appearing, there were hostile or ridiculing articles in newspapers and magazines on the idea of never spanking a child. In 1999, Arizona and Arkansas passed laws to remind parents and teachers that they have the right to use corporal punishment and to urge them to do so. There has also been a contentious debate in scientific journals on the appropriateness of corporal punishment. These developments made some advocates for children concerned that there is a backlash against the idea of no-spanking. However, there are several reasons for doubting the existence of a backlash in the sense of a reversal in the trend of decreasing public support for corporal punishment, or in the sense of non-spanking parents reverting to using corporal punishment.

One reason for doubting the existence of a backlash is that, each year, a larger and larger proportion of the American population opposes corporal punishment. In 1968, which was only a generation ago, almost everyone (94 percent) believed that corporal punishment is sometimes necessary. But in the last 30 years public support for corporal punishment has been decreasing. By 1999, almost half of US adults rejected the idea that spanking is necessary.

The Advocates Are Long-Time Supporters

In 1968, those who favored corporal punishment did not need to speak out to defend their view because, as just indicated, almost everyone believed it was necessary. The dramatic decrease in support for corporal punishment means that long time advocates of corporal punishment now have reason to be worried, and they are speaking out. Consequently, their recent publications do not indicate a backlash in the sense of a change from being opposed to corporal punishment to favoring it. I suggest that it is more like dying gasps of support for an ancient mode of bringing up children that is heading towards extinction.

The efforts of those who favor corporal punishment have also been spurred on by the increase in crime in many countries. The rise in youth crime in the United States, although recently reversed, is a very disturbing trend, and it has prompted a search for causes and corrective steps. It should be no surprise that people who have always believed in the use of corporal punishment believe that a return to their favored mode of bringing up children will help cure the crime problem. They argue that children need "discipline," which is correct. However, they equate discipline with corporal punishment, which is not correct. No-corporal punishment does not mean no-discipline. Delinquency prevention does require, among other things, discipline in the sense of clear rules and standards for behavior and parental supervision and monitoring and enforcement. To the extent that part of the explanation for crime, especially crime by youth, is the lack of discipline, the appropriate step is not a return to corporal punishment but parental standards, monitoring, and enforcement by non-violent methods. In fact, as the studies reviewed here indicate, if discipline takes the form of more corporal punishment, the problem will be exacerbated because, while corporal punishment does work with some children, more typically it boomer-

angs and increases the level of juvenile delinquency and other behavior problems.

The criticism in scientific journals of research on corporal punishment is also not a backlash. It has to be viewed in the light of the norms of science. A standard aspect of science is to examine research critically, to raise questions, and to suggest alternative interpretations of findings. This results in a somewhat paradoxical tendency for criticism to increase as the amount of research goes up. There has recently been an increase in research showing long-term harmful effects of corporal punishment. Given the critical ethos of science, it is only to be expected that the increased research has elicited more commentary and criticism, especially on the part of those who believed in corporal punishment in the first place.

Three Paradoxes About Corporal Punishment

Three paradoxical aspects of the movement away from corporal punishment are worth noting. The first is that, although approval of corporal punishment had declined precipitously in the last generation, almost all parents continue to spank toddlers. The second paradox is that professionals advising parents, including those who are opposed to spanking, generally fail to tell parents not to spank. They call this avoiding a "negative approach." Finally, and most paradoxically of all, focusing almost exclusively on a so-called "positive approach," unwittingly contributes to perpetuating corporal punishment and helps explain the first paradox.

Paradox 1: Contradictory Trends. Some aspects of corporal punishment have changed in major ways. A smaller and smaller percent of the public favors spanking (Straus and Mathur, 1996). Fewer parents now use belts, hairbrushes and paddles. The percent of parents who hit adolescents has dropped by half since 1975. Nevertheless, other aspects of corporal punishment continue to be prevalent, chronic, and severe. The 1995 Gallup national survey of parents (Straus and Stewart, 1999) found that:

- Almost all parents of toddlers (94 percent) used corporal punishment that year
- Parents who spanked a toddler, did it an average of about three times a week
- 28 percent of parents of children age 5–12 used an object such as a belt or hairbrush
- Over a third of parents of 13-year-old children hit them that year

The myths about corporal punishment in *Beating The Devil Out Of Them* provide important clues to understanding why parents who "don't believe in spanking" continue to do so. These myths also undermine the ability of professionals who advise parents to do what is needed to end corporal punishment.

Paradox 2: Opposing Spanking but Failing to Say Don't Spank. Many pediatricians, developmental psychologists, and parent educators are now opposed to corporal punishment, at least in principle. But most also continue to believe that there may be a situation where spanking by parents is necessary or acceptable (Schenck, 2000). This is based on cultural myths. One myth is that spanking works when other things do not. Another is that "mild" corporal punishment is harmless. All but a small minority of parents and professionals continue to believe these myths despite the experimental and other evidence showing that other disciplinary strategies work just as well as spanking, even in the short run and are more effective in the long run as shown by the first four of the studies described earlier in this article.

Consequently, when I suggest to pediatricians, parent educators, or social scientists that it is essential to tell parents that they should never spank or use any other type of corporal punishment, with rare exception, that idea has been rejected. Some, like one of America's leading developmental psychologists, object because of the unproven belief that it would turn off parents. Some object on the false belief that it could be harmful because parents do not know what else to do. They argue for a "positive approach" by which they mean teaching parents alternative disciplinary strategies, as compared to what they call the "negative approach" of advising to never spank. As a result, the typical pattern is to say nothing about spanking. Fortunately, that is slowly changing. Although they are still the exception, an increasing number of books for parents, parent education programs, and guidelines for professionals advise never-spanking.

Both the movement away from spanking, and an important limitation of that movement are illustrated by publication of the "Guidelines For Effective Discipline" of the American Academy of Pediatrics. This was an important step forward, but it also reflects the same problem. It recommends that parents avoid corporal punishment. However, it also carefully avoids saying that parents should *never* spank. This may seem like splitting hairs, but because of the typical sequence of parent-child interaction that eventuates in corporal punishment described in the next paragraph, it is a major obstacle to ending corporal punishment. Omitting a never-spank message is a serious obstacle because, in the absence of a commitment to never-spank, even parents who are against spanking continue to spank. It is important to understand what underlies the paradox of parents who are opposed to spanking, nonetheless spanking.

Paradox 3: Failing To Be Explicit Against Spanking Results in More Spanking. The paradox that fewer and fewer parents are in favor of spanking, but almost all spank toddlers reflects a combination of needing to cope with the typical behavior of toddlers and perceiving those behaviors through the lens of the myth that spanking works when other things do not.

When toddlers are corrected for misbehavior (such as hitting another child or disobeying), the "recidivism" rate is about 80 percent within the same day and about 50 percent within two hours. For some children it is within two minutes. One researcher (who is a defender of corporal punishment) found that these "time to failure" rates apply equally to corporal punishment and to other disciplinary strategies (Larzelere, et al., 1996). Consequently, on any given day, a parent is almost certain to find that so-called alternative disciplinary strategies such as explaining, deprivation of privileges and time out, "do not work." When that happens, they turn to spanking. So, as pointed out previously, just about everyone (at least 94 percent) spanks toddlers.

The difference between spanking and other disciplinary strategies is that, when spanking does not work, parents do not question its effectiveness. The idea that spanking works when other methods do not is so ingrained in American culture that, when the child repeats the misbehavior an hour or two later (or sometimes a few minutes later) parents fail to perceive that spanking has the same high failure rate as other modes of discipline. So they spank again, and for as many times as it takes to ultimately secure compliance. That is the correct strategy because, with consistency and perseverance, the child will eventually learn. What so many parents miss is that it is also the correct strategy for non-spanking methods. Thus, unless there is an absolute prohibition on spanking, parents will "see with their own eyes" that alternatives do not work and continue to find it is necessary to spank.

"Never-Spank" Must Be The Message

Because of the typical behavior of toddlers and the almost inevitable information processing errors just described, teaching alternative disciplinary techniques by itself is not sufficient. There must also be an unambiguous "never-spank" message, which is needed to increase the chances that parents who disapprove of spanking will act on their beliefs. Consequently, it is essential for pediatricians and others who advise parents to abandon their reluctance to say "never-spank." To achieve this, parent-educators must themselves be educated. They need to understand why, what they now consider a "negative approach," is such an important part of ending the use of corporal punishment. Moreover, because they believe that a "negative approach" does not work, they also need to know about the experience of Sweden. The Swedish experience shows that, contrary to the currently prevailing opinion, a never-spank approach has worked (Durrant, 1999).

In short, the first priority step to end or reduce spanking may be to educate professionals who advise parents. Once professionals are ready to move, the key steps are relatively easy to implement and inexpensive.

> Parent-education programs, such as STEP, which are now silent on spanking, can be revised to include the evidence that spanking does *not* work better than other disciplinary tactics, even in the short run; and to specifically say "*never* spank."

The Public Health Service can follow the Swedish model and sponsor no-spanking public service announcements on TV and on milk cartons.

There can be a "No-Spanking" poster and pamphlets in every pediatrician's office and every maternity ward.

There could be a notice on birth certificates such as:

WARNING: SPANKING HAS BEEN DETERMINED TO BE DANGEROUS TO THE HEALTH AND WELL BEING OF YOUR CHILD—**DO NOT EVER, UNDER ANY CIRCUMSTANCES, SPANK OR HIT YOUR CHILD**

Until professionals who advise parents start advising parents to *never* spank, the paradox of parents becoming less and less favorable to spanking while at the same continuing to spank toddlers will continue. Fortunately, that is starting to happen.

The benefits of avoiding corporal punishment are many, but they are virtually impossible for parents to perceive by observing their children. The situation with spanking is parallel to that of smoking. Smokers could perceive the short run satisfaction from a cigarette, but had no way to see the adverse health consequences down the road. Similarly, parents can perceive the beneficial effects of a slap (and, for the reasons explained in the previous section, fail to see the equal effectiveness of alternatives), they have no way of looking a year or more into the future to see if there is a harmful side effect of having hit their child to correct misbehavior. The only way parents can know this would be if there were a public policy to publicize the results of research such as the studies summarized in this article.

Another reason the benefits of avoiding spanking are difficult to see is that they are not dramatic in any one case. This is illustrated by the average increase of 3 or 4 points in mental ability associated with no-corporal punishment. An increase of that size would hardly be noticed in an individual case. However, it is a well established principle in public health and epidemiology that a widely prevalent risk factor with small effect size, for example spanking, can have a much greater impact on public health than a risk factor with a large effect size, but low prevalence, for example, physical abuse. For example, assume that: (1) 50 million US children experienced CP and 1 million experienced physical abuse. (2) The probability of being depressed as an adult is increased by 2 percent for children who experienced CP and by 25 percent for children who experienced physical abuse. Given these assumptions, the additional cases of depression caused by CP is 1.02 times 50 million, or 1 million. The additional cases of depression caused by physical abuse is 1.25 time 1 million or 250,000. Thus CP is associated with a four

times greater increase in depression than is physical abuse.

Another example of a major benefit resulting from reducing a risk factor that has a small effect, but for a large proportion of the population, might be the increase in scores on intelligence tests that has been occurring worldwide. Corporal punishment has also been decreasing worldwide. The decrease in use of corporal punishment and the increase in scores in IQ tests could be just a coincidence. However, the results of the study described earlier in this article which showed that less spanking is associated with faster cognitive development suggest that the trend away from corporal punishment may be one of a number of social changes (especially, better educated parents) that explain the increase in IQ scores in so many nations.

The other four prospective studies reviewed in this article and the studies in *Beating the Devil Out of Them* show that ending corporal punishment is likely to also reduce juvenile violence, wife-beating, and masochistic sex, and increase the probability of completing higher education, holding a high income job, and lower rates of depression and alcohol abuse. Those are not only humanitarian benefits, they can also result in huge monetary savings in public and private costs for dealing with mental health problems, and crime.

I concluded the first edition of *Beating the Devil Out of Them* in 1994 by suggesting that ending corporal punishment by parents "portends profound and far reaching benefits for humanity." The new research summarized in this article makes those words even more appropriate. We can look forward to the day when children in almost all countries have the benefit of being brought up without being hit by their parents; and just as important, to the day when many nations have the benefit of the healthier, wealthier, and wiser citizens who were brought up free from the violence that is now a part of their earliest and most influential life experiences.

Suggested Further Readings

Brezina, Timothy. 1999. "Teenage violence toward parents as an adaptation to family strain: Evidence from a national survey of male adolescents." *Youth & Society* 30: 416–444.

Durrant, Joan E. 1999. "Evaluating the success of Sweden's corporal punishment ban." *Child Abuse & Neglect* 23: 435–448.

Gershoff, Elizabeth Thompson. In press. "Corporal punishment by parents and associated child behaviors and experiences: A meta-analytic and theoretical review." *Psychological Bulletin.*

Gunnoe, Marjorie L., and Carrie L. Mariner. 1997. "Toward a developmental-contextual model of the effects of parental spanking on children's aggression." *Archives of Pediatric and Adolescent Medicine* 151: 768–775.

Larzelere, Robert E., William N. Schneider, David B. Larson, and Patricia L. Pike. 1996. "The effects of discipline responses in delaying toddler misbehavior recurrences." *Child and Family Therapy* 18: 35–37.

Neisser, Ulric. 1997. "Rising scores on intelligence tests: Test scores are certainly going up all over the world, but whether intelligence itself has risen remains controversial." *American Scientist* 85: 440–447.

Schenck, Eliza R., Robert D. Lyman, and S. Douglas Bodin. 2000. "Ethical beliefs, attitudes, and professional practices of psychologists regarding parental use of corporal punishment: A survey." *Children's Services: Social Policy, Research, and Practice* 3: 23–38.

Simons, Ronald L., Kuei-Hsiu Lin, and Leslie C. Gordon. 1998. "Socialization in the Family of origin and male dating violence: A prospective study." *Journal of Marriage and the Family* 60: 467–478.

Straus, Murray A., and Anitia K. Mathur. 1996. "Social change and change in approval of corporal punishment by parents from 1968 to 1994." Pp. 91–105 in *Family violence against children: A challenge for society.*, edited by D. Frehsee, W. Horn, and K-D Bussmann, New York: Walter deGruyter.

Straus, Murray A., and Mallie J. Paschall. 1999. "Corporal punishment by mothers and children's cognitive development: A longitudinal study of two age cohorts." in *6th International Family Violence Research Conference*. Durham, NH: Family Research Laboratory, University of New Hampshire.

Straus, Murray A., and Julie H. Stewart. 1999. "Corporal punishment by American parents: National data on prevalence, chronicity, severity, and duration, in relation to child, and family characteristics." *Clinical Child and Family Psychology Review* 2: 55–70.

Straus, Murray A., David B. Sugarman, and Jean Giles-Sims. 1997. "Spanking by parents and subsequent antisocial behavior of children." *Archives of pediatric and adolescent medicine* 151: 761–767.

Murray A. Straus is professor of sociology and co-director of the Family Research Laboratory at the University of New Hampshire. He is the author or co-author or editor of 18 books including Stress, Culture, and Aggression. *This article is adapted from Chapter 12 of* Beating the Devil Out of Them: Corporal Punishment in American Families and Its Effects on Children, *2nd edition, published by Transaction.*

From *Society*, September/October 2001, pp. 52-60. © 2001 by Transaction Publishers. Reprinted by permission.

FAMILY MATTERS

THE NEW BUZZ IN PSYCHOLOGY IS THAT PEERS ARE MORE IMPORTANT IN SHAPING A CHILD'S PERSONALITY THAN PARENTS ARE. BUT A 13-YEAR STUDY IN DOMINICA, OF ALL PLACES, SAYS HOME LIFE IS GROUND ZERO FOR MENTAL HEALTH

BY MEREDITH F. SMALL

LOPING THROUGH THE VILLAGE OF BWA Mawego, on the Caribbean island of Dominica, Mark Flinn looks and acts like a slimmer, bespectacled Al Gore stumping on the campaign trail. He stops at each house to chat. He shakes hands, touches shoulders. He asks parents about their children in lilting Creole and talks of his own three young boys back home. At the University of Missouri, where Flinn teaches anthropology, he is an admittedly aloof and distant colleague. But here in Bwa Mawego, everyone knows everything about everybody—"If you talk about someone and you don't see them soon," one villager says, "they are either in jail or in the cemetery"—and that suits Flinn just fine. In fact, his research depends on it. As Flinn makes his way up the crest of a ravine on a winding dirt road, he runs into two boys, aged 10 and 7, on their way to school. The boys have on the requisite brown shorts and pale yellow shirts and carry book bags. "Have time to spit?" Flinn asks.

Flinn gives each boy a stick of Wrigley's spearmint gum, and they chew and spit into plastic cups. Next, an elderly matriarch named Evelyn comes up the road

and lends a hand. Moving like a veteran lab assistant, she takes a plastic pipette, deftly sucks up five milliliters of saliva from one of the boys' cups, and transfers the saliva to a labeled tube. Finally, Flinn turns to the boys and asks them how things are at home. "When did you get up? Did anybody fall this morning? Did you sleep at your grandmother's or at home?"

The whole sequence, described in that way, sounds faintly absurd. Yet every action here has a reasonable purpose, and Flinn's lines are hardly non sequiturs. He is studying the relationship between stress and health in children, and two of the best ways to gauge stress are by asking personal questions and by measuring a hormone called cortisol, found in saliva. Since 1988, Flinn has collected more than 25,000 saliva samples from 287 children in this village—an average of 96 samples per child. He has tracked the children's growth and measured their immunoglobulin levels to see if their immune systems are healthy. He has checked their health records and sent out an assistant to see who's sick. Perhaps most important, he has watched, listened, and asked questions. The result is a year-by-year, day-by-day, and sometimes

even hour-by-hour glimpse of these children's lives. It's also a compelling rebuttal to one of the most widely publicized new theories in developmental psychology.

According to that theory, propounded by psychologist Judith Harris in her controversial 1998 book *The Nurture Assumption*, parents have relatively little power to shape a child's character. Studies of identical twins raised apart since birth have proved "beyond a shadow of a doubt that heredity is responsible for a sizable portion of the variations if people's personalities," Harris writes. At the same time, she points to a number of studies that seemed to suggest that the rest of a child's personality is shaped more by peers than by parents. How else—to take one example—could the children of non-English-speaking immigrants speak perfect English?

After generations of child-centered parenting books, Harris's argument immediately captured the media spotlight, perhaps mostly because it lets parents off the hook. If *The Nurture Assumption* is right, parents can all relax, put their kids in day care, and stop worrying that a little scolding will damage them for life. As an article in *The New Yorker* put it: "In some key sense, parents don't much matter."

Flinn's work makes an altogether different point—one as unfashionable as it is reasonable. His thousands of data points can be grouped into any number of constellations, but one pattern shines through all the others: Families matter more than anything else in a child's life. When a family has problems, it sends stress hormones coursing through a child's system. When family members get along, or have numerous relatives to call on, they can shelter a child from the worst social upheavals in the outside world. Emotionally and physiologically, family life is ground zero for a child's health.

BWA MAWEGO IS THE PERFECT SETTING for such research. (For the sake of privacy, the names of the village and all villagers have been changed.) Life is lived in the open here, making it far easier to meet people and follow them around, and many incidental sources of stress are naturally filtered out. There is no traffic, no rat race, no threat of war. The forest is fragrant with bay leaf bushes, the winding paths littered with ripe mangoes, the houses clustered in picturesque hamlets overlooking the sea. Of course, poverty, poor roads, and exposure to the elements take their own toll, but local people—some 700 of them, all of mixed African, Carib, and European descent—are unlikely to blame their stress on their surroundings.

Take Kristen, a 4-year-old in town. Every morning she wakes up to a billion-dollar view: Her house is built on stilts, on a volcanic cliff overlooking the Atlantic. In the front yard, clean laundry hangs on the trees that dot the hard-packed mud, chickens run about, and a soft Caribbean breeze wafts the smell of roasting coffee beans across the porch. With her large brown eyes, sweet smile, and quiet manner, Kristen is a child anyone would want to hug, and lots of people do—her mother, grandparents, and a multitude of relatives all live within walking distance.

Yet Kristen's life has its share of stress. Before she was born, her mother, Julianne, was single and going to high school in the city. When Julianne became pregnant, she had to move back home and hasn't worked since. Although Robbie, a nice guy and an old friend of Julianne's, has since become a kind of stepfather to Kristen, Julianne still worries about the opportunities she missed by not getting an education. In Bwa Mawego, as in most places, life can be

tough for a single mother. And today Kristen has a cold.

Flinn sees no coincidence there. "In the village, illness among children increases more than twofold following significant stress," he says. "About 30 percent of the children in the village have the current cold, even though most of them have been exposed to the pathogen. So why are only certain ones sick? In the West we think it is mostly contact—send your child to preschool and expect them to get sick. But I am convinced that resistance is more important than contact frequency."

The reason is as complex biologically as it is emotionally. When a person is in trouble, Flinn explains, the brain automatically sends signals to the sympathetic nervous system, initiating a "fight or flight" response. First adrenaline and then cortisol are secreted by the adrenal glands, revving up the body and the sustaining the energy flow to different systems. The lungs pump faster and the heart starts to race; blood pressure rises, charging up the muscles and sharpening the mind; the stomach gets jumpy and the rush of endorphins numbs the body. At the same time, the appetite, libido, and immune system shut down, and the energy they would normally consume is diverted to muscles that will help the body fight the immediate threat.

This is all well and good—unless the perceived threat persists. In that case, adrenaline washes out of the body quickly, but cortisol may linger for days, weeks, or even years, keeping the immune system and other important functions depressed. Children are especially vulnerable to stress. Their bodies are "nothing other than a long-term building project," says Robert Sapolsky, a stress researcher at Stanford University. Yet chronic stress is "constantly telling them, 'Don't fix stuff now, do it tomorrow, do it tomorrow.'" In the long term, too much cortisol can slow down a child's growth, brain development, and sexual maturation. In the short term, it can make a child prone to upper-respiratory infections and diarrhea, diseases that are often fatal at that age.

Stress can make you sick.

THANKS TO CORTISOL, MEASURING STRESS is as easy as a lab test or two. But only patient, detailed, long-term work like Flinn's can untangle its myriad causes. Hormone levels differ from child to child, Flinn says, and they fluctuate naturally over the course of a day. "The old dogma was that if you got a sample once a day, collected between 8 to 10 a.m., that was enough. But I've

found that controlling for time of day is not enough. If you have a tough kid who is habituated to the mundane, giving a saliva sample in a lab would be a bore. You need to know what happened to this kid the day before: Is he burned out? What are his reserves? What's the context?"

The payoff for Flinn's 13-year study is a startlingly intimate view of childhood and its discontents

---

Taking repeated measurements, as Flinn does, is expensive, complicated, and time-consuming. But the payoff is a startlingly intimate view of childhood and its discontents. One summer, for instance, Flinn took samples from a group of cousins, aged 3 to 8, who were playing house. Valerie and Kathy decided to be the parents, and they made Jane the child—a role of lowly status. Jane wasn't happy being the child. Worse, she felt betrayed: Valerie was *her* best friend. Why had she sided with Kathy? So Jane organized the other children into a game of jump rope, ruining Valerie and Kathy's plans.

A ruckus ensued. Kathy, still playing parent, told Jane she was being disobedient and threatened to beat her; Jane and her jump-rope partner swung the rope and hit Kathy in the face by mistake. Soon the children were yelling and their mothers were running over and accusations were flying. Kathy even threw a rock in Jane's direction as they parted.

If children's personalities are largely shaped by their peers, this should have been a traumatic event. Harris cites an informal study by sociologist Anne-Marie Ambert, of York University in Ontario, in which 37 percent of the students in a class blamed their most depressing experience on peers, while only 9 percent blamed it on parents. As evidence of peer influence, she also notes that siblings grow up to be very different adults; that adopted children are more like their biological parents than their adopted parents in terms of such traits as criminality; and that adolescents from poor neighborhoods are more likely to be delinquents that adolescents from middle-class neighborhoods, whereas being from a broken home as no effect on delinquency. Troubles with peers, Harris concludes, have a much deeper effect on children than do troubles at home.

Flinn's work shows just the opposite. Soon after Jane, Kathy, and Valerie's fight, he collected saliva from each of the participants. None of them had high levels of cortisol. "None," he repeats. "And this is typical of mild peer conflicts." Yet several weeks later, when Jane returned home late from a shopping errand, her saliva told a different story. This time it was her real mother, rather than Kathy, who did the scolding, and though Jane quietly went about her schoolwork afterward, her cortisol rose 60 percent above normal.

Flinn has seen the same pattern time and again. He has taken cortisol measurements from children engaged in 30 different types of activities—from "family fight" to "fight with peer"—and they consistently show that families cause more stress than peers do. Only major fights with friends elevate cortisol levels as much as family troubles do.

FLINN'S WORK GETS AT A FUNDAMENTAL truth about children, one that distinguishes them from the offspring of almost any other species. Most mammals are weaned within days or weeks of their birth. But human infants have to nurse for months, and they need a year just to learn how to walk. Their parents do more than usher them into the world; they feed, clothe, shelter, and protect them for a good portion of their lives. "Humans have the luxury of extended families who can care for these mental larvae," Flinn says. "And because of that protection, children can afford to have a brain that is in the process of growing." At the same time, he adds, children are designed to be exquisitely attuned to their caregivers: "There is nothing more important to a child than figuring out what makes those close to them happy, and what makes them sad."

Contrary to the studies that Harris cites, Flinn has found that children who live with both biological parents clearly do best. They have lower average cortisol levels, weigh more, and grow more steadily than those living with stepparents or single parents with no support from kin. Flinn has also found that boys from households without fathers (though not girls) have cortisol levels that are *too* low in infancy and grow slower than boys with fathers at home. Once again, parents do matter; their impact is sometimes just too deep to notice.

We expect our children to be happy-go-lucky and resilient, but Flinn has found

that they aren't as adaptable as we think. In Bwa Mawego, for instance, Aretha and Arnie Belle have five children, three of them still at home. But Arnie fools around, and so Aretha left him in the fall of 1990 and stayed with her sister in Martinique. During Aretha's absence, her children's cortisol levels shot up and did not come down until she came home a year later. It seems the children never adapted to living in a single-parent home.

Children with such chronically high cortisol levels can suffer permanent damage. In Romania, for instance, orphans raised under the dictatorship of Nicolae Cesusesscu were often so completely neglected—aside from perfunctory feedings and diaper changings—that they became withdrawn and temperamental, prone to rocking in place and staring blankly at visitors. Psychologist Elinor Ames, of Simon Fraser University in British Columbia, studied two groups of orphans. Those in the first group were adopted by American families by the age of 4 months; the second group spent eight months or more in an orphanage. Three years after adoption, the children in the first group had caught up to their peers in terms of size and maturity. But many of those who spent the longest time in the orphanage still suffered from depression and withdrawal.

ONE SUNNY MORNING IN JANUARY, A chubby little girl named Maryann, from the apartment downstairs, toddles up to Flinn's apartment and crawls onto his sofa. Maryann has on a bright pink dress and her hair is pleated into cornrows topped with plastic bows, but she isn't feeling quite so sunny. She has been running a fever and coughing all night, her grandmother explains, as several adults jump up with a tissue to wipe the girl's runny nose.

"She's had this cold for a few days," Flinn guesses. But unlike so many illnesses he has seen these past 13 years, this one probably wasn't exacerbated by stress. Day and night, Maryann is surrounded by loving family members, he says. "It seems like she's related to everyone in town." Such extended families, in turn, allow for much more flexibility in child care. In Bwa Mawego, 36 percent of households with children changed composition at least once between 1990 and 1995—a statistic not unusual for the Caribbean; over the same period about a third of the children lived in more than one household. Fathers often spend the late summer and fall working on farms in Canada; mothers work away from the village at resorts; children go to the city

to live with their grandparents. But even when children change houses, many of them are still with relatives who know all about them—and they are demonstrably healthier for it. Children with many kin connections, Flinn has found, are both taller and heavier for their age than children with few relatives.

> SOME STUDIES SUGGEST that stress can make children develop subtle asymmetries in their bodies. To check for such problems, Mark Flinn and his graduate student David Leone set up in front of the local school and use calipers to measure students. After the measuring, each child gets a little money to bring home and a lollipop from Dave, the "Poppie Man."
>
> Data gathered on 238 children over the past four field seasons have shown that children who live with a stepfather—a situation often rife with stress—weigh less than others but are surprisingly more symmetrical. There seems to be no relationship, so far, between stress and growth asymmetry in these children.

There may be an underlying lesson here for Dominica's more industrialized neighbors: Although nuclear families are the bedrock of Western societies, they're also prone to rifts and tremors—and children tend to fall through the cracks. In that sense, Harris may be partly right, and her differences with Flinn are partly a function of the different cultures they study. In the United States, families are an infant's first peer group, but children soon grow out of them. Without cousins, grandparents, and other relatives nearby to fill out their lives, they have to find their role models on the playground. In Bwa Mawego, by contrast, families tend to be fluid, amorphous entities, with kin networks extensive enough to guide and support children well past adolescence.

Maryann probably caught her cold from her father, a taxi driver. But with everyone in her family keeping close watch, Flinn knows that she will be fine soon. Money may be scarce here on Bwa Mawego, and health care may not be up to Western standards. But when it comes to avoiding stress, a happy family is a child's greatest asset—greater even than nice friends and billion-dollar view, and a house by the sea in a small slice of paradise.

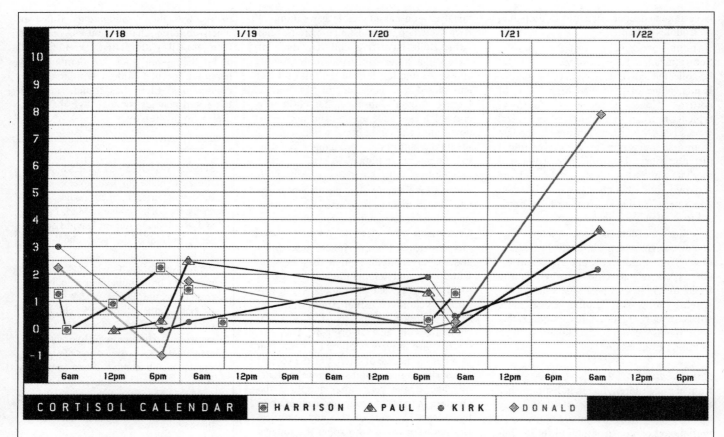

CORTISOL CALENDAR   ◉ HARRISON   ◭ PAUL   ◉ KIRK   ◈ DONALD

THIS WEEK, THE CABOT FAMILY IS A LIVING experiment in the physiology of stress. Their middle child, 6-year-old Harrison, was born with one leg shorter than the other—a handicap so severe that he can't walk to school. Now, after working and saving for many years, Harrison's father, John, is taking him to Shriner's Hospital in Tampa Bay, Florida, for an operation. Afterward, Harrison must undergo four months of intense physical therapy before he and John can return home. Meanwhile, Harrison's mother, Joyce, will have to care for his three brothers, Kirk, Paul, and Donald, as well as the new baby Louise. To see how the family is coping, Mark Flinn measures the boys' cortisol several times a day before and after the departure and talks to them about how they feel. Although the brothers act as if Harrison's trip is no big deal, their cortisol levels (adjusted according to their natural daily fluctuations) tell a different story. In the chart above, the mean cortisol level for the village is zero. Anything above that indicates unusual stress. Over the nine years that he has been following the Cabots, Flinn has found them to be relatively stable, loving, and relaxed—"just a real happy family"—with a mean cortisol level of -0.29. Yet in the week before Harrison's departure their mean level rose to 1.32, and on the morning after Harrison left, 4-year-old Donald's cortisol rose nearly eight standard deviations above the mean. "That's pretty darn dramatic," Flinn says. "You might see that only once every 10,000 cases. Obviously, their brains are kind of working to see how they are going to deal with the new situation,"

—M.F.S.

WHO'S RAISING BABY?

Challenges To Modern-Day Parenting

Anne R. Pierce

Drive through the empty streets of our neighborhoods and ask yourself not merely where the children have gone but where childhood has gone. It is most unlikely you will see such once-familiar scenes as these: a child sitting under a tree with a book, toddlers engaged in collecting leaves and sticks, friends riding bikes or playing tag, parents and their offspring working together in the yard, families (in no hurry to get anywhere) strolling casually along. Today's children are too busy with other things to enjoy the simple pleasures children used to take for granted. Preoccupied with endless "activities" and diversions, they have little time for simply going outside.

Where are the children and what are they doing? They are in day-care centers, now dubbed "learning centers." They are in "early childhood programs" and all-day kindergarten. They are acquiring new skills, attending extra-curricular classes, and participating in organized sports. They are sitting in front of the computer, the TV, and the Play Station. They are not experiencing the comfortable ease of unconditional love, nor the pleasant feeling of familiarity. They are not enjoying a casual conversation, nor are they playing. They are working—at improving their talents, at competing with their peers, at "beating the enemy" in a video game, at just getting by, at adapting to the new baby-sitter or coach, at not missing Mom or Dad. They, like their computers, are "on." Being, for them, is doing, adjusting, coping. Parenting, for us, is providing them with things to do.

Young children expend their energy on long days in group situations, in preschool and after-school programs, in music and athletic lessons. For much-needed relaxation, they collapse in front of the TV or computer, the now-defining features of "homelife." Relaxation no longer signifies quiet or repose. The hyperactive pace of children's television shows and video games, always accompanied by driving music, exacerbates and surpasses the fast pace of modern life. Children stare at the screen, though the inanity, violence, and doomsday sociopolitical messages of the programming are anything but reassuring.

From doing to staring, from staring to doing. There is little room in this scenario for idle contentment, playful creativity, and the passionate pursuit of interests. Alternatives to this framework for living are provided neither in thought nor in deed by busy parents who, themselves, end their rushed days with television and escapism.

Before nursery school starts, most children who can afford it have attended "classes," from gymnastics to ballet, piano, or swimming. Infant "swim lessons," in which an instructor in diving gear repeatedly forces screaming babies underwater so that they are forced to swim, are now commonplace. Day-care centers claim to give toddlers a head start in academic advancement and socialization. Increasing numbers of bright young children spend time with tutors or at the learning center to attain that ever-elusive "edge."

Children in elementary school now "train" and lift weights in preparation for their sports. Football and track are new options for first-graders. A recent trend in elementary athletic programs is to recruit professional coaches, due to the supposed competitive disadvantage of amateur coaching done by parents. It is more common for young children to "double up," participating in two team sports at a time. A constantly increasing selection of stimulating activities lures modern families, making downtime more elusive.

What used to be "time for dinner" (together) is, more often than not, time for family members to rush and scatter in different directions. A typical first-grade soccer team practices two evenings a week, from 6:00 to 7:30. The stress involved in getting six-year-olds fed and in gear by practice time and, after practice, bathed and in bed at an appropriate hour is obvious. And yet, if you attend a first-grade soccer game, you'll likely find parents eager to discover the activities of other people's children and anxious to sign their children up for—whatever it might be. Some parents appear to be jealous of the activities others have discovered.

THE NEW CONFORMISM—AFRAID OF MISSING OUT

In asking scores of parents about the purpose of all this activity, I have never received a clear or, to my mind, satisfactory answer. The end, apparently, is unclear apart from the idea, often expressed, that if one's child starts activities later than other children, he (or she) will be "left behind." Some of the more cohesive explanations I have received are these: A mother described herself as being "swept along by the inevitable"; she didn't want her young daughter to be "the only one missing out." A couple explained their determination to expose their toddler to a wide variety of opportunities so that he would know which sports he excelled in "by the time things get competitive." A father said, simply, that he saw his role in terms of making sure his children were "the best at something," and with all the other kids starting activities at such an early age, this meant that his kids "had to start even earlier."

In effect, this is the "do what everyone else does, only sooner and more intensely" theory of child rearing. This theory creates a constant downward pressure upon children of a younger and younger age. This was evident to me when my youngest son entered kindergarten and I discovered he was within a small minority of boys who had not *already* participated in team sports. Only five years earlier, my oldest son was within the sizable majority of kindergartners whose parents had decided kindergarten was a little too early for such endeavors. (First grade was then the preferred starting point.)

The more families subscribe to this "lifestyle," the more there is another reason for pushing kids off to the races: If no children are around to play with, then, especially for only children, organized activities become their only opportunity to "play" with other kids. Playing is thus thoroughly redefined.

The philosophy of child rearing as a race and of homelife as oppressive for women compels families toward incessant action. Love, nurture, and, concomitantly, innocence have been demoted as compared to experience and exposure. The family is viewed as a closedness to experience, the nurturing role within the family as the most confining of all. Indeed, busyness supplants togetherness in many modern families.

One legacy of Freud, Piaget, Pavlov, and the behaviorists, neodevelopmentalists, and social scientists who followed them has been the decreasing respect for the child's being and the increasing emphasis upon his "becoming." The child is seen as "socializable" and is studied as a clinical object whose observable response to this or that "environmental stimulus" becomes more important than his deeper, more complicated features. With the clinical interpretation of childhood, social engineering projects and "activities" that make the child's world more stimulating gain momentum.

In addition to the advantage that all this activity supposedly gives children, there is also the element of convenience. If parents are too busy to supervise their children, it behooves them to keep the kids so busy and under the auspices of so many (other) adults that they are likely to "stay out of trouble." Such is the basis of many modern choices. Children spend much of their time exhausted by activities, the purposes of which are ill construed.

> *Conformism, convenience, and new interpretations of childhood are, then, contributing factors in the hectic existence and the premature introduction to academics that parents prescribe for their children.*

Conformism, convenience, and new interpretations of childhood are, then, contributing factors in the hectic existence and the premature introduction to academics that parents prescribe for their children. For example, before the 1960s, it was generally believed that placing young children in out-of-home learning programs was harmful. The concern for the harmfulness of such experiences was abandoned when these learning programs became convenient and popular.

EDUCATION AS 'SOCIALIZATION'

In *Miseducation: Preschoolers at Risk*, David Elkind expressed dismay at the fact that age-inappropriate approaches to early education have gained such momentum despite the undeniable evidence that pushing children into formal academics and organized activities before they are ready does more harm than good. He lamented, "In a society that prides itself on its preference for facts over hearsay, on its openness to research, and on its respect for 'expert' opinion, parents, educators, administrators, and legislators are ignoring the facts, the research and the expert opinion about how young children learn and how best to teach them.... When we instruct children in academic subjects, or in swimming, gymnastics, or ballet, at too early an age, we miseducate them; we put them at risk for short-term stress and long-term personality damage for no useful purpose."

Elkind pointed to the consistent result of reputable studies (such as that conducted by Benjamin Bloom) that a love of learning, not the inculcation of skills, is the key to the kind of early childhood development that can lead to great things. These findings, warned Elkind, point to the fallacy of early instruction as a way of producing children who will attain eminence. He noted that with gifted and talented individuals, as with children in general, the most important thing is an excitement about learning: "Miseducation, by focusing on skills to the detriment of motivation, pays an enormous price for teaching infants and young children what amounts to a few tricks."

He further observed that those advocating early instruction in skills and early out-of-home education rely upon youngsters who are very disadvantaged to tout early education's advantages. "Accordingly, the image of the competent child introduced to remedy the understimulation of low-income children now serves as the rationale for the overstimulation of middle-class children."

Dr. Jack Westman of the Rockford Institute, renowned child psychiatrist Dr. Stanley Greenspan, and brain researcher Jane Healy are among the many unheeded others who warn of the implications of forcing the "childhood as a race" approach upon young children. Laments Westman, "The result is what is now referred to as the 'hothousing movement' for infants and toddlers devoted to expediting their development. This is occurring in spite of the evidence that the long-term outcomes of early didactic, authoritarian approaches with younger children relate negatively to intellectual development."

In an interview for Parent and Child *magazine, Dr. Greenspan insisted that young children suffer greatly if there is inadequate "emotional learning" in their daily lives.*

In an interview for *Parent and Child* magazine, Dr. Greenspan insisted that young children suffer greatly if there is inadequate "emotional learning" in their daily lives. Such learning, he explained, is both a requisite for their ability to relate well with others and the foundation of cognitive learning. "Emotional development and interactions form the foundation for all children's learning—especially in the first five years of life. During these years, children abstract from their emotional experiences constantly to learn even the most basic concepts. Take, for example, something like saying hello or learning when you can be aggressive and when you have to be nice—and all of these are cues by emotions."

In *Endangered Minds: Why Children Don't Think and What We Can Do About It*, Healy states the case for allowing young children to play with those who love them before requiring them to learn academic skills. She intones, "Driving the cold spikes of inappropriate pressure into the malleable heart of a child's learning may seriously distort the unfolding of both intellect and motivation. This self-serving intellectual assault, increasingly condemned by teachers who see its warped products, reflects a more general ignorance of the growing brain.... Explaining things to children won't do the job; they must have the chance to experience, wonder, experiment, and act it out for themselves. It is this process, throughout life, that enables the growth of intelligence."

Healy goes so far as to describe the damaging effect on the "functional organization of the plastic brain" in pushing too hard too soon: "Before brain regions are myelinated, they do not operate efficiently. For this reason, trying to 'make' children master academic skills for which they do not have the requisite maturation may re-

sult in mixed-up patterns of learning.... It is possible to force skills by intensive instruction, but this may cause a child to use immature, inappropriate neural networks and distort the natural growth process."

Play is a way for children to relish childhood, prepare for adulthood, and discover their inner passions.

Play is important for intellectual growth, the exploration of individuality, and the growth of a conscience. Play is a way for children to relish childhood, prepare for adulthood, and discover their inner passions. Legendary psychoanalyst D.W. Winnicott warned us not to underestimate the importance of play. In *The Work and Play of Winnicott*, Simon A. Grolnick elucidates Winnicott's concept of play.

> Play in childhood and throughout the life cycle helps to relieve the tension of living, helps to prepare for the serious, and sometimes for the deadly (e.g., war games), helps define and redefine the boundaries between ourselves and others, helps give us a fuller sense of our own personal and bodily being. Playing provides a trying-out ground for proceeding onward, and it enhances drive satisfaction.... Winnicott repeatedly stressed that when playing becomes too drive-infested and excited, it loses its creative growth-building capability and begins to move toward loss of control or a fetishistic rigidity.... Civilization's demands for controlled, socialized behavior gradually, and sometimes insidiously, supersedes the psychosomatic and aesthetic pleasures of open system play.

When we discard playtime, we jeopardize the child's fresh, creative approach to the world. The minuscule amount of peace that children are permitted means that thinking and introspection are demoted as well. Thought requires being, not always doing. Children who are not allowed to retreat once in a while into themselves are not allowed to find out what is there. Our busy lives become ways of hiding from the recesses of the mind. Teaching children to be tough and prepared for the world, making them into achieving doers instead of capable thinkers, has its consequences. Children's innate curiosity is intense. When that natural curiosity has no room to fulfill itself, it burns out like a smothered flame.

In an age when "socialization" into society's ideals and mores is accepted even for babies and toddlers, we should remember that institutionalized schooling even for older children is a relatively new phenomenon. Mass education was a post-Industrial Revolution invention, one that served the dual purposes of preparing children for work and freeing parents to contribute fully to the industrial structure. No longer was work something that families did together, as a unit.

The separation of children from the family's work paved the way for schools and social reformers to assume the task of preparing children for life. This is a lofty role. As parents, we need to inform ourselves as to what our children are being prepared *for* and *how* they are being prepared.

Although our children's days are filled with instruction, allowing them little time of their own, we seem frequently inattentive as to just what they are learning. As William Bennett, Allan Bloom, and others have pointed out, recent years have been characterized by the reformulation of our schools, universities, and information sources according to a relativist, left-leaning ideology saturated with cynicism. This ideology leaves students with little moral-intellectual ground to stand on, as they are taught disrespect not only for past ideas and literary works but for the American political system and Judeo-Christian ethics. Such works as *The Five Little Peppers and How They Grew* and *Little Women* are windows into the soul of a much less cynical (and much less hectic) time.

Teaching children about the great thinkers, writers, and statesmen of the past is neglected as the very idea of greatness and heroism is disputed. Thus, the respect for greatness that might have caused children to glance upward from their TV show or activity and the stories about their country's early history that might have given them respect for a time when computer games didn't exist are not a factor in their lives. The word *preoccupied* acquires new significance, for children's minds are stuffed with the here and now.

THE DEVALUATION OF HOMELIFE

The busyness of modern child rearing and the myopia of the modern outlook reinforce each other. The very ideas that education is a race and that preschool-age children's participation in beneficial experience is more important than playing or being with the family are modern ones that continually reinforce themselves for lack of alternatives. Our busy lives leave insufficient time to question whether all this busyness is necessary and whether the content of our childrens' education is good.

The possibility that children might regard their activities less than fondly when they are older because these activities were forced upon them is not addressed. The possibility that they may never find their own passionate interests is not considered. (I came across an interesting television show that discussed the problem middle-school coaches are having with burned-out and unenthusiastic participants in a wide range of sports. The coaches attributed this to the fact that children had already been doing these sports for years and were tired of the pressure.)

One needs time to be a thinker, freedom to be creative, and some level of choice to be enthusiastic. Families can bestow upon children opportunities for autonomy while at the same time giving them a stable base to fall back upon and moral and behavioral guidelines. Having a competitive edge is neither as important nor as lasting as the ability to lead a genuine, intelligently thought-out, and considerate life.

Some of the best learning experiences happen not in an institution, not with a teacher, but in a child's independent "research" of the world at hand.

Some of the best learning experiences happen not in an institution, not with a teacher, but in a child's independent "research" of the world at hand. As the child interprets the world around her, creates new things with the materials available to her, and extracts new ideas from the recesses of her mind, she is learning to be an active, contributing participant in the world. She occupies her physical, temporal, and intellectual space in a positive, resourceful way. Conversely, if she is constantly stuffed with edifying "opportunities," resentment and lack of autonomy are the likely results.

In *The Erosion of Childhood*, Valerie Polakow insists upon the child's ability to "make history" as opposed to simply receiving it. Lamenting the overinstitutionalization of children in day care and school, she warns, "Children as young as a year old now enter childhood institutions to be formally schooled in the ways of the social system and emerge eighteen years later to enter the world of adulthood having been deprived of their own history-making power, their ability to act upon the world in significant and meaningful ways." She adds, "The world in which children live—the institutional world that babies, toddlers and the very young have increasingly come to inhabit and confront—is a world in which they become the objects, not the subjects of history, a world in which history is being made of them."

Day care provides both too much stimulation of the chaotic, disorganized kind, which comes inevitably from the cohabitation of large numbers of babies and toddlers, and too much of the organized kind that comes, of necessity, from group-centered living. It provides too little calm, quiet, space, or comfort and too little opportunity to converse and relate to a loving other.

Imagine, for example, a parent sitting down with her child for a "tea party." As she pours real tea into her own cup and milk into her child's, the "how to do things" is taken seriously. The child is encouraged to say "thank you" and to offer cookies to his mother, and their chat begins. Although they are pretending to be two adults, the ritual is real; it occurs in a real home setting; it provides the child with real food and a real opportunity for "mature" conversation. The mother says, "I'm so glad to be here for tea. How have you been?" The child, enjoying the chance to play the part of his mother's host, answers, "Fine! Would you like another cookie?" "Oh yes, thank you," answers his mother. "These cookies are delicious!" The child is learning about civilized behavior.

Children living in the new millennium need a refuge from the impersonal, the mechanical, and the programmed. We must provide them with more than opportunities for skill learning, socialization, and competition.

Then, picture the toy tea set at the learning center. Two children decide "to have tea." They fight over who has asked whom over. When one child asks, "How have you been?" the other loses interest and walks away. Too much of this peer-centered learning and not enough of adult-based learning clearly has negative implications for social development. The child simply cannot learn right from wrong, proper from improper, from other children who themselves have trouble making these distinctions.

Homelife that provides a break from group action has innumerable advantages for older children as well. Think of the different learning experiences a child receives from sitting down at the dinner table with his family and from gulping down a hamburger on the way to a nighttime game. In one case, the child has the opportunity to learn about manners and conversation. In the other, he is given another opportunity to compete with peers. (This is not to deny the benefits of being part of a team but simply to state that homelife itself is beneficial.) I hear many parents of high-school students complain about the compet-

itive, selfish manner of today's students. And, yet, most of these students have not a moment in their day that is not competitive.

How can we expect children to value kindness and co-operation when their free time has been totally usurped by activities wherein winning is everything? At home, winning is not everything (unless the child expends all his time trying to "beat the enemy" in a video game). At home, a child is much more likely to be reprimanded for not compromising with his siblings than for not "defeating" them. If homelife provides children with time to define their individuality and interact with family members (and all the give-and-take implied), then it is certainly an invaluable aspect of a child's advancement.

Children living in the new millennium need a refuge from the impersonal, the mechanical, and the pro-grammed. We must provide them with more than oppor-tunities for skill learning, socialization, and competition. Otherwise, something will be missing in their human-ness. For to be human is to have the capacity for intimate attachments based upon love (which can grow more inti-mate because of the closeness that family life provides); it is to reason and to have a moral sense of things; it is to be capable of a spontaneity that stems from original thought or from some passion within.

We must set our children free from our frenetic, goal-oriented pace. We must create for them a private realm wherein no child-rearing "professional" can tread. Within this secure space, the possibilities are endless. With this stable base to fall back upon, children will dare to dream, think, and explore. They will compete, learn, and socialize as the blossoming individuals that they are, not as automatons engineered for results.

Anne R. Pierce is an author and political philosopher who lives in Cincinnati with her husband and three children. As a writer, she finds that bringing up children in the modern world gives her much food for thought.

Father Nature:
The Making of a Modern Dad

It takes a lot more than testosterone to make a father out of a man.
New research shows that hormonal changes in both sexes help shape men
into devoted dads. If testosterone is the defining hormone of masculinity,
it's time to redefine manhood.

By Douglas Carlton Abrams

"One of my first memories growing up was wishing that my father would be home more," recalls Andrew Hudnut, M.D., a family doctor in Sacramento, California. "I was 8, and we had just returned from a canoe trip. I remember thinking, 'I don't want a bigger house or more money. I just want my dad around.'"

When his wife gave birth, Hudnut arranged his practice so he could be home to take care of his son, Seamus, two days a week; he sees patients on the other three workdays. "It was a very natural transition," he reports. "I'm grateful to have the opportunity my father never had."

Part of a new generation of men who are redefining fatherhood and masculinity, Hudnut, who is 33, is unwilling to accept the role of absentee provider that his father's generation assumed. With mothers often being the breadwinners of the family, many young fathers are deciding that a man's place can also be in the home—part-time or even full-time.

According to census figures, one in four dads takes care of his preschooler during the time the mother is working. The number of children who are raised by a primary-care father is now more than 2 million and counting. By all measures, fathers, even those who work full-time, are more involved in their children's lives than ever before. According to the Families and Work Institute in New York City, fathers now provide three-fourths of the child care mothers do, up from one-half 30 years ago.

Is Father Nurture Natural?

Many men and women wonder if all of this father care is really natural. According to popular perceptions, men are supposedly driven by their hormones (primarily testosterone) to compete for status, to seek out sex and even to be violent—conditions hardly conducive to raising kids. A recent article in *Reader's Digest,* "Why Men Act As They Do," is subtitled "It's the Testosterone, Stupid." Calling the hormone "a metaphor for masculinity," the article concludes, "…testosterone correlates with risk—physical, criminal, personal." Don't men's testosterone-induced chest-beating and risk-taking limit their ability to cradle and comfort their children?

Two new Canadian studies suggest that there is much more to masculinity than testosterone. While testosterone is certainly important in driving men to conceive a child, it takes an array of other hormones to turn men into fathers. And among the best fathers, it turns out, testosterone levels actually drop significantly after the birth of a child. If manhood includes fatherhood, which it does for a majority of men, then testosterone is hardly the ultimate measure of masculinity.

In fact, the second of the two studies, which was recently published in the *Mayo Clinic Proceedings,* suggests that fathers have higher levels of estrogen—the well-known female sex hormone—than other men. The research shows that men go through significant hormonal changes alongside their pregnant partners, changes most likely initiated

The Daddy Dividend

Beyond birth and infancy, researchers are finding, a father's presence makes a big difference in a child's long-term development. Ross Parke, Ph.D., a psychologist at the University of California at Riverside, explains that children of involved fathers regulate their own emotions better.

They also have better social skills than children whose fathers are not involved in their lives and have better success in school. "It is clear that fathers affect their children's social, cognitive and emotional development," he says.

A father's influence seems to come, at least in part, through the unique ways that fathers play and interact with their children, says Kyle Pruett, M.D., a child psychiatrist at Yale. "Fathers are more likely to encourage their kids to tolerate frustration and master tasks on their own before they offer help," he explains, "whereas mothers tend to assist a fussing child earlier."

More than any particular social or cognitive skill, however, a father's love and affection may be the most significant gift he can give his children, says Ronald Rohner, Ph.D., a psychologist-anthropologist at the University of Connecticut, who for the past 40 years has been studying the effects of father love on children's development. "A father's love is often a significant buffer against depression, conduct problems and substance abuse," he finds.

"Children who experience their father's love are often more emotionally stable, less angry, have better self-esteem and have a more positive worldview," Rohner says. To his surprise, he discovered that "father love is often as influential as mother love on a child's happiness and sense of well-being." Rohner and his colleagues reviewed 100 U.S. and European studies; their results can be found in the *Review of General Psychology*.

Although researchers are just beginning to study the children of involved fathers, there is a mountain of research on the children of absent fathers. Those children are at a higher risk for school failure and dropout, drug use, teen pregnancy, delinquency and teen suicide. Fathers clearly play an important role in the psychological and social survival of their kids. —D. A.

by their partner's pregnancy and ones that even cause some men to experience pregnancylike symptoms such as nausea and weight gain. It seems increasingly clear that just as nature prepares women to be committed moms, it prepares men to be devoted dads.

"I have always suspected that fatherhood has biological effects in some, perhaps all, men," says biologist Sue Carter, Ph.D., distinguished professor at the University of Maryland. "Now here is the first hard evidence that men are biologically prepared for fatherhood."

The new studies have the potential to profoundly change our understanding of families, of fatherhood and of masculinity itself. Being a devoted parent is not only important but also natural for men. Indeed, there is evidence that men are biologically involved in their children's lives from the beginning.

Is Biology Destiny for Dads?

It's well known that hormonal changes caused by pregnancy encourage a mother to love and nurture her child. But it has long been assumed that a father's attachment to his child is the result of a more uncertain process, a purely optional emotional bonding that develops over time, often years.

Male animals in some species undergo hormonal changes that prime them for parenting. But do human dads? The two studies, conducted at Memorial University and Queens University in Canada, suggest that human dads do.

In the original study published last year in *Evolution and Human Behavior*, psychologist Anne Storey, Ph.D., and her colleagues took blood samples from 34 couples at different times during pregnancy and shortly after birth. The researchers chose to monitor three specific hormones because of their links to nurturing behavior in human mothers and in animal fathers.

The first hormone, prolactin, gets its name from the role it plays in promoting lactation in women, but it also instigates parental behavior in a number of birds and mammals. Male doves who are given prolactin start brooding and feeding their young. Storey found that in human fathers, prolactin levels rise by approximately 20 percent during the three weeks before their partners give birth.

"THIS IS THE FIRST EVIDENCE THAT MEN ARE BIOLOGICALLY PREPARED FOR FATHERHOOD."

The second hormone, cortisol, is well known as a stress hormone, but it is also a good indicator of a mother's attachment to her baby. New mothers who have high cortisol levels can detect their own infant by odor more easily than mothers with lower cortisol levels. The mothers also respond more sympathetically to their baby's cries and describe their relationship with their baby in more positive terms. Storey and her colleagues found that for expectant fathers, cortisol was twice as high in the three weeks before birth than earlier in the pregnancy.

Biologist Katherine Wynne-Edwards, Ph.D., who conducted the research with Storey explains that while cortisol is seen as the "fight or flight" hormone, it might more accurately be described as the "heads-up-eyes-forward-something-really-important-is-happening" hormone. It may help prepare parents for approaching birth. Cortisol levels normally increase in women as pregnancy advances; indeed, a cumulative rise in stress-hormone levels sets off labor and delivery.

The third hormone, testosterone, is abundant in male animals during mating but decreases during nurturing. If bird fathers are given testosterone, they spend more time defending their territory and mating than taking care of exist-

Hormones vs. Culture By Michael Lamb, Ph.D.

The view that fathers are reluctant caregivers may be a thing of the past. New findings show that hormonal changes of parenting are not limited to mothers. The reason we haven't discovered the hormonal changes in human fathers before now lies in a combination of scientific progress and cultural change.

Early studies on rats found that males could learn to become involved fathers after prolonged exposure to their pups but did not experience any hormonal changes. The fact that these reluctant dads could learn to nurture led to the so-called bonding hypothesis. It claimed that fathers, including human fathers, could *learn* to become competent caregivers.

But changes in mothers' work roles have forced a redefinition of fathers' nurturing roles. When I began studying families in the mid-1970s, half the fathers had never changed a diaper. Now, most dads do diaper duty. A father's role is increasingly multifaceted. He is, ideally, a breadwinner, a coach, a moral guide, a source of love and inspiration.

Here's the shocking news: In 90 percent of birds and the majority of fish, fathers care for the young. Mammals are the only major group of vertebrates in which mothers are more involved. Among mammals, 90 percent of fathers take off after conception or birth. But the offspring usually are either self-sufficient from the start or can survive with the sole care of the mother.

So why should human dads stick around and burp a baby? It turns out there's a big evolutionary advantage for the kids who get coddled.

Father care seems to boost the chances of survival significantly for human babies. Born helpless and dependent, babies demand an enormous amount of care. Having two parents to provide food and protection increases the odds an infant will function well and make it to adulthood.

Most children today survive physically, whether or not they have an involved father. But this may not have always been the case. In hunter-gatherer cultures the presence of a father counted heavily.

Even in advanced industrial societies, where food and physical survival are rarely the issue, social survival still is. Children who grow up without their fathers are at greater risk for everything from school failure to teen suicide (see "The Daddy Dividend").

So why, if fathers have a hormonal connection to their children, aren't all fathers more involved dads? "There are cultural scripts that have precluded fathers from being involved," observes Jay Belsky, Ph.D., a psychologist at the University of London. "A generation ago fathers weren't allowed into birthing rooms and didn't change diapers. When social norms work against father involvement, hormones may have less of an effect on their actual behavior." Men have moderate to high contact with infants in only 40 percent of cultures, according to an international survey.

In other words, humans aren't held in hormonal thrall—research suggests that hormones simply facilitate a transition into fatherhood. The definition of that fatherhood will no doubt depend on culture.

Michael Lamb, Ph.D., is at the National Institute of Child Health and Human Development.

---

ing offspring. Research has shown that human males experience a surge in testosterone when they win sporting events and other competitions.

> "MY BEST GUESS IS THAT WOMEN'S HORMONE LEVELS ARE TIMED TO THE BIRTH—AND MEN'S HORMONE LEVELS ARE TIED TO THEIR PARTNERS"

In Storey's study, testosterone levels plunged 33 percent in fathers during the first three weeks after birth. Levels then returned to normal by the time the babies were four to seven weeks old. However brief the dip in testosterone, it may have effects that endure for the life of the child. According to University of California at Riverside psychologist Ross Parke, Ph.D., it may "let the nurturing side of men come to center stage." The dip may set in motion the more-cooperative, less-competitive enterprise of parenting. By encouraging fathers to interact with their kids, the brief hormonal change might actually induce the bonding process.

Estrogen and the Daddy Brain

Wynne-Edwards and graduate student Sandra Berg designed another, just-published study to test Storey and Wynne-Edwards' earlier findings. They measured the hormone levels of the fathers over a longer period of time and incorporated into the study a control group of men who had never had children. The control group was matched by age, season and time of day tested—all of which can affect hormone levels. Finally, by using saliva samples instead of blood draws, they were able to test the fathers and the men in the control group much more frequently.

In addition to confirming the earlier findings for testosterone reduction and cortisol change the researchers also found that the fathers had elevated levels of estrogen. The increase started 30 days before birth and continued during all 12 weeks of testing after birth. Although estrogen is best known as a female sex hormone, it exists in small quantities in men, too. Animal studies show that estrogen can induce nurturing behavior in males.

Acting in the brain as well as in other parts of the body, estrogen in men, and testosterone in women, makes humans extremely versatile behaviorally. "We spend an awful lot of time looking for differences between the sexes and trumpeting them when we find them," observes Wynne-Edwards, "but our brains are remarkably similar, but from the same DNA."

In fact, going into the study, Wynne-Edwards predicted that the "daddy brain" would use the same nerve circuits, triggered by many of the same hormones, as the "mommy brain." "If Mother Nature wanted to turn on parental behavior in a male," she reasoned, "the easiest thing would be to turn on pathways already there for maternal behavior."

The studies also found that a father's hormonal changes closely paralleled those of his pregnant partner.

The Intimacy Effect

The researchers believe that intimate contact and communication between partners may induce the hormonal changes that encourage a father to nurture his children, Storey explains. "My best guess is that women's hormone levels are timed to the birth—and men's hormone levels are tied to their partners."

Exactly how this occurs is unknown. There may be actual physiological signals exchanged between partners in close contact, such as the transmission of pheromones. Similar to odors, pheromones are volatile chemical substances that animals constantly give off through their skin or sweat but that are undetectable. Pheromones can stimulate specific reactions—especially mating—in other animals. Think of a female dog in heat attracting all those barking male dogs in the neighborhood.

Classic studies show that menstruation is communicated, and synchronized, through pheromones among dorm mates in college. If women in dorms respond to one another's pheromones, then a man and a woman who share intimate space could certainly communicate chemical messages. These pheromones could biologically cue a man that his partner is pregnant and kick off the hormonal changes that prompt him to be a dad in deed as well as in seed. Pregnancy certainly could, in fact, be signaled.

The level of intimacy within a couple seems to be a factor in how a mother's body chemically signals approaching birth to a father. All of the men tested were living with their pregnant partners. Emotional closeness may also generate hormonal changes, although the possibility was not examined in detail. Still, couples reported feeling closer to their partner if they were talking about the baby and sharing details about the pregnancy.

Whether this is the cause or the result of hormonal changes remains unknown for now. But the intimacy effect and the subsequent hormonal shifts may also be the reason many men experience pregnancylike symptoms.

Honey, We're Pregnant

When he is not taking care of Seamus, Hudnut treats both men and women in his practice. He recalls several patients who came to him complaining of such typical pregnancy symptoms as weight gain and nausea—all of whom were men. He remembers one second-time father who knew that his wife was pregnant even before she told him: He started having morning sickness, just as he had during her first pregnancy.

Pregnancy symptoms in men are actually more common than most people believe. Two studies found that approximately 90 percent of men experience at least one pregnancy related symptom, sometimes severe enough to prompt an expectant father to seek medical help.

According to a study reported in *Annals of Internal Medicine,* more than 20 percent of men with pregnant wives sought care for symptoms related to pregnancy "that could not otherwise be objectively explained." Unfortunately, like pregnancy symptoms in women, there is little that can be done to make the symptoms go away—except wait.

"PREGNANCY SYMPTOMS IN MEN ARE GENERALLY DISMISSED AS BEING ALL IN THE FATHER-TO-BE'S HEAD, NOW IT SEEMS THEY MAY ALSO BE IN HIS HORMONES"

Pregnancy symptoms in men, however well documented, are generally dismissed as being all in the father-to-be's head. Now it seems they may also be in his hormones. Storey and her colleagues found that the men who experienced more pregnancy symptoms actually had higher levels of prolactin. They also had a greater reduction in testosterone after exposure to sounds of crying and other "infant cues" that simulated the experience of being with an actual baby.

For men who feel nauseated or gain weight, no one yet knows for sure whether the changes in hormones are to blame. Surging hormones, however, have long been blamed for women's morning sickness and other pregnancy side effects. The fact that men also experience hormone changes suggests it is more than empathy that causes many of them to feel their partner's pain.

Changed by a Child

While it now seems a father may accompany his wife on her hormonal roller coaster during pregnancy, interacting with the baby may keep his hormones spinning even after the birth.

It's no secret that hormone levels can change in response to behavior. Sex, sports and work success can all send testosterone production spiraling upward. Might not nurturing a child—or conversely, the sight, sound and smell of a newborn—also change fathers' levels of testosterone?

In the original study, the researchers asked couples to hold dolls that had been wrapped in receiving blankets worn by a newborn within the preceding 24 hours. (After their wives gave birth, fathers held their actual baby.) They listened to a six-minute tape of a real newborn crying and then watched a video of a baby struggling to breast feed. The investigators took blood from the men and women before the test and 30 minutes later.

What they found is startling. Men who expressed the greatest desire to comfort the crying baby had the highest prolactin levels and the greatest reduction in testosterone. And testosterone levels plummeted in those men who held the doll for the full half-hour.

Even though scientists have long observed changes in animal and human behavior as a result of shifting hormone levels, they do not yet understand exactly how hormones accomplish such changes. The hormone-behavior link remains one of the great mysteries of the brain. Perhaps hormones stimulate more neuron connections in the part of the brain responsible for nurturing. Or perhaps hormones encourage neurons in nurturing pathways to fire more quickly.

Wynne-Edwards thinks hormones might turn a two-lane pathway in the father's brain into a four-lane superhighway. A neural road expansion might make fathers better able to recognize the smell or sound of their baby. It might even act on smell receptors in the nose to mitigate the smell of a baby's dirty diaper. Countless are the ways in which hormones could influence a father's brain to be more responsive to his baby.

Home on the Range
Although testosterone may be the "primary" male sex hormone, the new research makes it clear that other hormones are also significant, especially during the transition into fatherhood. Wynne-Edwards believes the new research is "a validation of the experiences that many men know they have had. It also goes a long way to bumping testosterone off its pedestal as the only hormone that is important to men."

Parke believes that the research suggests something even more radical: "Men are much more androgynous than we think. We have the capability to be aggressive and nurturing. The traditional view of men as predominantly aggressive really sells men short and denies their capability to experience the range of human emotions."

The new research suggests that a man's hormones may play an important role in helping him experience this full range of emotions, especially in becoming a loving and devoted dad. In fact, it offers the first evidence that to nurture is part of a man's nature.

Douglas Carlton Abrams writes frequently on men, sexuality and parenting. He has recently completed Touching the Moon: A Boy, His Father, and the Discovery of Wonder, *a manuscript about his experiences as a primary care parent.*

What about Black Fathers?

By placing so much emphasis on marriage, public policy could set back efforts to bring unmarried fathers into more constructive contact with their children.

BY RONALD B. MINCY

Emboldened by the reduction in the welfare rolls, conservatives have renewed their demands that our welfare system reflect traditional family values, specifically marriage. But if marriage becomes the heavily favored family strategy of welfare policy, family-service providers and other supporters of responsible fatherhood will find it harder to help families as they actually exist—families that are not always headed by married couples.

President Bush, an outspoken supporter of strong marriages, has responded to this conservative social agenda with several policy initiatives. First, the administration's new welfare-reform proposal adds a few key words to the fourth goal of the 1996 welfare-reform act: "to encourage the formation and maintenance of healthy two-parent *married* families and responsible fatherhood [emphasis added]." Next, it dedicates $300 million in federal funds to support marriage-promotion efforts. Then, the plan encourages states to provide (pared-down) child support and commits the federal government to share in the costs.

This proposal may soften the opposition from some women's groups to the marriage emphasis. However, the plan only pays lip service to responsible fatherhood and provides no dedicated federal funds to support such efforts. Thus, responsible-fatherhood groups will have to rely exclusively upon Temporary Assistance for Needy Families or other state funds, for which there are many competing priorities.

Anticipating this new political and policy climate, several fatherhood groups that work in predominantly black communities are preparing to expand services to include marriage. The most important and innovative groups include the Center for Fathers, Families and Workforce Development (CFWD), the National Center for Strategic Nonprofit Planning and Community Leadership (NPCL), and the Institute for Responsible Fatherhood and Family Revitalization (IRFFR).

CFWD is a community-based responsible-fatherhood program that also provides job placement and wage- and career-growth services to disadvantaged fathers in Baltimore. The goal is to encourage fathers, whether married or not, to become more involved in their children's lives, both emotionally and financially, and to develop a better relationship with the child's mother. NPCL is a national intermediary organization that has trained more than 2,500 community-based practitioners and agencies that sponsor them. It works, through federally funded demonstration projects, to combine child-support enforcement and workforce-development efforts in support of fragile families, so that fathers have both the means and the commitment to contribute to the support of their children. The organization's recent international conference brought together more than 1,200 responsible fatherhood practitioners from the United States and around the globe. Both organizations are now developing marriage curricula. IRFFR, founded in the 1980s, is perhaps the oldest community-based responsible-fatherhood program in the country. These groups, and others with roots in the black community, did not need to be persuaded by the current political climate that marriage was vital to rebuilding strong black families.

Some observers may accuse them of opportunism or of selling out to the conservative agenda. However, few of these groups opposed marriage in principle, though they did object when the early rhetoric made marriage seem like a panacea—and when proposals began to surface to make marriage a condition of services or bonus payments. The rhetoric has now become more reasonable. The Bush administration intends to promote "healthy, stable, and happy marriages" and will target its marriage-promotion efforts at couples who choose to receive such services. Like most Americans, black fatherhood groups support this and wish that all the unwed parents who come to them for help were in a position to benefit from such services. As Andrew Billingsley points out in his book *Climbing Jacob's Ladder*, blacks generally have strong family values; however, they often struggle under difficult conditions that make it tough to act on those values. For this reason, Billingsley argues, black communities have had more diverse and complex family systems than whites for as long as blacks have been in this country.

UNMARRIED BUT NOT UNINVOLVED

Fatherhood groups who work in low-income black communities see this diversity and complexity every day. They also know that many young unwed parents, especially fathers, simply are unprepared to assume the responsibilities that would produce the kind of marriages that increase child well-being. For this reason, these groups have expanded their services to help fathers make positive contributions to their children, even while unmarried, and to position themselves to assume the responsibilities that would make it possible for them to one day sustain happy marriages. The new services focus on job retention, wage and career growth, and job placement. Besides employment services, groups are providing legal, educational, team-parenting, substance-abuse, child-support, health, mental-health, spouse-abuse, and other services to meet the needs of clients and their families. They are also improving their capacity to measure program outcomes and diversifying their staff or strengthening existing staff, in hopes that welfare reauthorization would provide additional resources to improve their work with fathers and families. These efforts are consistent with the 1996 goal of encouraging the formation and maintenance of two-parent families.

B UT NOW THE BUSH ADMINISTRATION HAS RAISED THE standard to emphasize marriage per se. And responsible-fatherhood groups that seek to promote marriage in predominantly black communities will find it hard to achieve this higher standard for several reasons. First, there are demographic realities. The percentage of black women of childbearing age (say, 15 to 44 years old) who have never married (41 percent) is just about double the percentage of comparable white women. Second, although cohabitation and unwed births have been rising while marriage has been declining among all race and ethnic groups, these trends are far from convergent for whites, blacks, and other groups.

For example, unwed births are more common among cohabiting Puerto Rican women than among black or non-Hispanic white women. However, an unwed first birth hastens the transition to marriage among non-Hispanic white cohabiting women, has no effect on the transition to marriage among black cohabiting women, and reduces the prospects of marriage among Puerto Rican cohabiting women.

Given these apparent differences in family formation by race and ethnicity, our research team at Columbia University and Princeton University has been using data from a new birth cohort survey to study the likely effects of the administration's approach on black and nonblack children and families. We assume that marriage is the best option even for the children of unwed parents, if only because marriages tend to last longer than cohabiting relationships. However, we also acknowledge the diversity of family systems. In particular, we acknowledge that in black communities (both here and abroad), father-child contact often occurs through nonresidential, visiting relationships between unwed parents, which are less stable than cohabiting relationships. This means that, unlike traditional models of family formation, unwed parents have four options to choose from: no father-child contact, some father-child contact, cohabitation, and marriage. Moreover, it turns out that Billingsley's metaphor powerfully predicts what could happen if the Bush administration's marriage initiatives could be used flexibly to strengthen families, because these options resemble a ladder leading to more intense and enduring forms of father-child contact.

That is, policies often have unintended effects. Thus, the responses of some unwed parents to policies that promote marriage may fall short of the administration's ideal but still result in more intense and enduring forms of father-child contact than would have occurred otherwise. For example, throughout the past two decades, the fraction of low-skilled men who are either working or looking for work has shrunk, despite strong economic growth interrupted by brief recessions. If welfare programs were able to help these men find jobs, some fathers who are not now in regular contact with their children might begin to be. Other fathers who now visit their children might live with them. And still other fathers who are living with their children (and their children's mother) would be married. Moreover, such a policy might have large effects on family formation and father-child contact for black unwed parents and, to a lesser extent, for nonblack unwed parents. Other policies might have the same effects on family formation and father-child contact for black and nonblack unwed parents.

STRENGTHENING FAMILIES AS THEY EXIST

Our study shows that fathers' employment benefits black and nonblack children, no matter where their parents begin on the ladder to more intense and enduring forms of father-child contact. Compared with children whose fathers did not work, children with working fathers were more likely to have some contact with their fathers, more likely to live with their fathers (and mothers in cohabiting relationships), and more likely to live with their fathers in a traditional married family. Having children with one partner rather than multiple partners also increases the odds of maintaining relationships with children, all the way up the ladder, in black and nonblack families alike. However, a mother's work history prior to giving birth increases the odds of cohabitation and marriage among black unwed parents but has no statistically significant effect on the odds of moving up the ladder for nonblacks. Thus, by providing employment services (for men as well as women) and an emphasis on preventing out-of-wedlock births, welfare policy could increase marriage and other forms of father-child contact for blacks and increase (or leave unchanged) the same outcomes for nonblacks.

Other policies would affect these groups or outcomes differently. Higher cash benefits increase the odds that black and nonblack fragile families have some father-child contact and the odds that they cohabit, but have no effect on the odds that they marry. By contrast, more effective child-support enforcement increases the odds of marriage among nonblacks but reduces the odds of father-child contact, without affecting the odds of marriage among blacks.

UNFORTUNATELY, THESE PROMISING POLICY INSTRUMENTS have been sidelined in the current debate. Instead, the administration is placing its entire emphasis on promoting marriage. Our research suggests such efforts would produce mixed results. They might encourage some unwed mothers to marry. We find, for example, that nonblack unwed mothers with some religious affiliation are more likely to marry the fathers of their children than those without a religious affiliation. Black unwed mothers affiliated with faith communities that hold conservative views on family issues are more likely to marry the fathers of their children than are black unwed mothers with no religious affiliation.

However, great caution is required before black communities would embrace such approaches—because the approaches are likely to celebrate the virtues of marriage while stigmatizing unwed births, something blacks traditionally have not done because of historical experience. Although rates have risen in recent decades, single motherhood has been much more common among black families for more than 100 years. The reasons for this are complex. Some black women became single mothers because they (and the fathers of their children) violated social and religious prohibitions against nonmarital sex. Others became single mothers because they were raped or their husbands were lynched. Still others became single mothers because their husbands migrated north in search of employment but never returned after job discrimination dashed their hopes.

Often in the painful history of race relations in this country, desertion and victimization were as likely the causes of single motherhood as was moral failure. In any individual case, who could know? Who would ask? In response, the black community developed a tradition of embracing all of its children, even the fair-skinned ones. Under these circumstances, stigmatizing unwed births was impossible. Fortunately, in many respects the circumstances have changed.

THERE IS MOUNTING EVIDENCE THAT CHILDREN ARE BETTER off if they grow up in healthy, married-couple families. This poses a unique challenge for the black community, because the substantial retreat from marriage in the black community has created extraordinarily high rates of childbearing and child rearing among unwed blacks. Marriage proponents would be wise to let this evidence prick the conscience of the nation with this question: How did we allow childbirth and child rearing to divorce themselves from marriage? The diverse race and ethnic groups that now constitute America will have different answers—and different strategies for creating or re-creating the most supportive family arrangements for children.

As they wrestle with this question, each group will be forced to reflect on its past and its future and to develop responses. If the issue is forced by heavily subsidizing marriage, the response that is easiest for whites but hardest for blacks will only provide a common threat against which blacks will rally. This will only distract them from the kind of private, searching dialogue the black community needs to reach into its own soul and find what is best for all its children, those whose parents marry and those whose parents do not.

RONALD B. MINCY *is the Maurice V. Russell Professor of Social Policy and Social Work Practice at Columbia University.*

Unmarried, With Children

Today's single mothers may be divorced or never-wed, rich or poor, living with men or on their own. But with traditional households in decline, they're the new faces of America's family album.

BY BARBARA KANTROWITZ AND PAT WINGERT

JUST IMAGINE WHAT WOULD HAPPEN IF JUNE AND WARD Cleaver were negotiating family life these days. The scenario might go something like this: they meet at the office (she's in marketing; he's in sales) and move in together after dating for a couple of months. A year later June gets pregnant. What to do? Neither feels quite ready to make it legal and there's no pressure from their parents, all of whom are divorced and remarried themselves. So little Wally is welcomed into the world with June's last name on the birth certificate. A few years later June gets pregnant again with the Beav. Ward's ambivalent about second-time fatherhood and moves out, but June decides to go ahead on her own. In her neighborhood, after all, single motherhood is no big deal; the lesbians down the street adopted kids from South America and the soccer mom next door is divorced with a live-in boyfriend.

Figures released last week from the 2000 Census show that this postmodern June would be almost as mainstream as the 1950s version. The number of families headed by single mothers has increased 25 percent since 1990, to more than 7.5 million households. Contributing to the numbers are a high rate of divorce and out-of-wedlock births. For most of the past decade, about a third of all babies were born to unmarried women, compared with 3.8 percent in 1940. Demographers now predict that more than half of the youngsters born in the 1990s will spend at least part of their childhood in a single-parent home. The number of single fathers raising kids on their own is also up; they now head just over 2 million families. In contrast, married couples raising children—the "Leave It to Beaver" model—account for less than a quarter of all households.

Demographers and politicians will likely spend years arguing about what this all means and whether the shifts are real or just numerical flukes. But one thing everyone does agree on

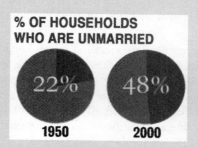

% OF HOUSEHOLDS WHO ARE UNMARRIED

22% 1950   48% 2000

Not Sure Yet It's 'Right'

When they moved in together, Susannah Wolverton, 24, and James Hoefert, 29, had been dating for more than a year. Their daughter, Elizabeth, was born last month. But the Albuquerque, N.M., couple is not quite ready to take the big step into matrimony. "We want to make sure we're doing the right thing," said Wolverton, who also has a 4-year-old daughter, Rachel, from a previous marriage.

is that single mothers are now a permanent and significant page in America's diverse family album. "We can encourage, pressure, preach and give incentives to get people to marry," says Stephanie Coontz, author of "The Way We Never Were" and a family historian at the Evergreen State College in Olympia, Wash. "But we still have to deal with the reality that kids are going to be raised in a variety of ways, and we have to support all kinds of families with kids."

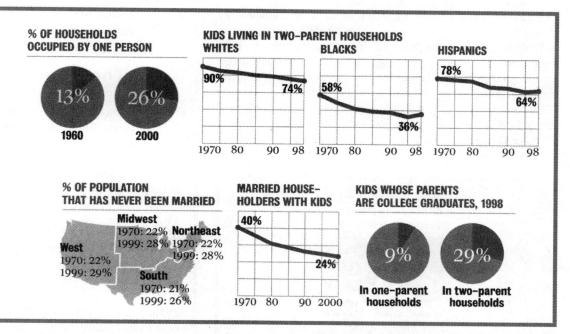

The Census Consensus

Traditional households are waning, but single parents aren't the only reason. Later marriages and births and longer life spans have also contributed.

SOURCES: U.S. CENSUS BUREAU, AMER.ASSOC. FOR SINGLE PEOPLE, AMERISTAT, PUBLIC AGENDA. RESEARCH BY JOSH ULICK AND NEWSWEEK RESEARCH CENTER

% OF HOUSEHOLDS OCCUPIED BY ONE PERSON
13% 1960   26% 2000

KIDS LIVING IN TWO-PARENT HOUSEHOLDS
WHITES: 90% ... 74%
BLACKS: 58% ... 36%
HISPANICS: 78% ... 64%
1970 80 90 98

% OF POPULATION THAT HAS NEVER BEEN MARRIED
Midwest 1970: 22% 1999: 28%
Northeast 1970: 22% 1999: 28%
West 1970: 22% 1999: 29%
South 1970: 21% 1999: 26%

MARRIED HOUSEHOLDERS WITH KIDS
40% ... 24%
1970 80 90 2000

KIDS WHOSE PARENTS ARE COLLEGE GRADUATES, 1998
9% In one-parent households
29% In two-parent households

This new breed of single mother doesn't fit the old stereotype of an unwed teen on welfare. She's still likely to be financially insecure, but she could be any age and any race. The median age for unmarried mothers is the late 20s, and the fastest-growing category is white women. She may be divorced or never-married. Forty percent are living with men who may be the fathers of one or more of their children; as the Census numbers also showed, there's been nearly a 72 percent increase in the number of cohabiting couples, many of whom bring along children from previous relationships. She may also be a single mother by choice. Unwed motherhood has lost much of its stigma and has even been glamorized by celebrity role models like Rosie O'Donnell and Calista Flockhart. "Twenty years ago middle-class women believed it took a man to have a child, but that's no longer true," says Rosanna Hertz, chair of the women's studies department at Wellesley College. "We've reached a watershed moment."

More women are better educated and better able to support themselves—so a husband is no longer a financial prerequisite to motherhood. That's a huge social change from the past few decades. Carolyn Feuer, 30, a registered nurse from New York, decided not to marry her boyfriend when she became pregnant with Ryan, now 6. "It wouldn't have been a good marriage," she says. "It's better for both of us this way, especially my son." Her steady salary meant she had choices. "I had an apartment," she says. "I had a car. I felt there was no reason why I shouldn't have the baby. I felt I could give it whatever it needed as far as love and support and I haven't regretted it for even a minute since."

For many women, the barrier to marriage may be that they care too much about it, not too little, and they want to get it right. If they can't find the perfect soulmate of their dreams, they'd rather stay single. So they're postponing that walk down the aisle until after college, grad school or starting a career and putting a little money in the bank. "Paradoxically, more people today value marriage," says Frank Furstenberg, professor of so-

ciology at the University of Pennsylvania. "They take it seriously. That's why they're more likely to cohabit. They want to be sure before they take the ultimate step." The average age of first marriage is now 25 for women and 27 for men—up from 20 and 23 in 1960. That's the highest ever, which leaves plenty of time for a live-in relationship to test a potential partner's compatibility. "Today it's unusual if you don't live with someone before you marry them," says Andrew Cherlin, a sociologist at Johns Hopkins University. "Before 1970, it wasn't respectable among anyone but the poor."

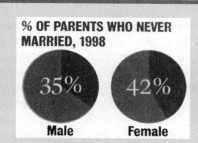

% OF PARENTS WHO NEVER MARRIED, 1998
35% Male   42% Female

Finding Great Kids But Not a Guy

Ten years ago, while vacationing in Costa Rica, Laura Carroll crossed paths with a poor, pregnant teenager who posed a question: can anyone in the United States adopt my child? Carroll, a lawyer, ultimately adopted Louisa herself and brought her home to Boston. Three years later, in 1995, Carroll adopted Annalin from China. Finally in 1998, when she was 45 years old, she became pregnant with James. "My grandfather would have been appalled if he were alive," says Carroll. Annalin, now 5, who has heard the story of Prince Charming, sometimes spots a male parishioner at church and nudges her mother: "What about him? He'd be OK."

Some of these women are adult children of divorce who don't want to make their own offspring suffer the pain of watching a parent leave. They see living together as a kind of trial marriage without the legal entanglements that make breaking up so hard to do—although research indicates that cohabiting couples don't have a much better track record. "They're trying to give their marriages a better chance," says Diane Sollee, founder of the Coalition for Marriage, Family and Couples Education. "They're not trying to be immoral and get away with something."

% OF SAME-SEX FEMALE HOUSEHOLDERS WITH KIDS*

14% 1990

17% 1998

* CHILDREN UNDER 15, ALL OTHERS, CHILDREN UNDER 18

In Spirit, If Not in Law

When talking to other people, Gwen Baba, 44, and Nicole Conn, 39, of Los Angeles refer to each other as "partner" or "spouse" and hope some day the law will allow gays and lesbians to legally marry. Their 1-year-old daughter, Gabrielle, was conceived by fertilizing eggs from both women; Baba, then, brought her to term. "The result is that it's *our* baby," said Baba.

And if the first (or the second) relationship doesn't work out, many women think there's no reason to forgo motherhood. Wellesley researcher Hertz has been studying middle-class single mothers older than 35. Most of the 60 women she has interviewed in depth became pregnant "accidentally." While their babies may have been unplanned, they were not unwanted. Hertz says that for many of these women, the decision to become a mother was all about the modern version of "settling." In the old days a woman did that by marrying Mr. Almost Right. Now settling means having the baby even if you can't get the husband. "When I started this project in the mid-'90s," Hertz says, "these women were tough to find. Now they're all over— next door, at the playground, in your kid's classroom. They've become a normal part of the terrain."

Not all single mothers by choice wait for a serendipitous pregnancy. There are so many options: sperm banks, adoption. New Yorker Gail Janowitz, a market researcher in her mid-40s, decided to adopt two years ago. She always wanted to be a mother, but never married. "As I got older," she says, "I didn't know if the timing of meeting a man was going to work out. I thought, well, I'll do the child part first." A year ago she adopted Rose, now 18 months old, in Kazakhstan. Although there have been difficult moments, Janowitz says she has no regrets. "I've never stopped knowing it was the right thing to do,"

she says. "I think I will still have the opportunity or the option, hopefully, to get married. But right now, I have a family."

The Family Test Tube

Television has always been ahead of the curve when it comes to depicting unconventional households. Some high points:

1968: Diahann Carroll was Julia Baker; a nurse who moved to L.A. after her husband died in Vietnam. Left to raise son Corey alone, Julia handled motherhood with humor.
1969: A 7-year-old played matchmaker in The Courtship of Eddie's Father: Girlfriends varied, but the song said father and son remained 'best friends.'
1970: An oddly cheery widow raised the rockin' Partridge Family, the show that practically launched 'Behind the Music.'
1975: On *One Day at a Time*, divorcée Ann Romano raised two headstrong teens alone. Style point: short hair = feminist advocacy.
1987: It's a *Full House* when widower Danny Tanner (Bob Saget) gets his goofball friend and rock-and-roller brother-in-law (John Stamos) to help raise his three girls
1988: When reporter *Murphy Brown* declined marriage, Dan Quayle took her on. Guess who won?
1999: One plus one make six on *Once and Again* when a divorced (and very sexy) father of two starts dating a newly separated (and equally hot) mother of two.

Even under the very best of conditions, single motherhood is a long, hard journey for both mother and children. No one really knows the long-term consequences for youngsters who grow up in these new varieties of single-parent and cohabiting homes. Much of the research in the past on alternative living arrangements has concentrated on children of divorce, who face very different issues than youngsters whose mothers have chosen to be single from the start or are cohabiting with their children's fathers or other partners. "We need to start paying attention to how these kids" living in cohabiting homes are doing, says Susan Brown, a sociologist at Bowling Green State University in Ohio. "All the evidence we have suggests that they are not doing too well."

Single mothers in general have less time for each individual child than two parents and cohabiting relationships are less stable than marriages. That means that children living in these families are more likely to grow up with a revolving set of adults in their lives. And the offspring of single parents are more likely to skip the altar themselves, thus perpetuating the pattern of their childhood. "Children living outside marriage are seven times more likely to experience poverty and are 17 times more likely to end up on welfare and to have a propensity for emotional problems, discipline problems, early pregnancy and abuse," says Robert Rector, a senior research fellow at the Her-

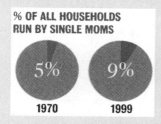

% OF ALL HOUSEHOLDS RUN BY SINGLE MOMS

5% — 1970   9% — 1999

Wary About Rewedding

Although Melaney Mashburn, 42, is engaged, marriage will have to wait. Mashburn, who lives in New York City, says she probably won't remarry while her children, Jesse, 14, and Skylar, almost 12, are still living at home. With a fiancé who also has two children, it might be disruptive "trying to create some fake family," she says. The engagement, she adds, symbolizes their mutual commitment.

itage Foundation, a conservative think tank. "It can be a recipe for disaster."

The average kid in a single-parent family looks much the same emotionally as children who grow up in the most conflicted two-parent homes, says Larry Bumpass, a sociologist at the University of Wisconsin. But, he adds, "the average is not the script written for every child. The outcomes are not all negative; it's just a matter of relative probability ... the majority will do just fine." Lyn Freundlich, who is raising two boys in Boston with their father, Billy Brittingham, says her home is as stable as any on the block. Freundlich and Brittingham have no plans to marry even though they've been living together for 13 years. "It's not important to me," says Freundlich, 36, who works for the Boston AIDS Action Committee. "Marriage feels like a really unfair institution where the government validates some relationships and not others. I can't think of any reason compelling enough to become part of an institution I'm uncomfortable with." When she was pregnant with their first son, Jordan, now 6, Brittingham's parents "waged a campaign for us to get married," she says. His father was relieved when they decided to draft a will and sign a medical proxy. These days, the possibility of marriage hardly crosses her mind. "I'm so busy juggling all the details of having a two-career family, taking care of my kids, seeing my friends and having a role in the community that it's just not something I think about," she says.

If Freundlich isn't thinking about marriage, a lot of politicians are—from the White House on down. In a commencement address at Notre Dame on Sunday, President George W. Bush planned to stress the need to strengthen families and assert that "poverty has more to do with troubled lives than a troubled economy," according to an aide. Bush believes funding religious initiatives is one way Washington can foster family stability. Policies to encourage marriage are either in place or under discussion around the country. Some states, such as Arizona and Louisiana, have established "covenant" marriages in which engaged couples are required to get premarital counseling. It's harder to get divorced in these marriages. Utah al-

Why I think I'm Still Right

Since the flap over 'Murphy Brown,' American families have come under even more pressure.
BY DAN QUAYLE

In 1992, I caused quite a stir by criticizing a television sitcom whose main character got pregnant by her ex-husband and then sent him packing. This was not an attack on single mothers, but a rallying cry for the role fathers should play. It just bothered me that the character didn't seem to care that there would be no father to help raise the child—fathers were presented as irrelevant. My concern has always been for the welfare of the child. Clearly, it is best to have a mother and a father, preferably in a happy monogamous relationship, actively involved in rearing and nurturing their child.

The recent Census numbers reflect what we already know: there is extraordinary turmoil and dysfunction in families today. What has caused this? Time pressure is one reason. With the "in touch" world we live in, the outside world intrudes on every waking hour. Time formerly spent in family activities is now spent on the computer, in front of the television, on the phone, in the car and at the mall. We are a harried society. Economic pressue is another reason. Most of our 21st-century innovations are costly, so more parents are working. Our mobile society has caused more families to live far away from the support system of their extended families. Add to this the fact that pop culture focuses too much on tearing down institutions that give us a sense of stability, and it is no wonder the traditional family structure is in decline.

Even so, there are encouraging signs in the Census report. The number of teenage pregnancies is in decline. Then there is the rise in the number of single dads. That is a cultural shift in which women—and the courts—are more comfortable giving custody to the parent best able to care for the child. It is heartening to see men asking to be given more caregiving responsibility for their children. Still, we should hope and pray that both parents would stay deeply and positively involved in the rearing of their children.

> "We need to expand the idea of extended family to include neighbors, friends and community. We each need to look around."

Children must have hope. Hope comes from a good education, good values, self-respect and living in a society that values every person, expects the best from each of us and does not tolerate abhorrent behavior. Faith in God fosters hope by providing a rationale for living. A two-parent household, with a mother and a father, is still the best place to raise a child. Current reality is that many children are not being raised by two parents. Since the support system of extended families, which in the past helped to fill the void, in most cases does not exist today, we need to expand the idea of extended family to include neighbors, friends and community. We each need to look around our community and see who needs nurturing. Is there a child who needs a grandparent figure, a father figure, a mother figure or a doting aunt or uncle? Fill that void for them.

The sense of belonging, of being a part of a greater whole, is what is sorely needed by so many. With the wisdom and love that is passed to others, with the hope that is engendered in a child's soul, we, as a nation, will be placed on a better path to the future.

lows counties to require counseling before issuing marriage licenses to minors and people who have been divorced. Florida now requires high-school students to take marriage-education classes that stress that married people are statistically healthier and wealthier.

Is It Healthy For the Kids?

Unconventional families can give children the love, stability and support they need—but it's much tougher

BY KAREN SPRINGEN AND PAT WINGERT

CASSIE DENHAESE'S MOTHER'S DIVORCE worked out so well for her, Cassie is already thinking about her own, in case she ever needs one. DenHaese, now 15, was 1½ when her father left, and she's seen him only twice since. "The cons? I don't think there really are any," she says. A man her mother dated for four years "is still like a father to me," even though her mother has a new boyfriend; group activities with Parents Without Partners stood in for an extended family. Cassie's mother, Becky Medicus—a staff training officer for the U.S. Army Reserves—found that single parenthood worked better than the alternative: "I didn't have to worry about whether my husband agreed. I made the rules, and the rules stood." Compared with the trauma of her teenage friends whose parents are going through their first divorces, DenHaese thinks she's got the better deal: even though she believes "very firmly in the whole marriage-family thing... if I was going to have a divorce, I'd have it when my kids were younger."

DenHaese's tale illustrates at least two important truths about the continuing evolution of American families: the resilience kids bring to their lives, and the powerful hold the "whole marriage-family thing" still exerts on their expectations. "All different kinds of structures work for kids, as long as there's love, adequate supervision, structure and consistency," says Barbara Howard, a pediatrician at Johns Hopkins. But those are four big requirements; not all "nontraditional" families can meet them. And, says child psychiatrist Elizabeth Berger, there is no escaping the "psychological reality of something in every child's heart that wants to say, 'Mommy, Daddy, me'."

Until recently, the dysfunctionality of nontraditional families was a self-fulfilling assumption; children without a biological mother and father were stigmatized and shunned. Now, in all but the most conservative milieus, that is no longer true. Still, to state the obvious, two parents are better than one by reason of simple logistics (although many parents would add that even two is a ridiculously inadequate number). "It pays to have two committed, able-bodied parents popping out of bed in the morning," says Berger. "Then one relieves the other."

Money, relatives and sheer effort can help substitute for the missing spouse. But they are of less value in providing the stability that children need even more than another person to drive them to ballet class. On that basis, says Howard, the children of lesbian couples can fare as well as those of heterosexual couples; lesbian relationships tend to be very stable and long-lasting. Howard also believes that single women who choose to have babies, whether by donor insemination or adoption, generally make successful mothers. "They're determined," she reasons. "They've got the financial resources. They're not downtrodden or depressed because they've been abandoned."

'Why Marry? I Had the Kids'

Natashya Brooks, 39, of Berkeley, Calif., supports her three kids—Katiri, 5; Razen, 10; and Paolo, 15—on a welfare check of $768 a month and $220 in food stamps. The kids have three different fathers, but Brooks has never been married and isn't looking to be. "When [the kids] see the stability of a nuclear family they ask me, 'Hey Mom, why don't you get married?' And I answer; 'Why get married? I already had the kids'."

KIDS WITH A SINGLE PARENT EARNING UNDER $12,500, 1998

17% % living with fathers

41% % living with mothers

In contrast, children of divorce often do feel abandoned, or, perhaps worse, responsible. "It is the nature of the childlike mind to believe the world revolves around them," says Berger. "They may think, 'If only I hadn't interrupted Daddy's nap'." But probably the most problematic situation for children is a series of relatively short-term relationships—a new man to call Daddy every few years. "We're much happier without a man in the house," says

Janice Brooks, 41, a benefits manager in Houston, who lives with two daughters by two different men—one of whom she never married—and a 2-year-old granddaughter. Her daughters' attitude toward her second husband, she recalls, was: "You're not my father, so you can't discipline me." Susan Brown, a sociologist at Bowling Green State University, has been studying cohabiting families in terms of kids' behavior and emotional problems. "Generally, kids living with cohabiting parents are not doing too well," she says, compared with those whose parents are married. The gap widens above the age of 6, which Brown attributes to "the cumulative effects of family instability. The older they get, the less likely they are to be living with two biological parents anymore."

Children in cohabiting families may also be at higher risk of abuse from their mothers' boyfriends—although researchers are still debating the question. Jill Glick, medical director of child protective services at the University of Chicago, says that more than half the serious brain injuries her hospital sees in infants are inflicted by "paramour perpetrators"—men who lack the biological and emotional connection that inhibits parents from hurting their own children. Recognizing that children's health can be affected by the stresses of growing up in a single-parent family, or with a succession of stepparents or revolving-door boyfriends, the American Academy of Pediatrics is introducing the concept of "family pediatrics." "We're not saying pediatricians need to take care of all the problems," says Dr. Edward Schor, "but they should be identifying them."

But while these circumstances "may make it more difficult to have good outcomes for children," Schor admits "it's nowhere near impossible." It's reassuring to know that millions of children of divorced, never married or gay and lesbian parents can hope to lead happy and productive lives as adults—which, after all, is a goal that can elude the offspring of even the most conventional families. It may be, as Berger says, that every child yearns to be part of a triad of Mommy, Daddy and me. But then again, who do you think psychoanalysis was invented for?

Some researchers who study the history of marriage say that such efforts may be futile or even destructive. "Giving incentives or creating pressures for unstable couples to wed can be a huge mistake," says family historian Coontz. "It may create families with high conflict and instability—the worst-case scenario for kids." Other scientists say that lifelong marriage may be an unrealistic goal when humans have life expectancies of 80 or older. In their new book, "The Myth of Monogamy," David Barash and Judith Lipton say that in the natural world, monogamy is rare. And even among humans, it was probably the exception throughout much of human history. In "Georgiana: Duchess of Devonshire," biographer Amanda Foreman details bed-hopping among the 18th-century British aristocracy that would make even a randy Hollywood icon blush.

If a long and happy marriage is an elusive goal for couples in any century, most women—even those scarred by divorce—say

it's still worth pursuing. When Roberta Lanning, 37, of Woodland Hills, Calif., became pregnant with her fifth child after a bitter divorce, she decided not to marry her boyfriend and raise Christian, now 9, on her own. As a child of divorce herself, she never wanted to raise a family on her own. "Single motherhood is not a good thing," she says. "It's definitely one hurdle after another." And despite everything, she hasn't given up. "It's been my heart's desire to have a father and mother in a structured home situation" for Christian, she says. "It just hasn't happened for me. Believe me, I've certainly been looking." If she finds the right man, chances are he'll probably have a couple of kids of his own by now, too.

With JULIE SCELFO, KAREN SPRINGEN, ANA FIGUEROA, MARTHA BRANT AND SALLY ABRAHMS

Adoption by lesbian couples

Is it in the best interests of the child?

The report of the American Academy of Pediatrics in February[1] supporting the introduction of legislation to allow the adoption by co-parents of children born to lesbian couples sparked enormous controversy not only within the medical profession but among the public as well. Almost without exception, only the mother who gives birth to or adopts the child may currently be the legal parent, even in cases where a couple plan a family together and raise their child in a stable family unit. The academy has taken the view that children in this situation deserve the security of two legally recognised parents in order to promote psychological wellbeing and to enable the child's relationship with the co-mother to continue should the other mother die, become incapacitated, or the couple separate. This position is based on evidence derived from the research literature on this issue.[2] The *Washington Times* described the stance of the academy as "an unfortunate surrender to political expediency" and accused the academy's Committee on Psychosociological Aspects of Child and Family Health of sacrificing scientific integrity in order to advance an activist agenda.[3] Is it the case that children born to lesbian couples "can have the same advantages and the same expectations for health, adjustment, and development as can parents who are heterosexual," as stated by the academy? Alternatively, is the academy simply pandering to a politically correct agenda?

Two main concerns have been expressed in relation to lesbian mother families: firstly, that the children would be bullied and ostracised by peers and would consequently develop psychological problems, and, secondly, that they would show atypical gender development such that boys would be less masculine in their identity and behaviour, and girls less feminine, than boys and girls from heterosexual families. Lack of knowledge about these children and their parents in the light of a growing number of child custody cases involving a lesbian mother prompted the first wave of studies in the 1970s. This early body of research focused on families where the child had been born into a heterosexual family and then moved with the mother into a lesbian family after the parents' separation or divorce. Regardless of the geographical or demographic characteristics of the families studied, the find-

ings of these early investigations were strikingly consistent. Children from lesbian mother families did not show a higher rate of psychological disorder or difficulties in peer relationships than their counterparts from heterosexual homes. With respect to gender development, there was no evidence of confusion about gender identity among these children, and no difference in sex role behaviour between children in lesbian and heterosexual families for either boys or girls.[4][5]

A limitation of the early investigations was that only school age children were studied. It was argued that sleeper effects may exist such that children raised in lesbian mother families may experience difficulties in emotional wellbeing and in intimate relationships when they grow up. Further, they may be more likely than other children to themselves adopt a lesbian or gay sexual orientation in adulthood, an outcome that has been considered undesirable by courts of law. To address this question, a group of children raised in lesbian mother families in the United Kingdom was followed up to adulthood.[6][7] These young adults did not differ from their counterparts from heterosexual families in terms of quality of family relationships, psychological adjustment, or quality of peer relationships. With respect to their sexual orientation, the large majority of children from lesbian families identified as heterosexual in adulthood.

In recent years, attention has moved from the issue of child custody to whether lesbian women should have access to assisted reproduction procedures, particularly donor insemination, to enable them to have children without the involvement of a male partner. The findings from studies of these families, where the children grow up without a father right from the start, indicate that the children do not differ from their peers in two parent, heterosexual families in terms of either emotional wellbeing or gender development.[8-11] The only clear difference to emerge is that co-mothers in two parent lesbian families are more involved in parenting than are fathers from two parent homes.

A limitation of the existing body of research is that only small volunteer or convenience samples have been studied, and thus mothers whose children are experiencing difficulties may be under-represented. Nevertheless, a substantial body of evidence indicates that children raised by lesbian mothers do not differ from other children in key aspects of psychological development. On the basis of this evidence it seems that the American Academy of Pediatrics acted not out of political correctness but with the intention of protecting children who are likely to benefit from the legal recognition of their second parent. At present in the United Kingdom, lesbian women are individually eligible to adopt children, whether living with a partner or not. However, members of parliament have recently voted to allow unmarried couples, whatever their sexual orientation, to adopt children jointly.

References

1. Committee on Psychosocial Aspects of Child and Family Health. Co-parent or second-parent adoption by same-sex parents. *Pediatrics* 2002;109:339–40.
2. Perrin EC. Technical report: coparent or second-parent adoption by same-sex parents. *Pediatrics* 2002; 109:341–4.
3. Dobson JC. Pediatricians vs children. *Washington Times* 2002 Feb 12.
4. Patterson CJ. Children of lesbian and gay parents. *Child Dev* 1992;63:1025–42.
5. Golombok S. Lesbian mother families. In: Bainham A, Day Sclater S, Richards M, eds. *What is a parent? A socio-legal analysis*. Oxford: Hart Publishing, 1999.
6. Golombok S, Tasker F. Do parents influence the sexual orientation of their children? Findings from a longitudinal study of lesbian families. *Dev Psychol* 1996;32:3–11.
7. Tasker F, Golombok S. *Growing up in a lesbian family*. New York: Guilford Press, 1997.
8. Flaks DK, Ficher I, Masterpasqua F, Joseph G. Lesbian choosing motherhood: a comparative study of lesbian and heterosexual parents and their children. *Developmental Psychology* 1995;31:105–14.
9. Golombok S, Tasker F, Murray C. Children raised in fatherless families from infancy: family relationships and the socioemotional development of children of lesbian and single heterosexual mothers. *J Child Psychol Psychiatry* 1997;38:783–91.
10. Brewaeys A, Ponjaert I, Van Hall E, Golombok S. Donor insemination: child development and family functioning in lesbian mother families. *Hum Reprod* 1997;12:1349–59.
11. Chan RW, Raboy B, Patterson CJ. Psychosocial adjustment among children conceived via donor insemination by lesbian and heterosexual mothers. *Child Dev* 1998;69:443–57.

Susan Golombok *professor*
Family and Child Psychology Research Centre, City University, London EC1V 0HB (S.E.Golombok@city.ac.uk)

WHY WE BREAK UP WITH OUR SIBLINGS

As baby boomers age, more are becoming estranged from their brothers and sisters. And they feel the loss especially during the year-end holidays

BY LISE FUNDERBURG

JONDA CYNECKI HASN'T SEEN HER TWIN sister Wanda in 13 years and doesn't hold out much hope that she ever will. Their last contact came at a family gathering in Ohio for Christmas, after which Wanda returned to her home in Key West, Fla. Then she disappeared. She didn't call, didn't write and couldn't be reached. When her parents died several years later, her siblings had to use intermediaries to get through to her. She called to borrow money about a year ago. Since then, the only sign she's still alive is that no one has heard anything to the contrary. And yet Jonda, 54, a school librarian, says wistfully of Wanda, "There isn't a day that goes by that something doesn't remind me of her."

Usually that something is doing the laundry. Whenever Jonda goes down to her basement to wash clothes, she sees, tucked under the stairs, an old tandem stroller. Her father crafted it from spare parts, painted it white and wrapped rubber around its wooden wheels. Jonda won't get rid of the stroller, even though it provokes sorrow and anger toward the sister who walked out on her family. What Jonda doesn't know—and might never know—is why.

Estrangement from siblings is a powerful ache not only for Jonda but for millions of other Americans as well—especially during the year-end holidays, when the absence of relatives is most poignant. Many of the 77 million baby boomers, now well into middle age, live farther from their

brothers and sisters than did previous generations. And with each passing year, they face more of the life passages that often trigger splits with siblings, particularly arguments over the care of elderly parents or over their estates. At the same time, boomers have more divorces and fewer children and are less tethered to neighbors than were their parents and grandparents, so they are more in need of strong relationships with sisters and brothers—the most-enduring ties many of us have in our lives. Eighty-five percent of adult Americans have at least one sibling, yet an estimated 3% to 10% have completely severed contact with a brother or sister.

Such absolute estrangements may not be the norm, but experts who study family relationships believe they are on the rise. Psychologist Carol Netzer, author of *Cut-offs: How Family Members Who Sever Relationships Can Reconnect*, thinks that today's broader cultural freedoms have made it easier for people to say goodbye to traditions and to relatives. "The nuclear family is not as tight as it once was," she says. Some rifts reflect larger trends. The Woodstock generation, Netzer explains, was full of young people leaving their families to lose themselves in drugs or join religious groups, political movements and communes. "Often, when that ripple in the culture passes," says Netzer, "people go back to their families." Terry Hargrave, family therapist and author of *Families*

and Forgiveness, believes that while the psychological self-help movement has been largely positive, "it teaches the individual that 'you're the most important thing; family is not.'"

The origins of a sibling breach often can be traced to childhood. Psychologist Stephen P. Bank, co-author of *The Sibling Bond*, observes that eldest children who are expected to care for younger siblings may feel overburdened and resentful. Children born too many years apart, says Bank, may never share common interests or developmental stages. For them, slender ties are sometimes easy to cut.

Nancy B. (who asked that her full name not be used) is a management consultant with a sister older by six years and a brother older by 12. She doesn't speak to either of them but for differing reasons. "The age gap was so significant," she says. As a child, she worshiped her brother, whose trips home from college were cause for celebration. A few years ago, he stopped returning her calls. She doesn't know why.

On the other hand, she was never comfortable with her sister. "There was always tension between us," Nancy, now 52, says. "I couldn't figure it out." Nancy ended contact after the sister attached herself to yet another violent man, and Nancy felt relegated to the role of caretaker—for someone who didn't want to be helped. The three siblings were last together 25 years ago at their mother's funeral. Nancy still feels the loss, she says, "but my heart isn't breaking anymore. I've figured out a way to be in the world without trying to make love happen where it isn't."

Yet in other families, psychologist Bank says, large age differences can help alleviate competition for toys, friends and parental attention. Some older siblings enjoy being caregivers, often in exchange for adoration. Studies show bonds among sisters tend to be strongest, epitomized by Bessie and Sadie Delany, co-authors of *Having Our Say: The Delany Sisters' First 100 Years*. And when parents are absent, neglectful or abusive, siblings often fill the void by forming tight bonds, as did the brothers in the movie *Radio Flyer*.

Major life changes such as marriage, divorce, birth, illness or death can trigger a separation, Netzer says, but usually only if tensions have been building for years. Consider, for example, the case of Michael Carr, 42, a money manager, and his older brother Steven, who ended contact with each other two years ago. When they were growing up, Michael saw Steven, two years older, as his best friend and guardian angel. "We were really close," Michael says. "He was the ringleader in the neighborhood. He was my hero." (Steven did not respond to requests for an interview.)

In the early '70s, Michael says, Steven became temperamental and less reliable, no longer resembling the person Michael had admired. Steven wasn't crazy, Michael says, just increasingly moody and self-centered. About six years ago, their father was hospitalized, and the brothers went to Florida to see him. They stayed with their stepmother, with whom Steven had a quarrel. Steven told Michael he was going to the hospital to tell their father about it. "It was ridiculous," Michael says. "My father was at death's door, and my brother wanted to complain to him about my stepmother! I had to physically restrain him from going."

Their father died that night, and Michael hasn't seen his brother since the funeral. "I wouldn't be surprised if I never see him again," Michael says. "If I saw him on the street I would talk to him, but I wouldn't let him back in my life. I don't know who he is."

Money issues are a common source of strife between brothers and sisters: Why wasn't that loan repaid? Who can afford the bigger house? How should the family business be run? Behavior outside the family's value system can also trip the switch: coming out of the closet, marrying interra-

cially or converting to a new religion. Then there are cutoffs linked to extreme emotional states, the reasons for which—such as untreated mental illness, substance abuse, incest and violence—may never be brought out into the open.

Wanda's older brother Charles Bucklew has only a few clues as to what might have caused his sister's self-banishment, including her drinking in the midst of their nearly teetotaling Lutheran family. Wanda, who no doubt has her own analysis of the split, never explained; her siblings never asked. And she could not be located by TIME reporters in Key West and New York. "There may be some reason out there that if you knew, it'd bring you to your knees, and you'd say, 'Oh, my God!'" says Bucklew. "But I don't know."

The drive to create sibling bonds or something like them is to some experts primordial—even for an only child. Parents always have a disproportionate power over offspring, but siblings teach peer-level tolerance, loyalty and constancy—qualities that later apply to colleagues, friends and lovers. In moderation, sibling discord is useful, says psychologist Bank. "If the frustration is too great, it cripples you. But we all need a level of frustration in our lives in order to move ahead."

IN A 1996 STUDY OF PEOPLE AGES 18 TO 86, 33% of those surveyed described their sibling relationships as "supportive," and only 11% were "hostile," with the rest falling somewhere in between. "I understand that there is sibling rivalry because I have two brothers and a sister," says Robert Stewart, chairman of the psychology department at Michigan's Oakland University. "But if something came up, and I needed to be on the other side of the country because one of them called, I'd go. There's not a whole lot of people in the world I'd do that for." Most people think of "rivalry" and "siblings" as synonymous and negative, he says, "but I think of it as a close affectional relationship where affection is not necessarily shown in a Hallmark card kind of way."

The sibling relationship of D.B. (who asked that her name not be used) won't ever be confused with a greeting card. As a child, she looked up to her brother, 3½ years older. After his marriage broke up, though, D.B. didn't like the way he treated his ex-wife. Well after the two divorced, he abandoned their original settlement agreement, demanding half the house and full custody of their daughter. D.B. saw his de-

mands as unfair—and didn't think much of his parenting skills. "I just felt he was such a pig," she says. So she stopped talking to him—for seven years. "I come from a long line of grudge holders," she says. "They like their grudges. They air them and walk them and make jokes about them—embellish them."

The silence ended, though, when an aunt died, and D.B. and her brother were the only relatives left to arrange her burial. "I remember thinking, Damn, now I have to see my brother." But the two reconciled somewhat and now talk occasionally on the phone. D.B., now 54, says if she ever needed money, she wouldn't hesitate to ask him for it. She has no money to offer him if the situation were reversed but says, "I would give him lots of time."

Often, estranged siblings are struck by a sudden yearning to reconnect. Says Bank: "Your children leave home, your friends are sick, the leaves fall off the trees, and you say, 'Well, what do I have from my past?' And for better or worse, you've got this sibling who might have been a pain in the neck but who probably knows more about what it was like to live in your childhood home than anybody else."

Yet even for siblings who wish to reconcile, breaking the ice is hard. "The difficulty most of us have is how do you pick up the telephone after so many years?" says Stewart. "People get into a pattern, and even though they're not comfortable in it, they can't imagine an alternative. Or the amount of courage and energy it would take to try to change may be beyond what they're capable of doing right now."

The ability to overlook imperfections for the sake of a relationship is one hallmark of maturity. Siblings may decide to forgive one another once they have their own children. For Mark Horton, 44, a recent falling-out he had with his eldest sister still baffles him. He's not sure what happened or why. Now that they are back in tentative contact, they still haven't talked about it. "It was kind of a *Twilight Zone* episode," he says. But he does hope things heal. Horton (whose sister declined to be interviewed) says she has done remarkable things for him—sending him money when he was a poor college student and then being the only one to show up at his Harvard graduation. And he wants his four children to know their aunt. "It places them in the world," he says. "They're not comets flying through space randomly; they're part of a solar system."

Reconciliation, experts say, is almost always worth an attempt. But about 40% of the families in Hargrave's clinical practice fail at reconciliation, mostly because when difficult issues get stirred up, no one is willing to take responsibility for what happened. Says Hargrave: "The person who has left just seals off again."

For Douglas Matthews, 49, a human-resources consultant, finally breaking off from his parents and three brothers three years ago brought immense relief—and not just to him. "I see it as the best thing he could have ever done for himself," says his wife Teri-Ann, "and for me and the kids."

MATTHEWS HAS ALWAYS BEEN reluctant TO discuss his family situation because he felt that well-meaning people just wouldn't get it that his parents and siblings were harmful to his happiness. "I learned early on that very few people understand the positive aspects of estrangement," he says. For decades, Matthews waffled between trying to be part of the family and retreating. He would try to initiate changes but says no one was willing to join in. Over time, and with therapy, he discovered that the yearning he felt was based on an unrealizable ideal of what his three brothers might have been to him. "A real brother would be there no matter what," Matthews says, "and not have an agenda for you—just accept where you are

and listen. But it would be unconditional—nothing could break it. And also do the stupid things, you know. Go to a ball game together." But what Matthews has with his wife and two sons is no fantasy. "I have a home," he says, "and that's what I didn't have before. And I cherish it."

Cutting off can be beneficial in some cases, says psychology professor Stewart, if what you're getting is nothing but negativity or grief. But it's "escape learning," he says, and if the other people involved are ever willing to work on the problem, "you won't know it because they're gone."

For 15 years Keith Bearden, 33, had given up on his family, including his elder brother Dean, 38. Their parents' divorce cleaved the family into separate camps, and Keith wanted no part of either one. "I was really angry," he says. He also felt that he, a self-described "meek intellectual," had nothing in common with his tattooed, motorcycle-riding, machinist brother. Then Dean started telephoning a couple of years ago, just to see how Keith was doing. Keith, to his surprise, was happy to get the calls. Dean says he had no particular plan, that he had never even thought about the years when they were out of contact. "If you were never close," he says, "you never miss it."

But becoming a parent got Dean thinking about family, and as Keith says, Dean

was never judgmental or bitter about what had happened in childhood. Now the brothers talk regularly. They visit each other every few months and have realized they have the same sense of humor, the same taste for adventure, and they notice the same things—someone's weird shoes on the subway or a cute woman in a bar.

Keith says he's much happier accepting rather than resenting the differences in his family, that it's helped him with all his relationships and that Dean deserves the credit for helping him reconnect. "Dean kept the door open, and I eventually walked back in," he says.

Jonda Cynecki hasn't closed the door on her sister but is at a loss as to how anyone can pass through it. Since the death of their parents, Jonda has felt an increasingly acute sense of the irreplaceable nature of family. "There's that line that connects you," she says of her missing twin, "and I don't know if it'll ever be broken. Certainly when one of us passes away—and she could be gone now—I don't know if I'll ever know that." Cynecki pauses, wipes away tears, and collects herself. "Someday, I really need to find her. But just not today. Not today."

—*With reporting by Rachele Kanigel/ Oakland*

The importance of partners to lesbians' intergenerational relationships

The strong likelihood of parental disapproval of a daughter's lesbianism indicates that for gay women intergenerational dynamics may be uniquely challenging and complex. In this qualitative study, 40 lesbians in 20 couples were interviewed about their relationships with their parents and their partner's parents. Respondents reported that since coming out, their parents' attitudes about their lesbianism shifted over time from profound disapproval to ambivalence. Partners emerged as a beneficial influence on most of the respondents' intergenerational relationships. Social workers assisting lesbians with intergenerational difficulties are advised to include the client's partner in treatment. Additional clinical implications are discussed.

Key words: **family therapy; intergenerational issues; lesbian couples; parents**

Michael C. LaSala

In describing family relationships, Bowenian theory delineates the need for balance between the life forces of individuality and togetherness (Kerr & Bowen, 1988). Practitioners of Bowenian family therapy use the term differentiation of self to describe how an individual establishes autonomy from his or her family members while also maintaining meaningful connections with them (Bowen, 1978). Problems arise when family members sublimate their own needs to avoid conflict, or distance themselves by emotionally cutting off from one another. In turn, unresolved emotional issues from problematic, family-of-origin relationships are often projected onto spouses, resulting in marital strain (Kerr & Bowen).

The available research sheds some light on the connection between intergenerational relationships and heterosexual marriage. Good relationships with parents (Lewis, 1989) as well as frequent intergenerational contact (Burger & Milardo, 1995) have been found to be associated with harmonious marital relations. On the other hand, parental disapproval may be associated with being distrustful, critical, and negative toward one's spouse (Driscoll, Davis, & Lipetz, 1972); can influence mate choice (Jedlicka, 1984); and may impede the progression of a relationship from dating to marriage (Leigh, 1982). Compared with those who had maintained relationships with their parents, adult children who were emotionally cut off from their parents were found to be less satisfied with their marriages (Dillard & Protinsky, 1985).

Some have postulated that coming out may be an important component of the differentiation process for lesbians (Iasenza, Colucci, & Rothberg, 1996; LaSala, 2000). Nevertheless, in applying Bowen theory and the aforementioned findings to the families of lesbians, one must consider how parents feel about their daughters' sexual orientation. On coming out, lesbians have been known to face parental reactions from guilt and disappointment to rejection, verbal threats, and even physical violence (D'Augelli, Hershberger, & Pilkington, 1998; "Results of Poll," 1989; Warshow, 1991). Whereas parent-child relationships have been found to improve with time following the initial disclosure, parental disapproval often persists (Beeler & DiProva, 1999; Ben-Ari, 1995; Bernstein, 1990; Cramer & Roach, 1988; Muller, 1987; Warshow, 1991). These findings suggest that parental attitudes toward a daughter's lesbianism are complex and warrant further study.

Not surprisingly, parental feelings may affect lesbians and their unions. For young lesbians, self-esteem and comfort with being gay have been found to be correlated with maternal acceptance (Floyd, Stein, Harter, Allison, & Nye, 1999; Savin-Williams, 1989a, 1989b). Among a sample of 124 coupled lesbians, relationship quality was found to be significantly associated with parental acceptance (Caron & Ulin, 1997). Conversely, parental negativity can have adverse affects on gay women and their relationships. Among a sample of 1,925 lesbians, Bradford, Ryan, and Rothblum (1994) discovered that difficulties with family was one of the top five problems listed by their respondents and the second most common reason for seeking mental health services. In a sample of 706 lesbian couples, women listed problems with relatives as the third greatest challenge to their relationships (Bryant & Demian, 1994). In a qualitative study of 20 partnered lesbians, 20 percent reported that their parents' disapproval adversely affected their relationships (Murphy, 1989).

The available clinical and empirical literature begins to explain the variety of ways coupled lesbians might cope with parental disapproval. From a Bowenian perspective, family therapists have described how some lesbians might react to parental disapproval by sublimating their own independence needs and prioritizing their relationships with their parents, resulting in conflict with their partners (Iasenza et al., 1996; Krestan & Bepko, 1980). Parental hostility also might lead lesbians to distance themselves from their families, which in turn could result in couple difficulties, as unsettled intergenerational problems get projected onto partners (LaSala, 2000). Kurdek and Schmitt (1987) compared samples of 79 heterosexual, 50 gay male, and 56 lesbian couples and discovered that, in contrast to heterosexuals, gay and lesbian couples were less likely to list family members as major sources of support. In a follow-up study, Kurdek (1988) found that emotional support from friends was more important than that of family to the relationship satisfaction and psychological well-being of gays and lesbians. These findings suggest that lesbians (and gay men) cope with family disapproval by finding alternative sources of support. However, it is also possible that they are disavowing the importance of family. Although it may be possible to compensate for a lack of closeness to one's family by cultivating supportive friendships, Bowenian theory would suggest that those who distance themselves from their parents and deny the importance of parental relationships may be prone to dysfunctional interactions with partners or friends who restimulate unresolved issues with parents (Kerr & Bowen, 1988). Most likely, it is desirable to have a network of good relationships that includes not only friends, but also family. Clearly, more research is needed to better understand how gay women cope with parental attitudes toward their lesbianism and relationships.

The purpose of this exploratory research was to develop new understandings that would add to the knowledge describing the intergenerational dynamics of coupled lesbians. More specific research questions included: How do coupled lesbians perceive their parents' feeling and opinions about their lesbianism? How do coupled lesbians respond to or cope with their parents' attitudes? What, if anything, helps lesbians and their parents maintain relationships that are meaningful and developmentally appropriate? I anticipated that the results of this study could suggest how to intervene with lesbians and their families sensitively and effectively.

METHOD

To obtain "thick descriptions" of lesbians' family dynamics in all of their complexity (Lincoln & Guba, 1985), qualitative methods were used.

Participants

The sample consisted of 40 self-identified lesbians in 20 couples. All of the women lived in the New York City metropolitan area; 17 couples resided in central and northern New Jersey; one couple lived in Brooklyn, another on Staten Island, and a third on Long Island. Thirty-five of the 40 women were non-Hispanic white, three were African American, and two were Latina. Household incomes ranged from $12,000 to $240,000 with a median of $80,000. The age range of the respondents was 26 to 49 years with a mean of 37 (SD = 5.10). The lengths of time couples were together ranged from one to 22 years with a mean of 6.5 (SD = 3.65). For the purpose of this study, *coming out* to parents was defined as explicitly telling a parent she was gay, and by this definition all but one woman had come out to at least one of her parents. The intervals from the coming-out disclosure to the time of the interview ranged from two to 27 years with a mean of 11 years (SD = 6.17).

Criteria

To be included in this study, both members of each couple had to agree to participate. The respondents needed to be living together and to have been in their relationship for at least one year. In addition, at the time of the interview both members of the couple needed to have at least one living parent.

Data Collection

A convenience sample was gathered (Fortune & Reid, 1998). Researchers have recommended that those who study lesbians recruit respondents from multiple sources to maximize the potential diversity of their samples (Institute of Medicine, 1999). An advertisement for this study was placed in a newsletter received by members of a gay/lesbian community center that serves central New Jersey. In addition, flyers were distributed at a dance for lesbians sponsored by this community center. This advertisement also was posted on a listserv subscribed to by lesbian and gay male graduate students, faculty, and alumni of a large public university in central New Jersey. To attract respondents who did not own computers, were not members of a gay organization, and were not affiliated with the university, an announcement was posted in restaurants and coffee shops in central New Jersey and New York City.

Potential participants contacted the interviewer by telephone or e-mail, at which time they were screened to determine if they met the study criteria. The primary reason for a couple not meeting the criteria was that one or both women's parents were deceased. Potential participants were told that their identities and responses would be kept confidential. In addition, each respondent was informed that she would be paid $20 for participating.

Only one couple canceled a scheduled interview appointment, stating that they did not have the time to participate. All others who scheduled an interview completed the study.

My assistant, a lesbian and first-year MSW student, and I, a gay man, collected data over a five-month period. I developed a standardized interview protocol of open-ended questions (Patton, 1990). Women were asked their perceptions of their parents' attitudes about their lesbianism, how their parents and in-laws felt about their partner relationships, and how their parents' and partner's parents' opinions affected their relationships. We took thorough notes during the interviews, which also were audiotaped.

I anticipated that members of a couple might disagree about the intergenerational effects on their relationship and that a participant might censor certain responses in the presence of her partner. Therefore, partners were interviewed privately in separate rooms of each couple's home.

Data Analysis

Coding of Data. Once we collected all the data, I read the quoted responses to a related set of questions. After reviewing the answers of eight to 10 interviewees, I was able to establish initial codes. Examples of these preliminary codes were as follows: parental shame, parental fear, parental guilt, parental support, assertive coping, partner encouraging parental contact, partner acting as buffer, and partner helping to set boundaries. I sorted quoted responses by code using word processing software. As coding of responses within and across targeted areas continued, it became apparent that several codes could be combined to form secondary or axial codes (Glaser, 1978). For example, partner encouraging contact and partner acting as a buffer could be combined into a broader code called partner facilitation.

Glaser (1978) defined memos as "the theorizing write-up of ideas about codes and their relationships as they strike the analyst while coding" (pp. 83-84). Toward the end of the coding process, I wrote memos to identify and elaborate emerging themes, such as the role of the partner in parental relationships. Memos also served as drafts of the Results section of this article.

Reliability. Several authors have described the benefits to data collection and analysis if the researchers and respondents share demographic and social similarities (Lofland & Lofland, 1984; Martin & Knox, 2000). Because we had common experiences and could speak the language of the gay culture, it was relatively easy to establish the necessary rapport to encourage participants to discuss these potentially painful areas of their lives. However, we ran the risk of allowing our views of gay life to bias our perceptions. To minimize this possibility, coded segments of the interview transcripts were reviewed regularly with gay and heterosexual clinical and research colleagues throughout data collection and analysis. As a result of these reviews, I revised several codes. For example, after some preliminary coding, I was alerted that I might have been bringing a bias to my analysis that might have led me to judge parents too dichotomously, categorizing them as either disapproving or supportive. I was advised to more thoroughly review the segments of the transcripts describing perceived parental reactions and, in doing so, I became aware of how most of the respondents saw their parents as having a complicated mix of feelings about their lesbianism.

The research assistant independently sorted written and tape-recorded data into key codes that emerged during the data analysis. Although codes were not changed as a result of these reliability checks, there were a few incidents when our sorting choices for a particular response did not agree. At these times we both reread entire transcripts of the interview in question and then discussed the responses. As a result several responses were recoded. The final overall agreement between her codes and mine was 92.3 percent with a range of 8 percent to 97 percent across key codes.

FINDINGS

Shift in Parental Reactions

On coming out, lesbians are almost certain to face parental and in-law antipathy. This has been reported in earlier research (D'Augelli et al., 1998; "Results of Poll," 1989) and by the women of this study. Thirty-four of the women encountered disapproval on coming out to their parents, with 23 women experiencing hostile or rejecting reactions. However, as time passed, their parents' attitudes seemed to improve. Most of the respondents indicated that their parents' feelings at the time of the interviews were a blend of support and disapproval. When parents were negative, it was because they felt guilty, embarrassed, or ashamed of their daughters' lesbianism. Furthermore, participants reported that parents worried for their daughters' well-being, fearing that the respondents would grow old alone or that they would experience discrimination. Nevertheless, respondents stated that their parents liked their partners and supported their relationships. As a matter of fact, besides feeling relieved about not having to hide their lesbianism, these women reported that the support and validation offered by their parents was a primary benefit of being out to them.

As stated by a 31-year-old respondent who had been out to her parents and also with her partner for five years:

> They would say they like her but they'd rather me be married with children. My mother would say she's embarrassed. She's said this.

However, she reported that her parents included her partner in family events and that this benefited her relationship with her partner. Another respondent who was 37, out to her parents for eight years, and currently in a three-year relationship reported:

> My mother claims she is embarrassed in her natural surroundings. They're [mother and father] only open in her immediate family…. They're afraid of what others would think.

Nevertheless, this same respondent described how her father bought her a plane ticket so she could relocate to be with her lover. Also, she reported that her mother allowed her teenage sister to visit the couple overnight and she perceived this to be evidence that her parents had accepted her lesbianism. A 33-

year-old respondent who had been out to her parents for nine years and was currently in a two-year relationship noticed that neither her mother nor her mother-in-law had told their extended families about their daughters' lesbianism. She believed this to mean they both were ashamed. Still, both sets of parents included both partners in family events. She reported: "Family is important to me, and being accepted as a couple helps by knowing we have our family to support us." Thus, although most of the women perceived their parents to be embarrassed about their lesbianism or worried for their well-being, their parents also demonstrated support for their relationships, and this support benefited their unions.

Parental Disapproval and Boundary Setting

The majority of women indicated that parental disapproval did not substantially affect their relationships. In all but two couples, there was at least one member who described how she protected the relationship from parental or in-law disapproval. In response to a minor incident, such as if a parent said something insensitive, couple members might ignore it or discuss it among themselves. However, when parents were perceived to be invalidating the relationship, the women responded assertively. For example, one respondent's mother wanted to visit her for an extended stay but requested that her daughter and her partner sleep separately for the duration of the visit. The interviewee adamantly refused, telling her mother, "This is our house and we'll do it by my rules."

Several women mentioned that a partner assertively affirming the couple's relationship to her parents was seen as a sign of her love and commitment: "The fact that she took that stand with her parents showed me how much she cared for me."

For many of these women, their relationship with their partners catalyzed the developmentally appropriate restructuring of their intergenerational relationships. The following woman who had been out for four years and with her current partner for one year, stated,

> They used to have expectations of me. They would expect I would stay with them on vacations and to come stay with them. Ever since I was with Fran, I don't do that anymore. They've adjusted to it. They accept I can't spend a lot of time with them.

After being out and with her partner for 13 years, this woman described what appeared to be a developmentally appropriate change in her relationship with her parents:

> It's become stronger. I'm not so much their "daughter" anymore as much as their adult friend. This is due to me being happy with Cheryl.

Some of the women gave examples of how their partners actively encouraged or helped them to set boundaries with their parents. A 41-year-old graduate student who had two children

from her heterosexual marriage, and who was currently in a four-year relationship, recounted:

> Mom took pictures and made an album with no pictures of Marie. Marie and I talked about it and decided how we would deal with her. I wrote her a letter and told her I was offended.

In speaking of her parents' and her partner's parents' disapproval, she stated, "Our relationship is sealed against outside influences. Our primary commitment is absolutely to each other, and nobody fucks with that. If anybody tries ... we deal with it." Early in their relationship, the following couple had argued because one of the women's parents insisted that the couple spend all of the holidays at their home. As stated by one of the women: "If we were a straight couple, her [partner's] family wouldn't mind her splitting the holidays with her in-laws."

At her urging, her partner asserted herself to her parents: "As I got older and when I realized Lisa was the one, I made it clear to them. That changed me. I will not allow anything to cause us problems."

Partner Facilitates Parental Relationships

The positive influence of partners went beyond merely providing a reason to set boundaries with parents. Anger or guilt in response to parental disapproval could potentially lead a gay woman to excessively distance and even cut off from her family of origin. However, 27 of the women reported that their relationships with their parents had improved since they had been with their partners, and 35 of the women described specific ways their partners facilitated parental relationships. This facilitation could simply be urging the partner to contact her parents: "She thinks I should go see my mother more than I do."

In addition, partners often acted in ways to buffer the problematic parental relationship. The following 33-year-old respondent pushed her partner of two years to "lighten up" on her own mother: "I am more tolerant of her mother. I feel she is very short with her at times. I have told her." In speaking about her relationship with her father, whom she described as homophobic, this 29-year-old woman stated:

> My father and I had a terrible relationship when I was a teenager. It's evolved since then because my father has worked really hard on it. Toni is a good buffer between us ... she puts up with his irritability and temperament. She's very calm and patient with him and tries to get special things for him; bake him things.... [As a result] he's always asked about her feelings. He's including her in family finances. Now my relationship with him is good, loving, and supportive.

Another woman talked about how she convinced her partner to soften her position regarding her own mother:

> When Kathy and her mother and her sister have conflict, I try to explain Mom's point of view. I remind

Kathy her mother is mourning [her heterosexual image of] her daughter, and I tell her to be more patient as she mourns.

She went on to say: "It makes me feel good that I can act as a buffer between Kathy and her mother."

For a 45-year-old respondent, her relationship with her partner helped her work through her anger at her mother for not protecting her from childhood sexual abuse perpetrated by her stepfather. For years, she and her mother were unable to speak without arguing about her childhood. When asked how her relationship with her parents had changed since she had been with her partner, she replied, "in a positive way. I am not as furious with her [mother]. Marge and I had a daddy-girl relationship, and I worked through my dad issues."

At times, a partner's actions could create some mild conflict, as it did for the following couple. One partner reported, "I keep telling her not to shout at her mother." And this was echoed in the responses of her partner who said, "If I say something nasty to my mother, she says: 'You can't say that to your mother!' I do the same." Even though she sometimes got slightly annoyed at her partner for seeming to take her mother's side, she conceded: "I like the fact that my partner respects my mother."

Thus, on the basis of the reports of these respondents, it seems that a partner's encouragement and coaching might have prevented the distancing that would be expected between disapproving parents and their lesbian daughters.

Couple and Family-of-Origin Discord

Sometimes the partner's involvement resulted in conflict, particularly when parents were strongly disapproving of their daughter's lesbianism. In couples in which one woman had a profoundly negative relationship with her parents, pushing the partner to have more contact or to improve her relationship with her parents resulted in conflict. One respondent described how her partner urged her to have contact with her rejecting mother and how this created tension between them: "We argue weekly, she wants me to call my mother. I'll say no, and we go back and forth with that." Another described her partner's mother as very hostile, yet she implored her partner to call her mother:

I think Julie's missing a lot, and I would like her to make an attempt [to contact her disapproving mother]. On Mother's Day I bug her all day to call her mother, and by the afternoon she does it. By the end of the call she is so upset, and she's saying, 'Why do I subject myself to this?'"

Thus, although pushing for contact and intergenerational harmony benefited most of the couples in this study, for women with the most negative parents, this action could strain the couple's relationship.

DISCUSSION

According to Bowen (1978), individuals in functional families are intimately connected yet allow each other the autonomy

to define or differentiate themselves and develop relationships with significant others. Because they are able to distinguish between thoughts and feelings, differentiated family members are able to disagree without letting their emotions interfere with their ability to negotiate and compromise. As a result, differing points of view can be tolerated without threatening family relationships (Kerr & Bowen, 1988).

Conversely, *fusion* describes the inability to separate thinking from feeling (Kerr & Bowen, 1988). The fused person is immersed in emotionality, as are her or his relationships, and is unable to understand accurately or tolerate the discomfort that arises when family members disagree. Attempting to control others through destructive arguments, distancing, or sublimating one's needs for the sake of harmony are ways family members undermine their own and each other's independence and maintain a fused homeostasis. Conceptually, fusion as defined by Bowen is not to be confused with the high levels of intimacy found in many lesbian relationships (Green, Bettinger, & Zacks, 1996). Fusion actually impedes intimacy; people struggling with fusion are so overwhelmed with their own anxiety and dependency needs that they are unable to recognize and attend to the needs of their partners.

Bowen (1978) and Kerr and Bowen (1988) believed that even the healthiest family's differentiation levels could diminish in a crisis, and the profoundly negative parental reactions experienced by the respondents on coming out suggest that such a regression may have occurred. However, despite their ongoing shame and worry about their daughters' lesbianism, many parents' attitudes improved to the extent that they were able to support their daughters' relationships. Maintaining connections despite differing points of view, as these parents did, is a hallmark of differentiation. In a related manner, lesbians who come out could be seeking to differentiate themselves because they are defining who they are and risking parental disapproval in the hopes of eventually establishing a more honest closeness. Asserting oneself when necessary, as did the women in this study, could be seen as one way a lesbian avoids the pitfalls of fusion and maintains appropriate intergenerational boundaries.

Boszorymenyi-Nagy and Spark (1973) claimed that for marriages to flourish individuals must place their relationships with their spouses ahead of those with their parents. However, it is reasonable to imagine that in the face of parental disapproval, gay women might hide or minimize the importance of their long-term partner relationships to maintain intergenerational peace. Such prioritization of parents would, in turn, be expected to lead to conflict in the partner relationship. However, for the women in this study, parental disapproval did not affect their relationships, thanks to their own boundary-setting behavior. In addition, the respondents' partners seemed to facilitate functional intergenerational relationships by helping the interviewees affirm appropriate intergenerational boundaries when parental hostility threatened to interfere with the partner relationship.

Furthermore, partners pushed respondents to maintain contact with family when, presumably, they perceived too much strain or distance between generations. For some women, their partners helped them see their parents in a more objective way. Thus, partners may have functioned in ways to minimize the potential for fusion and encourage healthy, intergenerational relating. According to Bowen (1978) *differentiation* describes an appropriate balance between connection and autonomy among family members, and the partners' support of not only protective intergenerational boundaries but also harmonious parental connections could be interpreted as efforts to help the respondents establish or maintain appropriate levels of differentiation.

The emergence of the women's partners as an important resource in the respondents' parental relationships was somewhat surprising considering that the literature on coming out to parents generally does not address how partners can help or hinder intergenerational relationships. In addition, according to Bowenian theory, a person's differentiation level is a product of past family relationships (Bowen, 1978; Kerr & Bowen, 1988). The findings from this study raise the possibility that a strong partner relationship might increase the basic level of differentiation and improve an individual's relationship with her parents. Certainly, this is an important topic for future research.

Fusion was evident in some of the respondents' parental and partner relationships. It seemed that parents who were continuously antagonistic were unable to put aside their own feelings to have meaningful relationships with their daughters, and this suggests a lack of differentiation. Several of the women with hostile parents were emotionally distant or cut off from their families. However, their partners pushed them to relate to their parents, even when this seemed to hurt their relationships with each other. Bowen (1978) believed that fusion was transmitted across generations by the tendency of people to marry others whose low differentiation levels matched their own. Some of the women from troubled families may have pushed their partners to the point of conflict because they were projecting their own unresolved issues with their parents onto their partners and in-laws. In addition, putting herself between her partner and her partner's hostile parents by arguing the parents' viewpoint could have given the troubled partner an outlet to express her anger without threatening the homeostasis of the problematic intergenerational relationship. In these circumstances, partner encouragement did not help parental relationships and actually strained partner relationships.

Additional research is needed to determine the relationships between parental disapproval, intergenerational discord, and relationship satisfaction for lesbian couples. In the meantime, social workers and other clinicians helping lesbians heal their relationships with their parents need to understand that whereas parental feelings and opinions about a daughter's lesbianism may improve from the initial disclosure, parental shame and worry can persist. Even if her parents never fully accept her sexual orientation, helping a lesbian client set intergenerational boundaries can assist her in maintaining healthy relationships with her parents and her partner. In addition, the often helpful but at times problematic role of the partner in encouraging intergenerational relationships found in this study suggests that social workers and family therapists need to assess the partner's potential as a resource for their lesbian clients' parental relationships carefully.

Caution should be taken in generalizing the findings from this small, mostly white sample. The family dynamics of lesbians of color may differ from those of their white counterparts. For example, Greene and Boyd-Franklin (1996) pointed out that for African Americans, the family serves an important protective function by buffering its members against the economic and psychological burdens of racism. As a result, an African American lesbian might be less willing to risk the family rejection that can occur if she chooses to live outside of the closet. An African American respondent from this study decided to terminate her relationship in the face of intergenerational pressure, and perhaps her fear of losing this special, protective family support contributed to her decision.

Research findings suggest that Latinos, African Americans, and Asian Americans may be more reluctant to come out to their parents, fearing that the antigay sentiment within their cultures makes parental rejection likely (Chan, 1989; Merighi & Grimes, 2000; Tremble, Schneider, & Appathurai, 1989). Clearly, more information is needed regarding family issues that are unique to lesbians of various races and ethnicities.

These findings support and in some ways add to those of earlier studies (Ben-Ari, 1995; D'Augelli et al., 1998) that found that parental attitudes toward their daughters' lesbianism that were initially very negative seemed to improve as time passed from the initial disclosure. However, the qualitative methods used in this study helped add to this information by identifying the blend of perceived parental feelings that included shame, fear, and support. It should be noted that this was a study not of actual parents' attitudes but of their daughters' perceptions of those attitudes. Interviews with parents could better elicit their feelings and opinions about their gay daughters. The qualitative approach also was useful in identifying what may be the important facilitative role of the partner in improving relationships with parents.

Researchers who study the issues and concerns of lesbians have called for more investigation of the effects of family relationships on lesbians' well-being (Institute of Medicine, 1999). Clearly, more quantitative and qualitative examination of how lesbians negotiate intergenerational family dynamics is needed to inform family scholars about this variant family form and to help social workers and other mental health professionals understand the distinct clinical needs of this understudied population.

REFERENCES

Beeler, J., & DiProva, V. (1999). Family adjustment following disclosure of homosexuality by a member: Themes discerned in narrative accounts. *Journal of Marital and Family Therapy, 25*, 443–459.

Ben-Ari, A. (1995). The discovery that an offspring is gay: Parents', gay men's and lesbians' perspectives. *Journal of Homosexuality, 30*, 89–112.

Bernstein, B. (1990). Attitudes and issues of parents, gay men and lesbians and implications for therapy. *Journal of Gay & Lesbian Psychotherapy, 1*, 37–53.

Boszorymenyi-Nagy, I., & Spark, G. (1973). *Invisible loyalties: Reciprocity in intergenerational family therapy.* New York: Harper & Row.

Bowen, M. (1978). *Family therapy in clinical practice.* New York: Aronson.

Bradford, J., Ryan, C., & Rothblum, E. (1994). National lesbian health care survey: Implications for mental health care. *Journal of Consulting and Clinical Psychology, 62,* 228–242.

Bryant, A. S., & Demian. (1994). Relationship characteristics of American gays and lesbians: Findings from a national survey. *Journal of Gay & Lesbian Social Services, 1,* 101–117.

Burger, E., & Milardo, R. (1995). Marital interdependence and social networks. *Journal of Social and Personal Relationships, 12,* 403–415.

Caron, S. L., & Ulin, M. (1997). Closeting and the quality of lesbian relationships. *Families in Society, 78,* 413–419.

Chan, C. (1989). Issues of identity development among Asian-American lesbians and gay men. *Journal of Counseling and Development, 68,* 16–20.

Cramer, D., & Roach, A. (1988). Coming out to mom and dad: A study of gay males and their relationships with their parents. *Journal of Homosexuality, 15,* 79–91.

D'Augelli, A. R., Hershberger, S. L., & Pilkington, N. W. (1998). Lesbian, gay, and bisexual youth and their families: Disclosure of sexual orientation and its consequences. *American Journal of Orthopsychiatry, 68,* 361–371.

Dillard, C., & Protinsky, H. (1985). Emotional cutoff: A comparative analysis of clinical versus nonclinical populations. *International Journal of Family Psychiatry, 6,* 339–349.

Driscoll, R., Davis, K., & Lipetz, M. (1972). Parental interference and romantic love: The Romeo and Juliet effect. *Journal of Personality and Social Psychology, 24,* 1–10.

Floyd, F., Stein, T., Harter, T., Allison, A., & Nye, C. (1999). Gay, lesbian, and bisexual youths: Separation—individuation, parental attitudes, identity consolidation, and well-being. *Journal of Youth and Adolescence, 28,* 719–736.

Fortune, A. E., & Reid, W. J. (1998). *Research in social work* (3rd ed.). New York: Columbia University Press.

Glaser, B. G. (1978). *Theoretical sensitivity: Advances in the methodology of grounded theory.* Mill Valley, CA: Sociology Press.

Green, R. J., Bettinger, M., & Zacks, E. (1996). Are lesbian couples fused and gay male couples disengaged? Questioning gender stereotypes. In J. Laird & R. J. Green (Eds.), *Lesbians and gays in families: A handbook for therapists* (pp.185–230). San Francisco: Jossey-Bass.

Greene, B., & Boyd-Franklin, N. (1996). African American lesbians: Issues in couples therapy. In J. Laird & R. J. Green (Eds.), *Lesbians and gays in families: A handbook for therapists* (pp. 251–271). San Francisco: Jossey-Bass.

Iasenza, P., Colucci, P., & Rothberg, B. (1996). Coming out and the mother-daughter bond: Two case examples. In J. Laird & R. J. Green (Eds.), *Lesbians and gays in families: A handbook for therapists* (pp. 123–136). San Francisco: Jossey-Bass.

Institute of Medicine. (1999). *Lesbian health: Current assessment and directions for the future.* Washington, DC: National Academy Press.

Jedlicka, D. (1984). Indirect parental influence on mate choice: A test of psychoanalytic theory. *Journal of Marriage and the Family, 46,* 65–70.

Kerr, M., & Bowen, M. (1988). *Family evaluation: An approach based on Bowen theory.* New York: W. W. Norton.

Krestan, J., & Bepko, C. (1980). The problem of fusion in the lesbian relationship. *Family Process, 19,* 277–289.

Kurdek, L. A. (1988). Perceived social support in gays and lesbians in cohabitating relationships. *Journal of Personality and Social Psychology, 54,* 504–509.

Kurdek, L. A., & Schmitt, J. P. (1987). Perceived emotional support from family and friends in members of homosexual, married and heterosexual cohabitating couples. *Journal of Homosexuality, 14,* 57–68.

LaSala, M. C. (2000). Lesbians, gay men and their parents: Family therapy for the coming-out crisis. *Family Process, 39,* 67–81.

Leigh, G. (1982). Kinship interaction over the family life span. *Journal of Marriage and the Family, 44,* 197–208.

Lewis, J. (1989). *The birth of the family: An empirical inquiry.* New York: Brunner/Mazel.

Lincoln, Y. S., & Guba, E. G. (1985). *Naturalistic inquiry.* Beverly Hills, CA: Sage Publications.

Lofland, J., & Lofland, L. (1984). *Analyzing social settings: A guide to qualitative observation and analysis.* Belmont, CA: Wadsworth.

Martin, J. I., & Knox, J. (2000). Methodological and ethical issues in research on lesbians and gay men. *Social Work Research, 24,* 51–59.

Merighi, J. R., & Grimes, M. D. (2000). Coming out to families in a multicultural context. *Families in Society, 81,* 32–41.

Muller, A. (1987). *Parents matter: Parents' relationships with lesbian daughters and gay sons.* Tallahassee, FL: Naiad Press.

Murphy, B. C. (1989). Lesbian couples and their parents: The effects of perceived parental attitudes on the couple. *Journal of Counseling & Development, 68,* 46–51.

Patton, M. Q. (1990). *Qualitative evaluation and research methods* (2nd ed.). Newbury Park, CA: Sage Publications.

Results of poll. (1989, June 6). *San Francisco Examiner,* p. A19.

Savin-Williams, R. (1989a). Coming out to parents and self-esteem among gay and lesbian youths. *Journal of Homosexuality, 18,* 1–35.

Savin-Williams, R. (1989b). Parental influences on the self-esteem of gay and lesbian youths: A reflected appraisals model. *Journal of Homosexuality, 17,* 93–109.

Tremble, B., Schneider, M., & Appathurai, C. (1989). Growing up gay or lesbian in a multicultural context. *Journal of Homosexuality, 17,* 253–267.

Warshow, J. (1991). How lesbian identity affects the mother/ daughter relationship. In B. Sang, J. Warshow, & D. Smith (Eds.), *Lesbians at midlife: The creative transition* (pp. 81–83). San Francisco: Spinster Books.

Michael C. LaSala, MSW, PhD, is assistant professor, School of Social Work, Rutgers—The State University of New Jersey, 536 George Street, New Brunswick, NJ 08901–1167; e-mail: mlasala@rci.rutgers.edu. The author thanks Annmarie Agosta for her data collection assistance.

From *Social Work Research,* March 2001, pp. 27-35. © 2001 by National Association of Social Workers, Inc., Social Work Research. Reprinted by permission.

UNIT 4

Crises—Challenges and Opportunities

Unit Selections

Key Points to Consider

- How does an abusive relationship develop? What, if anything, can be done to prevent it?

- If you felt your sexual relationship was troubled, how would you act? Would you discuss it with your partner? Explain.

- What is the best way to work out the competing demands of work and family?

- What would you give up to care for your parents? How do/should we respond to uncertain losses like a stillborn child?

 **Links: www.dushkin.com/online/**
These sites are annotated in the World Wide Web pages.

Alzheimer's Association
http://www.alz.org

American Association of Retired Persons
http://www.aarp.org

Caregiver's Handbook
http://www.acsu.buffalo.edu/~drstall/hndbk0.html

Children & Divorce
http://www.hec.ohio-state.edu/famlife/divorce/

Parenting.com
http://www.parenting.com/parenting/

National Crime Prevention Council
http://www.ncpc.org

Widow Net
http://www.fortnet.org/WidowNet/

*S*tress is life and life is stress. Sometimes stress in families gives new meaning to this statement. When a crisis occurs in families, many processes occur simultaneously as families and their members cope with the stressor and its effects. The experience of a crisis often leads to conflict and reduces the family members' ability to act as resources for each other. Indeed, a stressor can overwhelm the family system, and family members may be among the least effective people in coping with each other's responses to a crisis.

Family crisis comes in many forms; it can be drawn out or the crisis event can be clearly defined. The source of stress can be outside or inside the family, or it can be a combination of both. It can directly involve all family members or as few as one, but the effects will ripple through the family, affecting all of its members to one degree or another.

In this unit, we consider a wide variety of crises. Family violence is the initial focus. "Hitting Home" argues that greater awareness of the cycle of violence and the complexity of an abusive relationship can only benefit us as a nation.

The next subsection deals with problems in sexuality and sexual relationships. A good sex life is important to the life of a relationship, yet the underlying meaning attributed to it makes it difficult to discuss. In "Sex & Marriage," ways in which a couple can improve their sex life are addressed. The next article, "Is Your Dog (Cat, Bird, Fish) More Faithful Than Your Spouse?" presents six examples of affairs that indicate specific underlying problems between spouses.

The subsection that follows looks at the work/family connection, with interesting results. "The Politics of Fatigue: The Gender War Has Been Replaced by the Exhaustion of Trying to Do It All" addresses gender differences in the workplace and the impact on family life as well as the overwhelming nature of the struggle to balance work and home. "What Kids (Really) Need" addresses the risks and benefits of day care.

Mental illness is the focus of the next section, and is addressed in "The Binds That Tie—and Heal: How Families Cope With Mental Illness." As this article clearly shows, families can add to the stress of mental illness, but they can also be a major factor in the management of the illness.

Divorce and remarriage are the subjects of the next two subsections. In the first article, E. Mavis Hetherington presents an overview of "Marriage and Divorce American Style." Then Benedict Carey, in "Is Divorce Too Easy?" says that women are paying the price of easy divorce, which has led a coalition of feminists and conservatives to want to change divorce laws in order to make breaking up more difficult to do. A somewhat different view is presented in "The Happy Divorce: How to Break Up and Make Up," which argues that methods of easing the changed relationship after divorce can only benefit both partners and any children they may have. The other side of divorce—re-

marriage—is the focus of the next two articles. "Divorced? Don't Even Think of Remarrying Until You Read This" provides insights on what should be dealt with before one remarries, while "When Strangers Become Family" addresses issues that arise when stepfamilies are formed.

The nature of stress resulting from caring for others in the family is the subject of the final subsection. "Elder Care: Making the Right Choice" presents a variety of methods by which family members can provide aid to an elderly family member. The next article addresses a particular loss to death that often is not discussed—"Still Birth." Finally, the special needs of children are discussed in "After a Loss, Kids Need to Mourn and Be Reassured."

Hitting Home

Domestic violence is the issue that embarrasses traditionalists. Today, despite greater awareness and a variety of model programs, partner abuse is still far too prevalent.

BY CARA FEINBERG

A LEATHERY WOMAN WITH A DARKENING BLACK eye smokes cigarettes through the spaces of her missing front teeth and tells the police how her boyfriend slapped and bit her because he didn't like her grandchildren. Another woman tells a counselor at a shelter that she's tried to leave her husband 15 times in the two years that she's been married to him. Still another can't speak at all, her moans incoherent as she's wheeled out of her house on a stretcher covered in blood, her cheek slashed into two loose flaps from the corner of her mouth.

These graphic details of domestic abuse come to us courtesy of documentary filmmaker Frederick Wiseman, whose camera has been mercilessly recording the often unpleasant aspects of our social reality for three decades. In the years since 1967, when his first documentary, *Titicut Follies*, garnered artistic awards and journalistic respect—and an injunction from the Massachusetts Superior Court, which banned the film in the state for the next 24 years—Wiseman has captured everything from the crumbling walls of a housing project to the locker-lined hallways of a high school, from a ballet company to a state prison for the criminally insane. Using his signature cinema verité style—there is no narration, music, or overt editorializing in his films—Wiseman has become a barometer of our values and mores, revealing our culture and progress by observing our social organizations, institutions and institutional practices.

It is therefore telling that Wiseman has chosen to take on the issue of domestic violence at precisely this moment. While the scenes from his latest film, *Domestic Violence*, are explicit, we've seen these types of images before. Hardly a news cycle goes by nowadays without a domestic-violence story. The

media attention is a salutary development; not long ago, domestic violence didn't exist as a legal or social concept.

Yet while we've come incredibly far in our struggle to recognize domestic violence as a national, public problem, battered women now face a new set of challenges—preeminent among them, the religious right's efforts to portray marriage as the panacea for all social and moral problems. If only we could all just pair up in happily heterosexual matrimony and stay that way, the logic goes, social ills such as violence, crime, and poverty would simply wither away.

While ample data suggest the social and personal benefits of a happy marriage, the get-married-and-stay-married-at-all-costs ethos often ignores the damage that bad marriages can do both to adults and to children. And domestic abuse? Social conservatives often pretend that the problem would disappear if only more people got and stayed married. They make it more difficult for women to leave abusive relationships—not only by steeling social attitudes against divorce but by making it contractually harder (through such vehicles as "covenant marriages") for domestic-violence victims to escape.

> "Everyone asks why she continues to stay; no one thinks to ask, 'Why does he hit her in the first place?'"

Moreover, social conservatives tend to confuse marriage policy with welfare policy; indeed, they would like to replace the latter with the former. This is the "get-married-and-stay-married-and-you-won't-need-welfare" argument. Robert Rector, a senior fellow at the Heritage Foundation, argues that marriage incentives must be built into Temporary Assistance for Needy Families (TANF)—the basic federal welfare program, designed to provide assistance and work opportunities—and that divorced and out-of-wedlock mothers should get diminished levels of welfare assistance for not being married. This is a typical conservative argument that not only gets the relationship between poverty and welfare backward—and this is a great source of liberal-conservative argument generally—but also makes it much harder for wives to leave their abusive husbands, for fear of being financially penalized.

DOMESTIC VIOLENCE AND THE LAW

It is this sort of rhetoric that threatens to roll back the heroic—and remarkably recent—achievements of the battered-women's movement. As late as the 1960s, if you looked at American newspapers, police reports, medical records, and legal texts, you would find little mention of domestic violence anywhere. "In the last few decades, there has been a great surge in attention to this issue," says Clare Dalton, Northeastern University's Matthews Distinguished University Professor of Law, who is a leading feminist legal scholar and a pioneer in the development of legal education about domestic violence. A founder of Northeastern's domestic-violence clinical program and the Domestic Violence Institute (an interdisciplinary educational, research, and service organization), Dalton served as a consultant on Wiseman's film and led discussions about the issue at several showings of *Domestic Violence* in the Boston area.

"Right up into the 1980s, we still had states in the Union with out-of-date immunity laws based on common law from the 1800s, protecting men who beat their wives," Dalton says. "It was only 10 years ago now that the Supreme Court was even ready to recognize the severity of domestic violence in our country—only eight years ago that Congress addressed it on a federal level with the Violence Against Women Act [VAWA]."

... the number of women dying in domestic-violence situations hasn't changed. The problem is as widespread as ever.

That legislation, passed initially in 1994 and renewed by Congress in 2000, was a milestone: It was the first federal law ever to address the issue, and it came at the problem with a variety of solutions, including funding for women's shelters, a national domestic-abuse hot line, rape education-and-prevention programs, training for federal and state judges, new remedies for battered immigrants, and criminal enforcement of interstate orders of protection.

As Dalton points out, VAWA would have been impossible without the work that began with the feminist movement of the 1960s and 1970s. "Our latest campaign against domestic violence grew directly out of the movement," she says. "For the first time, women were getting together and talking about their experiences and discovering the great prevalence of these unspoken terrors. Emerging feminist theory allowed women to connect with each other and to the ideas that feminists had been arguing for all along: that women's legally sanctioned subordination within the family was denying them equality."

Taking their cue from the civil-rights and antiwar movements earlier, feminist activists began to see the law not only as an important tool for protecting victims but as a way to define domestic violence as a legitimate social problem. Local legal groups and grass-roots advocacy organizations began to develop legal remedies based on the link between sexual discrimination and violence. Starting in the sixties, lawyers began to seek civil-protective or restraining orders to keep batterers away from their victims. Courts began to create special rules for domestic-violence cases and custody cases involving children from violent homes. And by the mid-1990s, Congress had passed VAWA. Today, feminist advocates for battered women have begun to draw important interconnections among battering, poverty, welfare reform, homelessness, immigration, employment, gun control, and many other areas of concern. They are working with all sorts of organizations to step up education and reform.

THE PSYCHOLOGY OF ABUSE

While the stories of domestic violence in Wiseman's film are horrifying, even the most compassionate viewer's sympathy can run thin when victims shun opportunities to abandon their own torture chambers. Of the three women in the opening scene who have called the police, not one is prepared to listen to advice about legal options or free social services. Rather, each one simply continues recounting her abuse, speaking as if she had never even heard the officers' recommendations.

"We have always looked at the victim and said, 'Well, why doesn't she just leave?'" says Lynn Rosenthal, executive director of the Washington, D.C.-based National Network to End Domestic Violence. "We've got cops and judges and lawyers who get upset when victims don't flee, or fail to report their abusers, or don't show up in court to press charges." This past January, a judge in Lexington, Kentucky, sparked outrage among victims' advocates when she fined two women for contempt of court because they returned to their alleged abusers despite having obtained protective orders against them. "But this attitude places the burden on the victim, not the abuser," Rosenthal says. "Everyone asks why she continues to stay; no one thinks to ask, 'Why does he hit her in the first place?'"

Dr. Judith Lewis Herman, an associate clinical professor of psychiatry at Harvard Medical School and the training director of the Victims of Violence Program at Cambridge Hospital, has been fighting to change this perception of victims for more than 30 years. "The tendency to blame the victim has always influ-

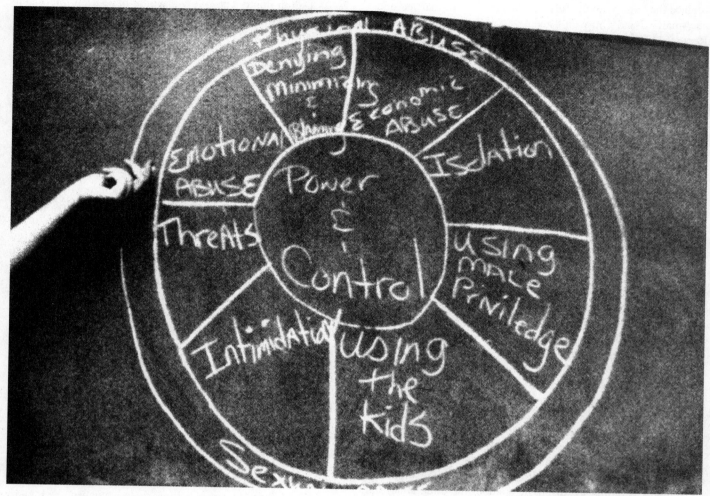

Frederick Wiseman's film Domestic Violence shows the "Power & Control" wheel, a chart summarizing abuser's primary tactics.

enced the direction of psychological study," Herman said in an interview in her office at Harvard. "Research had always looked at what the woman did to provoke her batterer, or it focused on her own 'personality disorders.'" In 1964, for example, researchers conducted an egregious study of battered women called *The Wife-Beater's Wife*, in which the inquiries were directed toward women simply because the men refused to talk. The clinicians identified the women as "frigid" or "indecisive" and went on to *treat* the women so they would stop "provoking" their husbands.

In the mid-1980s, when the diagnostic manual of the American Psychiatric Association came up for revision, this misdiagnosis of victims—and the tendency to blame them for their partners' violence—became the center of a heated controversy. A group of male psychoanalysts proposed that "masochistic personality disorder" be added to the manual to describe any person "who remains in relationships in which others exploit, abuse, or take advantage of him or her, despite opportunities to alter the situation"—a proposal that outraged women's groups around the country. Herman was one of the leaders in the fight to formulate a new diagnosis that accurately described the psy-

chological conditions of battered women. Herman proposed "complex post-traumatic stress disorder," which describes a spectrum of conditions rather than a single disorder, and is now listed as a subcategory of post-traumatic stress disorder in the latest edition of the standard diagnostic manual.

ALTHOUGH WISEMAN RECOUNTS NONE OF THIS POLITICAL or legal history explicitly in *Domestic Violence*, the evidence of these years of struggle pervades every frame he shoots. In the opening sequence, a lean, tattooed, middle-aged man wearing only his undershorts asks, "Why do you always take the woman's word?" as police officers cuff and arrest him.

"When it comes to domestic violence," they respond, "that's the way it is. If she says you hit her, you hit her."

This brief exchange may not seem particularly significant—after all, if a stranger had assaulted a woman in a parking lot, we would expect the police to haul him away. But the very fact that the Tampa, Florida, officers responded immediately to a call for domestic violence and then removed the batterer from his home without hesitation or an arrest warrant is a testament to the progressive laws, police training, and legislative reform developed and implemented in the past 30 years.

According to Elizabeth M. Schneider, a professor at Brooklyn Law School and the author of *Battered Women and Feminist Lawmaking* (2000), one of first and most important legal issues to come to the attention of the feminist movement in the 1960s was the failure of police to protect battered women from assault. By the 1970s, class-action lawsuits were filed in New York City and Oakland, California. All of a sudden, domestic violence was considered a crime against the public and the state, not just the individual.

Yet even these victories and others like them initially made little headway in police attitudes and practices. Nineteen years ago, a woman named Tracey Thurman was nearly beaten to death in Torrington, Connecticut, before the police came to her aid. Though Thurman had reported her estranged husband's threats and harassment to the police repeatedly for over a year, it wasn't until she called in utter desperation, fearing for her life, that the police responded. They sent only one officer, however, who arrived 25 minutes after the call was placed, pulled up across the street from Thurman's house, and sat in his car while Thurman's husband chased her across the yard, slashed her with a knife, stabbed her in the neck, knocked her to the ground, and then stabbed her 12 more times.

Permanently disfigured, Tracey Thurman brought what became a landmark case to the Supreme Court, which found that the city police had violated her 14th Amendment right to "equal protection of the laws" and awarded her $2.3 million in compensatory damages. Almost immediately, the State of Connecticut adopted a new, comprehensive domestic-violence law calling for the arrest of assaultive spouses. In the year after the measure took effect, the number of arrests for domestic assault increased 92 percent, from 12,400 to 23,830.

"We'd all like to look at our progress and be optimistic," says Clare Dalton. "But if you look at the most recent statistics from the Justice Department, the number of women dying in domestic-violence situations hasn't changed. The problem is as widespread as ever.

"But there is one interesting thing here," Dalton notes. "While the number of deaths among women hasn't changed, fatalities among men have dropped significantly. This, in truth, is our first real triumph. If women feel they can get help—if they believe the police will come when they call them, if they understand they will get support and have a place to go where they will be safe with their children—then fewer are pushed to the wall. Fewer will resort to killing or dying at the hand of their abuser."

THE TAMPA EXAMPLE

Such wisdom has not been lost on the City of Tampa Police Department, whose progressive, community-wide response to the problem Frederick Wiseman chose to film for *Domestic Violence*. Tampa's network of coordinated, cooperative services—from law enforcement, to social services, to the legal system—is a model example of similar programs around the country.

"We now have a zero-tolerance policy toward domestic violence here in Tampa," said Lieutenant Rod Reder, a 24-year veteran of the Hillsborough County Sheriff's Office in Tampa, when reached by phone. A former supervisor for the Sex Crimes Division and onetime member of the Governor's Domestic and Sexual Violence Task Force, Reder is now widely considered to be an expert in the field of domestic and sexual violence. Under the auspices of the U.S. Department of Justice, he runs training sessions for law-enforcement officers at conferences nationwide. "We discovered there were so many simple things we weren't doing... to help victims of domestic violence," Reder said. "And we found there really is only one way to make things work. All the community players have to come to the table; otherwise, it's the victim's safety that gets compromised."

> "In the past, many officers looked at domestic-violence calls as a waste of time or a private family matter. Now we consider them some of the most dangerous calls there are."

The catalyst for Tampa's adoption of community cooperation was a woman named Mabel Bexley, who in 1981 pushed Reder to bring police practices in line with new domestic-violence laws, and who two years later became the director of a women's shelter called the Spring. In her 19-year tenure there, Bexley, now 65 and recently retired, expanded the Spring—which is the focus of much of Wiseman's documentary—from a three-bedroom house with more than a dozen women and children huddled inside to a 102-bed facility with 120 employees and a $4-million budget.

Reder and Bexley teamed up again in 1995, when Tampa hit an all-time high in domestic-violence-related homicide, to work alongside members of the state attorney's office and the 13th Judicial Circuit Court to form the zero-tolerance campaign against domestic abuse. Reder and the Hillsborough County police then formed a special domestic-violence unit and developed a three-day training seminar for all seven local law-enforcement agencies.

"We do all sorts of things now to make the system work," said Reder. "When police answer a domestic-violence call, they are required to file a report—even if there is no arrest—just so the incident is documented. We had deputies who would walk away from incidents saying, 'No harm, no foul,' and would leave with no report," he recalled. "But now officers are required to document domestics by state law. You start dinging a few deputies and taking disciplinary action, and word gets out real quick: If you go to a domestic, write a report."

According to Reder, Tampa officers have also become very aggressive about arrests: "We used to think we were doing the right thing by not arresting the man—we didn't want to get him any angrier than he already was. In the past, many officers looked at domestic-violence calls as a waste of time or a private family matter. Now we consider them some of the most dangerous calls there are."

Hillsborough County has also addressed other gaps in the system. "We've sent advocates to go pick up victims at their homes so they'd be sure to get to court," said Reder. "We used to have communal waiting rooms in the courthouse, but now we have separate ones so victims won't have to face their abusers before their trial begins. To file an injunction, you used to have to fill out a complicated 25-page form that was only available in English. This alone used to scare people away, so now we have bilingual advocates and lawyers available to help people fill them out."

This is where the Spring comes in. Though most victims who arrive at the shelter are running for their lives and have no desire even to consider legal action against their abusers at that point, the facility employs an on-site attorney to help them navigate the judicial system and pursue the available options. In addition, each one of the Spring's hot-line operators is a deputy of the court who can file injunctions at any hour of the day or night. This is crucial, because the most dangerous time for abuse victims actually begins the moment they choose to leave their homes. "The Bureau of Justice statistics say that one-third of all women murdered in the U.S. are killed by an intimate," says Jennifer Dunbar, who works at the Spring. "But of those 30 percent, 65 percent are murdered when they leave. It's our job to make sure [victims are] protected at this point."

NEARLY 40 YEARS AFTER THE FIRST FEMINIST ACTIVISTS in the women's movement brought domestic violence to the nation's attention, the policies have largely been set and the laws are finally on the books. Now it's a question of making sure that the systems work and helping the larger community to understand, recognize, and accommodate the needs of battered women. "Right now, we're working on expanding efforts into other systems, like job placement, affordable housing, welfare reform, and child-protective services," says Lynn Rosenthal of the National Network. "A number of states now have special domestic-violence provisions within their welfare systems and housing programs. For instance, under the original job-placement programs in the TANF program, people who showed up tardy three times to the program would lose their benefits. A battered woman might have tremendous problems meeting these criteria—her husband could still be sabotaging her efforts." Rosenthal adds: "It's easy to see how our own well-intended programs could send her right back to her batterer."

... in communities where awareness of partner abuse remains limited... reform movements lag well behind their counterparts in more progressive places.

Throughout the country, states have begun to integrate their systems and have developed new, progressive programs to deal with domestic violence. Though they vary in their specific reforms, many have expanded their legal definition of domestic violence to include nonmarried and nontraditional couples. And some, shifting their focus from punishment to rehabilitation, have begun to examine the root causes of violence in the first place. Programs like EMERGE in Cambridge, Massachusetts, work with batterers to find nonviolent ways to express their anger; many others educate children and teens—ideally, before any battering starts. A number of states have created specialized domestic-violence courts so that the judges hearing these cases are not only familiar with and sympathetic to the special circumstances surrounding battering cases but can follow them from start to finish.

Yet for all the progress that has been made in addressing domestic violence, Wiseman's film makes clear that there is a long way yet to go. One problem is how practically and psychologically difficult it can be for a victim to leave her batterer. But another is the complexity of the political environment itself. As elected officials come and go, their varying agendas affect the winds of legislative change and shift fiscal priorities along with idealistic convictions. According to Robin Thompson, the former executive director of the Florida Governor's Task Force on Domestic Violence, in order for a state to stay vigilant in its fight against domestic abuse there must be "a bedrock of political commitment"—be it a designated task force or a group of grass-roots activists invested in educating and uniting their community. Awareness alone is not enough.

And while states may have implemented great judicial and law-enforcement reforms, if these are not closely monitored and coordinated, they can still fall short of their goals. For instance, if an accused batterer is arrested right away but then must wait six months for a trial, the victim is still largely unprotected. Or if a judge orders a defendant to participate in an intervention program but no one checks to see if he complies, the sentence may be useless.

Obstacles to reform certainly don't fall neatly along partisan lines. A liberal judge might opt for a surprisingly lenient sentence for a defendent, while a conservative judge might make an equally counterintuitive ruling, viewing the court as the woman's traditional protectorate. Yet in communities where awareness of partner abuse remains limited—and partisan issues such as welfare, gun ownership, and "family values" remain entwined with domestic violence—reform movements lag well behind their counterparts in more progressive places.

So far on a national level, what little government funding there is for community-based programs like the community courts or the Spring has not been cut by the Bush administration. But Rosenthal remains worried about the potential for an "unholy merger" between social conservatives and the growing movement for fathers' rights. Though she respects much of the work that fathers' rights groups have done in calling for more paternal responsibility and accountability, she fears that some men will latch on to the claims of right-wingers who resent gains by the battered-women's movement—and by the feminist movement generally—and will seek to cripple these movements' effectiveness by demanding their defunding.

In a tableau that echoes the opening scene of *Domestic Violence*, Wiseman returns at the end of his documentary to police officers responding to a call. This time, it seems, the outcome will be more hopeful: The call was placed not by a battered woman but by a potential batterer seeking intervention—a last-ditch effort to stave off the violence brewing in his household. But when the police arrive, the couple refuses to listen to their suggestions or take any steps to change the situation. When nei-

ther the man nor the woman agrees to leave the premises, the police ultimately return to their squad car shaking their heads, leaving behind only words of advice and a volatile couple "afraid of what they might do." It is an ominous ending to a celebration of progress—an eerie mirror of the problem we continue to face.

Prospect *assistant editor* CARA FEINBERG *writes the "World Responds" column for Porspect Online.*

SEX
& Marriage

Experts say sex is vital to healthy relationships. Why is it so difficult for couples to do what's good for them?

By Patricia Chisholm

Max is recalling what sex was like before the big job, kids and mortgage. "I was a walking hormone," he says, laughing a little with his wife, Julie, in the basement of their comfortable Montreal home. The thirtysomething parents of two young children, who asked that their real names be withheld, used to fool around at least five times a week. Now, they say, they are lucky to make love that many times a month because they are either physically exhausted or mentally distracted by their demanding daytime roles—his as a boss, hers as a stay-at-home mom. Unlike many couples, though, Max and Julie haven't lost their sense of humour about what they view as a temporary decline in their physical intimacy. "It's a little sad—sex is such an enjoyable, amazing experience, " Max says. "We still really enjoy it. But now I find I'm often just too tired at night. I can get it up, but I just can't get up off the couch." Ah, sex. It's one of the few pleasures left that doesn't bloat the waistline, cause cancer or break the family budget. Researchers claim it even helps prevent wrinkles, and psychologists say it can rejuvenate the most tired relationship. According to a 1998 *Maclean's*/CBC poll, 78 per cent of married Canadians (as opposed to 61 per cent of single respondents) said they were sexually active, and 87 per cent of married Canadians said they were "satisfied" with their sex lives. Sexual monogamy has never been easy, though, and that fact has become depressingly clear to the great glut of baby boomers who grew up with the pill and unprecedented sexual freedom but now are struggling with aging bodies, sexual bore-

dom, marital spats and plain old exhaustion. So much for the Summer of Love.

There is no easy way out, either. The divorce rate is falling as concerns about splintered families and AIDS prompt more people to recognize that breaking up really is hard to do. Statistics Canada reported this year that the number of divorces has fallen for four years in a row, from 78,880 in 1994 to 67,408 in 1997—a 14.5-per-cent drop. Edward Laumann, a University of Chicago sociologist who studies sexual dysfunction, says people appear to be staying together longer, despite lots of problems with sex, because they are realizing that changing partners costs huge amounts of time, money and energy, with no guarantees. "They are aware that divorce is not a one-year experience," he says.

Of course, some passions cannot be revived, and some couples find it's easier to stay put and just be celibate. But in general, therapists say good sex is a hallmark of solid, long-term relationships. It's an opportunity to relax, to put everyday pressures aside and, especially, to reinforce emotional intimacy and physical closeness. More couples are turning to sex aids like toys and videos to ignite passions, while others are exploring unconventional options like long-term affairs and group sex. The permutations may be endless, but one thing is clear: sex, or the lack of it, still speaks volumes. "If you want to look at what is going on in your relationship, look at your sex life—it won't lie to you," advises Sig Taylor, a Calgary marriage counsellor. "It's a barometer, and it's usually the last thing to go. If couples get to the point where there is no sexuality anymore, the relationship is pretty much dead."

Most people are reluctant to talk about an unconventional or problematic sex life, making it one of the last real taboos. But in fact, problems of one kind or another are strikingly common. One of Laumann's recent studies found that, over a one-year period, 43 per cent of women and 31 per cent of men between the ages of 18 and 59 experienced some kind of sexual impediment, including lack of desire, erectile dysfunction and pain during intercourse. "These are huge numbers," he said, "and it's probably an underestimate—people don't like to admit they have problems with sex."

No wonder people don't want to talk about their troubles—the message in the media is that only losers are sitting it out. Explicit, even kinky sex now permeates movies, magazines and the Internet. *Eyes Wide Shut*, the late Stanley Kubrick's heavily hyped film, features the unlikely scenario of a married couple descending into the depths of their own, profoundly disturbing sexual fantasies. Against that backdrop, simple sex with a partner who never changes—except to acquire a few more sags and bags every year—can start to seem, well, ordinary.

What's to be done? Experts say the vast majority of aging-related sexual ailments—erectile dysfunction, pain during intercourse and lack of lubrication—can be cured medically. But lasting solutions have to start with talk. "If couples pretend nothing is wrong, it only prolongs the problem," says Laumann. "Discussing it takes the edge off." The consequences of not talking can blight a life. "At the beginning of our marriage, things were great," says Frank, a 68-year-old retired Ontario businessman who asked for anonymity. "We had sex a couple of times a week and we were great friends." But their sex life declined sharply after they started having kids—he and his wife now have three grown children. "I felt I was inadequate," he says. "There were so many times I quietly hid my face under the sheets and cried."

He and his wife separated, but they have since struck an uneasy truce and now live together, although their sex life never resumed. Recently, he learned from a TV talk show that it is common for sexual appetites to fluctuate widely from year to year, and that the combination of life pressures and hormones is usually to blame. "I think we need to talk more about sex," he says now. "If I had known this was her body and not me, I would have done everything to fight for her."

The elation people experience at the beginning of a relationship is really more akin to a drug-induced high

Hormones can be responsible for the ups as well as the downs. The elation people feel early in a relationship is akin to a drug-induced high and is just about as sustainable, experts say. "The amount of adrenaline in the body is so great, you can get by with almost no sleep," says Richard Dearing, director of the Marriage Therapy Program at the University of Winnipeg. "You just don't have the energy to keep that going for more than a few months."

As passions abate, couples stand back and take a hard look at one another. Details of character and temperament kick in, and partners begin to make decisions based on compatibility. They may also notice that sex plays different roles in their respective lives. Libidos can differ wildly, partly because of natural hormonal levels—testosterone in men, androgen in women—and partly because of the approach that individuals take to sex. Dearing, like many therapists, has found that, typically, men use sex to feel good, while women need to feel good before they get into bed. The result when life gets stressful? He wants to, she doesn't.

Of course, there are no rigid categories when it comes to sex drive, and for many couples the roles are reversed. In either case, a mismatch can create big problems. Sipping a glass of white wine on a restaurant patio in Vancouver, a 38-year-old woman reflects on the recent breakup of her four-year, live-in relationship. "I realize that sex can't always be the priority," she says. "But for me, it's a way to let go of the day's hassles. You can get into it, just for the sake of pure, physical pleasure." She stayed with her partner for two years after their sex life ended, a phase that began when he was laid off. Despite her repeated efforts, it never resumed. "There was nothing I could do to reach him, and after a while I stopped trying because the rejection was too hard to take. It was horrible," she recalls. "A relationship to me is a partnership—you play as a team. When something as basic as your physical intimacy breaks down, it's impossible to think of yourself that way anymore. One of you has broken the contract."

Even when two people agree on what they want out of life, and seem to be getting it, sex can suffer. Phil Bentley, 44, and John Doleman, 37, have lived together in Toronto for more than a decade. Unlike many couples, gay or straight, their early years together were tough because they decided to put all their efforts into paying off a large mortgage. They took in boarders and each worked at two jobs. "The house was always full of people so we didn't have many opportunities to be alone," says Bentley. Now, they have more time for one another, and that has translated into better sex. "After this amount of time being together, we are more honest with each other about our sexual needs," says Doleman.

National TV sex-show host Sue Johanson bursts into laughter when the subject of sex and marriage is raised. "The two are not simpatico, " she chortles, only half in jest. But this grandmother has listened to thousands of tales of woe, and she believes there are many ways to revive flagging sexual appetites. As a first step, she says, couples should set aside time for the occasional date. She counsels couples to play games, such as hide-and-seek—in the nude and in the dark. Sex toys can rev things up as well, she contends, although she has found that men are often threatened if a woman buys a vibrator. "They say, 'What do you need that thing for, you've got Mr. Ever Ready here.' But once men use it to stimulate their partner, they're home free—they think it's great."

In fact, there is something of a revolution under way in the area of sex aids, especially for women. Shops like Womyns' Ware in Vancouver and Good For Her in Toronto coax women inside with tasteful decor and shelves free of hard-core videos and magazines, or cheap, crudely made products. At Womyns' Ware, for instance, a sound system plays warm jazz in a light-filled room where merchandise is arranged so that those browsing for lubricants can avoid coming face-to-face with customers sampling handcuffs and leather floggers.

There is also a relatively new line of erotic videos aimed at women, called Femme. Developed by retired porn star Candida Royalle, 48, the videos feature complex story lines and shun sex scenes that degrade women. "There's a lot more out there that is couple-oriented," notes Montrealer Josey Vogels, who writes a syndicated weekly column called *My Messy Bedroom*. "Women want to explore their sexuality more, but they don't want to go to some sleazy hole in the wall—they don't want to feel creepy."

But bedroom toys cannot save a sex life that is undercut by marital conflict or fatigue. "Women are angry because they are aware that they are doing much more of the housework than men are," Johanson says. "A couple gets into bed and he has this copulatory gaze and she just looks at him and thinks, 'This is just one more person to service.' " If they want more sex, she says, men will "have to pick up more of the slack around the house—enough of this nonsense."

Leslie, a mid-40s Victoria-area mother of two young boys, can relate. With a demanding managerial job, and jammed off-hours—daily commutes to two schools, plus appointments for tutoring, soccer, sailing—Leslie says she retreats to the bedroom with one thing in mind. "By the time my head hits the pillow, I'm ready to pass out," she says. Her husband helps a lot with the kids, she says, but she is still the one who knows if it's pizza day at school or whether the dog needs a rabies shot. Too often, sex simply falls to the bottom of her "to-do" list. "Making a date with your mate is good advice, but I also know I should be doing two miles a day on the treadmill," she says wryly. "Trying to recapture the fun you had when you were young is like trying to remember Grade 9 chemistry—you know what apparatus to use, but you're not sure which chemicals you need to get a reaction."

Experts say there are peaks and valleys in everyone's sex life. Claude Guldner, professor emeritus at the University of Guelph and one of Canada's leading sex therapists, says desire tends to follow a U-shaped pattern in most marriages: it is intense during the courtship phase, dips down with the arrival of children and—if couples are lucky—swings strongly upward again when children are older. Often, those at the bottom of the U fail to realize that they may be devoting too much energy to parenting at the expense of their marriage. "We need to educate people that 'husbanding and wifing' continues, even though you are now fathering and mothering," he says.

Some people understand that lesson without being taught. Cheryl, a 40-year-old Halifax hairdresser, and Bob, 43, who works in the offshore gas industry, have been married for 10 years. When their now-five-year-old son was born, the first three months were "challenging," recalls Cheryl, who with her husband requested anonymity. "We just realized that every time we would get intimate, our son would start crying. That was a given and we would just laugh." She says grabbing a few moments here and there is enough to keep sex alive. "Even if it's five minutes in the shower in the morning, when junior is having his catnap, it's better than nothing," she says.

Cheryl says she and her husband have ups and downs, and that things can be especially difficult when her husband arrives home after a month offshore. "I always think of my relationship as the hardest thing I will do in my life, as well as the best thing," she muses. "It's hard to keep yourself present with somebody, to keep yourself vulnerable and open. It's hard to be intimate."

Mutual neglect can do much more than lead to bad sex—it can torpedo a marriage if it spawns infidelity. Guldner, who specializes in counselling couples grappling with the fallout from cheating, says that except for chronic philanderers, affairs are rarely about sex. Usually, the cheater is avoiding another issue: they are turned off by a partner's weight gain, for instance, or they are too often left alone by a spouse obsessed with work. "Many, many people say that sex in the affair isn't nearly as good as it was with their partner," Guldner says. But if couples are willing to confront one another with their problems, they often survive an event that, in the past, was widely viewed as unforgivable. That is partly because cultural shifts have weakened old notions of sexual possessiveness. "There is less exclusivity to the sexual act now because so many people have had premarital sex," Guldner points out.

Some see a discreet affair as a viable alternative. Susan, a Toronto manager in her late 30s who requested anonymity, is deeply committed to her family, even though she has carried on a secret affair for nine years. What she gets from her lover is not better sex, she explains, but intellectual companionship and support in her professional life. Despite that, she has no intention of leaving her husband, with whom she has three school-age children. "Marriage is such a difficult, complex relationship," she says. "I would just be exchanging one set of problems for another if I left. And I think that children have the right to grow up in a home with both parents."

The payoff for couples who remain intimate through a marriage's stress-plagued middle years can be extraordinary

The payoff for couples who remain intimate through a marriage's stressful middle years can be extraordinary. Dartmouth, N.S., residents Les and Joan Halsey have treated sex as a precious, fragile wonder that is integral to the success of their 44-year marriage. "We realized early that it was very important," says Les, 65. "Once a month, we would go out for a candlelight dinner. Taking the time is so important—it's not just going to the bedroom and saying, 'OK, let's have sex now.'"

Joan, 64, recalls times when life got in the way of their physical intimacy—job changes, caring for their three children, periods of depressed libido. And she candidly admits that it was sometimes work for a couple married at 21 to keep themselves from straying. "The seven-year itch, living in suburbia, wild parties—it's only by the grace of God we didn't go that route," she says. And she has some advice for those still battling it out in the trenches. "Don't just have a home, children, work," she advises. "Do things that interested you before you were married. We always had a little bit of something just to ourselves—it keeps us healthy. And now that our family has left the nest, we have this whole new journey together." The motto for marriage, then, is "better sex than sorry."

With Ruth Atherley and Chris Wood in Vancouver,
and Susan McCelland in Toronto

Is Your
Dog (Cat, Bird, Fish)
More Faithful than Your Spouse?

Affairs are never just about sex.

by Emily M. Brown

An affair is not about whether or not your spouse loves you. An affair sends a message about a particular problem between spouses. Six examples follow:

1. Nice couples who never fight. In reality, they're terrified to be anything but nice for fear that conflict will lead to abandonment. They never resolve their differences, so their marriage erodes.

2. Couples who are frightened of intimacy. These couples are afraid of being emotionally vulnerable, so they keep the barriers high between them by fighting. Frequent and intense battles are the emotional connection between them. Sometimes they are verbal, accentuated by slamming doors or other dramatic actions—and in other cases these fights escalate into physical violence. These couples fear closeness more than conflict. They fear that if they let their emotional guard down, they will get hurt, or even be abandoned, or feel trapped.

3. Spouses who use affairs to fill the emptiness inside—much as alcoholics use alcohol—are sexual addicts. Sexual addiction is often viewed as a joke, or as an excuse to be promiscuous, but sexual addiction is real. It is not about sex, however, nor is it about romantic love. Charlotte Kasl, a psychologist, says, *"Sexually addicted adults are seeking parents to love them unconditionally"*.

4. Spouses who are sick of sacrificing their own feelings and needs to take care of others. The affair begins when someone comes along who stirs the vestiges of life in one of the spouses. The affair is serious, long-term and passionate. Once fully involved, the betraying spouse struggles to decide between the marriage and the other person.

This kind of affair is often regarded as midlife crisis, but it is much more. Your spouse was not looking for an affair, but the years of not attending to his own feelings made him a prime candidate. He was charmed and excited when a friendship with a colleague began to blossom. He had been starving emotionally, so he acted impulsively, although not without the sense of betraying a trust. He and his colleague became seriously involved—even while he was trying to decide which one was the right person for him. He doesn't really want to end his marriage. Yet he certainly doesn't want to end the affair, although he knows he should. So change lies ahead.

5. Exit Affairs. An exit affair is the *vehicle* for ending the marriage—not the reason. This is the kind of affair that a spouse launches when the marriage is deteriorating, and endings are hard for him. The affair provides a way of sliding out the door.

What you need to do is understand what each of you contributed to the collapse of your marriage. However, it is unlikely that you will put this kind of marriage back together.

6. What about affairs that are not acted upon sexually? Are they really affairs, or are they only friendships? These relationships should be considered as affairs when they consume time and energy that would more appropriately be going into the marriage. These relationships have a sexual current, even if sexual activity is not involved.

You may overlook the seriousness of your spouse's non-sexual affair, however, you would do well to pay attention to two common danger signals: If your spouse is spending more quality time with the other person than with you, and if your

140

spouse's primary confidant is the other person, and not you. If either of these patterns is present, get help now, before the non-sexual affair becomes a sexual affair.

You probably know, consciously or unconsciously, whether your spouse is having an affair. You know deep down that your marriage is off track, but you really don't want to know, so you explain away the evidence you see.

The signs often show up on long-distance phone bills or charge accounts. Or suddenly, your spouse starts criticizing you, your sex life changes, a friend's name suddenly drops into the conversation (or drops out); your spouse's physical appearance suddenly spiffs up, or your spouse becomes moody and unavailable. Sometimes the third party tells you of the affair, hoping to provoke you into ending the marriage.

When you are ready for the truth, it is time to confront your spouse. But if you don't have hard evidence, simply say, *"I think you're having an affair"*, and wait for an answer. It will be more difficult for your spouse to lie if you make a statement than if you asked, *"Are you having an affair?"* This question asks for only a yes or no. Make your statement, then stay silent, and wait for your spouse to respond. Don't give your spouse time to come up with a "good answer", or you'll miss your spouse's initial reactions.

Is there an embarrassed silence? Is there fumbling denial or a beating around the bush? Are there questions that put you on the defensive, such as *"What makes you say that?"*

Any of these responses is probably a "yes". If your spouse does not admit to the affair—and your jealousy is not working overtime—there could be another big secret, but it's not an affair.

Usually, when there's a secret, it's an affair. In the few instances when the secret is not an affair, it is a secret with relevance for your marriage, such as a large financial gift made to a relative without your knowledge.

If your spouse confesses to an affair, you will feel shock—edged with relief, to be followed by pain and fury. Your heart doesn't really want to believe what your head knows is the truth. You're afraid of what will happen next: Will your marriage survive? Will you survive?

Even though you're increasingly furious, ignore the advice of friends and relatives to rush to the nearest divorce attorney. *Legal proceedings don't resolve emotional issues.* See if you can keep your focus on your own pain and anger rather than on attacking your spouse. And whatever you do, leave your children out of it for now. There is time enough later for deciding how to talk with the children about the turmoil in the family.

Forget the temptation to separate immediately. Going home to visit your mother for a few weeks so that you don't have to deal with the situation—or telling your spouse to leave—will not help. Fleeing gives the illusion that you can avoid your pain, but the pain goes with you. Separate bedrooms in the same house are OK for a while. Each of you may need some space when you feel so raw and vulnerable. Just don't separate.

"I can't trust you" is a common theme. Of course you can't. Right now, neither of you can trust each other. You need to express your pain, and you need for your spouse to hear it.

Your spouse will probably want to appease you in order to avoid having to witness your pain. However, resist any attempts by your spouse to get you to "be nice", and suppress your anger. Don't let your voice be shut off by a quick *"I love you"* or a guilty *"I'm sorry"*. Neither love nor guilt makes it OK. If your spouse offers a lame excuse, such as, *"She came after me, and I didn't know what to do"*, don't believe him. You want it to be over, but blaming the third party won't work. It's your spouse who betrayed you.

But don't assume divorce—though it might seem like the only answer. It's not. It's not even the most common result of an affair. An affair doesn't automatically mean divorce. You have a variety of choices, and you owe it to yourself to take plenty of time to check them out so that you can choose a solution that fits you.

This is not the time for major decisions, because you can't see the whole marriage if you're looking at only one part—and decisions driven by an emotional crisis tend to be poor ones.

You may find that neither of you wants the marriage to end. Or it may be that your spouse's affair really is the announcement that your marriage is ending—that life as you know it is over.

But if your marriage has a chance of making it, your next moves are critical. It is easy to sabotage yourself by asking your spouse question after question about the affair: *"Why didn't you tell me if you thought things weren't right? When did you see her last? Are you still seeing her? How can I believe that?"*

You wake up your spouse at three in the morning, insisting, *"We have to talk now!"* You ask, *"Do you love her? How many times did you have sex? What does she have that I don't have? How could you do this to me?"* No matter what your spouse says, you lose: If he says he loves her, you're devastated, and if he says he doesn't love her, you don't believe him. You think about the affair so much that it becomes your life. You're so obsessed that it's as if you're having an affair with the affair.

Getting over the obsession with the affair requires that you express your anger, pain and powerlessness:

If you tell your spouse that he's lower than low, and ask, *"How could you do this to me?"* this is a statement of your thoughts about your spouse, not an expression of your anger. Anger sounds more like this: *"I am furious at you!"* or *"I am angry at you for lying to me!"* Pain might sound like this: *"I am so hurt that you've done this"*. Powerlessness might be: *"I don't know what to do. Nothing I do makes any difference right now."* See whether your words and your tone of voice are connected to what you are feeling inside. You don't need to scream to convey just how hurt and angry you are—neither do you have to explain nor justify your anger.

Moving beyond obsession is harder when your spouse is leaving the marriage, especially when your spouse is leaving to be with the third party. You are facing a double whammy: It will be hard to resist the temptation to blame it all on your spouse (or the third party). Doing that, however, would be a tragedy. Opportunities are often created out of painful circumstances. This is the time to grow rather than to make yourself a living monument to betrayal. Letting go of obsession is more difficult when you have been married for a long time, and have sacrificed parts of yourself along the way. If you have put aside your needs for the good of your spouse or your marriage, you may feel as if you have little self left, but as you reclaim the lost parts of yourself, you will be able to let go of the obsession.

If the affair was with your best friend, it is not quite incest, but it may feel close to it. When this happens, shock waves wipe out one of your main sources of psychological support. Even so, you must give up the friendship. That is a violation of friendship that goes too deep to be rectified.

Many affairs are with a work colleague. Knowing that the spouse who betrayed you will continue to have daily contact with the third party makes it hard to believe that the affair has really ended. Yet many times it has. It's even harder when you have to have contact with the third party on a regular basis, as for example when that person answers the phone in your spouse's office. If your spouse really seems to have ended the affair, and is working on the marriage, see if you can rise above the temptation to be rude. Make yourself a class act. While it is

not always possible or practical for your spouse to change jobs, it is something the two of you might seriously consider for business as well as personal reasons.

In a few cases, the third party won't let go. There are phone calls, letters or other attempts to contact your spouse. Sometimes, this means the affair is continuing, but in other situations, it's because the third party is having difficulty giving up the affair. If your spouse is clear and firm about ending the affair, these contacts should end fairly soon.

How *do* you go about rebuilding your life? Will you ever be able to trust again? Will your marriage survive? If it does, will you feel that bond of belonging that you crave? How *do* you rebuild trust?

Rebuilding involves ruling out separation and divorce for now. By the end of three months, you will know whether you can make the marriage fit you both. However, for the two of you to work together, the affair must be over—physically and emotionally.

You're ready to work on rebuilding trust when the following indicators are in place:

- The affair has been revealed.
- The affair has ended.
- Any ongoing contact between the affair partners, such as at work, is being handled openly and appropriately.
- You still like and care about each other.
- You know how the two of you created an opening for the affair.
- You are both committed to working on yourselves and on the marriage, knowing that it will be painful, and will take longer than you want, and that you have no guarantees of how it will all come out.

If you and your spouse want your marriage, you will both need to

make changes in how you interact with each other. One spouse can't rebuild the relationship alone. There is no healing without willingness to risk, but you've got a good chance of rebuilding a better relationship when you both can discuss the changes needed, and share your emotional ups and downs.

Your emotions are critical in connecting with your spouse. Trust is rebuilt by each of you developing the skills of intimacy: Being honest, becoming emotionally vulnerable, and developing reasonable expectations for your marriage.

The affair doesn't mean that your ability to love and care are gone. They were overshadowed by your pain and anger. Your spouse was looking outside your relationship for what he didn't know how to find inside. Thus an important part of rebuilding is looking inward at yourself and at your marriage.

Intimacy doesn't mean constantly being with your spouse. So you must tell each other when you need some physical or emotional space, and when you'll be available again.

Expect your rebuilding process to have its ups and downs. It takes tremendous energy to change habits. Sometimes there is sadness at letting go of your dreams of your perfect future together. Giving up your dreams hurts, but it frees you to move on to new dreams that are based on reality—that are a better fit for who you are today.

Emily M. Brown, LCSW, MSW, is the founder and director of the Key Bridge Therapy and Meditation Center in Arlington, VA. She is a noted international expert on the issue of affairs.

The Politics of Fatigue

The gender war has been replaced by the exhaustion of trying to do it all

By Richard Morin and Megan Rosenfeld
Washington Post Staff Writers

Men and women have declared a cease-fire in the war that raged between the sexes through much of the last half of this century. In its place, they face common new enemies—the stress, lack of time and financial pressure of modern life.

A new national survey has found that after nearly a generation of sharing the workplace and renegotiating domestic duties, most men and women agree that increased gender equity has enriched both sexes. But both also believe that the strains of this relatively new world have made building successful marriages, raising children and leading satisfying lives ever more difficult.

The problem that now unites them, as warehouse operations manager James Lindow, 35, of Green Bay, Wis., puts it, is "the lack of time you spend with your life."

Large majorities of more than 4,000 men and women questioned in a series of surveys last fall placed high importance on having a successful marriage and family. At the same time, equally large majorities of working men and women said they felt bad about leaving their children in the care of others, and wished they could devote more time to their families and themselves.

Surprisingly, although men and women agreed they should have equal work opportunities, and men said they approved of women working outside the home, large majorities of both said it would be better if women could instead stay home and just take care of the house and children.

Majorities of men and women believe there still are more advantages to being a man rather than a woman, and that most men don't understand the problems women face. And the survey shows that in some areas, the reality of daily existence for two-career families still has not caught up with changed attitudes.

Most men in the polls said they were happy to share child care and domestic chores with wives who work outside the home. Yet household duties remain sharply divided along gender lines. Working mothers still do twice as much housework as their husbands, and more than half of all women questioned expressed at least some dissatisfaction with the amount of help their husbands provide around the house.

"I think men are beginning to get it, at least some are, some of the time," says survey respondent Traci Hughes-Velez, 34, of Brooklyn, N.Y., director of compensation for a major corporation. "But there are times they don't. My husband just doesn't seem to get it when I tell him that I feel I'm always on duty. When we're at home, I'm the one who always has an eye out for our son, making sure he's eating on time, things like that."

The survey shows that real differences in perspective and perception remain between the sexes. Men are more likely to support increases in defense spending; women more favorably disposed toward health care for uninsured children. Women are more likely than men to be religious and to value close friendships; men are more likely than women to want successful careers and wealth, and more likely to value an "active sex life."

But rather than emphasizing their differences and blaming many of life's problems on each other, men and women share a sense of conflict and confusion about how to make it all work under today's pressures. To a large extent, the politics of resentment have become the politics of fatigue.

The Washington Post is examining how men and women are managing in this transformed world based on a series of five nationwide surveys sponsored by The Washington Post in collaboration with researchers from Harvard University and the Henry J. Kaiser Family Foundation.

The people surveyed came from all walks of life and all parts of the country. They included people like B. J. Sande, a 32-year-old mechanical engineer from Chattaroy, Wash., and Phyllis Wilkes, a 68-year-old San Franciscan retired from waitressing in a restaurant called Clown Alley. A sewing machine operator, a preschool teacher, a woman on welfare, a man looking for a job—they all spoke with conviction about how their lives are mostly better but definitely harder.

This story describes some of the consequences of the gender revolution, as revealed in survey data, in conversations with men and women, and in interviews with social scientists.

percent, sociologists Suzanne Bianchi and Daphne Spain reported in their recent book "Balancing Act."

Changes in Gender Roles

Men and women agree that the changes in gender roles in recent years have been both good and bad, and nostalgia for the lifestyle of the 1950s lingers, according to a new series of national surveys by The Washington Post/Henry J. Kaiser Family Foundation/ Harvard University.

Q. How much change do you think there has been in recent years in the relationship between men and women in their roles in families, the workplace and society?

	Men	Women
A great deal	36%	33%
Quite a lot	**40**	**43**
Only some	20	21
None at all	4	3

Q: Do you think these changes have been mainly good for the country, mainly bad, or have they been both good and bad?

	Men	Women
Mainly good	23%	13%
Mainly bad	14	12
Both good and bad	**62**	**72**
No difference	1	1

Q: Considering everything, do you think it would be better or worse for the country if men and women went back to the traditional roles they had in the 1950s, or don't you think it would make a difference?

	Men	Women
Better	**35%**	**42%**
Worse	35	33
No difference	29	21

Changed Roles Make Things Harder

For each of the following aspects of life, please tell me whether you think this change [in the relationship between men and women in their roles in families, the workplace and society] has made things easier or harder for people in this country, or whether it hasn't made much difference:

	Men	Women
For parents to raise children		
Easier	12%	14%
Harder	**80**	**80**
Not much difference	6	5
For marriages to be successful		
Easier	12%	15%
Harder	**70**	**72**
Not much difference	13	11
For families to earn enough money to live comfortably		
Easier	31%	22%
Harder	**60**	**69**
Not much difference	7	8
For men to lead satisfying lives		
Easier	22%	30%
Harder	**53**	**44**
Not much difference	22	21
For women to lead satisfying lives		
Easier	42%	34%
Harder	**44**	**50**
Not much difference	10	14

IN JUST THE PAST THREE DECADES, MOST AMERICANS agree that changing gender roles have dramatically altered their lives at work and at home.

Government statistics confirm what they see every day: The world of work is increasingly a man's and a woman's world. Between 1970 and 1995, the percentage of women ages 25 to 54 who worked outside the home climbed from 50 percent to 76

Other numbers tell a richer story. The percentage of lawyers and judges who are women doubled to 29 percent between 1983 and 1996, while the percentage of female physicians increased from 16 to 26 percent. Today, nearly a third of all professional athletes are women—almost double the proportion in 1983.

Women currently make up nearly half of all entry- and mid-level managers in American corporations, up from 17 percent in 1972. But the executive suite remains disproportionately male: A 1995 survey of Fortune 500 corporations found that only 1 in 10 corporate officers and fewer than 3 percent of all chief executive officers are women.

In higher education, gender equity is a reality. Slightly more than half of all bachelor's degrees were awarded to women last year, and the percentage of doctoral degrees granted to white women has increased from 25 percent in 1977 to 44 percent in 1993. Among African Americans, women receive more of the doctorates.

At home, men do more around the house than their fathers ever did. But the burden still falls on women: On average, working mothers do about 20 hours of housework a week, down from 30 hours two decades ago, while their husbands are doing 10 hours a week, up from five hours, Bianchi said in the book. And it's still women who say they're responsible for the way the house looks, according to the Post-Kaiser-Harvard polls.

The survey of couples with children found that women still do most of the food shopping, laundry, cooking, cleaning, arranging for child care and babysitters, and taking children to appointments or after-school activities—even when both parents work full time. Men tend to mow the lawn, shovel the snow and take out the trash, the survey found.

IN IMPORTANT WAYS, THE SURVEY SUGGESTS THAT we have yet to find new patterns of living that recognize the real workloads of two-career couples with children, and some resentment, nostalgia and fatigue are reflected in the survey results.

"I work, my husband works, I come home and I work. I clean the house and I do my laundry," says Susan Gehrke, 44, a tenant assistant for the elderly in La Crosse, Wis. "Someone comes over and the house is a mess, they don't look at the man and think, 'What a slob,' they look at her and say, 'What a slob.'"

Says Lindow, 35, the Green Bay warehouse operations manager, whose wife also works full time: "Your kids are going to the day care, or wherever they are taken care of by somebody else. By the time you get done with your job, you've got to rush home and make supper, do whatever, and then you have to run your kids somewhere else. You don't get enough time to spend with your wife anymore, either, because you are both working. You're lucky if you get to see your wife one or two hours a day. What kind of quality time is that?"

Age, more than sex, shapes attitudes toward the changing roles of men and women, the survey suggests. Younger men and women were far more likely than their elders to say the change in gender roles has made their lives better.

"These changes have made a lot of people's lives better and it's made some people's lives worse," says the 32-year-old Sande, who is single. He adds: "Any time there is a change like there has been in my generation, there is always going to be some growing pains. But as a whole I think it's moving toward the direction of making things easier, better."

Powerful social and economic forces nourish and sustain the trends that create these tensions. Two out of three men and women surveyed agreed that it takes two incomes to get by these days; about half the respondents—men and women—said they work mostly because they must.

ONE OUT OF EVERY FIVE WORKING WOMEN SAID she would cheerfully quit her job if only she could afford to—but so did 1 in 5 men surveyed. Today, even mid-career crises are gender-neutral.

"I did stay home with my daughter the first couple years, but financially you just can't make it on one salary anymore," says Kelly Lynn Cruz, 22, of Henderson, Md., who is between jobs and has one child and another on the way. "It's hard on my family, anyway. I don't get to spend as much time with my child. The housework isn't always done, which makes me feel like I'm not always doing my job."

Why is the housework her work? "It just is," she says with a laugh, adding that "he helps. But it's mainly my job. I take care of the inside, he takes care of the outside."

Perhaps not even the '50s housewife worked this hard at home: "I've had grandmothers tell me their daughters work far harder and spend more time with their children than they did" in the 1950s, says Sharon Hays, a sociologist at the University of Virginia who studies family structure.

Many Americans say that mounting pressures to be it all and to have it all put many relationships on the rocks. In the survey, 7 in 10 said there's too much pressure on both men and women today to realize the American ideal: marriage, family and a successful career. Many survey respondents in subsequent interviews said they put the pressure on themselves. Not surprisingly, those who felt this tension most acutely also were more likely to say it's harder to make marriages and families work.

"There's too much pressure on everyone, period, whether they're men or women," says Karen Mapp, a 42-year-old PhD candidate and researcher in Boston.

In response to these pressures, 4 in 10 of those surveyed said, it would be better to return to the gender roles of the 1950s, a dimly remembered world of television's Ozzie and Harriet and their blithe suburban existence.

"I definitely think it would be good to go back," says Rose Pierre-Louis, 40, a social worker in Brooklyn, N.Y., who was among those interviewed in the poll. "Kids aren't being raised, they're just growing up. Nobody's getting married anymore. There's no respect between men and women, [or from] children for their parents."

BUT JUST AS MANY AMERICANS SAY THEY AREN'T eager to go back—particularly young people, who do not bear the burden of their parents' nostalgia.

"I've never been under the impression that I couldn't do something because I was a woman," says Jennifer Wedberg, 25, a graphics designer who lives in Lisle, Ill. "It would be a shame if things went back to the way they were in the '50s.... It's easier to grow up knowing that some day you're just going to get married and be a mom or a wife, and now it's more complex, you have to figure out what you want to do with your life.... But I think more choices is always a good thing."

Young women like Wedberg have many of the same conflicts— over whether to stay home or take an outside job after having children—that their mothers might have had. But they also believe they are entitled to be full participants in areas of life their mothers had to fight to enter, and they assume their personal identity includes a job or a career.

Similarly, young men generally accept that their lives at work and in the home have changed, and with these transformations have come new duties, responsibilities and rewards. "I'd just as soon stay home with the kids," says Lindow, who adds that it doesn't bother him that his wife has a better job than he does.

"I think a lot of the problems we hear of now are because we have raised our standards," says Christopher M. Moeller, 22, a radio reporter in Des Moines. "We're more involved in each other's lives.... We value equality, we value everybody wanting to have self-esteem, to get everything they want, and I don't see where imposing a limit on more than half of our population accomplishes that."

Washington Post assistant director of polling Claudia Deane and staff researcher Robert Thomason contributed to this report.

What Kids (Really) Need

**Here's a question to drop in the center of the breakfast table and break in two:
What if day care makes our children smarter—and meaner?**

BY NANCY GIBBS

It is the season again for working parents to brace themselves and shudder as the latest study on child care lands in the headlines to stoke their quiet fears. But not just theirs. Last week's survey, funded by the National Institutes of Health and the largest ever on the subject, had something awful for just about everyone.

17% of kids who spend more than **30 hours** a week in day care have aggressive tendencies by kindergarten

---

The more hours children spend away from their mothers, researchers concluded, the more likely they are to be defiant, aggressive and disobedient by the time they get to kindergarten. Kids who are in child care more than 30 hours a week "scored higher on items like 'gets in lots of fights,' 'cruelty,' 'explosive behavior,' as well as 'talking too much,' 'argues a lot' and 'demands a lot of attention,'" said principal researcher Jay Belsky. It didn't matter if the children were black or white, rich or poor,

male or female, and—most confounding—whether the care was provided by a traditional child-care center, a nanny, a grandmother, even Dad. Only Mom will do.

But just in case those stay-at-home moms found comfort in the choices and sacrifices they have made, the study also suggests that kids in strong child-care programs tend to develop better language and memory skills, are in certain respects better prepared for school. Would you take that trade, Mom and Dad?

The news refueled some ancient rivalries, revived the most basic questions about what price our children pay for the hours we work and the choices we make. Parents peered into the data looking for themselves, but clear distinctions were hard to find. So far, the unpublished study has offered us only two kinds of children: those raised at home by their mothers (about 1 in 4 children) and everyone else. Which begs the question that the researchers didn't even pretend to answer: Why would kids who are cared for by anyone other than Mom develop disruptive behaviors, and what should we do about it?

For that matter, should we even be worried at all? The researchers noted that almost all the "aggressive" toddlers were well within the range of normal behavior for four-year-olds. And what about that adjective, anyway? Is a vice not sometimes a form of virtue? Cruelty never is, but arguing back? Is that being defiant—or spunky and independent? "Demanding attention" could be a natural and healthy skill to develop if you are in a room with 16 other kids.

Some experts in the field argue that the problem is not child care but bad child care. Across the nation there is a numbing range in child-care quality, rules and regulations. Some states allow only six babies in one room, others allow 20. States require all different kinds of licensing and accreditation. Child-care workers get paid about $7 an hour on average, roughly the same as parking-lot attendants; no wonder good care is hard to find. "There is a crisis in this country," says Mary Kakareka, a child-care consultant in Rockville, Md. "Middle-class families pay a lot to get into bad centers—and then down the line, pay again to get their kids in special programs to help solve the problems."

But what constitutes good care, whether in the home or outside it? What is the healthiest way for children to spend their time, especially in the years before school soaks up most of the day? Many anxious parents, wanting the best for their children and willing to pay for it, fill their kids' days with oboe lessons and karate classes, their rooms with phonics tapes and smart toys. And yet if you ask the experts to name the most precious thing you can provide your child, they often cite things you cannot buy: time and attention, the appreciation that play is children's work. Maybe, as the study results suggest, mothers have a special gift for giving that kind of gentle company. But it's hard to believe they are the only ones who can, as anyone with a great baby sitter, grandmother, husband or day-care provider can tell you.

This is the challenge to busy parents, working long hours, strung out at home. What would it take to create an easy, quiet space where you can just hang out with your kids, read a story or make one up, build a fort, make something goopy together? If in the process your children grow secure in the knowledge that you will forgive them for whatever they break or spill or forget, if they learn to share because you are sharing, if they don't have to fight for your attention, those skills may serve them better in the adventure that is kindergarten than being able to distinguish the octagon from the hexagon or fuchsia from lilac. The best news about raising a super child is that the secret to doing it is not to try too hard.

THE BINDS THAT TIE—AND HEAL: HOW FAMILIES COPE WITH MENTAL ILLNESS

Psychologist Herbert Gravitz, Ph.D., talks about the importance of families for the mentally ill. While the family may not cause mental illness, it may be one of the most powerful factors affecting the outcome.

By Herbert Gravitz, Ph.D.

When I lean back in my chair and think about the Parker family, I know they have changed. Instead of fear, isolation and shame, there is love, connection and meaning. And most important, hope has replaced dread and despair. Millions of families throughout the country suffer just as the Parkers did, but many aren't as fortunate. These families are ignored at best and blamed at worst by a society that doesn't understand their needs. But the Parker family (not their real name) is an example of what can happen.

Our first family meeting took place on a cool November afternoon four years ago in my Santa Barbara office. To my left sat Paul Parker, a young man unable to perform his duties as a bookkeeper. He had lost two jobs in one month. In this time, other self-care behaviors had deteriorated as well, making it hard for him to live independently. He had become so increasingly bizarre that he was a concern and embarrassment to his entire family. To my right sat Paul's parents, Tom and Tina. And next to them were their two younger children, 16-year-old Jim and 23-year-old Emma.

Paul has a neurobiological disorder (NBD) and psychiatric illness caused by a brain dysfunction. NBDs currently include major depression, schizophrenia, bipolar disorder and obsessive-compulsive disorder. Although different types of mental illnesses present different challenges, there are similarities in the way these illnesses impact family members and loved ones.

The session unfolded. "You just don't understand, doctor," Paul's father bursted out. "Nobody listens to us, his family. It's not easy dealing with Paul. I hate to say this, but he can be such a burden. My wife and I can't do anything without considering its effect on Paul—and he is 30 years old. Half the time we feel crazy." Tom added, "Paul seems like a stranger to us. It's as though aliens have taken our son and left an impostor."

Almost mindless of the children, Tom and Tina shared the devastation of Paul's illness on their marriage. They were so drained and so angry with each other that they rarely made love, and they seldom went out together. When they did, they argued about Paul. Tom thought that many of Paul's problems were exaggerated and that he was taking advantage of them. Like many mothers, Tina was more protective and accommodating of her son, especially during the early years. These differences led to quarrels in front of the children, which the family dreaded almost as much as Paul's strange and peculiar behavior. Both parents had little compassion left for Paul or each other. Even less time was left for Jim and Emma, because they seemed so normal and caused no problems.

Without warning Jim interrupted, "Not again. Why does Paul get all the attention? I never feel important. You always talk about him." Ignoring her own fears, Emma tried to reassure the family that Paul would be okay. "We've handled Paul's problems before," she pleaded. There were many unspoken feelings, such as the overwhelming responsibility Tom and Tina suffered, the resentment that Emma and Jim felt, as well as the family's guilt, exhaustion and demoralization. And there was a half-wish that Paul would just disappear.

Despite everything, the family loved Paul. They each had powerful—even fierce—loyalties toward him. This was evident when Tom explained: "We brought Paul here, we care what happens, we sit in the waiting room while his life is on the line, and we will take care of Paul when everything is said and done." Paul was important to all of them.

Stopping the hurt

The family had sought help from other mental health professionals. Paul's parents recounted being blamed for his disorder by several professionals, and they reported feeling confused and helpless. Emma and Jim felt like outcasts, they were ignored by their parents and shunned by their friends. Everyone wanted the hurt to stop. At the very least, the family wanted someone to recognize their pain and say, "This must be very hard for all of you."

The Parkers are not rare or unusual. One in five Americans has a psychiatric disorder at any given time, and half will have one at some point in their lifetime.

More than 100 million Americans have a close family member who suffers from a major mental illness. Of the 10 leading causes of disability, half are psychiatric. By the year 2020, the major cause of disability in the world may be major depression. Further, it has been estimated that only 10 to 20% of those requiring care in the United States receive it in institutions; the rest receive their primary care from the family.

Devoted to their ill member, the family may be the best-kept secret in the arsenal of healing. Yet, family members are considered the support team; they are not known as the stressed and the grieving. These tired mothers and fathers, daughters and sons, husbands and wives deserve attention as well.

Mental illness can weave a web of doubt, confusion and chaos around the family. Unwittingly, the person with mental illness can dominate the entire family through control and fear or helplessness and incapacity. Like a bully, the mental illness bosses the primary sufferer as well as the loved ones. Instability, separation, divorce and abandonment are frequent family outcomes of mental illness.

Under the influence

I have observed five factors that bind families to the despair of their loved one's illness: stress, trauma, loss, grief and exhaustion. These factors provide a useful framework to understand the underlying structure of the family under the influence.

- Stress is at the foundation of the family experience of mental illness. There is constant tension, dread and worry because the illness can strike at any time. It's common for family members "to walk on eggshells." The Parkers liken the atmosphere to a pressure cooker and the possibility of the ill loved one "going off the deep end" looms. Stress accumulates and leads to psychosomatic illness. Tom has high blood pressure, while Tina suffers ulcers.
- Trauma also lies at the core of the family's experience. It can erode members' beliefs about control, safety,

meaning and their own value. While victims of NBDs rarely assault others physically, they do assault with words, and their words can pull apart the family. Another form of trauma is "witness trauma," where the family watches helplessly as loved ones are tortured by their symptoms. This type of family atmosphere can often induce the development of traumatic symptoms like invasive thoughts, distancing and physical disorders. The result can be traumatic stress or posttraumatic stress disorder. Much of the family's despair results from trying to manage and control what it cannot. Knowing when to intervene is one of most difficult lessons a family must learn.

- Loss lies at the very nature of family life. Family members report losses in their personal, social, spiritual and economic lives. They suffer losses in privacy, freedom, security and even dignity. "What we miss most is a normal life," said Mrs. Parker. "We have lost being just an ordinary family." The family may be the only place where we cannot be replaced. So it can be devastating if we cannot have effective family relationships.
- Grief occurs from this steady diet of loss. Family members can go through protracted grieving, which often goes undiagnosed or untreated. Grieving centers around what life will not be. "It's as if we are in a funeral that never ends," said Tom. Grieving can become compounded because our culture does not sufficiently acknowledge and legitimize the grief of those under the influence of mental illness. A lack of appropriate entitlement can follow. "I really have no right to feel bad. Paul is the one who is ill," said Tom. Therefore, mourning fails to occur, preventing acceptance and integration of loss.
- Exhaustion is the natural result of living in such an atmosphere. The family becomes an endless emotional and monetary resource, and must frequently monitor the concerns, issues and problems of the ill loved one. Worry, preoccupation, anxiety and depression can leave the family drained—emotionally, physically, spiritually, economically. Tina summarized it, "There's no rest." Tom added, "We can't even get a good night's sleep; we lie awake wondering what Paul is doing. This is 24 hours a day, 365 days a year."

Leaving it to fate

Living in an environment of chronic stress, trauma, loss, grief and fatigue can also lead other family members to their own parallel disorder. Parallel disorders of family members are also known as secondary or vicarious traumatization. The family members can develop symptoms including denial, minimization, enabling, high tolerance for inappropriate behavior, confusion and doubt, guilt and depression, and other physical and emotional problems.

Other more recent terms include learned helplessness, which occurs when family members find that their actions are futile; depression fallout, the consequence of living in close proximity to a loved one's despair; and compassion fatigue, burnout that comes from intimate relationships when family members believe they cannot help their loved one and are unable to disengage from the illness long enough to get restored. "I'm just too tired to care," said Tina.

The symptoms of families under the influence of NBDs can be devastating, but they are also very treatable. Research consistently shows that four elements lead to healing: information, coping skills, support and love.

Healing begins with an accurate diagnosis; from there core issues can be confronted. The family moves beyond their loved one's illness—not away from their loved one.

In response to pain, the family can learn to develop a disciplined approach to dealing with their situations. Tina, for example, has embraced spirituality and has learned to ask herself, "What is the lesson that I am supposed to learn in this very moment?" Tom adds, "When I gave up caring about what was supposed to be, I got back my footing and now have something to offer Paul other than my temper."

To create a new life, the Parkers made five key transitions that facilitated healing. Although not every family member made all of these shifts, most family members made enough of them to change their lives. First, to transform the way they thought and felt, they shifted from denial to awareness. When the reality of the illness was confronted and accepted, healing began. The second transition was a shift in focus from the mentally ill person to attention to self. This shift requires the establishment of healthy boundaries. The third transition was moving from isolation to support. Facing the problems of living with mental illness is too difficult to do alone. Family members worked within a framework of love. This makes it easier to relate to the illness with distance and perspective. The fourth change is family members learning to respond to the person instead of the illness itself.

The fifth and final shift toward healing occurs when members find personal meaning in their situation. This elevates the personal, private and limited stories of the family to a much larger and more heroic level. This shift doesn't change what happened or even take the hurt away, it just makes people feel less alone and more empowered. It creates choices and new possibilities.

It has been a little over three years since my first encounter with the Parker family. Yesterday, I met with them for the first time in over a year. As they sat in their familiar seats, I reminisced. I remembered the moment the family's denial was broken: when Tina said to her son Paul, "I have your pain and I have my pain—I have both."

When we first met, they were trying to save a past; now they are building a future. The session was punctuated by laughter as the Parkers learned to reduce their expectations to more realistic levels. They also learned to take better care of themselves. Because family members who get help and support demonstrate healthier functioning, Paul has become more responsible for his own recovery.

Change has occurred for many other reasons. Newer medications, for example, have helped Paul significantly. Almost 95% of what we have learned about the brain has occurred in the last 10 years. Initially, family members couldn't talk to one another. Now, they turn to each other and speak openly about their concerns. Tom and Tina have found a new life through their advocacy and support group work. Emma has married. And Jim is studying to be a psychologist and wants to help families.

Healing a family entails discipline. With love and commitment, family members can break the spell of the illness by broadening their sense of meaning. And meaning can be found in such diverse areas as religion, raising children, contributing to charities, forming organizations, developing a 12-step program, writing, running for office, or helping the boy next door who lost his father.

Families like the Parker's are among a growing number of people who are recognizing that they have been impacted by the mental illness of a loved one. They are choosing to acknowledge their plight, grieve their losses, learn new skills and connect with others.

Living under the influence of mental illness calls us to confront the darker as well as deeper sides of life. It can be a terrifying, heart-breaking, lonely and exhausting experience or it can forge the latent, untapped strengths of individuals and families. There is more hope than ever for families. And it is never too late to have a happy family.

Said Tina Parker, "While I don't believe life is a bowl of cherries, it isn't a can of worms anymore either." And Tom adds, "Hardly a day goes by where I am not grateful for my family and being alive. I savor the good days and let the bad ones pass. I have learned to make the most out of every moment."

READ MORE ABOUT IT

The Burden of Sympathy: How Families Cope with Mental Illness By David A. Karp (Oxford University Press, 2001)

Obsessive Compulsive Disorder: New Help for the Family By Herbert Gravitz (Healing Visions Press, 1998)

Herbert L. Gravitz, Ph.D., practices in Santa Barbara, California. He is a founding board of director for the National Association for Children of Alcoholics.

Marriage and Divorce American Style

A destructive marriage is not a happy family.

By E. Mavis Hetherington

On average, recent studies show, parents and children in married families are happier, healthier, wealthier, and better adjusted than those in single-parent households. But these averages conceal wide variations. Before betting the farm on marriage with a host of new government programs aimed at promoting traditional two-parent families and discouraging divorce, policy makers should take another look at the research. It reveals that there are many kinds of marriage and not all are salutary. Nor are all divorces and single-parent experiences associated with lasting distress. It is not the inevitability of positive or negative responses to marriage or divorce that is striking, but the diversity of them.

Men do seem to benefit simply from the state of being married. Married men enjoy better health and longevity and fewer psychological and behavioral problems than single men. But women, studies repeatedly have found, are more sensitive to the emotional quality of the marriage. They benefit from being in a well-functioning marriage, but in troubled marriages they are likely to experience depression, immune-system breakdowns, and other health-related problems.

We saw the same thing in the project I directed at the Hetherington Laboratory at the University of Virginia, which followed 1,400 divorced families, including 2,500 kids—some for as long as 30 years—interviewing them, testing them, and observing them at home, at school, and in the community. This was the most comprehensive study of divorce and remarriage ever undertaken; for policy makers, the complexity of the findings is perhaps its most important revelation.

GOOD MARRIAGES, BAD MARRIAGES

By statistical analysis, we identified five broad types of marriage—ranging from "pursuer-distancer" marriages, (which we found were the most likely to end in divorce), to disengaged marriages, to operatic marriages, to "cohesive-individuated" marriages, and, finally, traditional marriages (which had the least risk of instability).

To describe them briefly:

- Pursuer-distancer marriages are those mismatches in which one spouse, usually the wife, wants to confront and discuss problems and feelings and the other, usually the husband, wants to avoid confrontations and either denies problems or withdraws.

- Disengaged marriages are ones where couples share few interests, activities, or friends. Conflict is low, but so is affection and sexual satisfaction.

- Operatic marriages involve couples who like to function at a level of extreme emotional arousal. They are intensely attracted, attached, and volatile, given both to frequent fighting and to passionate lovemaking.

- Cohesive-individuated marriages are the yuppie and feminist ideal, characterized by equity, respect, warmth, and mutual support, but also by both partners retaining the autonomy to pursue their own goals and to have their own friends.

- Traditional marriages are those in which the husband is the main income producer and the wife's role is one of nurturance, support, and home and child care. These marriages work well as long as both partners continue to share a traditional view of gender roles.

We found that not just the risk of divorce, but also the extent of women's psychological and health troubles varies according to marriage type—with wives in pursuer-distancer and disengaged marriages experiencing the most problems, those in operatic marriages significantly having fewer, and those in cohesive-individuated and traditional marriages the fewest. Like so many other studies, we found that men's responses are less nuanced; the only differentiation among them was that men in pursuer-distancer marriages have more problems than those in the other four types.

The issue is not simply the amount of disagreement in the marriage; disagreements, after all, are endemic in close personal relations. It is *how* people disagree and solve problems—how they interact—that turns out to be closely associated with both the duration of their marriages and the well-being of wives and, to a lesser extent, husbands. Contempt, hostile criticism, belligerence, denial, and withdrawal erode a marriage. Affection, respect, trust, support, and making the partner feel valued and worthwhile strengthen the relationship.

GOOD DIVORCES, BAD DIVORCES

Divorce experiences also are varied. Initially, especially in marriages involving children, divorce is miserable for most couples. In the early years, ex-spouses typically must cope with lingering attachments; with resentment and anger, self-doubts, guilt, depression, and loneliness; with the stress of separation from children or of raising them alone; and with the loss of social networks and, for women, of economic security. Nonetheless, we found that a gradual recovery usually begins by the end of the second year. And by six years after divorce, 80 percent of both men and women have moved on to build reasonably or exceptionally fulfilling lives.

Indeed, about 20 percent of the women we observed eventually emerged from divorce enhanced and exhibiting competencies they never would have developed in an unhappy or constraining marriage. They had gone back to school or work to ensure the economic stability of their families, they had built new social networks, and they had become involved and effective parents and socially responsible citizens. Often they had happy second marriages. Divorce had offered them an opportunity to build new and more satisfying relationships and the freedom they needed for personal growth. This was especially true for women moving from a pursuer-distancer or disengaged marriage, or from one in which a contemptuous or belligerent husband undermined their self-esteem and child-rearing practices. Divorced men, we found, are less likely to undergo such remarkable personal growth; still, the vast majority of the men in our study did construct reasonably happy new lives for themselves.

As those pressing for government programs to promote marriage will no doubt note, we found that the single most important predictor of a divorced parent's subsequent adjustment is whether he or she has formed a new and mutually supportive intimate relationship. But what should also be noticed is that successful repartnering takes many forms. We found that about 75 percent of men and 60 percent of women eventually remarry, but an increasing number of adults are opting to cohabit instead—or to remain single and meet their need for intimacy with a dating arrangement, a friendship, or a network of friends or family.

There is general agreement among researchers that parents' repartnering does not do as much for their children. Both young children and adolescents in divorced and remarried families have been found to have, on average, more social, emotional, academic, and behavioral problems than kids in two-parent, non-divorced families. My own research, and that of many other investigators, finds twice as many serious psychological disorders and behavioral problems—such as teenage pregnancy, dropping out of school, substance abuse, unemployment, and marital breakups—among the offspring of divorced parents as among the children of nondivorced families. This is a closer association than between smoking and cancer.

However, the troubled youngsters remain a relatively small proportion of the total. In our study, we found that after a period of initial disruption 75 percent to 80 percent of children and adolescents from divorced families are able to cope with the divorce and their new life situation and develop into reasonably or exceptionally well-adjusted individuals. In fact, as we saw with women, some girls eventually emerge from their parents' divorces remarkably competent and responsible. They also learn from the divorce experience how to handle later stresses in their lives.

Without ignoring the serious pain and distress experienced by many divorced parents and children, it is important to underscore that substantial research findings confirm the ability of the vast majority to move on successfully.

It is also important to recognize that many of the adjustment problems in parents and children and much of the inept parenting and destructive family relations policy makers have attributed to divorce actually are present *before* divorce. Being in a dysfunctional family has taken its toll before the breakup occurs.

Predicting the aftermath of divorce is complex, and the truth is obscured if one looks only at averages. Differences in experience or personality account for more variation than the averages would suggest. A number of studies have found, for instance, that adults and children who perceived their pre-divorce life as happy and satisfying tend to be more upset by a marital breakup than those who viewed the marriage as contentious, threatening, or unfulfilling. Other studies show that adults and children who are mature, stable, self-regulated, and adaptable are more likely able to cope with the challenges of divorce. Those who are neurotic, antisocial, and impulsive—and who lack a sense of their own efficacy—are likely to have these characteristics exacerbated by the breakup. In other words, the psychologically poor get poorer after a divorce while the rich often get richer.

The diversity of American marriages makes it unlikely that any one-size-fits-all policy to promote marriage and prevent divorce will be beneficial. Policy makers are now talking about offering people very brief, untested education and counseling programs, but such approaches rarely have long-lasting effects. And they are generally least successful with the very groups that policy makers are most eager to marry off—single mothers and the poor.

In their recent definitive review of the research on family interventions, Phil Cowan, Douglas Powell, and Carolyn Pape Cowan find that the most effective approaches are the most comprehensive ones—those that deal with both parents and children, with family dynamics, and with a family's needs for jobs, education, day care, and health care. Beyond that, which interventions work best seems to vary, depending on people's stage of life, the kind of family or ethnic group they are in, and the specific challenges before them.

Strengthening and promoting positive family relationships and improving the many settings in which children develop is a laudable goal. However, policies that constrain or encourage people to remain in destructive marriages—or that push uncommitted couples to marry—are likely to do more harm than good. The same is true of marriage incentives and rewards designed to create traditional families with the husband as the economic provider and the wife as homemaker. If our social policies do not recognize the diversity and varied needs of American families, we easily could end up undermining them.

E. MAVIS HETHERINGTON *is a professor of psychology at the University of Virginia and the co-author (with John Kelly) of* For Better or for Worse: Divorce Reconsidered.

is divorce too easy?

We have stopped taking marriage seriously, say the experts and women are paying the price. That's why a surprising coalition of conservatives and feminists want to make breaking up harder to do.

By Benedict Carey

HE MUST HAVE BEEN RELIEVED to get out of the house and into the open. He'd tried to be casual, waiting until breakfast was over, when the kids were preparing for school, waiting until his wife, almost ready for work herself, came to the door to see him off. What was it he had said? "We're getting a divorce. Give me a call later." The basics, anyway. Then he was gone.

"It was an announcement, not a conversation," Susan Blumstein, now remarried, says of the day her first husband left, in 1990. "We talked that day, and then that same week we went to see his brother the lawyer, who had already prepared papers. It was a done deal."

> "I have heard divorce described as a kind of death," Susan Blumstein says. "That sounds right to me."

Susan had assumed all along that their marriage was the done deal—an assumption, she now concedes, that may have blinded her to her husband's discontent. After 18 years of partnership, after raising two children to adolescence, after all the diapers and dishes and damp dental floss, one does indulge a few simple faiths. "You don't just *think* of yourself as a married person," she says, "you *are* a married per-

son. It's part of what you are, everything you do." But the family's life together vaporized in less time than it takes to put out the recycling bins, and there was nothing she could do about it.

She had no idea what might be next, no notion of what slights the world reserves for a divorced, middle-aged mother of two. She had to break the news to everyone: her friends, her coworkers, her boss. She lost her place in her social group. Many mornings she woke up afraid, profoundly unsure of who she was. "I have heard divorce described as a kind of death," Blumstein says. "That sounds right to me."

She kept the Birmingham, Alabama, house and got custody of their two children, a girl, then age 17, and a boy, 11. She dropped several rungs on the economic ladder. (Divorce on average leaves ex-wives 20 to 30 percent poorer than ex-husbands, mainly because child support doesn't cover all of a child's living expenses.) Once comfortable, the family was suddenly strapped. And she had scant expectation of starting a new relationship; divorced mothers who retain custody don't get bachelor pads and long nights out in the bargain.

It would have come as no surprise to Susan to hear that, compared to married people, divorced individuals are three times as prone to depression, twice as likely to drink heavily, and three times more liable to commit suicide. She might have been too overwhelmed to care that

they're also at higher risk of developing cancer or heart disease. "We have been studying this subject for a long time now," says Linda Waite, a University of Chicago sociologist whose book, *The Case for Marriage*, is due out next year. "Being married changes people's behavior in ways that make them better off."

Susan did gain one thing from her divorce: a set of previously undreamed-of anxieties about her children's future. The kids were suddenly subdued, spending more time at friends' houses. "They just didn't want to be here," she says. But they were old enough, fortunately, to understand what was happening; kids under the age of ten don't fare as well. Sociologists have found that children who grow up in split families are twice as likely to eventually divorce, twice as likely to drop out of school earlier, and much slower to support themselves.

Americans sometimes toast their own divorces, but few would celebrate their country's distinction as the world's divorce leader. Between 40 and 50 percent of first-time marriages break up in the United States. Perhaps a third of divorces end poisonous unions to the benefit of everyone involved, say researchers. In the other two-thirds, the vital security of family life is evident only after it has been irrevocably lost. Women in particular pay the price, financially and emotionally.

For decades now, legislators, religious leaders, and social reformers have debated

Making Divorce Work

My husband and I divorced when our son Patrick was four and our daughter Morgan was six. Patrick cried and asked for cookies, then couldn't eat them. "I told you not to do this," said Morgan.

"I know, baby," I said, tears sliding down my face. This was my first taste of that curious callousness of a mother. I would have died for them, but I would not, for their sake, go on living with a good man I no longer loved.

Jim was 21 years my senior–he had been my college English professor–and we had begun to grow apart. He once snapped off a radio I was listening to, saying he had only a finite number of hours left on earth, and did not want to spend any of them listening to rock music. I snapped it back on.

One day while sitting at a red light, I realized I was no longer in love, and hadn't been for some time. It seemed to me then reason enough to leave. It still does. But I went home and cried, desperately afraid of what I was about to do–to him, to the kids, to myself, condemning us all to the bitterness and the pain of divorce.

Shortly after I made my decision, a comment from an acquaintance took me by surprise. "I think it's terrible when people give up like that," she said. "I can't respect that at all." Her parents had been married for 45 years, she said, through some very hard times. She respected that kind of commitment. Anything short of it was giving up.

I respected it, too; it seemed to me an immense achievement. But what my husband and I were doing also struck me as immense. We were attempting to divorce without destroying the family.

"You should know joint custody works in only 10 percent of cases," said the first lawyer I spoke to. I found another lawyer.

Jim kept the kids Sunday through Wednesday night, and they were mine the rest of the week. By the time the divorce papers came thumping through the mail slot, several years after we had separated, Jim and I were neighbors. I had moved into the flat below his so we could raise the kids together more easily. It took civility, effort, and luck, but we made it work.

Would my kids have been happier had we stayed together? Of course. But they're doing fine. Over the years, we've developed an odd kind of extended family. The other night we had our usual Sunday dinner together: My husband of seven years, Bill, grilled steaks, Jim brought down fresh strawberries, Morgan had a tofu burger, and Patrick, now 19 and 6 foot 3, ate an entire T-bone before heading out to his summer restaurant job. Afterward, as I was getting ready to go to the movies, I heard Morgan tell a friend on the phone, "All of my parents are going out. Want to come over?"

—ADAIR LARA

how to lower the divorce rate. It is a very tall order. No policy can re-create the society of the 1950s that supported traditional households. No one is going to abolish the economic sovereignty and independence women have earned in the past few decades, which has given them the freedom to leave an unbearable marriage. And no advertising campaign can convince a nation of divorced people to seriously stigmatize divorce.

But legislators can change laws, and they are beginning to do just that. In August 1997 the state of Louisiana started allowing people to choose a marriage option more binding than the standard no-fault contracts that have governed marriage and divorce in most states since the 1970s. Called covenant marriage, the new statute is a favorite among religious conservatives. What's surprising is that some feminists and many progressives have allowed themselves to be counted among the faithful–especially those who, like Waite, have studied the consequences of divorce for women.

Diane Sollee is founder and director of the Coalition for Marriage, Family, and Couples Education, a group of professional counselors, researchers, educators, and policy-makers. "No-fault laws were originally meant to give people an easy way out of a bad marriage," she says, "but

we've been using the statutes to make a quick exit from any marriage."

Covenant marriage is sometimes called "I do, and I really mean it" marriage. It differs from the conventional contract in two important ways. First, it requires that couples receive professional marital counseling—before the wedding and, if it comes to it, prior to filing for divorce. Second, the law prohibits a mutually agreed-upon, no-fault split until husband and wife have lived apart for two years. Currently, in most states, the waiting period for a divorce can range from six to 18 months and can be waived altogether. The only way to dissolve a covenant marriage in less than two years is by going to court and proving that your spouse committed adultery, a felony, or physical or sexual abuse, or has moved out for a year and won't return.

The agreement gives leverage to spouses who want to preserve their marriage, says the statute's composer, Katherine Spaht, a law professor at Louisiana State University in Baton Rouge. "What we have now amounts to legalized abandonment," she says. "This law says, 'You leave me, I set the terms.'"

Spaht's zeal derives from what she has witnessed among Louisiana's modern professional class of lawyers, doctors, and academics. "I was seeing friends of mine, women in their forties and fifties, being

left behind when their husbands decided they were tired of them. A man I know, a surgeon, just left his wife of 23 years for a younger woman. He was just up and gone. I believe that is simply not right. It shouldn't be that easy," she says. "Many of these women chose to raise their children. Even if they kept working, they made significant sacrifices to put their families first. What's a woman supposed to think when half of all marriages fail and here's a man proposing to her, asking her to give up a career? It's crazy."

In 1996 Spaht met a state representative named Tony Perkins who shared her view. Together they drew up the covenant bill, which passed by a vote of 99 to 1. "We had liberal Democrats with us from very early on," says Perkins, a Republican. "Here was a bill that commits people to at least try to make their marriages work, and it's voluntary. It was hard to vote against."

NOT LONG AGO, voting against marriage counseling would have been easy. New York State had laws on the books in the 1960s and early 1970s that required couples to get therapy, yet the effect on the divorce rate was negligible. If anything rates increased, helping to expose marriage counseling for what it then was: a profession as starved for answers and direction as its clients.

"The professional stance of the American Association for Marriage and Family Therapy was neutrality," says Sollee, a past associate director. "That meant we were neither pro-marriage nor pro-divorce. We thought we should be working for what was best for each spouse. Often the so-called marriage therapist would be advising couples to divorce."

Nine years ago when Susan met Chris Blumstein, the man who would become her second husband, one of the things they talked about, besides the surreal suddenness of being abandoned (Chris had been, too), was the absence of effective counseling. Susan doubts it would have saved her first marriage, but she still feels cheated that they couldn't at least have given it a chance.

Chris and his first wife *did* seek advice—in vain. "We went to a professional counselor who said, 'Come back with a list of what you want most out of marriage.' Well, I came back with a list of 26 things, and she just had one: 'I want him to spend more time with the kids.' She was right. But our problems went deeper than that, and we refused to deal with them. So did our counselor. What kind of counseling is that?"

It's the traditional kind, Sollee says, and it's on the way out, thanks to ground-breaking marriage research done in the 1980s. Psychologists interested in relationship dynamics began using videotape to observe how couples spar over the small, I-thought-you-were-going-to-pack-that nuisances that often escalate into scalding arguments. The scientists also started using blood pressure monitors, stress hormone tests, and urinalysis to provide a record of physiological stress during these spats.

"The new technology allowed you to see what was going on inside," says Sollee, "even if you had stoic New Englanders there holding everything in."

These experiments demonstrated something astonishing: Couples who stayed together fought as frequently, and over precisely the same things, as did couples who split up. "Experiment after experiment showed this, until we couldn't avoid it," says Sollee. "We *all* have irreconcilable differences. Every couple has them. Those who have successful marriages simply have learned ways of talking about their problems. They may never solve them. But they know how to talk about them."

The importance of this discovery to the field of marriage counseling cannot be overstated. Most marriage advisers are

neutral no longer. Barring extreme circumstances, they don't put personal needs before the relationship. Most have abandoned the traditional emphasis on solving each spouse's individual problems in favor of what Sollee calls marriage education—a relationship course, in effect, that teaches skills and strategies for disarming emotional grenades.

The model is called PREP, for Prevention and Relationship Enhancement Program, developed in 1980 by clinical psychologist Howard Markman. Markman's methods are straightforward. For example, he coaches couples to discuss problems in what he calls speaker-listener technique, in which one person gripes, then the listener paraphrases the complaint, and vice versa.

In practice, this technique is not all that unnatural; it simply provides a framework for the sort of empathetic conversations most couples have had. Other tactics include taking time-outs when tempers flare, and spending an hour weekly to discuss your relationship.

In an ongoing Denver-area study, Markman found that 8 percent of couples who took his course broke up, separated, or divorced within five years. But that number rose to 16 percent of the couples in the control group. A similar trial in Germany reported that only 4 percent of a PREP group divorced after three years, compared to 24 percent of those who got no counseling. On every measure of marital stability—number of fights, amount of affection, level of trust—the couples who had taken the course were better off.

"I don't give people wedding presents anymore," says Sollee. "I give a weekend of marriage education. It's far more valuable than a table setting or a salad bowl."

The covenant statute doesn't specify any particular type of counseling; lawmakers decided against that. It is the binding promise to do *something*, however, that sells covenant marriage to people who otherwise wouldn't buy it.

Bob Downing, a Louisiana District Court judge, and his wife, Pamela, decided last year to renew their vows under the covenant license. "It was his idea," says Pamela, "and I asked myself, Why? I mean, my first vows were my vows, and this wasn't going to make them any more sacred. But I eventually decided that the counseling was a good safety valve, and I like the agreement up front to do it. If you can't agree to that, what kind of commitment do you have?"

NOT MUCH OF ONE, most married people would agree. But behind the commonsense appeal of the law, some see a dark trend: covenant marriage as a step back to the more acrimonious days of fault-based divorce. Back in the sixties, divorce laws were relaxed in the United States because they were out of step with people's behavior. Throughout this century, Americans who wanted out have found a way to make it happen—by heading off to Reno, by leaving the country, most of all by fabricating evidence of infidelity or abuse. No-fault laws made the system a more honest one.

They've also made the process more humane. "The most offensive thing to me is the suggestion that somehow no-fault divorces are easy," says Terry O'Neill, a law professor at Tulane University in New Orleans and past president of the Louisiana chapter of the National Organization for Women. "Just think of the divorced people you know. They all got divorces for reasons that were very important, very real for them. This covenant law is really all about punishment. It punishes people for wanting to get out of a marriage, even a bad marriage. As if it weren't already difficult enough to go through a divorce."

> "Our laws tell a story, and for 30 years now they've been telling us that committed marriage isn't that important."

Linda Waite doesn't deny the real pain of no-fault divorce; she's been through one herself. She's nonetheless concerned by a telling statistic: Thirty years ago, just 40 percent of Americans believed ending a troubled marriage could benefit a husband or a wife. These days, 80 percent share that belief, according to the General Social Survey, a government poll of social attitudes. "This amounts to a very large and very real change in attitudes toward committed marriage," she says.

Most Americans still want to be married; surveys are clear about that. The romantic ideal is intact. It is the reality of marriage, the thing itself, that has lost its place in the public imagination. All the mundane give-and-take that is part of a normal relationship can disappoint sentimental couples, Waite says. And the ease of walking out makes the union that much more fragile.

"When people are in more binding contracts they tend to invest more in the kids, and become more emotionally dependent on each other in the best ways," Waite says. "They put their well-being in a partnership, in a trust. They become part of a larger network of people, including spouses' parents, siblings, and friends. All of this helps enormously."

Katherine Spaht puts it more simply. "I believe our laws tell a story," she says. "And for 30 years now they've been telling us that committed marriage isn't that important."

Spaht's legislation tells an imperfect story, to be sure; experience suggests that many of these Louisiana covenants will blow up for perfectly valid reasons. But the law does provide for a different narrative than the one we've been hearing for de-cades. It challenges couples to honor their promises and marriage counselors to do their job, and has prompted lawmakers around the country to think seriously about the benefits of marriage preparation and rehabilitation. Deeper than that, the law says that there is more to marriage than romantic love.

ON VALENTINE'S DAY LAST YEAR, dozens of churches in Louisiana held collective ceremonies in which married parishioners renewed their vows. In Baker, near Baton Rouge, the Bethany World Prayer Center had 500 couples in attendance. Another 100 convened in the venerable First Presbyterian Church downtown. "I think we were all surprised at how emotional the ceremonies were," says Russ Stevenson, senior pastor at First Presbyterian. "One fellow came up to me and said, 'Reverend that was more beautiful than the first time.'"

The ceremonies had the feel of a mass public demonstration—a March for Marriage, so to speak—and the sensation persists in the humid delta air around the city. Says Pamela Downing: "Our own kids have so many friends whose parents are divorced that I felt this was a way to let them know we are in this for keeps."

She and husband Bob joined the Valentine's Day ceremonies, affirming 18 years of marriage. Katherine and Paul Spaht (28 years) also participated, along with Russ and Sherrill Stevenson (38 years). And at the Baton Rouge Christian Center Church, after seven years together, stood Susan and Chris Blumstein, ready to make the long walk down the aisle for the last time.

Benedict Carey is a contributing editor.

THE HAPPY DIVORCE

HOW TO BREAK UP AND MAKE UP

BY NORA UNDERWOOD

For a decade, Tom Cruise and Nicole Kidman were Hollywood's patron saints of marriage. When not giving relentless interviews about how they were each other's best friend, they were swinging their two children between them on sunny afternoon walks, posing in couture or snuggling at film openings. Whatever it really was, the marriage seemed like something out of a fairy tale. When it ended—suddenly, to the rest of the world—there were predictions about how ugly the divorce proceedings were going to be. Reportedly there was nastiness behind the scenes, but in public the Hollywood couple seemed to do divorce as perfectly as they'd done marriage. In a few hours one day last November, together at a final meeting with their lawyers, they hammered out how their considerable assets would be split and how custody of the children would be arranged. They even parted ways with an embrace. "We are great friends," Cruise said of Kidman in an interview with *People* magazine shortly after their divorce was negotiated. "She is someone who I love and always will."

> ## "If there are children or a business, friendly divorce is the way to go. But that means having to grit your teeth a little."

In a perfect world, we'd all live happily ever after with the people to whom we had pledged ourselves. Short of that, we'd divorce as (apparently) amicably as Kidman and Cruise did. In reality, 36 per cent of Canadian marriages are expected to end in divorce, a number that has remained relatively stable for decades; the average duration of a marriage that ends, according to Statistics Canada, is just under 14 years. (The oft-cited statistic of almost one in two marriages failing is in fact American—the figure is 43 per cent.) According to Diana Shepherd, editor of Toronto-based *Divorce Magazine*, most North American couples manage to divorce in a civilized way;

only 10 per cent are the nasty, bitter feuds that are the stuff of tabloids and made-for-TV movies. "If there are children or a business involved, a friendly divorce is the only way to go," says Shepherd. "And sometimes friendly means having to grit your teeth a little bit and get on with it, let it go."

Until recently there has been little recourse for couples who wanted to avoid the notoriously adversarial legal process for divorce. But a growing number of people are seeking out mediators to help broker a peaceful legal ending, or taking part in divorce ceremonies and rituals to help bring about emotional resolution. In addition, a kinder, gentler legal practice known as collaborative law, which started in the United States during the early 1990s, has moved north and is starting to spread through parts of Canada.

This evolution has been precipitated by a number of factors, not the least being the children of divorce. A growing body of research points decisively to the fact that kids have a much harder time adjusting to new family dynamics when their parents are bickering or engaged in full-scale war. "We did a video of children talking about the impact of divorce," says Rhonda Freeman, director of Families in Transition for the Family Service Association of Toronto. "A nine-year-old in the film said, with a very quizzical look on her face, 'If parents choose to live apart, why do they need to keep fighting?'" There is also strong evidence, Freeman says, that the kids who do best are the ones who feel free to have positive relationships with both parents—particularly parents who have moved on in their own lives. "And that includes ending the conflict," adds Freeman. "Because while you're involved in the conflict, you just don't have the emotional energy or time to devote to your children."

Martin and Deborah (unless full names are given, people cited have been given pseudonyms on request) met when they were 12, got married eight years later, started a retail business together, and raised two children. But 10 years ago, after two decades of marriage, each became involved with someone else. For the sake of the kids (now grown and away from home), as much as for their own, the Ontario couple decided to continue cohabiting—they have never divorced. "I think it's possible that people can go in different directions sometimes without losing the love for the person," explains Martin, who still lives with Deborah and the man Deborah fell in love with a decade ago. "The fact that it hasn't worked out exactly right doesn't mean you should lose sight of what brought you together in the first place."

There are usually other casualties when a long-term relationship breaks up, but Martin and Deborah have managed to maintain positive connections with each other's families as well as with all their friends. And while the community has never fully adjusted to the couple's decision to continue living together, it was best for the kids. "For them it was better than living separately," says Deborah. "They found it difficult to explain to their friends, but their friends all grew to really care about us and all of the weird stuff that people thought was going on was forgotten. Our daughter told us she's really proud of us."

While Martin knew rationally the new arrangement was for the best, it still took him about five years to feel completely comfortable with it emotionally. "But I was lucky that her partner was a person I found to be a very good man, who understood how it would be difficult for me for the love of my life to be with a different person." Martin, meanwhile, has had relationships; one girlfriend even joined the family for a while, but there was friction with Deborah over parenting issues. Overall, says Martin, the struggle was worth it. "Continuity is really important," adds Martin, who still runs a business with Deborah. "For me, a journey through life is far more interesting if you don't force dislocations into it that aren't necessary."

Calgary couple Kate and Tom had been married for 18 of their 20 years together. They had two children, now 17 and 14, and lived happily for a number of years. After a while, though, Kate started to feel lonely in the marriage—that Tom "wasn't there emotionally"—though she concedes she also played a role in the marriage's demise. Finally, just before Christmas two years ago, she asked him to move out.

Despite the grief and anger they both felt as they were separating, Kate and Tom discussed how they needed to manage the situation for the children's sake. "We've worked really hard at being civilized," says Kate, now 47 (Tom is 55). "We never, ever say anything bad about each other because of the kids and because it doesn't pay." The children spend more time with their mother, but Kate makes sure Tom knows everything that's going on at school and at her home. She even suspects the time may come when she and her ex-husband will be good friends. "We were together a very long time," she says, "and I don't think you stop loving someone."

The couple were clear from the beginning that an acrimonious parting wouldn't benefit anyone. "I don't think you can move on and build a life and have any fun if you're putting energy into being mean or being difficult—or even being right," Kate adds. "It just doesn't pay. Living and loving takes enough energy. Living and hating is just a huge waste of time."

Children may be one of the strongest incentives for divorcing couples to be civil to—or even friends with—each other. But there are other potent factors, among them the very real differences between how this and previous generations view divorce. "Many of the people who are getting divorced today were in fact children of parental divorce, so it does, in a sense, become normalized in a culture," says Robert Glossop, co-executive director of the Ottawa-based Vanier Institute of the Family. "One might speculate that having had the experience of divorce, they do understand how difficult or traumatic it can be. We may be maturing a little bit as a society that recognizes that relationships are fragile, vulnerable and do break up, and that we need to minimize the effects of divorce on children."

Glossop also speculates that because people tend to get married later than they used to, they might approach divorce more maturely. Until recently, there were few options to help people who weren't able to get along in marriage to make a proper go of divorce. But in recent years, more and more couples—and lawyers—are dropping their weapons and abandoning the court system. Divorce mediation is becoming increasingly prevalent, and a growing number of family lawyers are opting out of litigation.

Talking to a collaborative lawyer is like speaking to someone who has just seen the light. For many of the divorce and family lawyers who switch over to collaborative law, there's a profound sense of relief. Years of dealing with angry couples and displaced children take their toll. Traditional divorce, says Brampton, Ont.-based lawyer Victoria Smith, "is so expensive, it takes so long and the outcomes are so unpredictable." A collaborative divorce typically costs between $5,000 and $10,000, while a divorce that ends up in court could cost as much as $70,000. Ultimately, she adds, the things people really care about often aren't dealt with. "Most people who go into family law do it because they want to help," says Smith. "I was really having a sense that we lawyers are often making things worse. Our training is to get the biggest piece of the pie for our client, and in family matters that doesn't work. Relationships were damaged. We often made them worse."

Morrie Sacks's passionate desire to practise family law stemmed from the lingering effects of his own parents' divorce during the 1950s. But he often felt frustrated by the way the system worked. "In the adversarial model, you're waging war and there's this whole idea of victors

THE GAY BREAKUP: NOT SO GAY

Financial strain, intimacy and communication problems, loss of love, parenting differences— many of the issues that may ultimately divide a heterosexual union are identical to those that can split a same-sex relationship. But gay couples must grapple with additional challenges, both in their relationships and in the event of separation. Canadian figure skater Brian Orser famously illustrated one of those challenges in 1998 when his former partner, Craig Leask, brought a palimony suit against him. Orser tried, unsuccessfully, to have the court record of the case sealed, fearing that his career could be harmed once his sexual preference became public knowledge.

In fact, the issue of how "out" a same-sex couple is even when the partners are together can be an added source of stress. "I don't know of very many couples where both people are in the same place at the same time about how public they are about the relationship," says Lori, a health-care worker in her late 30s who, with her partner, social-services employee Lynn, has a two-year-old child (biological mother Lori became pregnant through artificial insemination). The Calgary couple has also experienced the lack of recourse a non-biological parent has to a child once the relationship with the biological parent is over. Lynn has a 13-year-old from a prior union, and had attempted to get legal guardianship of the child when he was five, a few years after she and the biological mother had broken up. But she was denied. Finally, when he turned 12, she tried again and won. Lynn has guardianship status with her child with Lori, but notes that it has less legal heft than adoption.

There are other unique parenting issues to resolve, according to Calgary mediator Lorri Yasenik. A lesbian couple, for example, may have allowed for some access between their child and the sperm donor. "Now we have to organize how it will look if they reorganize themselves into new couples—four mother figures and a donor who may come in and out of the picture," she explains.

Neither has there been, until recently, any precedent regarding spousal support and asset-splitting. But in 1999, in a case known as M versus H, the Supreme Court of Canada ruled it as unfair that a Toronto lesbian had no rights to sue a former partner for support. The following year, Ottawa passed Bill C-23, which ruled that same-sex couples were entitled to the same federally legislated benefits, obligations and status as heterosexual common-law couples.

As Toronto gay rights lawyer Douglas Elliott notes, each province protects the rights of same-sex couples to different extents, but at least now there is a constitutional imperative for support. Still, he adds, because there isn't as reliable a legal framework for same-sex couples, "It does create greater uncertainty and that can create a more contentious approach than would occur in a heterosexual situation." In addition, he says, AIDS may be a complicating factor because if one partner is disabled, the other may have a lifetime obligation to him.

Elliott strongly encourages same-sex couples to draw up prenuptial agreements. But that advice flies in the face of human nature, gay or straight. "I think it's pretty typical of all couples, regardless of their sexuality, to enter into a relationship in a very trusting manner and assume everything will be fine," says Lynn. "So there's not a lot of, 'Let's sit down and draw up a lot of forms—let's go see a lawyer'"

Nora Underwood

and losers—the wife looking for maximums and the husband trying to part with minimums," says the Vancouver lawyer. "In the collaborative model, the shift is to interest-based negotiation, how can problems be resolved. A win-win solution is the goal." Sacks found out about collaborative law two years ago from a client. "This was a gift from God as far as I was concerned," he adds. "We talk about a paradigm shift but that hardly does it justice. It's more like a quantum leap."

How it works—and it only works for people who are looking for a peaceable resolution, not for those hiding assets or out for revenge—is that each person hires a collaborative lawyer and all four proceed through the divorce as a team. Typically, collaborative lawyers also have like-minded child specialists, financial advisers and business valuators on call to help deal with particularly troublesome aspects. Going to court is not an option. "The belief is that people can make their own decisions," explains Smith. "You're still acting as that person's lawyer, but in addition you're acting as a facilitator, providing people with the support they need to make those decisions, making sure they have an opportunity to go beneath the positions they bring in the door and think about what's important in the long term."

John and his wife separated last summer after almost 10 years of marriage. The 36-year-old construction supervisor living in Brampton loves her but found they had little in common apart from their three children. "I could've stayed for the kids," says John. "But between the time I was 12 and 24, my parents went through that. They shot daggers at each other, and I hated it with a passion so I was not going to put my kids through that." Despite how angry his wife was with him—he had an affair before he and his wife separated—she wanted to mediate a settlement together. The couple's primary objective was to remain friends with each other. "It hurt, but the fact that we could sit at a table—and yes, there were tears shed—was a very positive experience," says John. "It was four people, all friends, trying to find solutions and coming up with suggestions."

In the end, according to Calgary mediator Janis Magnuson, that is really what most people prefer. "People want their marriage to end decently," says Magnuson, who runs a business called Constructive Divorce. "They don't want it to cost an arm and a leg and they don't want to hate each other. This process allows people to end relationships respectfully, effectively and efficiently."

A handful of couples are even turning to divorce ceremonies, rituals that signal the end of a relationship and the beginning of a new life apart. Such a ritual has existed in Judaism for millenniums: traditionally, a husband gives a *get* (the Hebrew word for the divorce document) to his wife to free her to remarry; now, in liberal congregations, either spouse can initiate a *get*. Phil Penningroth and his wife of 25 years, Barbara, whom he divorced in 1997, drew on that and other ceremonies for *A Healing Divorce*, their 2001 book about how to symbolically seal a divorce. "I don't think any relationship ends without a lot of strong feelings," says Phil, who lives in Longmont, Colo. "We did not want to let our conflicts carry us away into acrimony and bitterness and estrangement. There were a lot of good things in our relationship and we wanted to do our best to preserve those things, even as we decided to divorce."

In their ceremony, attended by friends, the Penningroths played a video tribute to the marriage, spoke of forgiveness and regrets and of the gratitude they felt for the relationship they'd had. "Marriages, funerals, bar mitzvahs—there are scads and scads of different rituals," he says. "The symbols involved in a ritual speak far more powerfully than the words in a divorce decree." Adds Penningroth: "When my father got divorced in the mid-1950s, as far as he was concerned it was just a fight. How can anyone be against something that creates harmony and peace, especially when there are children involved?"

But like any healthy marriage, a good divorce requires commitment and a lot of hard work. "It's still a relationship," says *Divorce* editor Shepherd. "Your marriage is ending but your relationship isn't ending if you have children. It needs to change but it's not over." The payoffs are big for divorced couples who have struggled through the anger and grief and made peace with each other. Judy Moody's first husband was her childhood sweetheart. She married him at 18, after she got pregnant, and within a couple of years they had a second child. But after about five years, the marriage fell apart, and Moody left. They struggled through a few years of arguing and bitterness, and even tried to reconcile once, but ultimately decided to build a post-marital friendship.

Around her Christmas table seven years ago were Moody and her children, her first husband, his wife, Moody's second husband, her in-laws and her former in-laws. "I was never so happy in my whole life because my whole family was there," recalls Moody, who lives in Sutton, Ont. Over the years since their divorce—Moody is now 56—she and her ex-husband have been through a lot together, including the death of their son, Andrew, in 1996. "Bill comes over and we sit and we talk about Andrew and what could have been and what was, and we cry and we laugh and we have a bond. He's the only person I can sit and talk to like that." To Moody and to others who have worked at having a good divorce, the relationship is a natural. "I have a history with him that I don't have with anyone else," says Moody. "When I see him, it's like seeing the best, oldest friend in the world, and I love him with all my heart."

From *Maclean's* January 21, 2002, pp. 25-29. © 2002 by Maclean Hunter Ltd. Reprinted by permission.

DIVORCED?

Don't Even Think of Remarrying Until You Read This

Divorce rates prove that conventional wisdom is wrong: The dirty little secret is that when it comes to relationships, experience doesn't count. Experts take a close look at why we don't learn from our mistakes and how we can start—right now.

By Hara Estroff Marano

Americans are an optimistic lot. Perhaps nowhere is our optimism more apparent than in our approach to marriage.

One of every two marriages can be expected to end in tears. Still, 90% of Americans marry. Surveys consistently show that marriage holds an honored place on our wish list, something we believe is necessary for attaining life happiness—or its slightly wiser sibling, fulfillment.

If our optimism steers us into marriage, it goes into overdrive with remarriage. Despite the disappointment and the pain and the disruption of divorce, most of us opt to get back on the horse. An astonishing 75% of the broken-hearted get married all over again. And if you count among the remarried those who merge lives and households without legal ratification, the de facto remarriage rate is even higher.

Yet a whopping 60% of remarriages fail. And they do so even more quickly; after an average of 10 years, 37% of remarriages have dissolved versus 30% of first marriages.

If divorce and remarriage rates prove one thing, it is that conventional wisdom is wrong: When it comes to remarriage, experience doesn't count. A prior marriage actually *decreases* the odds of a second marriage working. Ditto if you count as a first marriage its beta version, living together; three decades of a persistently high divorce rate have encouraged couples to test the waters by living together before marrying. But this actually dims the likelihood of marital success.

"It's so counterintuitive," says Diane Sollee, M.S.W., a family therapist and director of the Coalition for Marriage, Family and Couples Education, based in Washington, D.C. "It seems obvious that people would be older and wiser. Or learn from the mistake of a failed first marriage and do better next time around. But that's like saying if you lose a football game you'll win the next one. You will—but only if you learn some new plays before you go back onto the field."

Remarriage may look a lot like any other marriage—two people, plenty of hope, lots of love and sex, and a desire to construct some form of joint life. It even smells like an ordinary marriage—the kitchen is busy once again. But it has its own subversive features, mostly invisible to the naked eye, that make it more tenuous. It's not impossible to make remarriage work, but it takes a concerted effort.

Why Experience Doesn't Count

No, when it comes to relationships, people don't automatically learn from experience. There seems to be something special about relationships that prevents them from recognizing their failures. A close look at marriage suggests several reasons why.

• **Love deludes us.** The rush of romance dupes us into believing our own partnership uniquely defies the laws of gravity. "We feel that this new, salient, intense relationship fills the firmament for us," observes William J. Doherty, Ph.D., director of the Marriage and Family Therapy Program at the University of Minnesota and author of *The Intentional Family* (Avon, 1999). "You really think 'problems are for regular people and our relationship certainly isn't regular,'" Doherty adds. "Partners bring to remarriage the stupidity of the first engagement and the baggage of the first marriage."

• **Marriage deflects us.** Marriage, in fact, contains a structural psychological loophole: Being a two-party event from the get-go, it affords us the (morally slippery) convenience of thinking that any problems reside in our partner. We simply chose the wrong person last time. Or despite our shining presence and best efforts, the other person developed some critical character flaw or craziness. Either way, we focus—wrongly, it turns out—on the characteristics of our partner rather than on the dynamics of the relationship, by definition involving both people.

"Till our last dying breath we still think, 'Someday I'll meet a mensch and it will be perfect; he will fit with all my wonderfulness in such a way that it will all work,'" says Diane Sollee. "We indulge the illusion that, with the right partner, conflict will be minimal."

Jeffry Larson, Ph.D., psychology professor at Brigham Young University, confirms, "Partners don't reflect on their own role. They say 'I'm not going to make the same mistakes again.' But they do make the same mistakes unless they get insight into what caused the divorce and their role in the marriage failure." Larson is quick to admit that our culture generally provides us with no road map for assessing ourselves or our relationships. And some people are just too narcissistic to admit they had any role in the relationship's failure. They will never understand what went wrong. And that makes them lousy bets as new partners.

What's more, we are deeply social creatures, and even distant rumblings of a threat to our most intimate social bond are intolerable. When problems develop, marriages become so painful that we can't bear to look at our own part in them.

• **Conflict confuses us.** Our ability to learn about relationships shuts down precisely when marriage begins to get tough—and they all get tough. Conflict is an inevitable part of relationships. But many people have no idea how to resolve the conflict; they see it instead as a sign that there's something wrong with the relationship—and their partner. With low expectations about their own ability to resolve conflict, explains psychologist Clifford Notarius, Ph.D., professor of psychology at Catholic University in Washington, D.C., people go into alarm mode. This distorts the couple's communication even further and prevents any learning from taking place. "When a husband hears 'let's talk about money,' he knows what's coming," says Notarius. "He doesn't think anything different can happen. He shuts down."

• **Conflict rigidifies us.** Arguments engage the Twin Terminators of relationship life: blame and defensiveness. These big and bad provocateurs destroy everything in their path, pushing partners further apart and keeping them focused on each other.

Invariably, marriage experts insist, whether in the first marriage or the fourth, couples tend to trip over the same mistakes. No. 1 on the list of errors is unrealistic expectations. A decline in intensity is normal and to be expected, says Notarius. In its own way, it should be welcomed. It's not a signal to bail out. "You will be disappointed—but that opens the potential for a relationship to evolve into something wonderful, a developmental journey of adult growth. Only in supportive relationships can we deal with our personal demons and life disappointments. We get the reassurance of having a partner who will be there no matter what, someone who can sit through our personal struggle for the hundredth time and support us. The promise of long-term relationships is the sharing of the secret self."

Absent this awareness, partners tend to start down the road to divorce as soon as the intensity wanes. Happiness, observes Pat Love, Ph.D., a marital therapist based in Austin, Texas, is the ratio between what you expect and what you get. "You have to suffer the clash of fantasy with reality in some relationships," adds Notarius. "Either you do it in the first relationship or you have 10 first relationships."

How To Remarry

Why is remarriage so difficult? The short answer is because it follows divorce. People who divorce are in a highly vulnerable state. They know what it's like to have a steady dose of love, that life's burdens are better when shared. But, says Love, "They go out, so they're hungry. And when you're hungry, you'll eat anything." The longing for comfort, for deep intimacy, impels the divorced to rush back into a married state. Says Love: "People tend to want to go back into the woodwork of marriage."

Yet prospective remarriage partners need to build a relationship slowly, experts agree. "They need to know each other individually and jointly," says Robert F. Stahmann, Ph.D., professor of family sciences and head of the Marriage Preparation Research Project at Brigham Young University. "This means time for bonding as a couple because the relationship will be under stress from each partner's various links to the past," none more tangible than children and stepchildren.

Couples also need enough time to allow for the cognitive and emotional reorganization that must take place. Says Love, "You've got to replace the image in your head of what a man or a woman is like based on your ex. It happens piece by piece, as with a jigsaw puzzle, not like a computer with the flick of a switch."

When choosing a mate the second time around, people typically look for traits and tendencies exactly opposite those of their first partner. A woman whose first husband was serious and determined will tend to look for someone more fun. "Unfortunately," observes Howard K. Markman, Ph.D., "to the extent that they are making conscious choices, they are looking at the wrong factors." At the University of Denver, where he is professor of psychology, Markman and his colleagues are videotaping couples in a second marriage who were also studied in a first marriage.

"The motivation to do it differently is there," says the researcher, "and that is good. But they don't know exactly what to do differently. They're not making changes in how they conflict, which is predictive of relationship quality."

Further, he notes, both parties need to use the second marriage to become better partners themselves. "They both need to nourish the relationship on a daily basis…and refrain from things [such as hurling insults at one another] that threaten the marriage in the face of disappointments."

- **Learn to Love Complexity.** There is even more opportunity for conflict and disappointment in remarriages because the challenges are greater. "There are always at least four people in bed," says Love. "Him, her, his ex and her ex. Not to mention the kids." The influence of exes is far from over with remarriage. Exes live on in memories, in daydreams, and often in reality, arriving to pick up and deliver the kids, exerting parental needs and desires that have to be accommodated, especially at holiday and vacation times. The ex's family—the children's grandparents, aunts, uncles and cousins—remains in the picture, too. "When you remarry," says Brigham Young's Larson, "you marry a person—and that person's ex-spouse." It just comes with the territory.

- **Defuse Anger, Vent Grief.** Nothing keeps exes, and the past itself, more firmly entrenched in the minds of one-time spouses than anger. But we can minimize anger by finding ways to minimize the impact of ghosts from the past.

Unless people grieve the loss of the prior relationship and the end of the marriage, they are at risk of staying covertly attached to it. "When they don't grieve, often they remain angry," Larson says. "Exploring the feelings of sadness, and understanding the ways in which the first marriage was good, is a way of unhooking from it."

Many are the sources of loss that require acknowledgment:

The loss of an attachment figure. "It has nothing to do with how you were treated," says Love. "You lost someone you once cared about."

Loss of intact family. We all harbor the idea of a perfect family, and it's one in which emotions and biology are drawn along the same tight meridians.

A sense of failure. "A powerful element contributing to vulnerability in a second marriage," observes Love, "is a sense of shame or embarrassment stemming from the relationship's failure," denial of any role in the marital breakdown notwithstanding.

"There is pain and fear from the fact that former relationships did not go well," adds Hawkins, "which inhibit commitment to the new relationship and distort communication between partners."

A sense of grief. Grief is bound to be especially great for those who were dumped by their first spouse. "You can't grieve and try to get used to a new relationship at the same time," says Jeff Larson, who recommends waiting at least one or two years after a divorce before remarrying.

Digging Up the Past

Stahmann emphasizes that for remarriage to be successful, couples need to look at their previous relationships and understand their history. How did they get into the first marriage? What were their expectations, hopes and dreams? Through the soul-searching, people learn to trust again.

"It is essential that they do this together," Stahmann says. "It helps each of them break from the past relationship and sets a precedent for the foundation of the new one."

Pat Love stresses that this joint exploration must include a look at the partners' own role in the failure of the past relationship. "You have to list what you didn't like in your partner and own your own part in it. If you don't understand your part, then you are bound to do it again."

"When you do something that reminds me of my old partner," Love explains, "I project all the sins of that partner onto you. If you don't want sex one night, then you are 'withholding,' just like the ex." The fact is, Love insists, "the things you didn't like in your old partner actually live on in you."

But such joint exploration doesn't always take place. Couples are often afraid that a partner who brings up the past will get stuck there. Or that a discussion will reignite old flames, when in fact, it helps extinguish them. "Couples often enter remarriage with their eyes closed more than the first marriage," reports Hawkins. "It's as if they are afraid the marriage won't happen if they confront the issues."

Once a couple has opened up and explored their past, they need to bring the kids in on the discussion. "Kids don't have the same understanding of how and why the prior relationship ended," explains Stahmann. "Yet they need it." On the agenda for discussion: how the adults got together, why the past failed, how contact with the biological parents will be maintained, and all the couple's dreams and hopes for the future. Most experts would reserve this conversation for after the wedding.

- **Clearing Customs.** In any marriage, each partner to some degree represents a different culture with different traditions and rituals and symbols. The two distinct sets of highly structured traditions are not simply deeply emotionally resonant; they carry the force of commandment. The subtlest departure from them can make anyone feel like an outsider in his own home. One or both partners is bound to feel bad, even unloved, when their current family does a celebration "the wrong way."

The problem is, culture clash is built in to marriage, says Frank Pittman III, M.D., an Atlanta-based family therapist whose most recent book is *Grow Up! How Taking Responsibility Can Make You a Happy Adult* (Golden Books, 1998).

That, however, is where the fun begins. "The conflict causes electricity and the need to discuss things and compare perspectives, and thus come to know one another and oneself. That is the source of a marriage's energy," he says.

It's wise for couples heading into remarriage to explicitly discuss and agree on which ritual styles will prevail when. Even the everyday ones: Will dessert be served with dinner? Are evening snacks allowed? Then there are the big celebrations sprinkled throughout the calendar, culturally designated as holidays but more likely hurdles of stress in remarriage households.

• **Negotiating External Forces.** As if there aren't enough internal hurdles, remarriage can be undermined by outside forces, too. "People who lived independently before remarriage often have jobs, friend networks and hobbies that are anti-relational," says Stahmann. "These are spheres in which they have come to invest a lot of themselves as a regular source of gratification." He counts among them learned workaholism. "Such individual-gratifying activities can be hard to give up. Couples need time to work out these patterns."

• **Coping with Kids.** Nothing challenges a remarriage more than the presence of children from a prior marriage, and 65% of remarriage households contain kids. Their failure rate is highest in the first two years, before these multiplex families have even sorted themselves out.

"All you need is one active conspirator," says Minnesota's Doherty. "It's not uncommon for an ex to play on the ambivalence or outright hostility that kids have for a remarriage, especially at the beginning. An ex can have you talking about him every day."

Take one of his clients for example: Bob, who is remarried, gets a visit from his two children. After the weekend, the kids mention to their mother that the house felt cold. She calls her ex-husband, furious. When he agrees to turn up the thermostat, the new spouse feels powerless in her own home and angry at her husband because she thinks he is not standing up for himself, or her.

With kids present, partners in a remarriage do not get time to develop as a couple before becoming parents. Their bond is immediately under assault by the children. Family experts agree that this is yet another reason for couples heading into remarriage to prolong the period of courtship despite the incentives to merge households.

Even noncustody can pose problems. "Custody is a legal solution," says Stahmann. "It implies nothing about the emotional reality of family. A parent who shares custody or one who has only visitation rights is already experiencing some degree of loss regarding the children."

And the children themselves are in a state of post-divorce mourning over the loss of an intact family and full-time connection to a parent. No matter which parent a child is with, someone is missing all the time. "This leads to upset, depression and resentment at the new marriage," says Emily Visher, Ph.D., a psychologist in California and co-founder of the Stepfamily Association of America. The resentment is typically compounded by the fact that the children do not have the same perspective as the adults on how and why their parents' marriage broke up.

Financial obligations add more stress. Many a stepfather thinks: "I don't want to be putting my money into your kids' college education when I didn't put it into mine."

"There is an existential, moral dimension to remarriage families that is not talked about," says Minnesota's Doherty. "The partners will always be in different emotional and relational positions to the children. One is till death do us part. The other is till divorce do us part. The stepparent harbors a deep wish that the children did not exist, the very same children the parent could not live without."

People need to develop "a deep empathic understanding of the different emotional worlds parent and stepparent occupy." To be a stepparent, Doherty adds, "is to never be fully at home in your own house in relation to the children, while the original parent feels protective and defensive of the children. Neither 'gets' it until each describes what the emotional world is for him or her." Each partner is always an outsider to the experience of the other.

The role of the nonbiological parent is crucial—but fuzzy. "Twenty plus years into the divorce revolution and remarriage is an incomplete institution," observes Andrew Cherlin, Ph.D., professor of sociology at Johns Hopkins University. "It's not clear what rules a stepparent should follow." In successful families, the stepparent is somewhere between a friend and a parent, what he calls "the kindly uncle role." Using first names can help enhance that relationship.

But most importantly, "the more a couple can agree on expected roles, the more satisfied they will be," says Carlos Costelo, a Ph.D. candidate focusing on the dynamics of remarriage at the University of Kansas.

The key to remarriage, says Stahmann, is for couples to be less selfish that they used to be. "They have to realize there is a history there. They can't indulge jealousy by cutting off contact with kids. They can't cut off history." Selfishness, he insists, is the biggest reason for failure of remarriages.

"We all have a lot to learn from them," notes Doherty. "Remarriage families hold the secrets to all marriage. Remarriage with stepchildren illuminates the divergent needs and loyalties that are always present but often invisible in original families."

It Takes a Village

With so much vulnerability, and the well-being of so many people at stake, prospective partners in a remarriage need a little help from others. "The impression of family and friends on whether this remarriage will work is important," says Stahmann.

Pat Love, herself in a remarriage, couldn't be more emphatic. "You've got to do it by consensus. It takes a village. You've got to listen to friends. You're in an altered state by way of infatuation. The failure factor is there, making you fragile."

In fact, Stahmann contends, the opinion of family members and friends is predictive of remarriage success. "Friends and family know who you are. They knew you married, and they can see how you are in the context of the new relationship." The trick is to listen to them.

READ MORE ABOUT IT

Stepfamilies: Love, Parenting and Marriage in the First Decade, James H. Bray, Ph.D., and John Kelly (Broadway Books, 1998)
How To Win as a Stepfamily, Emily B. Visher, Ph.D., and John S. Visher, M.D. (Brunner/Mazel, 1991)

Hara Estroff Marano is PT's editor-at-large and author of Why Doesn't Anybody Like Me? (*William Morrow, 1999*).

When Strangers Become Family

The art of being a stepparent, learned not easily but well

BY WRAY HERBERT

Tori La Londe hosts a large Thanksgiving gathering every year at her home, but she's never sure who will show up. It could include any combination of her four biological children from two marriages, her stepson, the two foster kids she raised, or the several strays the others bring home. Although La Londe has little contact with her two former husbands, she has a close, enduring relationship with Jud, the stepson she helped raise. She also has a strong friendship with Jud's mother (when the two get together one will quip, "How's our husband?"). Once, when she ran into Jud's grandmother—his mother's mother—they embraced warmly, and Jud's grandmother cheerily introduced Tori to her friends: "This is my ex-son-in-law's wife."

Ex-wife now, which means the U.S. Census Bureau doesn't count Tori La Londe's family as a stepfamily. Social scientists label it a broken stepfamily, but calling her a "step" mother presiding over a "broken" home belies the warmth and wholeness she sees in her recombinant family. Like many Americans, she considers the collection of children and in-laws she has inherited in her marriages as family, plain and simple. The ties may not be biological, but they are strong nonetheless.

In fact, La Londe's extended family and other stepfamilies of various configurations are becoming standard issue: The government estimates that stepfamilies will outnumber traditional nuclear families by the year 2007. But a more inclusive estimate of anyone in any kind of step relationship brings the number of people who are "steps" to about 60 percent of the population. Which means that sitting down this week to the final Thanksgiving dinner of the 20th century will be more than 5.5 million American stepfamilies.

Their stories have become familiar in the two decades since *Kramer vs. Kramer:* the uneasy navigation of strangers suddenly confronting each other at the breakfast table, over the holidays, on the way to the bathroom in the middle of the night. In interviews with *U.S. News,* they spoke of awkward intimacies, jealous anxieties—and the strange alliances that make stepparenting an experiment in heartbreak and joy. Many of them are prospering, instinctively coming up with strategies that social scientists and family experts have just begun to understand.

Name game. The challenges begin on the level of language: What do members of new stepfamilies call themselves? Consider Kris Allen, 18, of Boulder Creek, Calif. His mother is Kim Allen, Allen being the name she took from her ex-husband, Kris's father. But Kris's father only became an Allen when he himself became part of a stepfamily in his youth; his given name was Hoops, and Kris is thinking of taking Hoops as his name. Just to make it interesting, Kris's stepfather, Jerry Kaiser, was originally Jerry Cohen. His widowed mother changed his name to Kaiser when she remarried, when Jerry was 10.

As complicated as it is to deconstruct the Allen-Hoops-Kaiser-Cohen family tree, in practice they act like any old American family. Both parents are fully involved in family decision making and discipline, as they have been since Jerry and Kim got together eight years ago. Kris is a well-adjusted kid, no more directionless or cynical than the other 18-year-olds attending nearby Cabrillo College. Social scientists haven't studied this family, but if they did they would point to a couple of things that Kim and Jerry have done that most successful stepfamilies do. First, they talk openly and daily, anticipating and defusing many potential land mines. Jerry and Kim are both counselors, and the communication skills that they teach to corporate managers are the same ones they bring to parenting. They also developed their relationship very slowly at first. Jerry and Kris actually became friends before Jerry and Kim started dating—Kris attended a work-site day-care center where they worked—so he was excited when his mother told him that Jerry would be moving into their house. The 10-year-old had only one question: "Where's he going to sleep?"

The Kaiser-Allen family is typical of what psychologist James Bray calls "neotraditional" stepfamilies, the most successful stepfamilies he identified in his nine-year study for the National Institutes of Health. Their most striking characteristic is that they take a realistic—and flexible—approach to building a family out of strangers. They know they're not a 1950s-vintage nuclear family and don't try to be;

but they are also the type of stepfamily that after a few years most closely resembles the traditional nuclear family, in intimacy and unconditional support of one another.

But successful stepfamilies come in many different shapes. Brenda and Jeff Micka of Joseph, Ore., have staked out a bold position, perhaps at odds with what the experts counsel, but which works for them. All four of their boys—three from his first marriage and one from hers—call them Mom and Dad. They also call their other biological parents Mom and Dad—an arrangement that the kids seem comfortable with. But the Mickas are well aware that they have an unusual setup. For one thing, Jeff's ex lives eight hours away in Eugene, so every other weekend the three boys have to travel 16 hours round trip to visit their mother. Still, they've been able to turn this awkward arrangement into an acceptable routine. For Michael and Simone Humphrey of Overland Park, Kan., the sacrifice has been even greater: They recently moved their new family to Kansas from Dallas, following Michael's son and daughter and their mother—his ex-wife—who had relocated in 1996. Says Simone: "We were flying Jennifer and Matthew to Dallas and back once a month. It was just too much, and too little time with them."

Every successful stepfamily has stories about compromises and adjustments it has had to make. In the case of Drew Myers and Anne Marie O'Connell-Myers of Westport, Conn., a major issue was religion. Anne Marie and her daughter, Jackie, are practicing Catholics; Drew and his four kids—Brad, Carter, Garrett, and Libby—were not churchgoers when Drew and Anne Marie got together. Anne Marie had no interest in converting her new family, but she did think as a matter of shared values that it was important for all of them to attend church. So Drew and his children began attending the Congregational Church, where they now go on the first Sunday of each month. It was an adjustment at first for the formerly unchurched Myers kids, but now they sometimes choose to join Anne Marie and Jackie at their services, too.

Lifestyle change is inevitable when a new stepfamily is formed, and it can be especially difficult for only children. In the Micka family, for instance, Brenda's son, Cody, inherited three younger brothers overnight. "Cody had some difficulty at first," says Brenda Micka, "going from having me to himself to sharing a mother with three younger brothers." But the three younger boys' adoration of their new

"older brother" brought Cody around. For 10-year-old Jackie O'Connell, the adjustment had more to do with family finances. An only child who had lived with her single mom since birth, she had never really wanted for anything; when she joined the Myers clan, she inherited four siblings and a stepdad who was used to running a disciplined family budget. "We had to negotiate family finances," says Drew. "I was budgeting for four, and Jackie had been used to getting what she wanted."

Baby makes three. The arrival of new half-siblings can also be disruptive, although it doesn't have to be; indeed, it can be tonic if the parents involve the older children in the excitement of the pregnancy early on. That's certainly how 12-year-old Madeleine Schlefer of Brooklyn, N.Y., sees it. She and her 9-year-old sister, Gwen, live primarily with their mother, but her dad and stepmom live close by in the same Park Slope neighborhood. That proximity makes it easy for the two older sisters to stop by after school and check in on their baby sister, Juliet, who was born 10 months ago. Meg Schlefer, the girls' stepmom, credits their mother with helping to make Madeleine and Gwen's comings and goings uncontentious.

RELIGION, FAMILY FINANCES, DIET, DISCIpline—these are all issues that stepfamilies around the country are struggling with every day. And most of them are doing it gracefully. Even so, there is a sizable minority of stepfamilies in America that are not doing well at all. A variety of studies have demonstrated that stepkids do more poorly on a variety of measures than do kids who live in traditional, two-parent families—even adjusting for income level. They are more apt to repeat a grade in school, have disciplinary problems, and drop out of school altogether. In fact, these studies collectively indicate that stepchildren do about as well as kids who live with a single parent, which is to say much worse than kids in traditional nuclear families.

And that's not the worst of it. According to extensive research by Martin Daly and Margo Wilson of McMaster University in Ontario, stepchildren are more likely to be abused, both physically and sexually, and even more likely to be killed by a parent—100 times as likely—compared with kids being raised by two biological parents. Another line of research indicates that they are less likely to be provided for. For example, American children living with a stepparent are less likely to go to college and to receive family financial

support if they do. New research also shows that biological mothers around the world spend more of family income on food—particularly milk, fruit, and vegetables—and less on tobacco and alcohol, compared with mothers raising nonbiological children. The list goes on.

Unsolved mysteries. Just why these families fare so poorly as a group is a matter of dispute. It's widely accepted that kids in single-parent families have troubles at least in part because the parent—usually the mother—has money problems following divorce. Facing financial difficulties, she is more apt to be absent—actually or emotionally. But remarriage doesn't seem to ameliorate the children's problems. And while few doubt that the dislocating effects of the initial divorce contribute to the situation, many experts believe that these experiences cannot fully account for the problems.

Experts offer several ideas about what might be going on. For example, unsuccessful stepfamilies often overromanticize the new family. What psychologist Bray calls "romantic" stepfamilies picture themselves as the idealized nuclear family, and they do whatever they can to fit into that mold—usually with unhappy results. The main problem, Bray says, is that in their impatience to be seen as traditional, these families push things that should evolve slowly. In most families, for example, family members spend a fair amount of time apart, more and more so as the kids become teenagers. Romantic stepfamilies, on the other hand, spend a lot of time in forced camaraderie, and teens are especially quick to detect the falseness. The decidedly unromantic Kris Allen wasn't even comfortable being photographed for this article taking a walk with his parents. A friend asked him, "So, Kris, you mean that photographer dude tried to make you act normal doing stuff with your parents that you'd never do?" Kris: "Yeah. Like I'd ever be walking on the beach with my parents!" In extreme cases, stepfamilies actually pretend they are nuclear families, hiding their step-status from schools, for example. And the bottom line is that they break up at a higher rate than other stepfamilies.

The problem, experts say, is that stepfamilies are not nuclear families—even if they wish they were—and trying to squeeze into that mold can backfire. According to historian Stephanie Coontz, author of *The Way We Really Are: Coming to Terms With America's Changing Families,* stepfamilies are not a new phenomenon in

EVIL STEPMOTHERS

The uses and abuses of Cinderella

Who's the fairest of them all? asks Snow White's stepmother before plotting to kill her young, raven-haired competition. Hansel and Gretel head to the forest knowing their father's new wife would like to see them dead. Cinderella is relatively lucky: Her stepmother relegates her to the chimney corner, but at least she doesn't threaten her life. Similar tales starring evil stepmothers can be found in cultures around the world, leading social scientists to wonder if this archetype might be rooted in fact.

Indeed, scientists who study modern stepfamilies generally agree that families with a full-time stepmother do worse than families with a stepfather. It may be that stepmothering is simply harder, because the children's bond with the biological mother is often very powerful. As University of Nebraska–Lincoln sociologist Lynn White notes, a man can be a decent stepfather simply by being a provider and a nice guy, but a stepmother is often called upon to establish "gut-level empathy and attachment"—traits that are difficult, if not impossible, to fabricate. It's also possible, White adds, that the children have a poorer relationship with their father to begin with, a frailty that may weaken the basic foundation of the new family. Whatever the reason, stepmothers and stepchildren are the "big losers" in these reconfigured families.

Evil stepfathers? But such stepfamilies are actually quite rare. In fact, most stepfamilies are formed when a biological mother remarries. So why isn't literature filled with evil stepfathers instead? According to Martin Daly and Margo Wilson, authors of The Truth About Cinderella, stepfathers don't come off all that well either; they're often lustful as well as cruel. But there aren't as many of them, and Daly and Wilson speculate that stepmothers weren't always so vanishingly rare. In earlier times, when the mortality rate for women during childbirth was much higher, a lot of widowers ended up replacing their first wife with another. According to historian Stephanie Coontz, these stepfamilies were often plagued by feuds, divorces, and even murders—not infrequently because of competition over inheritance. In societies like those of medieval Europe, she says, where primogeniture ruled inheritance, "it makes sense for people to be obsessed with wicked stepmothers who might try to substitute their own (often older) children for the oldest biological child of the dad."

Daly and Wilson offer one additonal theory. If a story is to persist through the ages, they contend, it must serve some social purpose, not only for the audience but for the storytellers as well. The audience for stories like Cinderella and Snow-White was most likely children; the storytellers, however, were their mothers. It's not hard to imagine why mothers might prefer tales whose subtext runs: "Remember, my dears, that the worst thing imaginable would be for me to disappear and for your father to replace me with another woman."—W.H.

American life, but the dynamics have changed in important ways. Before divorce rates exploded in the 1970s, stepfamilies were usually formed after the death of a parent, and those stepfamilies could in effect create a second nuclear family. But modern stepfamilies are mostly the product of divorce (or out-of-wedlock births), and it's nearly impossible for these families to fit the traditional mold. Most have to deal with ex-spouses—the "ghost at the dinner table," in one expert's phrasing—and often with the exes' new families as well. These interactions can be complex under the most congenial circumstances, and more often than not the circumstances are not congenial. Meg Schlefer has found that humor goes a long way in navigating the tricky territory of step-relationships. When she's trying to get her stepdaughters to attend to chores, for example, she'll say: "Your wart-covered, foul-smelling, evil stepmother asks you, 'Please clean your room.'"

Biological nuclear families form gradually, allowing a couple time to negotiate rules, responsibilities, and traditions before children come along. But in stepfamilies these processes unfold helter-skelter.

From the point of view of the child, it can seem that one life has been torn away and replaced with another—and all without the child's vote. Jerry Kaiser, for example, was 10 when his widowed mother remarried. Seemingly overnight, he inherited two older siblings and had to share a room with one of them in a strange house. Perhaps most disconcerting, he lost his name and the name of the father he grieved for. He was Jerry Cohen one day, Jerry Kaiser the next. He was never clear on what he was supposed to call his stepfather—nobody ever told him—so he simply avoided addressing him at all. "I got very good," Kaiser recalls, "at positioning myself in the room so I didn't have to call him Norm or Dad."

If stepfamiles shouldn't pretend they're traditional intact families, how should they act? Nobody really knows, including stepparents. In one recent research project, adults were asked to rank various roles according to their importance as sources of their sense of self. Not surprisingly, "parent" topped the list, but "stepparent" ranked extremely low, below such identities as neighbor, in-law, or churchgoer. Because of the low regard accorded stepparenting, it's not surprising that many stepparents are tempted to put more of their time and energy into other roles, making their presence in the new family shadowy at best. But this can set in motion a vicious circle: When a stepparent lacks a clear mandate as the authority figure within the family, he or she may err on the side of disciplining too much—or too little, withdrawing from that traditional parental role completely. The result may be that the stepchildren receive less attention, monitoring, and supervision than children in nuclear families.

Being somewhat disengaged as a stepparent isn't always bad, however. The third type of stepfamily to emerge from Bray's study is what he calls "matriarchal" stepfamilies, and as the name suggests, the mother plays the dominant parenting role in these families. Matriarchal stepfamilies often come into existence when a single mom finally remarries; since she has been carrying the full parenting load, perhaps for several years, she often simply continues to do so. These stepfamilies usually do best when the new stepfather takes a somewhat marginal role; this is especially true if the stepchildren are teenagers, who are just beginning the psychological process of distancing themselves from parental authority. Indeed, matriarchal stepfamilies are more likely to experience problems when circumstances force the new father into a disciplinary role with which he is unfamiliar or uncomfortable.

WHEN PAUL AND GALE HALPERN DECIDED to end their marriage, Paul expected he would at least have some kind of continuing relationship with their 1-year-old daughter, Laurie. Although he was not the girl's biological father, he felt that he had been a committed "psychological parent": He had coached Gale through the birth and cut the umbilical cord; his name was on the birth certificate, evidence of the couple's intention to raise the child together. And he had been a stay-at-home dad since Laurie's birth. Indeed, she had even called him "Daddy."

No relationship. But when Paul Halpern petitioned for visitation rights, the California courts denied his request in what has become an often-cited legal landmark. Because he was a stepparent during the marriage, the dissolution of that union made him nothing more than a "nonparent" in the eyes of the court. The judge dismissed Paul and his claims with this terse comment: "He absolutely has no relationship to the child bloodwise or otherwise, and I can't accept I should burden all of the parties in this matter, including Mr. Halpern, with conflicts, struggles, and disruptions for years to come because of Mr. Halpern's present emotional state in connection with the child."

The Halpern case took place nearly two decades ago, but it has remained a symbol in the legal profession of the gross disregard and lack of protective laws that beset stepparents and stepfamilies. Sadly, the shaky status of stepparents is just as much a fact of life today as it was in the Halperns' time. Indeed, it is now under fresh assault: Conservative critics have recently embraced the sweeping biological indictment of stepfamilies proposed by evolutionary psychologists, who contend that parents have evolved over eons to care only about the welfare of their genetic offspring. The critics are using the scientific theory as ammunition to lobby for stronger "pro-family" social policies. If stepfamilies are so unnatural from a genetic point of view that they imperil children's welfare, the argument goes, then anything that can be done to prevent divorce and preserve traditional families ought to be. This includes a number of ideas proffered by the

nascent "marriage movement"—from pro-marriage tax policies to the so-called covenant marriages that are intended to make divorce (and thus remarriage) more difficult.

Biological determinists represent a minority viewpoint in family-policy debates. Other social critics contend that if there is a genetic predisposition that favors biological children over stepchildren, it's just that—a predisposition—and predisposition is not destiny. Creating social policies that keep unhappy families trapped in the same house, these critics argue, would be wrongheaded and far more risky psychologically than life in a stepfamily. What's needed, these critics argue, is not more stigmatizing of stepfamilies, but rather policies that strengthen stepfamilies and reduce any risks that might exist.

Changes in their legal status are one possibility. Like domestic partners, stepparents currently have almost no legal standing in most states, which means that even when they assume responsibility for their stepchildren—supporting them emotionally and financially, for example—they have no corresponding rights. If the marriage ends, the stepparent has no legal standing to ask for custody or visitation. Similarly, stepchildren rarely have rights—to life insurance benefits, for example—or, if the marriage ends, to continued support or inheritance. Existing family law has been challenged in various ways in different localities, but the resulting legal rulings have been inconsistent. In a case now pending before the Supreme Court, a child's grandparents are suing for visitation rights, but some legal experts believe that a ruling for the grandparents could be interpreted as an affirmation of stepparents' rights as well.

Many family experts are now arguing for legislation that explicitly spells out both the rights and responsibilities of stepparents, perhaps modeled on England's Children Act of 1989. That law gives stepparents who have been married to a child's parent for at least two years the right to petition the court for a "residence order," which conveys many of the same rights and responsibilities as the biological parents'. Children in these stepfamilies in effect have legal relationships with three adults: both biological parents and the stepparent. The theory is that giving the stepparent enhanced status will legitimate his or her role, both in the family and in society, and that the very process of asking for rights and responsibilities will bolster the stepparent-stepchild bond. (The law

only went into effect in 1991, so its effects are not yet known.)

MAKING STEPFAMILIES WORK

Taking it step by step

Some lessons experts have distilled from research on successful stepfamilies:

• **Don't go nuclear.** Parents often cling to the dream of being a nuclear family, but it's a mistake to push it too fast. The most successful stepfamilies are realistic about the challenges they face—dealing with ex-spouses, negotiating rules and traditions—and communicate openly about them.

• **Work on the relationship.** Stepchildren need attention, but the family won't last if the parents' relationship doesn't. Anyway, it's not normal for families to be together all the time.

• **Don't rush it.** It usually takes up to two years for the stepfamily to emerge from an initial period of conflict. It can be difficult for everyone if a stepparent tries to take on the role of full parent too quickly. Kids generally want their own parents to be responsible for them.

• **Define roles.** The stepparent and stepchild need to figure out what feels right. Some form close bonds over time, but in many cases both the parent and child are better off if the stepparent acts more like a kindly aunt or uncle.

—*W.H.*

Cultural connection. Ultimately, the changes that will strengthen stepfamilies will likely come from shifts in cultural prejudices. Such change is slow, but there are signs that some preliminary movement along this line is beginning to take place. For instance, Roger Coleman, a clergyman in Kansas City, Mo., performs marriage ceremonies specifically designed to include children when a parent remarries. In years of officiating second marriages, he says, he became acutely aware of the confusion and insecurities of the children, and the ceremony—which includes a special medallion worn by the child—aims to celebrate the "new family" and move the church beyond mere condemnation of divorce. This year, Coleman says, over 10,000 families across the country will use the medallion in their remarriage ceremony.

Similar changes are occurring in public schools around the country. One of the difficulties for stepfamilies is that schools and other public institutions have typically not recognized the stepparent as a legitimate parent; school registration forms, field trip permission slips, health emergency information—none of these required or acknowledged the stepparent. The message, whether intended or not, has been that only biological parents count. It's a message that the stepparent and stepchild internalize, undermining what's often an already difficult relationship, and one which the larger community takes as another sign of

the stepfamily's illegitimacy in American society. Through the efforts of the Stepfamily Association of America and other advocates, schools around the country have begun changing their policies to acknowledge the increasingly important role of stepparents.

Change is also evident in a marketplace eager to exploit this wide social trend. In a particularly American sign of the times, the Hallmark greeting card company, that longtime arbiter of normalcy, is about to launch a line of cards devoted entirely to nontraditional families. The cards never use the word "step," but most of the "Ties That Bind" line is clearly aimed at people who have come together by remarriage

rather than biology—or, as one card puts it, "Thrown together without being asked, no chance of escape." Some are straightforward ("There are so many different types and ways to be a family today"), while others are more elliptical ("It's like looking at a puzzle where the pieces aren't where they used to be"). But all are aimed at the vast and growing market of people who don't identify with the old definitions of family, and who—like the Mickas and Kaisers and Allens and Schlefers—are finding ways to make their new families work. Who knows—soon there may even be a card Tori La Londe can send to her ex-husband's ex-mother-in-law.

ELDER CARE: MAKING THE RIGHT CHOICE

Nursing homes used to be the only stop for seniors who need help. Now there are options

By JOHN GREENWALD

MARJORIE BRYAN'S HUSBAND DIED 14 YEARS AGO. THAT was when she lived in Mississippi, and for some time afterward she went on living on her own. Now she's 82. A few years ago, she started having trouble with her balance and taking falls. Bryan has a grown son in Georgia, but moving in with him didn't seem like the answer. It's one thing to have a roof over your head. It's another to have a life. "I didn't want to live with my children," she says. "I think it would bore me to death. I don't drive anymore. If I'd stayed there, I'd be sort of a prisoner during the day."

So Bryan went looking at the alternatives. It turned out there were more than she had imagined. A couple of decades ago, seniors like her who were basically healthy but needed some assistance had limited choices. Among them, they could move in with their grown children, if they had any and were willing to risk the squabbling and sulking. Or they could be bundled off to a nursing home that was like a hospital, only less inviting. All that began to change in the early 1980s with the growth of a new range of living arrangements for older people who want to live as people, not patients, without the physical confinement and spiritual dead air of many nursing homes.

Eventually Bryan came upon the Gardens of Towne Lake in Woodstock, Ga., a landscaped complex where about two dozen seniors live in their own apartments and have round-the-clock staff members to help with daily tasks such as dressing and bathing. There are regular social events. There's a beauty shop. "I love living here," she says. "I got out that first day to learn names."

The late 20th century has done for the retirement years what it did for TV channels and fancy coffee. It multiplied the choices but also the consumer bewilderment. For seniors who want to stay in their homes as long as they can, there is home care for the masses—agencies everywhere that provide nurses and aides who either come by your place on a regular basis or live in. Traditional nursing homes are still widely used, though they are evolving away from long-term care and toward rehabilitative facilities, for short-term stays following hospitalization. The

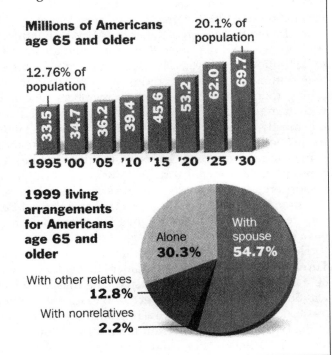

AGING IN AMERICA
The number of American seniors is growing. They're independent now, but it won't last forever

76
Currently the average life expectancy for Americans

43
Percentage of today's seniors who will use a nursing home in their lifetime

25
Percentage of elderly housing residents in assisted-living facilities now

Millions of Americans age 65 and older

12.76% of population

20.1% of population

33.5 | 34.7 | 36.2 | 39.4 | 45.6 | 53.2 | 62.0 | 69.7

1995 '00 '05 '10 '15 '20 '25 '30

1999 living arrangements for Americans age 65 and older

Alone 30.3%

With spouse 54.7%

With other relatives 12.8%

With nonrelatives 2.2%

most popular new options are assisted-living facilities. There are an estimated 20,000 to 30,000 such places in the U.S., according to industry figures. Assisted-living com-

THE OPTIONS	HOME CARE	CONGREGATE HOUSING	ASSISTED LIVING	CONTINUING-CARE FACILITIES	NURSING HOMES
WHAT IS IT?	■ Services ranging from shopping and transportation to physical therapy brought to the home	■ A private home within a residential compound, providing shared activities and services	■ Residential units offering private rooms, meals, 24-hr. supervision and other assistance	■ A variety of housing options and a continuum of services all in one location	■ Residential medical care for the aged who need continual attention
WHOM IS IT FOR?	■ Seniors who are able to continue living at home but need some help	■ Seniors in good health who want both independence and companionship	■ Seniors who may need help with bathing, dressing, medication, etc.	■ Seniors who want to provide for health needs as they age without having to relocate	■ Seniors with deteriorating mental or physical abilities or great difficulty with daily activities
WHAT DOES IT COST?	■ Some services are free; a home health-care visit can be $80	■ Often $1,200 to $2,000 a month, yet can cost much more	■ Averages $2,000 a month, but can be far more for high needs	■ $1,500 to $5,000 a month. Most require an entry fee	■ Average close to $50,000 a year
WHAT DOES IT OFFER?	■ Independence at home, but can be costly depending on level of care needed	■ The advantages of home, plus services like 24-hr. security and laundry	■ A greater level of care while maintaining some independence	■ Guaranteed care as a resident ages—at a relatively high price	■ About the only option for those who need constant care

plexes are home to one-fourth of the 2.2 million Americans who live in housing for seniors, according to the American Seniors Housing Association. Some are free-standing facilities. Some are part of continuing-care retirement communities, which offer increasing levels of help and medical supervision as residents move through the years.

"The assisted-living movement has really changed the way people age," says Karen Wayne, president of the Assisted Living Federation of America (ALFA), an industry trade group. "We've proved that people don't want to be in institutional settings." The facility provides each resident with a room or suite; meals, usually in a common dining room; and round-the-clock members who help with the no-big-deal chores of the day that can still defeat the mostly capable elderly—bathing, dressing, taking medication. Assisted living gives the elderly some measure of independence, a chance to socialize and needed privacy. Privacy for all sorts of things—sex has hardly disappeared from these seniors' lives. A survey released this month by the American Association of Retired Persons revealed that a quarter of those 75 or older say they have sex at least once a week.

The widening flood of Americans into later life—Tina Turner turns 60 this year!—guarantees that elder care will be a 21st century growth industry. The market, which was $86 billion in 1996, is expected to reach $490 billion by 2030. That potential is attracting such big developers as the Hyatt Corp. and Marriott International hotel operators. The 3,300 units of senior housing that Hyatt operates in 16 communities around the country are worth an estimated $500 million.

The old people that assisted living caters to are usually able to get out of bed and walk around. But their average age, estimated by ALFA, is 83, so they can also be frail. Almost half have Alzheimer's or some degree of cognitive impairment. (Alzheimer's patients tend to have their own, more closely supervised area.) John Knox Village, in Pompano Beach, Fla., is a not-for-profit continuing-care operation on a landscaped campus with meandering walks and duck ponds. In an arrangement typical of such places, the elderly buy a residence—studio apartments are $48,500; two-bedroom "villas" are $142,500—and a continuing-care contract that sets a monthly maintenance fee covering all services. While they may begin life there in a mostly independent mode, taking an apartment with meals, they can later move to assisted-care rooms or even the on-campus nursing home for about the same monthly maintenance fee, usually a fraction of what a regular nursing home demands.

Carl Kielmann, 73, is a retired banker and the second generation of his family to live at John Knox in the Health Center. He and his wife Lillian moved there in 1985, joining his mother, who was also a resident. His mother's contract with Knox allowed her to spend her last six years in the village medical center without eating up her savings. "In a lot of ways," says Kielmann, "this type of place is your ultimate insurance policy."

Other assisted-care facilities can be a single building. Sunrise Assisted Living in Glen Cove, N.Y., is a 57,000-sq.-ft. soft yellow mansion with white gingerbread trimmings. The 83 seniors who live there each pay between $2,850 and $4,800 a month. On a recent day the buttery smell of fresh popcorn wafted through the vestibule. On the door of its suites, framed "memory boxes" display mementos of the lives of the people who live behind those doors—family photos, military dog tags and other souvenirs of long lives. In the special section for residents with

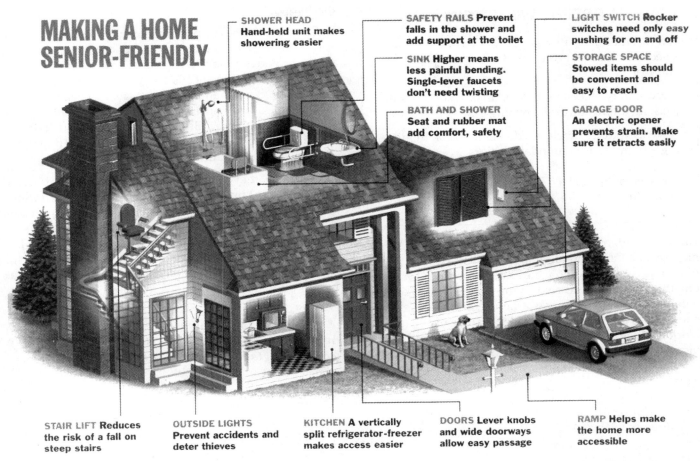

MAKING A HOME SENIOR-FRIENDLY

SHOWER HEAD
Hand-held unit makes showering easier

SAFETY RAILS Prevent falls in the shower and add support at the toilet

SINK Higher means less painful bending. Single-lever faucets don't need twisting

BATH AND SHOWER Seat and rubber mat add comfort, safety

LIGHT SWITCH Rocker switches need only easy pushing for on and off

STORAGE SPACE Stowed items should be convenient and easy to reach

GARAGE DOOR An electric opener prevents strain. Make sure it retracts easily

STAIR LIFT Reduces the risk of a fall on steep stairs

OUTSIDE LIGHTS Prevent accidents and deter thieves

KITCHEN A vertically split refrigerator-freezer makes access easier

DOORS Lever knobs and wide doorways allow easy passage

RAMP Helps make the home more accessible

TIME GRAPHIC BY ED GABEL
SOURCE: AARP

Alzheimer's, one area is stocked with old tool kits, weeding gowns and a crib with several dolls, haunting but therapeutic props meant to engage the minds of people who have returned in fantasy to younger days when they worked and raised families. "We want to create pleasant days for these folks," says Jennifer Rehm, who runs the busy activity room. "This is not usually a neat place by the end of the day."

Keeping the elderly connected to the larger world is a big part of the idea behind assisted living. At the Munné Center in Miami, where family gatherings are featured, residents look forward to seeing their neighbors' grandchildren as eagerly as they do their own. Cecilia Struzzieri, 95, recently moved into Munné after living with her daughter. "I was getting feeble, and she wanted her freedom," Struzzieri says with a sigh. "Here I get all the attention I need." Miami developer Raul Munné, who built the place, is a Cuban immigrant. "Where I grew up," he jokes, "the elderly sat on the porch and fought with the neighborhood kids. It gave them incentive to get out of bed in the morning." But in the U.S., he says, "old folks are told, 'Don't open your door and go out at night. You might get mugged.' So, many of them have no one to talk to all day. They can only sit and watch television."

Later life lived this way doesn't come cheap. The Del Webb company, which made its name building luxury spas and retirement communities in the Sun Belt, last year opened a Sun City retirement community in Huntley, near frost-belted Chicago, an acknowledgement that seniors increasingly prefer to locate near longtime friends and family and not move to far-off sunny climes. Prices range from $130,00 for a single-level fourplex to $750,000 for customized estate homes that include home theaters, Jacuzzis and wine cellars, where eminent Bordeaux can age along with its owners.

The typical assisted-living unit rents for about $2,000 a month, meals and basic services included. And prices can go much higher. Furthermore, assisted-living communities are not medical facilities, so their costs are not covered by Medicare or Medicaid, though 32 states do permit the limited use of Medicaid funds for assisted living. No wonder, then, that the average assisted-care resident has an income of $26,000 annually, while the typical retiree has $20,700.

The boomtown growth of the assisted-living industry has left it a bit rough around the edges. While nursing homes are federally regulated, assisted-living communities are overseen by the states and thus subject to widely

USEFUL WEBSITES

www.senioralternatives.com • A virtual tour of selected retirement communities around the country

www.elderweb.com • Lots of links to specific subjects, including a useful housing guide

www.aarp.org • Includes detailed tips on modifying a home to accommodate seniors

www.ec-online.net • Comprehensive information about Alzheimer's disease

varying standards. A federal study in four states (California, Florida, Ohio and Oregon) found "unclear or potentially misleading" language in sales brochures for about one-third of the 60 assisted-living homes surveyed. The most common problem was a failure to disclose the circumstances under which a resident can be expelled. One Florida home promised that seniors would not have to move if their health deteriorated, but the fine-print contract said physical or mental decline could be grounds for discharge.

Congress has begun poking into the problem, partly by way of its work to update the 1965 Older Americans Act, which provides penalties for scams on the elderly. "New services that meet the needs of our growing senior population are necessary and exciting," says Louisiana Senator John Breaux, ranking Democrat on the Senate Special Committee on Aging. "But the facilities are market driven and are susceptible to a bottom-line mentality that can lead to consumer fraud and abuse."

Of course, they are. Late-century American life is a social experiment in which we hope that market institutions can be fashioned to meet the most personal requirements. And sometimes they can be. New living arrangements for the elderly are still evolving. If that evolution isn't finished in time for all out parents to take advantage of, for many of us there will be a second chance—when it's our turn.

—Reported by Aixa M. Pascual/New York, Greg Aunapu/ Miami, Leslie Everton Brice/Atlanta, Anne Moffett/Washington and Kermit Pattison/ St. Paul

Still Birth

the story of one mother

by Robin Wallace

There is a gaping hole in the bottom of the city where I work. For a long time it was filled with the mangled ruins, the tortured debris of unspeakable loss.

Now it is cleaned out and smoothed over, and what is left is emptiness. Sometimes I think that we should leave that place as it is now, a yawning raw space. What better tribute to the loss that happened there than a giant empty hole standing for all the empty chairs at dinner tables, all the empty sides of the beds, all the empty holes in so many lives?

It may seem like the most self-indulgent of metaphors, to compare the anguished howling of a nation to the quiet, soundless loss of one tiny baby. But I see that hole in the ground, and I feel the canyon carved into my heart.

I know something about emptiness, about how a bright, gleaming symbol of promise, of humans at their most productive, can turn to dust in an instant, can become a grotesque monument to the unthinkable. I know that sometimes a loss can be so enormous that we have no choice but to embrace the space left behind, to revel in the emptiness, because it is only there, submerged in the cold, echoing hollow, that we can commune with the missing.

For me, it is my baby, my first child, my son Luke, born dead, a stillbirth, on June 12, 2001. It may seem like the most self-indulgent of metaphors, to compare the anguished howling of a nation to the quiet, soundless loss of one tiny baby. But I see that hole in the ground, and I feel the canyon carved into my heart. I imagine the dreams and hopes and futures entombed in that mass grave, and I see so many of mine buried beneath a tiny headstone in a New Jersey cemetery. I see all of those babies born without fathers, and I think of my partner, whose empty arms ache as much as mine.

I hear the ticking of my 35-year-old biological clock, and I hear the opposing voices debating what to do with that valuable but now sacred open land. If I want to be a parent, I have to do it now, but I am filled with ambivalence. I do not want to fill up the empty space, because that's all I have of Luke. People think I'm afraid of losing another baby, but what I'm afraid of is losing even more of the baby that is already gone. I don't want a baby, or another baby or a different baby. I want that baby. I can still feel his weight in the crook of my arm. I don't know if there is room in my life for another one. The emptiness is taking up so much space.

A full-term stillbirth is not the worst-case pregnancy scenario; it is the unfathomable. You skip that chapter in the pregnancy book not so much because the idea is too awful to consider but because it is too improbable, too horrible—you think—to actually ever happen. When it does, the knowledge that the unimaginable does happen and that there is no reason to think it can't or won't is a crushing burden. The basic human inclination to hope for the best, in times of hopefulness as well as fear, not only is exposed as a sham but is also no longer available to you. You have yourself become the proof of the foolishness and naiveté of such faith.

My son did not look dead. He was pink and round and perfectly formed and appeared only to be deep in a peaceful baby slumber. His eyes were closed, but there was the trace of an expression on his face, a thoughtful one, as if he had spent some time pondering his future or planning his entry into the world. The secret of who he would have been was permanently trapped inside him, but its presence was unmistakable: the potential my son would never have the chance to realize, potential from which the world would never benefit.

I see his face every minute of every day, and I cannot think of him without seeing some sort of payback, a restitution for past sins or transgressions. Yet I have no sense of any cosmic debt being paid, of karmic accounts being settled. Instead, he hovers above me like an angel of foreboding, a warning to heed the message of his death. But I cannot figure out what that message is, what lesson I was supposed to learn. The fear that until I decipher the message of my son's death the lessons will keep on coming is paralyzing.

There'd been no ovulation kits, no fertility treatments, no scheduled sex for my partner and me. I'd conceived immediately, beating my biological clock and breezing through 40 weeks of tests and examinations. My son was going to squeeze into the world two months before my 34th birthday, six weeks before our one-year anniversary. We were so very pleased with ourselves.

For me, pregnancy was not just a metamorphosis of the body but a spiritual transformation as well, a process that cast off my old self, with its mundane inadequacies and failings, and regenerated a spectacular new me in its place, a new me empowered with awesome, preternatural capabilities.

For us, the pregnancy was a validation of our destiny. My partner and I had both lived lives littered with foolish mistakes and bad choices, but in each other we'd both found the one person in the world who could inspire us to be our best selves, who would support us in being our true selves. We would be that for our children. Look at how amazing we are together, my swollen belly seemed to say. We would no longer be two but three; we could make a circle. We would be our own safe, sealed-off unit.

My life has instead become defined by a grotesque mutation of this experience: My proudest triumph now my most abject failure. It was not the onset of labor that sent me to the hospital but the eerie stillness of my child, the absence of his familiar squirms and kicks. Nine months were distilled into the few seconds it took for a doctor to say, "I'm sorry. There doesn't seem to be a heartbeat." Some essence of myself, something innocent and optimistic, drained away. All the planning, shopping, speculating; the debates over names; the choosing of hoodie towels. I felt ridiculous. I felt like a fool. I felt like I should have seen it coming.

Motherhood means different things to different women, but it is indisputably a defining moment. The purgatory straddling the worlds of motherhood and childlessness in which I've been stranded is a lonely place. I carried my baby inside me for nine months and pushed him into the world. I know the surge of all-consuming love and pride that rushes into every cell of a person's body the instant her child is placed in her arms. But I never fed my son or changed him. I never heard him cry or saw him smile.

Procreation among our social set is nonstop. Someone is always giving birth or announcing another pregnancy, and the news always hits me like a smack to the face. I imagine I can hear the cliquish scorn of the other mothers I thought I'd be joining: *You're not really one of us. What ever made you think you could be?* I had been the dutiful, faithful pledge of this elite sorority, but here I still am on the outside, my nose hard up against the glass. I've had a child but don't have my child. I fit in nowhere.

Sometimes, I feel as if the pregnancy did not actually happen, as if the whole ordeal was a disturbing, vivid dream or the product of my imagination. For a long time, I'd find myself, for just the briefest flash of a moment, thinking I was still pregnant and had not had the baby yet.

Sometimes, however, my whole body will just ache for my son, crave him. I'll dig out the blanket and knit cap he was wrapped in and inhale until my lungs are bursting. But these remnants of my baby are eerily odorless, not the slightest trace of a scent. Everything else in the world has a smell, or at least a scent that evokes its presence, but my son did not leave that expected association behind. I cannot have even that simple connection with him.

I sometimes see myself as the freakish subject of a nature documentary: the slow, sad female of a mutant species who, tricked by a cruel twist of biology into believing she has reproduced, spends her life roaming her habitat in search of her phantom offspring.

The saleswomen at the Betsey Johnson boutique are fawning over me. The dress looks fabulous. Standing self-consciously before them, obscenely overweight, I know they are lying. But I cannot wait any longer to purchase a dress for my brother-in-law's wedding, and this magenta-purple-beaded—*stretchy fabric*—affair in a size large is the only thing I've come across that fits both my body and my fashion sense.

I want to explain to these trendy, cool girls that I'm fat because I've just had a baby, but I can't do that because I don't have a baby. I cannot tell them that on the day after my due date, while I thought he was safe in my womb, my son tangled his umbilical cord around his neck and died before he was born. It's just not the thing you toss into casual conversation.

> I spent the next hours, even the next week, trying to celebrate Luke's birth while simultaneously mourning his death. I could not stop myself from brimming with new-mother pride.

Yet this socially correct silence is painful to comply with. I don't want to impose the burden of my personal tragedy on strangers, but I don't want to have to stand in circles at parties and weddings, baby showers and office bathrooms, denying who I am. *I craved oranges and had burning pelvic pain, too. My epidural also didn't take on the first try.* I want trendy, cool salesgirls to know that I've got a legitimate reason to temporarily not quite be my own trendy, cool self.

But of course, the natural progression of such remarks—congratulations, did you have a boy or girl? What's his name? How old is he?—makes such contributions impossible. So I stay quiet. With each incidence of this forced, unnatural muteness, of pretending I did not have a baby, I lose my son all over again.

You do not realize how many strangers you chatter with each day until you must guard each word so as not to offhandedly refer to the most significant event of your life. You cannot know how important your physical appearance is to you until you can't tell everyone with whom you come in contact why you are fat.

Luke was born at one o'clock in the morning. None of my dreams had prepared me for his beauty; none of this new horror could diminish the joy of holding our own child in our arms. He was still ours, he was so much ours. I remember the feel of his weight fitting perfectly into the bend of my arm and how, with that simple but sublime sensation, my entire body trembled, contorted, *writhed in agony*. But the thrill of seeing him for the first time, the mightiness of that thrill, had not been taken away from us.

I spent the next hours, even the next week, trying to celebrate Luke's birth while simultaneously mourning his death. I could not stop myself from brimming with new-mother pride. My hospital allowed parents like us unlimited access to their dead newborn, and I took extreme advantage. Luke was held by his grandparents and aunts, passed around my hospital room in a ritual that seemed perfectly sound to me at the time, but that probably permanently traumatized my ambushed relatives. They saw his long legs, his giant feet that had jabbed my ribs, his full head of red-brown hair. We baptized him and held a full burial service. I tried to be as much of a mother to my son as I had the chance to be.

Once, parents were not given this chance. Babies were discarded—no pictures, no holding, no baptism, no burial. Hospitals didn't know, or maybe didn't care, about grief counseling or emotional triage. But in this we were lucky.

We were lucky that I gave birth in a hospital with the enlightened policies mine had (even today, not all do); lucky that we had each other; lucky that I had a good job that paid me for my leave and put no pressure on me to return before I was ready.

I have, as this year has passed, thought often of all the women out there—the poor women, the women in abusive relationships—who've had to endure this suffering along with so many awful hurts and disappointments. And I've often thought of the places out there where certain parents—single mothers, teenager girls, gay couples—may not fit the perfect parent profile, who may be suffering a loss like this alone, outside the usual support systems, places that do not rush to wrap its arms around them the way ours did for my partner and me.

We were told in the hospital that men and women grieve differently. I was told that my partner's grief would need to be remembered, because so much attention would come to me. In a lesbian couple, the partner who did not carry the baby would of course have a different experience of grief than the partner who gave birth, but does that mean she would grieve like a father, like a man? Does the social worker at the hospital have a pamphlet for what would be her very unique kind of pain? Is there a male gay couple somewhere mourning the stillbirth of a child they were about to adopt? Or of a baby that a surrogate was carrying for them? Is anyone feeling their loss?

I often think that the best way to honor my son's memory would be to provide support to those parents who probably aren't getting it. It's just that I keep hoping, as time goes on, that I will want to move away from the experience, not toward it.

Still, for all we were able to do for Luke, all we really have of him is this suffocating sadness that has now, with time, yielded to emptiness. I've slowly come to realize that if I had to choose between there never having been a Luke at all or being able to have only this much of him, I would easily endure the whole thing again.

So though I struggle with the constant fear of likely doom that the loss of my son has unleashed in my life, I am comforted by the sadness, the quiet way in which it reminds me that my grief remains inconsolable, that I have not forgotten the gaping, empty hole in my life where my baby and I are supposed to be together, that unique brand of loneliness, that tells me I am still very much his mother. What I fear now is not that my grief will never heal. My greatest fear is that it will.

Robin Wallace is a writer and editor with Foxnews.com in New York City. She lives in Montclair, New Jersey.

From *And Baby*, September/October 2002, pp. 65-68. © 2002 by ANDBABY Magazine.

After a **loss**, kids need to mourn—and be reassured

By Katy Kelly

Sean Doss was 5 years old and his brother, Dustin, nearly 2 when their maternal grandmother died in 1993. The next year their parents decided to divorce and their paternal grandfather died. In 1996 their other grandparents died. The losses were so relentless, says their mom, Trish Ellermeyer-Doss-Candy, a social worker and student in Butler, Pa., that "it was like I could not catch my breath."

The sad, bad times are tough for grown-ups. They can be wrenching for children, particularly when parents are steeped in their own sadness and grief and are unable to offer reassurance or even clear explanations. When children face serious parental illness or lose a parent or close relative—to death or divorce—their faith in a world where all things can be righted is forever altered. These kids learn too soon that life isn't fair and that awful things can happen. However, research and two recent books show that thoughtful parents and caretakers can help soften the emotional blow and sometimes even fortify the child.

Death, illness, and divorce leave children with a terrific sense of loss, and parents should be direct and honest but not overly detailed in helping them cope with those events. "All involve getting through a period of grief," says Barbara Coloroso, a noted parenting educator and the author of *Parenting Through Crisis*. "The key is getting through it, not getting around it or over it or denying it." Don't try to manage the child's mourning, she says. "Give the headlines first. Then shut up and just be present for your children for whatever they need."

Range of emotions. How children respond varies depending on their age. An adolescent is likely to react to a death by being angry, says Coloroso. A 9-year-old may want details and facts, and a 5-year-old may say, "When he's done being dead, he'll be back." But many basic responses to loss are the same for anyone old enough to grasp what has happened. First comes piercing grief during which children may deny their parents are divorcing or that someone close to them has died. Denial is common, adds Mary Ann Emswiler, who with her husband, James, wrote *Guiding Your Child Through Grief* and founded the Cove, a program for grieving children. "The idea that a parent might disappear is inconceivable."

For most people, piercing grief lasts about a week and is followed by a period of intense sorrow, which can last six months to two years. "Normal things start happening again; parents return to work and kids go to school, but everything is colored with that steel-cold gray," Coloroso says. Children tend to grieve in spurts, and not always in obvious ways. A child may choose to watch *The Lion King* over and over "so they can be sad with Simba and then go out and play," Coloroso says. Finally, there's a balanced feeling when "sadness shares space with a quiet joy and a gentle peace. That's when it doesn't feel bad to feel good."

For most children, these serious losses are rare, preparations are few, and lessons are learned or lost along the way. Fears and other emotions can, and often will, creep out in daily life. Usually the child will follow the parent's positive or negative lead. Right after her separation, "I was very angry," says Ellermeyer-Doss-Candy. Two months later, "when I realized the kids were mimicking my attitude, I did a real about-face …. I decided to make a point of not discussing [any of it] in front of the kids."

Anger is a natural response to loss, but leaving it unexpressed in front of the kids is the better part of parenting, the experts say. "If you really want to help your kids, you have to act like an adult and parent your children," says Coloroso. "This might mean you might need to get some support, too. Let others help you."

To get beyond a loss, a child must be allowed to mourn and encouraged to have faith in better times to come. And stay true to the family routine. "Even when you've been brought to your knees in grief you can get up in the morning and fix breakfast," says Coloroso. These small actions reassure kids that life can go on. By showing that they are resilient and compassionate, parents can give their children the tools to mend their hearts.

Healing is an evolving state for most kids, but some need professional help. About one third of kids facing a trauma would benefit from therapy, says Emswiler. Signs that such help is needed include ongoing depression and severe anxiety, chronic anger, hostility, aggression at school or at home, or regression to the behavior of a child significantly younger. Other warning flags are trying to fill in for parents by taking on adult responsibilities or a consistent desire to stay home from school or away from friends. "We see a lot of preadolescent girls who have stomachaches or headaches," says Emswiler. "That's a sign they are struggling with something pretty profound."

Group healing. Even those who don't need individual therapy will likely benefit from a peer support group. The Doss boys found solace through the RAINBOWS program—an international nonprofit organization designed to guide children and adults through painful transitions—at Butler Memorial Hospital. With the help of a facilitator, kids in the program work through their

Where to learn more

• **Grief counseling.** Sponsored by the Barr-Harris Children's Grief Center in Chicago, *www.barrharris.org* offers an extensive book list for children and adolescents. Also visit *www.neclt.org*, run by the New England Center for Loss & Transition.

• **Words of wisdom.** Locate a RAINBOWS program or gather advice at *www.rainbows.org*.

• **Dealing with death.** This comprehensive site, *www.hospicenet.org*, includes articles on talking to children about death.

sense of isolation and learn ways to manage fear and anger. That helps them move past the loss. Being with other kids who have also suffered a loss and can understand is key, says Ellermeyer-Doss-Canedy.

Sean agrees. "At the beginning I didn't really want to go. But in the end I liked it. I could talk about it more." His brother, Dustin, adds, "I got happier because I knew I wasn't the only one in there that had my parents divorce."

In time and with help kids learn that life does indeed go on. At different ages and developmental stages they will need to revisit and recall the trauma. And even certain happy moments—like a graduation or a wedding—may also be a bit wistful for years to come. Coloroso considers an old saying: In the good times and the bad, remember, this too will pass. These children understand that "both are a part of life."

From *U.S. News & World Report*, January 8, 2001, pp. 51-52. © 2001 by U.S. News & World Report, L.P. Reprinted by permission.

UNIT 5
Families, Now and Into the Future

Unit Selections

Key Points to Consider

- After having charted your family's lifestyle and relationship history, what type of future do you see for yourself? What changes do you see yourself making in your life? How would you go about gathering the information you need to make these decisions?

- How have the events of September 11, 2001, affected your thinking about moral values, drug use, racism, family, and patriotism?

- What decision have you made about long-term commitments—marriage or some other relationship? How about children? Do you see divorce as a viable option, even before marriage? Do you expect to live "happily ever after"?

- Are you "happy"? Why or why not? What factors in your life have contributed to your present feelings?

- What is the state of rituals in your family? What rituals might you build in your family? Why? How might you use family gatherings and other traditions to build family integration?

 **Links: www.dushkin.com/online/**
These sites are annotated in the World Wide Web pages.

National Institute on Aging
   http://www.nih.gov/nia/
The North-South Institute
   http://www.nsi-ins.ca/ensi/about_nsi/research.html

*W*hat is the future of the family? *Does the family even have a future?* These questions and others like them are being asked. Many people fear for the future of the family. As previous units of this volume have shown, the family is a continually evolving institution that will continue to change throughout time. Still, certain elements of family appear to be constant. The family is and will remain a powerful influence in the lives of its members. This is because we all begin life in some type of family, and this early exposure carries a great deal of weight in forming our social selves—who we are and how we relate to others. From our families, we take our basic genetic makeup, while we also learn and are reinforced in health behaviors. In families, we are given our first exposure to values and it is through families that we most actively influence others. Our sense of commitment and obligation begins within the family does our sense of what we can expect of others.

Much writing about families has been less than hopeful and has focused on ways of avoiding or correcting errors. The seven articles in this unit take a positive view of family and how it influences its members. The emphasis is on health rather than dysfunction.

Knowledge is the basic building block of intelligent decisions regarding family. Jennifer Matlack describes the genogram, a useful technique for mapping out your family history so that you can anticipate, plan, and possibly change the choices you make in relationships and lifestyle. One way to gather this information is through interviews, and "Getting the Word" explains just how this can be done. "Generation 9-11" describes how positively adolescents have responded to the world following the terrorist attacks of September 11, 2001. "What's Ahead for Families:

Five Major Forces of Change," identifies five societal trends that Joseph Coates believes will have an impact on the future direction of families. Then, in "Happiness Explained," Holly Morris examines the science of contentment, happiness, and optimism. Family rituals can be a powerful force for family cohesion and change, and the nature of family rituals is described in "Examining Family Rituals." Concluding this volume, "Reconnect With Your Family," by Joyce Brothers, describes the ways in which family gatherings and other rituals can be used to strengthen families.

relationships

breaking free of
the family tree

Save yourself a lot of bark and spilled sap:
Branch out from the usual genealogical charts
by mapping your family's behavior tics.

BY JENNIFER MATLACK

Take a good look in the mirror.

Along with the color of your eyes and the shape of your face, you might also have your mother's quirky sense of humor and your father's artistic flair. And it doesn't stop there. One parent's debilitating depression or peculiar obsession may be as much a part of you as the nose on your face.

All families carry baggage. And when it comes to piling it on, families can be awfully generous. You may have ended up with emotional loads you don't even know you're carrying that will affect important relationships in your life and steer you off course in ways you can't imagine.

Lucinda and Dan (names have been changed), a professional couple in their 30s, were each reliving familiar family patterns—and didn't realize it. They only knew their marriage was in trouble, so they sought help from San Diego marriage and family therapist Sally LeBoy. To LeBoy, Lucinda complained that her husband would agree to do a household chore, such as lock the doors at night, and then forget to follow through. Moreover, he didn't seem to care, and his passivity made Lucinda feel as if she didn't have a partner. Dan, on the other hand, told LeBoy that he thought of his wife as a maddening little Miss Wiz—always taking control and getting things done. He was unhappy because it seemed as if Lucinda was constantly nagging him. "They weren't discussing divorce," says LeBoy, "but they knew they had to work out the problem before it got worse."

LeBoy began, as many therapists do, by exploring the family dynamics in the couple's background. Then she created a family diagram, or genogram, which charts patterns of behavior through several generations of a family. Along with normal behavior, distant or hostile relationships and serious mental or physical problems are diagrammed in symbols that appear on a chart. It becomes immediately clear if history is repeating itself. "We claim that we will never be like our parents and have the same relationships they had," says LeBoy. "But how we define ourselves in an intimate relationship comes from what we have learned in our families."

your family inheritance may be more than you bargained for. The emotional patterns of families can be handed down in the genes along with physical traits.

Genograms have more details than ancestral trees. They include not only three generations of a family but also live-in partners and other important nonfamily members. In addition to marriages, births, and deaths, genograms record extramarital affairs, miscarriages, abortions, financial problems, serious illnesses, and other major stressful events. The charts also note the personality traits of family members, such as whether someone is emotionally inaccessible, controlling, or passive.

"Think of it as if you're painting a picture of your family," says LeBoy. "The more detail, the better."

Genograms were created by the late psychiatrist Murray Bowen, M.D., developer of the family systems theory in the early 1950s. Bowen's work with schizophrenic patients and their families at the Menninger Clinic in Topeka, Kansas, and later at the National Institute of Mental Health near Washington, D.C., led him to radically depart from previous theories of human emotional functioning. Bowen saw the family as one emotional unit and the individual as part of that unit rather than as an autonomous psychological entity. Through his research, he discovered that an order and predictability in family relationships existed. The recent resurgence of genograms is due in part to New Jersey therapist Monica McGoldrick's use of the charts in family life cycle development and the popularity of her 1999 book, *Genograms: Assessment and Intervention* (W.W. Norton).

Genograms include details not found on the traditional family tree, such as extramarital affairs, abortions, and financial problems.

Behavioral patterns are passed down from generation to generation by parents, who teach their children how to relate to other people. Therapists also believe that learning interpersonal skills occurs on a subconscious level in children, and recent genetics research suggests that some character traits and behaviors, such as shyness and depression, are actually encoded on genes and thus physically transmitted to the next generation.

In Lucinda and Dan's case, the genogram study showed that their behavior toward one another was directly related to how they functioned subconsciously in their respective families. Lucinda came from a line of strong, reliable women and marginally functioning men. In her immediate family, her father was alcoholic and her mother, perhaps to compensate, was extremely reliable. Dan's family was dominated by his rigid, controlling father, who was determined that all his children should be successful. LeBoy also discovered that Dan left his parents' home at age 18 to attend college on the other side of the country, about as far away from home as he could get.

"For people who grow up in a situation where someone in the family didn't pull their weight, the tendency to overfunction is huge," says LeBoy. Clearly, that's what Lucinda was doing in her marriage.

Dan, on the other hand, according to LeBoy, learned to distance himself physically and psychologically from his overachieving, overbearing family. Thus, the more Lucinda demanded of Dan—as her mother had tried to do with her father—the more Dan withdrew, the same way he had always withdrawn from his own demanding father. Both were extremely ingrained in their particular "learned behaviors," that is, how they react in familiar situations.

LeBoy tried to help Lucinda and Dan unlearn some of their programmed behavior. For Lucinda, this meant dropping her mother's overfunctioning style. Dan's job was first to try to change the relationship with his father by relating to him as a responsible adult, rather than a rebellious child. Once Dan "grew up" and began to feel more autonomous, LeBoy believed he would be able to drop his defensive, passive-aggressive style with his wife, and when Lucinda demanded something of him, Dan would be more willing to cooperate. Becoming aware of the origin of their behavior enabled the couple to set their marriage on a steadier course.

Genograms help people see the big picture, which at times can be scary, and interpreting a baggage-laden lineage is not always easy. Professional guidance is recommended.

"If you do a genogram and discover patterns that you find are negative or disturbing, take this information and work with a therapist," says Ann Kramer, a family counselor in Tampa, Florida. "A professional will help you clarify what you're seeing and perhaps give you some insight you can't see on your own."

Certain key relationship patterns tend to surface repeatedly. One is called "emotional fusion," which occurs when family members fail to establish healthy differences between one another, and function in exclusively codependent ways. "Triangling" is another. It occurs when two people draw in a third person in an attempt to defuse stress and anxiety between one another. A "cutoff" is perhaps the most serious difficulty, which occurs when someone severs ties with his or her family completely. Another important factor to consider in genograms is birth order. Siblings' emotional places in the family are often duplicated in their subsequent intimate relationships. Firstborns, for example, tend to be responsible and serious adults, whereas the babies are more carefree and rebellious.

Sorting through past family relationships can be an emotional strain, but the rewards of such a cleansing are great.

As difficult as it is to sort through family dynamics and relationships, the rewards are great indeed. But before you can change a problem, you first must realize one exists. Too often, families live in cycles of despair and anger, feeling that there is no way out, and not realizing the door they seek may be the back door of their past.

Jennifer Matlack is a writer based in Wilton, Connecticut.

Generation 9-11

The kids who grew up with peace and prosperity are facing their defining moment

BY BARBARA KANTROWITZ AND KEITH NAUGHTON

I was a sleepy, gray afternoon—a challenge to any professor. And for the first few minutes of class last week, University of Michigan sociologist David Schoem had some trouble rousing the 18 freshmen in his seminar on "Democracy and Diversity." One student slurped yogurt while another stretched his arms wide and yawned. A few others casually took notes. But the lassitude ended abruptly when Schoem switched the discussion to America's war on terrorism. For the rest of the hour, the students argued passionately and articulately about foreign policy, racism and media coverage. Then, New Yorker Georgina Levitt offered one view that stopped the debate cold. "September 11 has changed us more than we realize," she said. "This just isn't going to go away."

At Michigan and campuses all around the country, the generation that once had it all—peace, prosperity, even the dot-com dream of retiring at 30—faces its defining moment. College students are supposed to be finding their place in the world, not just a profession but also an intellec-

tual framework for learning and understanding the rest of their lives. After the terrorist attacks, that goal seems more urgent and yet more elusive than ever. In the first week, they prayed together, lit candles and mourned. Now they're packing teach-ins and classes on international relations, the Mideast, Islamic studies, even Arabic. Where they once dreamed of earning huge bonuses on Wall Street, they're now thinking of working for the government, maybe joining the FBI or the CIA. They're energized, anxious, eager for any information that will help them understand—and still a little bit in shock.

REASON TO BELIEVE
Epstein reached out to students of many faiths, all struggling to understand their changing world.

It's too soon to tell whether 2001 will be more like 1941, when campuses and the country were united,

or 1966, the beginning of a historic rift. So far, there have been only scattered signs of a nascent antiwar movement; at Michigan and other campuses, students' views are in sync with the rest of the country's. In the NEWSWEEK Poll conducted last week, 83 percent of young Americans said they approved of President George W. Bush's job performance and 85 percent favored the current military action. These figures are consistent across all age groups. But students also understand that the future is increasingly unpredictable and that long-held beliefs and assumptions will be severely tested in the next few years. "Our generation, as long as we've had an identity, was known as the generation that had it easy," says Greg Epstein, 24, a graduate student in Judaic studies at Michigan. "We had no crisis, no Vietnam, no Martin Luther King, no JFK. We've got it now. When we have kids and grandkids, we'll tell them that we lived through the roaring '90s, when all we cared about was the No. 1 movie or how many copies an album sold. This is where it changes."

After September 11, even the school the cops attended felt out of date

Turning John Jay Into Terrorism U

By Peg Tyre

WHEN COLLEGE RECRUITMENT fairs resumed following September 11, Alan Weidenfeld, an admissions counselor for John Jay College of Criminal Justice in New York City, found that his information table wasn't attracting the usual handful of prospective students. Instead, it was drawing a crowd. "Students who might have looked at chemistry or biology at another college three months ago are checking our forensic-science program," says Weidenfeld, who estimates inquiries have tripled. Those prospective students, Weidenfeld says, are influenced by patriotism, but they're also thinking about their futures. "Many of them want to know, 'Will John Jay prepare me for the FBI, Secret Service and INS?'"

Professors and administrators at John Jay say the answer to that question is a resounding yes. Founded in 1964, John Jay is the only liberal-arts college in the nation devoted to criminal justice. Once of the 20 City University of New York campuses, John Jay has a reputation as a solid, if uninspiring, academic steppingstone for the uniformed professions. But its campus is also home to some unsung innovators in behavioral science, organized crime an forensics. In the days following September 11, those staffers, along with professors from other parts of the sprawling CUNY system, began to plan a terrorism institute on the campus of John Jay. "It's a new day in criminal-justice education," says college president Gerald Lynch.

The college already offers classes in risk assessment, cybercrime and terrorist cults to its 11,500 students, but next year it hopes to ramp up the toxicology lab and inaugurate nearly three dozen new courses—from analyzing biological assaults to the literature and art of terrorism.

Some ongoing classes have already undergone a mid-semester transformation. Before the attacks, students taking security design discussed threats to Manhattan landmarks. Following September 11, says student Peter Linken, "we needed to have an entirely new discussion on how to prevent the unexpected." At John Jay, that discussion is hardly academic. The school counts a staggering 110 current and former students killed in the World Trade Center. Those losses, says president Lynch, fuel their determination to better equip the crimefighters of the future.

VOLUNTEERS
September 11 has changed the curriculum at Michigan and elsewhere

What will they make of their moment? It's always tricky to generalize about a generation, but before September 11, American college students were remarkably insular. Careers were their major concern both during the high-tech boom (how to cash in) and after (how to get a job). According to the annual survey of college freshmen conducted by UCLA's Higher Education Research Institute, only 28.1 percent of last year's freshman class reported following politics, compared with a high of 60.3 percent in 1966. Nationwide, campus activism has been low key through the 1990s. That was true even at Michigan, the birthplace of SDS and a hotbed of antiwar protest during Vietnam. Alan Haber, a 65-year-old peace protester and fixture on the Ann Arbor campus since his own student days in the 1960s, says

that before September 11, there was no central issue that ignited everyone, just a lot of what he describes as "little projects": protests against sweatshops or nuclear weapons. He thinks that may change as these campus activists begin questioning the U.S. military efforts. "This situation," he says, "bangs on the head and opens a heart."

68% of young adults believe the terror attacks have made people their age more serious about their work and studies

Despite their perceived apathy and political inexperience, this generation may be uniquely qualified to understand the current battle. "I think they realize more than the adults that this is a clash of cultures," says University of Pennsylvania president Judith Rodin, "something we haven't seen in a thousand years." While their parents' high-school history lessons concentrated

almost exclusively on Western Europe, they've learned about Chinese dynasties, African art, even Islam. They are more likely than their parents to have dated a person from another culture or race, and to have friends from many economic and ethnic backgrounds. Their campuses as well are demographically very different from those of a generation ago. "It's gone from a more elite institution to more of a microcosm of the population," says David Ward, president of the American Council on Education, a national association of colleges and universities.

A DAY IN THE LIFE
After the attacks, Gagnon, editor in chief of The Michigan Daily, sent four reporters and two photographers to NY

Others argue that this spirit of tolerance can have a downside, particularly now. When author David Brooks, who wrote a widely discussed Atlantic Monthly article on

At UCLA, a national emergency means more opportunities to teach

Islam, Arabic and Afghanistan 101

BY DONNA FOOTE

THE EMERGENCY MANAGEMENT TEAM at UCLA normally convenes to deal with earthquakes. But at 10 a.m. on September 11 it met to handle an entirely different emergency. Though the campus of 60,000 people appeared to be in no physical danger after the East Coast attacks, the team of top administrators declared a "policy crisis" requiring a rapid response. "We agreed that it was important to connect the event with what we do here every day—which is teach and learn," recalls Brian Copenhaver, provost of UCLA's College of Letters and Science. Within the week an e-mail titled "Urgent Call to action" had gone out to all 3,200 faculty members, seeking volunteers to design and teach a series of one-unit, pass/fail seminars related to the events of September 11—without pay.

By the time the fall quarter began two weeks later, UCLA had some up with 50 (yes, 50) new courses taught by some of the marquee names on campus. Chancellor Albert Carnasale signed on to teach "National Security in the 21st Century." Copenhaver offered a course exploring the sue of terror in Machiavelli's "The Prince." Allan Tobin, director of the UCLA Brain Research Institute, teamed up with his wife, English professor Janet Hadda, to look at the neurobiological effects of terror on creativity.

Instead of hitting the streets with anti-war demonstrations, undergrads are hitting the books. Demand for courses in Arabic and Iranian studies is way up, and the series of 50 seminars, called "Perspectives on September 11," is almost completely full. that may be because the weekly, one-hour classes are part academic inquiry, part group therapy. Unlike most courses at UCLA, where enrollment is large and professors are distant, the new seminars are limited to 15 students to encourage discussion. Like many students, political-science major Grant Rabenn reacted to the September attacks was fear. "In most classes there is hardly any interaction," Rabenn says. "Here you just go and let out what's inside you."

Jordan Richmond, a music major, is enrolled in three September 11 seminars. On the first day of history professor Vinay Lal's analytic class on terrorism, Richmond recalled finding a Web site by 10:30 a.m. on September 11 that had already posted a WTC obit—noting both the date of the towers' completion and the date of their destruction. Seeing that cybertombstone, "I almost cried," he says. "The event was already contextualized. that blew my mind." The seminars, believes Richmond, have sent him on a journey to learn what he should have already known.

rampant pre-professionalism at Princeton last year, returned there after September 11, he found a surging interest in global affairs and issues of right and wrong—but also a frustration with the moral relativism of much of the curriculum (see this week's Web Exclusive at Newsweek.MSNBC.com). One student told him that he had been taught how to deconstruct and dissect, but never to construct and decide.

Michigan, one of the country's premier universities with more than 38,000 graduate and undergraduate students, has spawned campus groups reflecting virtually every corner of the globe and every world view, from the conservative Young Americans for Freedom to groups that still cling to dreams of a socialist utopia. There are also substantial numbers of Jewish, Arab and Muslim students who have made the politics of the Mideast a personal cause. But on the morning of September 11, senior Geoff Gagnon, editor of The Michigan Daily, the campus newspaper, thought an issue much closer

to home would be sparking angry debate that day. An athlete had been accused of sexual assault—a major story on a Big Ten campus—and Gagnon had been at the paper until well past 3 in the morning nailing down details. He was still groggy when his roommate burst in to tell him that NPR was reporting a "big plane crash in New York." Gagnon rushed from his apartment to the Daily newsroom, where he and his staff gathered around the TV. Soon, classes were canceled for the first time since the 1975 blizzard. "We just watched this thing unfold like everyone else," he says, "except we had to figure out what it meant for the 40,000 people here."

GIVE PEACE A CHANCE Charlotte Greenough chose Michigan for its diversity and was impressed by how so many students drew together in a crisis

Virtually everyone Gagnon spoke to knew someone who might be missing. One of the news editors worried about her mother and stepfather, who worked near the World Trade Center. A reporter who grew up near Pittsburgh was alarmed when she heard about the crash of Flight 93 in rural Pennsylvania. After the first plane hit, they heard an active Michigan alumnus, Jim Gartenberg, interviewed on ABC. Trapped on the 86th floor of the North Tower, he was on the air live, describing the scene just before he was killed in the collapse. Gagnon quickly sent four reporters and two photographers to New York. "We wanted things we weren't going to get from the AP," he says. One of the reporters, David Enders, talked to Gartenberg's pregnant widow, Jill. She said that on Saturday three weeks earlier, her husband woke up exhilarated because it was the start of the college-football season. "He lived for Michigan football," she told Enders.

That first night, nearly 15,000 students gathered for an impromptu

After decades of disrespect and worse, ROTC has become cool again

'They Know I'm About Something'

BY ALLISON SAMUELS

GROWING UP IN A POOR Los Angeles neighborhood that still shows scars from the 1992 riots, David Ramirez watched friends wind up in juvie, or worse, after getting involved in theft and other small-time crimes. He knew he was headed in the same direction if he didn't get a plan.

So in the ninth grade, David enrolled in the Army Reserve Officers' Training Corps program at Inglewood High School. Though he thought the olive uniforms were dorky, David liked the sense of purpose he'd seen in others who enrolled. "The more free time you got, the more you're bound to end up in some type of trouble," says David, now 17. "Plus, I didn't want to be home that

much. In ROTC, everyone's family." He likens his school's ROTC to a secret fraternity. "When I walk in my neighborhood now, the gang guys see me in my uniform and they leave me alone. They know I'm about something."

Dare we say it? ROTC is cool again. Started in 1916 when the United States was faced with world war, ROTC fell out of favor after Vietnam. But it found renewed popularity thanks to gulf-war patriotism and the skyrocketing costs of higher education (ROTC gives scholarships of up to $35,000 a year in exchange for a four- to eight-year commitment to the military). Today it has 200,000 students nationwide, an its ranks have increased considerably since September 11.

For many inner-city kids like David Ramirez, ROTC is sorely needed. The students at his school, divided evenly

among blacks and Hispanics, suffer more than their share of poverty and low self-esteem. "These kids are living very tough lives, and September 11 didn't change that a bit," says Sgt. 1/c Luis A. Melendez, who has headed the Inglewood program since 1994. Usually only a handful sign up each semester, but after September 11 the ranks at Inglewood swelled to 350. "Many of them know that the military was their best option, one way or the other, for any chance out of her," says Melendez.

An average to below-average student before ROTC, David now boasts a 3.5 GPA. He is second in command for the school's ROTC squad and plans to attend West Point next fall with the sponsorship of Rep. Maxine Waters. "I want to show people that someone from this community could get there and make it," he says.

candlelight vigil on the Diag, the main campus crossroads. Some in the huge crowd had spent much of the day anxious for news of relatives or friends. Charlotte Greenough, an 18-year-old freshman from Manhattan whose family lives a few blocks from the World Trade Center, had waited five hours to hear that her parents were safe. She was so frustrated by the constant busy signals that she threw a cordless phone across the room and broke it. "I've never been so scared in my life," she says. Greenough, a committed pacifist, chose Michigan because of its diversity. "You can learn about other people, take any sort of class or go to any religious service or any concert," she says. "I knew that whatever direction I decided to go in, whatever happened, I would be able to follow that up and define myself." When classes resumed on Sept. 12, Greenough was impressed by how students on the huge campus reached out to each other. "People came up to me constantly," she says, "gave me hugs and were so nice to me."

In the first few days after the attacks, everyone seemed to be look-

ing for ways to give and receive comfort. The bell tower played the national anthem. The Rock, a boulder along fraternity row that's often painted in school colors or bright neon hues, was adorned for weeks with American flags and "God Bless America." On Wednesday, junior Joanna Tropp-Bluestone's experimental-art instructor handed his class two huge wooden boards and asked the students to create a mural. Tropp-Bluestone, whose father died of heart disease when she was 10, knew exactly what she wanted to paint in her corner: a hollow red heart. "The only way you get through something like that is with love," she says.

Michigan's president, Lee Bollinger, had been in New York for a meeting on Sept. 11 and managed to get one of the last cars available from Hertz on 57th Street for the 10-hour drive home on Wednesday. As he drove, he was on his cell phone with the football coach, Lloyd Carr, debating whether Saturday's game against Western Michigan University should go on. Carr argued for the game, but Bollinger wasn't con-

vinced. As he sped across New Jersey, Pennsylvania and Ohio, he called colleagues for advice, including Peter McPherson, president of the university's archrival, Michigan State. Finally, as he neared Ann Arbor, Bollinger made his decision. The cavernous Michigan Stadium would be silent on Sept. 15. "It became clear to all of us," Bollinger says, "that the magnitude of this was so great that a few days would not separate ordinary life from this event. People would need to regain ordinary life over a longer period of time."

Young people say careers in medicine (48%), the military (46%) and science and tech (44%) will be more popular now

Over the next week, walk-in traffic doubled at the campus psychological-counseling center. Everyone was feeling vulnerable, says Jim Etzkorn, the clinical director. Many students were worried about being drafted if war erupted. There were also more intense cases of homesickness, especially among freshmen. On Sept. 19, 800 people jammed a panel discussion of the attacks by historians and political scientists who specialize in the Mideast. Even the most uninvolved students understood that they could no longer ignore what was happening on the other side of the world. The Daily was running foreign news on its front page almost every day, and many professors, encouraged by the administration, incorporated discussions of the events into classes on a wide range of subjects.

STAR SPANGLED
Areej El-Jawahir, a Muslim originally from Iraq, opposes bin Laden and supports bombing Afghanistan

For Michigan's Arab and Muslim students, the weeks after the attack brought unexpected terror. On September 11, Areej El-Jawahri, an 18-year-old freshman whose family moved here from Iraq four years ago, was still trying to check on friends in New York when she started receiving threatening e-mail. One said: "We will f--- you bastards for doing this." Later that week, when El-Jawahri mentioned the e-mails in her political-science class, two non-Muslim girls she didn't know well came up and hugged her, and they've since become good friends. "I love this country," she says. "I love the freedom." She supports the bombing of Afghanistan and says that the United States is "defending the Islamic religion from the disgrace of bin Laden." Brenda Abdelall, 20, a political-science and Islamic-studies major from Ann Arbor who is president of the Arab Students Association, said she received a death threat within two hours of the attack. Abdelall, pictured on NEWSWEEK's cover, was afraid to leave her apartment, and her mother

came and got her. Abdelall called the police soon afterward, but the e-mail couldn't be traced. "Walking around, I did feel people were looking at me," she says. She and a friend put together a campus wide teach-in on hate crimes that was attended by 500 people. "Only through education and knowledge can we defeat intolerance on campus," she says.

When he heard about the attacks, Aiman Fouad Mackie, a 21-year-old graduate student in public policy, had just one thought: "Please God, don't let it be Arabs." Since then, he says, many of his Arab friends have received death threats. Mackie is president of Michigan's Lebanese Student Association and he says many members do not show up for meetings now because they're afraid to walk around at night. But, he says, there have been encouraging changes as well. Instead of shouting at each other, pro-Palestinian and pro-Israeli groups are speaking in a more civilized way. Mackie always wanted to work for the government, but now he is even more sure that he'd like to represent the United States overseas, maybe in the Mideast. "The most positive thing coming out of this," he says, "is that Americans will have a better understanding of Islam and Arabs."

PLAYIN' IN THE BAND
Drum major Karen England has to comfort bandmates after an emotional patriotic halftime performance

Foreign students at Michigan and elsewhere have also felt the pressure of extra scrutiny. The university has 4,000 foreign students, the majority in graduate school. So far, officials say, only one is known to have withdrawn because of concerns about safety. However, proposals to tighten immigration and student-visa standards could affect Michigan in the future.

Many students say that something resembling normal life started returning to campus on Sept. 22, when the Wolverines finally met Western Michigan for the postponed match up. In a somber, patriotic tribute, the band formed an American eagle on the field while they played "America the Beautiful." They unfurled a giant flag on the 50-yard line. As she stood saluting, drum major Karen England was stunned by the crowd's reaction. Normally, Michigan football fans clog the aisles at halftime, racing for the concession stands and the restrooms. Instead, the crowd stood as one and sang. After they exited the field to a simple military drum tap, England had to comfort her sobbing bandmates. "I don't think anybody in the band realized the effect this would have," she says. "We were performing for something really important, our country. That week, we had a purpose." (Michigan won, 38–21.)

WE ARE FAMILY
Almost everyone at the Kappa Alpha Theta sorority house feels vulnerable on a campus where safety was taken for granted

Over the next few weeks, the flags that had sprung up over campus began to come down, but the wave of patriotism that swept the campus remains strong. No one felt the change more than the university's Navy ROTC students. Their captain, Dennis Hopkins, was a student at Michigan in the mid-1970s, when ROTC students "got rocks and bottles thrown at you," he says. But his students say that their non-ROTC classmates now view them with a mix of awe and curiosity. Jessica Ryu, a 21-year-old battalion commander from North Carolina, recalls a physical-fitness run across a bridge on campus with 23 other ROTC students—all wearing fatigues. "People stopped on the bridge and started clapping," she says. "Before, we were yelled at for being in the way." Ryu says it bothers her that "it took so many people to die to make others proud to be an American. I felt that from day one."

In late September, as Michigan was struggling with new realities, Bollinger was trying to figure out his own future. He was offered the presidency of Columbia University, and he and his wife, Jean, an artist and a Columbia graduate, spent long hours weighing the pros and cons of the new job. "It was extremely agonizing," he says. But September 11 actually helped tip the scales in favor of Columbia, where he'll take over next summer and where he hopes to do his part to help rebuild New York.

Two months after the attacks, many Michigan students say they're still trying to get back to "normal"—whatever that means now. At the Tau Epsilon Phi fraternity last week, headless Barbies decorated the entrance. The smell of stale beer from a Halloween party lingered in the air. But as they sat under a poster of a vo-

luptuous model, the frat boys seemed remarkably sober. Ben Weinbaum, a 19-year-old sophomore from San Diego, says many of his friends felt guilty going out and having fun. But he doesn't. "Life moves on," he says, "but moving on doesn't mean forgetting. We think about it every day." Joel Winston, a 20-year-old junior majoring in political science, says that although he'd been thinking about working for the government before September 11, he's now more sure than ever of his goal. He wants to help in a way he never imagined before. Even with a shaky economy, he says, "the government is always looking for bright people to do America's work."

Down the street, at the Kappa Alpha Theta sorority, an Arab and a Jew talked about their very different attempts to pick up their lives. The Arab, Rema Mounayer, a 20-year-old junior, was still feeling hurt after another sorority sister told her that her mother had directed her not to sit next to any Arabs on planes. She cried for days. "The fact that it happened in my own sorority killed

me," she says. Lately, she's been thinking of moving out of the sorority even though everyone in her house seems to be on her side. "I can't live in a place where I feel ashamed of who I am," she says. Mounayer says she always understood that in a diverse community like Michigan, there would be people who didn't agree with her, but she never expected to feel like an outsider.

Another sorority sister, Lee Raskin, a 20-year-old from New York's Long Island, is still mourning for her mother's best friend, a lawyer at Cantor Fitzgerald. As she chokes back tears, she says she now calls home many times a day and phones her mother at work "just to check in." When she sees a plane flying low, she worries. At the same time, she's learned to appreciate the moment. "I want to do everything now and not put anything on hold," she says. High on her list: time with her family and a trip to Australia. There's still a whole world to explore.

With JULIE HALPERT *in Ann Arbor and* PAT WINGERT *in Washington*

GETTING
the Word

Oral-history interviewing can enrich your family history and unlock your relatives' memories—if you go easy on the **who, where** *and* **when** *and focus instead on* **why, how** *and* **what.**

By Sharon DeBartolo Carmack

When I started to research my family history, I dutifully interviewed my grandmother, asking her questions like when and where she was born, the names of her parents, when and where they were born, the names and birth dates of her siblings, the names of her grandparents and when and where they were born and died. Then, as all the genealogy how-to books advised, I verified everything she told me in one record or another.

I hated doing oral history interviews. My grandmother hated being interviewed.

It was a long, long time before I tried again. By then, Grandma was gone, so I interviewed her cousin Isabel. I followed the same procedure, asking about names, dates and places. Finally Isabel had enough of my pestering for facts: "Please don't ask me any more questions," she said. "I've told you everything I know." She stopped answering my letters, and when I called she pretended I had the wrong number.

So much for quizzing relatives for genealogical data. Besides, why bother asking questions I could find the answers to in a record somewhere? What was the point?

"I learned to unlock my relatives' memories and to tap the family history that's not in the record books—people's thoughts, feelings and motivations."

Then I met a social historian who taught me a better way of doing oral history interviewing—the oral historian's way. Instead of asking *who, where* and *when*, I should have been asking *why, how* and *what*. I learned to unlock my relatives' memories and to tap the family history that's not in the record books—people's thoughts, feelings and motivations. Trust me, the census record enumerating Great-uncle Mortimer's family will still be around long after we're all dead and gone. But the sense of what life was like in the past, the memories that make a person unique, will go to the grave with that person—unless you ask the right questions.

The right questions to ask in an oral history interview go beyond "just the facts, ma'am":

- What were some of your grandfather's positive qualities?
- What about negative qualities?
- How did your grandparents meet?
- What kind of work did your grandfather do?
- What's your fondest memory of your grandfather?
- What do you think he would have wanted to be remembered for? Why?
- As you think of your grandfather, how do you remember him looking?
- How old was he then?
- What did you call him?
- What did his wife and friends call him?
- Tell me a story about your grandfather that shows what kind of a man he was.

Notice that none of these questions can be answered with a simple "yes" or "no." These questions require the person to think about the answers and will give you information that's more interesting than dry names and dates.

From who to why

When I interviewed my grandmother and poor Isabel, I was laboring under another misconception: that the right time to interview your relatives is when you're just beginning to research your family history. Actually, you should talk to relatives at least twice: once when you first begin, then again after you have gathered quite a bit of research.

The first interview should be short. Your goal is to gather the facts—names, approximate dates, places, and stories about the origins of the family—so you can begin researching in records. But don't belabor this interview, and let your relative know your limited goal. You'll be back again for more after you've done some research and found some records.

Focus the second interview on augmenting information in the records and getting historical content based on that person's life. Anything Great-aunt Esmeralda tells you about ancestors beyond her lifetime is just hearsay anyway. Concentrate on getting stories based on her own lifetime and what she remembers about the oldest people in her life.

You should prepare for this interview by thinking of questions you'll ask on events, emotions and what you found in the records, asking why did this happen, how did you feel about it, and what was it like? My favorite book for helping me to prepare questions is William Fletcher's *Recording Your Family History* (Ten Speed Press, out of print). He subdivides questions into these categories:

- family history
- childhood
- youth
- middle age
- old age
- narrator as parent
- grandchildren
- historical events
- general questions, unusual life experiences and personal philosophy and values
- questions for interviewing Jewish, black and Hispanic relatives

I use the questions Fletcher provides as a starting point, then tailor the questions to the individual I'm interviewing based on my prior or research knowledge. I write these questions out in advance, but I'm prepared to deviate if the person gives me details about a topic I hadn't considered. For example, a general question might be "Where did your father go to college?" Since I knew my subject's father went to Princeton, instead I asked her, "Did you father ever tell you stories about his Princeton years?" Even though I knew what her father did for a living, I still asked, "What kind of work did your father do?" to get her interpretation.

Getting them to talk

Before I actually begin interviews, I explain to my subjects that not all the material will be used in the family history I write and that they'll have a chance to see and approve what I write before it's published or distributed to other family members. You can't own another person's memories. Get written permission to use the material if you plan to publish or distribute parts of the interview.

interviewing
toolkit

PACKING FOR AN INTERVIEW

Before making a trip to visit and interview family members, stock a tote bag with these oral history essentials:

- Cassette tape recorder (microphone if not built in)
- Power cord
- Extension cord
- Cassette tapes and labels
- Extra batteries
- Note pad and pens
- List of questions or a book on oral history interviewing that has simple questions
- An address book to note names and addresses of relatives the person you are interviewing may give you
- Your research notebook with pedigree charts and family group sheets (you can download these from www.familytreemagazine.com/forms/download.html)
- A watch to make sure you're not overstaying your welcome
- Photocopies of any documents you've gathered to show the relative or photographs you need to identify
- Magnifying glass in case the relative needs it to view the photocopies
- Camera to photograph any documents or photographs you relative won't let you take out of the house to copy (you may also consider bringing a laptop computer and handheld scanner)

Label each tape and its storage case with identifying information:

- The person being interviewed
- The date
- The place

After the interview, immediately punch out the tab, making it impossible for someone to accidentally erase the tape or record over it.

I also try to put my interview "victims" at ease by telling them that they don't have to answer all the questions I ask. If it's too personal, just tell me. And if they later regret telling me something, they can contact me and I won't include it. This happened after an interview I did with a lady who commissioned me to write her family history. During the interview, she told me how she and her daughter didn't get along. Afterward, she had second thoughts about seeing that in print, so I left it out. Remember, you're a family historian, not someone out to write an exposé.

You can also put your subject at ease by beginning with a fun, easy question. If I know the person is also interested in genealogy, I ask how he became curious about his ancestry. Typically, fellow genealogy buffs make enthusiastic interview subjects. If I have a reluctant interviewee, however, who can't imagine why I'd want to interview him, I might begin by asking what he does for a living or about one of his hobbies or the family pet.

My aunt was one of those reluctant interviewees. She dreaded coming for a visit because she knew I wanted to interview her. By the second day, however, she informed her daughter who had come along, "You'll have to find something to do to entertain yourself. Sharon and I are going to do more interviewing because this is important, and we have to get this done." Usually, once the reluctant subject sees that I'm not asking for facts—especially about people long dead and buried—but instead for stories about her life and her memories of her parents and grandparents, the "victim" relaxes and thoroughly enjoys the attention.

An interview shouldn't last longer than an hour or two at a stretch. It's tiring for you and the person being interviewed. If you're with the relative only for a day or so, take frequent breaks during the interview, since an intensive interview like this can total six to eight hours. You may want to break up the interview with a visit to the cemetery or a walk around the old neighborhood to get more stories.

Try to interview only one person at a time, alone. People tend to talk over one another and finish each other's sentences—especially couples who've been married a lifetime—making it hard for you to keep up. If you're taping the interview, it's more difficult to transcribe or take notes from the tape with several people talking.

Ask a question, then wait and really listen to the response. Resist the urge to interrupt, to clarify a point or ask another question. Make a note and come back to it. Don't correct your subject. Even though you may have a contrary document, let your relative tell you the way he or she remembers the event and make a note of the discrepancy. Show interest in what your subject is saying by nodding, using appropriate facial expressions or occasionally saying "uh-huh."

Taping and notetaking

If the interviewee doesn't mind, it's always a good idea to tape the interview, but you should also take notes. Don't rely solely on the tape recorder. I've had recorders malfunction and lost portions of an interview because I wasn't taking notes. Recently I purchased a new tape recorder and was happily interviewing; then it dawned on me that we'd been going longer than the half hour for that side of the tape. The machine had come to the end

of the tape, but it didn't click off. My subject and I had to reconstruct about 20 minutes of the interview. If I'd been taking notes, that wouldn't have been necessary.

Videocameras:
Recording Words and Pictures

If you're recording an oral history interview with a videocamera, here are some secrets for success.

• Use a tripod for the videocamera and make sure it's placed in the least distracting spot you can find.
• If your videocamera has a light that flashes when it's recording, place a piece of black electrical tape over it. This light can be distracting to your subject and is a constant reminder that the camera is rolling.
• Pick a room that's brightly lit, or use lots of lights to ensure the best quality picture. But don't have the subject sit in front of a window, which will cause everything in front of it to photograph too dark. Do a "screen test" with the subject to make sure the lighting and sound are acceptable.
• Have visual materials ready (photographs, artifacts, historical documents) so you can get these items on the video when the narrator begins talking about them.
• Punch the tab on the tape as soon as you take it out of the camera, so it can't be accidentally recorded over with next week's "E.R."
• Make a copy of the tape and store in a cool, dry place.

Make a double-space printout of the questions you're planning to ask, then jot down answers and notes next to the questions. You'll want to verify spellings of names, places or unusual or archaic words, but do this at the end of the interview or at the end of a story—don't interrupt the speaker's flow.

Include in your notes a description of where you're conducting the interview. Detail what your subject is wearing, how she looks, whether she smiles over one question and frowns at another, how she fidgets. All these traits show personality, and unless you're videotaping, you won't get these recorded.

Audio taping, rather than videotaping, is the least intrusive to the interview. While videotaping (see box "Videocameras: Recording Words and Pictures") can capture a person's look, facial expressions and personality, some people are more intimidated by a camera than a tape recorder and behave unnaturally.

Always begin each tape with your name, the name of the person being interviewed, how you're related, the date of the interview, whether this is tape number 1 or 21, and where the interview is taking place. Also record this information on the tape or cassette case.

Getting personal

Some of the best questions to ask are personal—questions that may be slightly embarrassing or make the subject laugh or cry.

These are the questions no one has had the nerve to ask, the answers to which you won't find recorded anywhere, except maybe in a diary. Obviously, you don't want to start the interview with a question like, "So tell me what you and your husband used for birth control in the 1940s." Or, "Tell me about the automobile accident your son died in last year." Interviewing requires sensitivity and a sixth sense of what you can ask and when.

on the
bookshelf

READING ABOUT ORAL HISTORY

• *Family Tales, Family Wisdom: How to Gather the Stories of a Lifetime and Share Them With Your Family* by Robert U. Akeret (Henry Holt, out of print)
• *Transcribing and Editing Oral History* by Willa Baum (Altamira Press, $15.95)
• "Searching at Home and Talking With Relatives," in *The Genealogy Sourcebook* by Sharon DeBartolo Carmack (Lowell House, $16)
• *Oral History: From Tape to Type* by Cullom Davis, Kathryn Back and Kay MacLean (American Library Association, $46)
• *Record and Remember: Tracing your Roots through Oral History* by Ellen Epstein and Jane Lewit Lanham (Scarborough House, $10.95)
• *Recording Your Family History: A Guide to Preserving Oral History Using Audio and Video Tape* by William Fletcher (Ten Speed Press, out of print)
• *Nearby History: Exploring the Past Around You* by David E. Kyvig and Myron A. Marty (Altamira Press, $24.95)
• *Video Family History* by Duane and Pat Strum (Ancestry, out of print)
• *How to tape Instant Oral Biographies* by Bill Zimmerman (Betterway Books, $12.99, in bookstores or order direct from www.familytreemagazine.com/store)

Most out-of-print books can be obtained through bookselling Web sites such as www.amazon.com, www.bn.com or www.borders.com.

Often I'll phrase potentially embarrassing questions so they sound general, not personal: "Were many teenage girls in your day having premarital sex?" You may be shocked by the bluntness of the answer, though. One elderly lady responded to this question with, "Oh, sure, my boyfriend and I did it." Another lady told me much more about her sex life than I really wanted to know—but only after I turned off the tape recorder.

And move over, Barbara Walters—I can make the person I'm interviewing cry, too, though that's never my intention. You just never know what question may trigger an emotional response. In one interview, the question that triggered the tears

was, "Tell me how you heard World War II had begun." The tears took us both by surprise, but I just let her cry and waited while she composed herself. Uncomfortable? You bet. Hard to wait out the tears? Incredibly. Now I know how my therapist feels.

Photographs and memories

An oral history interview is the perfect time to bring along old photographs or ask your subject if he or she has any. Ask your interviewee to tell you about the people in the photograph and where and when it was taken. If your subject is also in the photo, ask if she remembers the events that led to the photograph being taken. Was it a special occasion? Did some people not want to be in the photograph? If so, who else was there? Who suggested the pose? What was the conversation before and after the photograph? Yes, these are tough questions, and it will be the rare person who can remember all these details. But it's always worth asking.

Also ask about family artifacts. My grandmother's cousin, Isabel, has the tea set my great-grandmother brought with her from Italy in 1910. I wanted to know whether it had been a wedding present or held some other special meaning and how often the set was used—on special occasions or every day. Perhaps there are interesting stories surrounding an item in your family.

Bring out photocopies of the documents you've been gathering and show them to your relatives. Isabel had never seen her name on the passenger arrival list when she came to this country. She got teary-eyed when I showed it to her, and even more excited when I gave her her own copy.

Using oral history

So what do you do with your interview materials after you leave your relative's house? First, you'll either need to transcribe your tapes or, if you didn't take notes during the interview, you should make notes from the tapes. Keeping the interview only on tape limits its usefulness to you and your descendants. Technology changes too fast, and the shelf life of an audio- or videotape is only about 10 years before it begins to deteriorate. The printed word is still the most widely used—and reliable—form of preserving history.

Transcribing entire tapes is incredibly time-consuming. To transcribe, edit and proof the transcript against the tape and make a final copy, plan to spend about 22–25 hours for every hour of an interview. I've never transcribed an oral history tape; instead, I take notes from the tape and pull particularly interesting quotes.

Once you have your notes or a transcript, you can combine information from the interview with the records you have researched and the general, relevant historical context to write a narrative account as part of the family history. Here's an example using oral history, a death certificate and historical information on tuberculosis:

Mary remembers visiting her cousin Ralph who had tuberculosis. "We used to visit him in the sanatorium. It was like a hospital, and because we were too young and it was a contagious disease, we weren't allowed to go up and see him. But he used to wave to us from the window as we played on the grounds." Tuberculosis was the leading cause of death in the 19th century and into the 20th century, when Ralph died from the disease in 1946. Not until 1882 was the tubercle bacillus identified, and doctors realized that the disease was infectious. Confining tuberculin patients in sanatoriums became popular in the late 1890s.[1]

Using footnotes or endnotes, make sure your readers and descendants know where all the information came from. For example:

[1]*Oral history interview with Mary Bart, October 31, 1997, Simla, Colo.; death certificate, Register of Deaths, Harrison, N.Y.; Sheila M. Rothman*, Living in the Shadow of Death: Tuberculosis and the Social Experience of Illness in American History (Baltimore: Johns Hopkins University Press, 1994),2, 43, 6, 179.

No source you consult while doing your genealogy is 100 percent accurate. Any record, from a birth certificate to even a tombstone, can be wrong. Oral history is no more or less reliable. Yes, memories are prone to lapses, distortions and mistakes. But it depends on the type of information you're seeking: If you're asking Great-uncle Mortimer the dates when all 12 of his brothers and sisters were born, or when they all got married, then you're also asking for trouble. If you're asking him to recount memories of the first car he owned—how did it smell? What did it feel like to get behind the wheel? What color and make was it? where did you first drive it to?—then you're on pretty safe ground.

You'll also find that talking to Great-uncle Mortimer about his memories can be personally rewarding—both for you and for your interview subject. Despite my rocky start as an oral history interviewer, I've come to really enjoy it. I now think of myself more as an oral history therapist, because it's so therapeutic for people to have my full attention for the length of the interview and to reflect on their lives and the lives of their parents and grandparents. One person I interviewed said I asked tough questions—"tough" because I made him think about his relationships, attitudes and feelings. Even though we both walked away from the interview feeling mentally drained, we felt good and knew we'd captured something that would have been lost otherwise.

As you prepare for an oral history interview, think of this African proverb: "When an old person dies, a whole library disappears." Don't let these libraries of memories disappear. With oral history interviewing, you can ensure that the why, how and what of your family's past will be remembered forever.

SHARON DEBARTOLO CARMACK is a Certified Genealogist who specializes in writing family history narrative. She is the author of *Organizing Your Family History Search* (Betterway), *A Genealogist's Guide to Discovering Your Female Ancestors* (Betterway) and *The Genealogy Sourcebook* (Lowell House).

From *Family Tree Magazine*, April 2000, pp. 29–33. © 2000 by ABM Publishing. Reprinted by permission.

What's Ahead for Families: Five Major Forces of Change

A research firm identifies key societal trends that are dramatically altering the future prospects for families in America and elsewhere.

BY JOSEPH F. COATES

No adequate theory in the social sciences explains how values change, so it is very difficult to anticipate changing social values. On the other hand, the social sciences are outstanding in reporting and exploring historic patterns of social change and in reporting contemporary social values through surveys, opinion polls, and observational research.

Identifying long-term shifts in values is complicated by the great deal of attention given to fads—that is, transient enthusiasms. A good example is "family values," a topic of great interest in recent political seasons. Both the family and values are undergoing shifts, and the challenge for futurists and other observers of social change is to identify the long-term trends and implications in both of these important areas. Social values are slowly evolving trends.

To help you understand the myriad of evolving patterns in families, this article describes several major trends and forecasts in families and values and suggests what they may imply for the future.

TREND 1

Stresses on Family Functions

The family in the United States is in transition. While the forces at play are clear and numerous, the outcomes over the next decades remain uncertain.

Anthropologists agree that the family is a central, positive institution in every society. It performs two functions: the nurturing and **socialization** of children and the regulation of the expression of **sexuality**. In European and North American society, the family serves another basic function: **companionship**. Also important are the **economic** functions of families, such as providing care for the elderly and sick and social support for unemployed members.

All of these family functions are being stressed by structural changes in society. Among the patterns that have long-term implications are:

• Increased life-spans mean that adults live well past the period in which nurturing and socialization of children is central to their lives. In many cases, longevity leads to the death of one spouse substantially before the other, creating a companionship crisis.

• Sexual behavior is increasingly being separated from its procreative function, thanks to reproductive technologies such as artificial insemination and *in vitro* fertilization, as well as contraceptives.

• New patterns of work and leisure mean that people are developing interests and activities that are different from other members of their family. In many cases, this leads to conflicting interests and expectations rather than convergence and mutual support. As a result, the companionship function of families comes under increasing stress.

• Television and magazines create images of lifestyles, which may influence people's expectations of each other and the roles of families.

• The anonymity of metropolitan life eliminates many of the social and community pressures on families. There are no watchful and all-knowing eyes in the big city that compare with those in smaller and more cohesive communities, where "What will the neighbors think?" is a critical socializing factor.

These forces will not wipe out the family or the commitment to family, but they will continue to reshape it.

Implications of Stress on Family Functions:

• **Substitutes for family functions will develop.** As family members seek other sources of companionship, and nurturing children becomes less important in matured families, institutions will have a challenge and opportunity to meet human needs. Already, people are finding companionship and even forming committed relationships on the Internet. Schools, businesses, and governments are all under more demand for meeting human services once provided in families, such as health and medical care, child care, retirement care, unemployment compensation, etc.

About the Report

This article expands on research prepared for "Social and Value Trends," the third in a series of reports by Coates & Jarratt, Inc., on critical trends shaping American business in the next 30 years.

The reports were collected under the general project title, American Business in the New Millennium: Trends Shaping American Business, 1993–2010, which was prepared for and sponsored by 15 U.S. organizations: Air Products and Chemicals, Battelle Pacific Northwest Laboratory, CH2M Hill, Discover Card Services, Dow Chemical Company, E.I. DuPont de Nemours & Company, Eastman Chemical Company, Motorola, Niagara Mohawk Power Corporation, NYNEX Corporation, Ohio Edison, Sony Corporation of America, Southwestern Bell Corporation, Goodyear Tire & Rubber, and U.S. West.

Other reports in the series covered trends in U.S. and world demography, politics, the global economy, science and technology, environment and resources, information technology, health and safety, transportation and habitats, and more.

For more information on the reports, contact: Coates & Jarratt, Inc., 3738 Kanawha Street, N.W., Washington, D.C. 20015. Telephone 202/966–9307; fax 202/966–8349.

• **Interest groups will proliferate**. Support groups have burgeoned in recent years to help people with special health or emotional problems. Similarly, special-interest groups such as book-discussion salons, travel and adventure societies, or gourmet dinner circles could see a renaissance as individuals seek others with similar interests outside their own families.

• **"Recreational sex" may become more acceptable** as the connection between sexual activity and child-bearing diminishes. Greater access to information on health and "safe sex" will allow people—including the very young and the very old—to engage in sexual activity more safely, both physically and emotionally.

TREND 2

Economics Drives Family Changes

The greatest changes in families have to do less with the family structure and more with economics. The change richest in implications is the rise of the two-income household. The United States has a way to go. Sweden and Denmark are the standards for mothers participating in the labor force. Sixty-five percent of U.S. mothers with children under age 18 are in the work force, compared with 86% in Denmark and 89% in Sweden. For children under 3, the figures are 53% in the United States, 84% in Denmark, and 86% in Sweden. Among the significant patterns emerging are:

• By 2000, women will make up just under half of the work force.

• Women are older when they marry and have their first child, deferring family formation until after they finish their education and get their first job. In 1988, the median age of mothers of firstborn children was 26, the oldest at any time in U.S. history.

• Although the average income of the family household has stayed relatively flat over the last 15 years, the growth of the two-income household is allowing couples to make a higher average income.

Enduring Family Values

(Percentage of adults saying these values are important)

Respecting your parents	70%
Providing emotional support for your family	69%
Respecting people for who they are	68%
Being responsible for your actions	68%
Communicating your feelings to your family	65%
Respecting your children	65%
Having a happy marriage	64%
Having faith in God	59%
Respecting authority	57%
Living up to your potential	54%
Being married to the same person for life	54%
Leaving the world in a better shape	51%

Source: *American Demographics* (June 1992), from the Massachusetts Mutual American Family Values Study, 1989.

Implications of Changes in Family And Economics

• **Two incomes, two decision makers**. Both breadwinning members of two-income households will have broader opportunities to start a new career or business initiative. Any change of job or relocation offer will thus affect two incomes rather than just one, making life/career planning doubly complicated.

• **Women disappear from the community**. Women's greater commitment to work means a long-term change in their commitment to home and the community. Like male breadwinners of the past, women may be rarely seen in stores, in their neighborhood, at home, and so on. In the shopping mall of the future, for instance, the only daytime customers may be the very old, the very young with their mothers or minders, and after-school teenagers.

• **A masculinization of the home** will spread to the community. Telecommuting allows one or both breadwinners of the dual-income household to work at home. Many men are choosing this option in order to be more available for domestic responsibilities such as cooking, cleaning, and chauffeuring

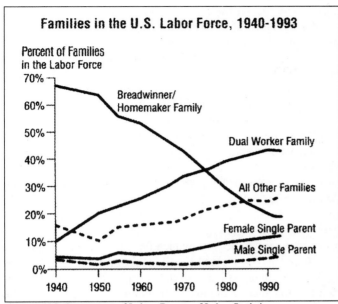

Families in the U.S. Labor Force, 1940-1993

Source: U.S. Department of Labor, Bureau of Labor Statistics.

children to various activities. Men may also increasingly become involved in volunteer activities, especially those that directly benefit their own families, such as neighborhood crime-watch groups and the PTA.

• **An economy of convenience will emerge**. A working lifestyle for most families will also continue to shape their preferences in eating, at home, for entertainment, and in shopping. Many families will be willing to pay a premium for convenience in all goods and services they purchase.

TREND 3

Divorce Continues

Divorce may be viewed as a way to correct social mistakes and incompatibility. In the 1940s, for example, there was a surge of marriage in the early 1940s as young Americans went off to war, and at the end of the war there was a surge of divorces in 1945–1947, apparently correcting impetuous mistakes. There was an even greater surge in post-war marriages.

Divorce is seen by many as the death knell of family values. On the other hand, a high divorce rate could be seen as a positive social indicator. It represents an unequivocal rejection of a bad marriage. For the first time anywhere in a mass society, the United States has had the income, the wealth and prosperity, and the broad knowledge base to allow people previously trapped in lifelong misery to reject that state and search for a better marriage. The evidence is clear, since the majority of divorced people either remarry or would remarry were the opportunity available.

Among the patterns emerging in divorce are:

• Divorce rates fell below 10 per 1,000 married women between 1953 and 1964, then surged to a high of almost 23 per 1,000 married women in 1978. Divorces have continued at about 20 to 21 per 1,000 for the last decade.

• Commitment to marriage continues, as demonstrated in the fact that the majority of divorced people remarry. One-third of all marriages in 1988 were remarriages for one or both partners. The average time until remarriage is about two and a half years.

• The shorter life-spans of many families has led to serial marriages. Almost surely there will continue to be people who have three, four, or five spouses, without any intervening widowhood. In the long term, it is much more likely that society will settle down into a pattern of later marriage, earlier sexual engagement, and much more careful and effective selection of life mates.

• **Marriages and families will be businesses**. Families may increasingly be treated as business units, which form legal partnerships and plan and evolve their own lifecycles as an integrated activity. Families may even incorporate to obtain tax and other benefits. Divorces will be handled as simple business or partnership dissolution. *[Ed. note: The rise of "families as businesses" was predicted by Lifestyles Editor David Pearce Snyder in his article, "The Corporate Family: A Look at a Proposed Social Invention," THE FUTURIST, December 1976.]*

U.S. Divorce Rate, 1940-1992

Source: National Center for Health Statistics.

• **Teenage sex—but not pregnancy—will** increase. Teenagers will observe and emulate their parents' distinct separation of sexuality and commitment.

• **Companies will share and care**. Businesses will offer their employees training in household economics and management, as well as family and divorce counseling. These courses could also be marketed as a service to the community.

• **Opportunities for marketing to new families will emerge**. Many of the families in the top income segments will include remarriages and second and third families, in which the parents will have a strong incentive to tie together the new relationships. Aiming at this concern could offer opportunities. For example, a new blended family may want financial planning

Divorce petition. Author Coates anticipates a movement to improve match-making in order to strengthen marriages and families.

and related services to reallocate its resources. Club memberships for the new family, new homes, etc., all could be important among this group.

• **A "pro-family" movement will take new directions**. One of the most important underlying causes of divorce is that no institution in the United States—school, church, Boy Scouts, or other—teaches and trains people about what it is like to be married, to live in a two-income household, or to share and be involved in a new division of domestic labor. The search for a good marriage is not supported by the right tools to aid that search. Over the next decade, society will focus more on creating more-effective families. A new "pro-family" movement will encourage better and more effective matchmaking, as well as better teaching and training on marriage lifestyles and on economic and household management.

TREND 4

Nontraditional Families Proliferate

A variety of nontraditional family forms are evolving in the United States, shaped by economic and social changes. For example, higher expectations for education mean young people

spend more years in the educational system and marry later. The greater tolerance of divorce and remarriage affects how often people dissolve and re-form families. Many people enter long-term cohabiting relationships before marriage. And many single-parent families are being formed among low- and middle-income communities, as a result of divorce, widowhood, or out-of-wedlock childbearing.

The emerging patterns include:

• More couples are cohabiting. In 1988, one-third of all women aged 15–44 had been living in a cohabiting relationship at some point.

• The number of "boomerang" families is increasing. Young people—post-high school or post-college children who would otherwise be on their own—are returning home to live with Mom and Dad. To a large extent, this is a money-saving move more commonly practiced by men than by women.

• Blended families are becoming the norm. Blended families result from divorced parents who remarry, either linking step-families together or linking the children of one partner to the subsequent children of both. It is estimated that, for nearly 16% of children living with two parents in 1990, one of those parents is a stepparent.

• Technology is creating new families. These may involve adopted children matched for similar genetic inheritance, children from surrogate parents, and eventually children from cloned embryos.

• Gay families are surfacing as a result of the new openness in society. Aside from the social approval so valuable to many in the gay community, acknowledgment offers substantial economic benefits in corporate or business health and recreation benefits packages. Time will make family resources available to members of nontraditional families.

• Group living, with or without sexual intimacy, is likely to remain a transitional life stage for an increasing number of people, often as an alternative to living alone.

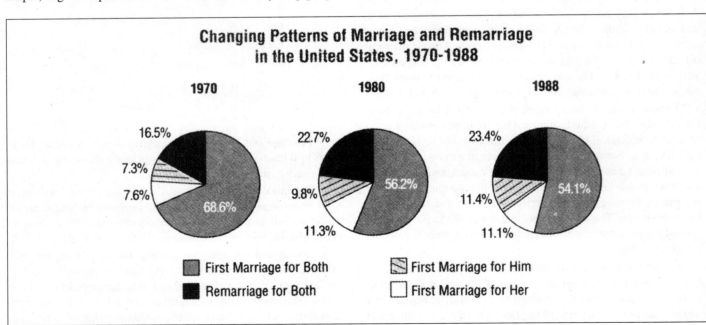

Changing Patterns of Marriage and Remarriage in the United States, 1970-1988

Source: Statistical Abstract of the United States, 1992.

• Single-parent families are increasingly common across all socioeconomic groups. The unmarried woman who bears a child is one of these family styles. It is unclear what the consequences are for middle- and professional-class mothers and children in these voluntary single-parent households. Evidence is strong that teenage childbearing, particularly by unmarried mothers, is socially destructive of the future well-being of both the mother and the child. Some single-parent families are single by divorce or separation.

Implications of the Proliferation of Nontraditional Families

• **Rearranged families will rearrange the workplace**. The work force will continue to be profoundly affected by new family structures. The proliferation of family arrangements will create new pressures on employers to be flexible and responsive in relation to working hours.

• **Businesses will make attitude adjustments**. Employers will be hard-pressed to justify accepting one type of family arrangement among their employees and not another. One company decided to offer benefits to gay couples because they could *not* get married and deny them to male-female couples living together because they *could*. Workers did not accept this justification.

• **"Nonfamily" families will gain in status**. Many groups of people consider themselves families, even though they do not fit traditional definitions (e.g., gay couples, unmarried couples with or without children, foster parents, long-term housemates, etc.). This has implications for business and nonbusiness issues, for example in marketing, housing codes and covenants, loans, billing, leasing, and so on.

• **Family-oriented organizations will reinvent themselves**. For example, Parent-Teacher Associations may broaden into Family-Teacher or Community-Teacher Associations. Schools may provide more counseling for students in nontraditional families.

• **Flexible architecture will be mandatory**. Housing will become more flexible, with walls that can be easily taken down and rearranged to form new rooms depending on the needs of new family members.

TREND 5

An Aging Society Will Redefine Families

The traditional family in past decades was the nuclear family: a working father, a homemaker mother, and children. As the children aged and left home, the traditional family was two adults with no children living at home; then one or the other died, leaving an elderly single person alone.

Aging creates a crisis in traditional families' lifecyles. The patterns to watch now include:

• Death rates of men are relatively high compared with women. Men also tend to marry women younger than themselves. As a result, at age 75 and older, 66% of men but only 24% of women are living with a spouse. At age 65, for every 100 men there are 150 women. At age 85, for every 100 men there are 260 women.

• The savings rate among working adults is now just 4.1% of personal income, compared with 7.9% in 1980; this low rate bodes ill for Americans' economic status in retirement.

• Voting rates among seniors are traditionally higher than for younger people (60.7% of those 65 years and older voted in 1994, compared with 16.5% for 18- to 20-year olds and 22.3% for 25- to 34-year olds). It is likely that the baby boomers' influence on public policy will gain strength as they approach retirement years.

Implications of Age and Family

• **The end of retirement?** A combination of several factors may lead to the end of retirement: the emotional need of seniors to feel useful when their families no longer demand their daily attention, the financial needs of seniors who didn't save enough during their working years, the improved mental and physical health of older people, and the need in businesses for skilled, experienced workers.

• **Economic priorities shift away from children**. There is already concern among the elderly about balancing their economic assets against commitments to their children. Personal savings during their working years for their kids' college education may have left them ill-prepared for retirement.

• **Parents will "boomerang" back to their kids**. Just as adult children of the 1980s and 1990s moved back into their parents' home for economic security, elderly parents in the twenty-first century may increasingly move into the homes of their grown children. "Granny flats" and mother-in-law apartments will be common additions to houses.

• **No retirement from sex**. The sexual experimentation characteristic of baby boomers' youth may be brought to their old age. New drugs and therapies, such as penile implants, will help.

• **Elders will have roommates** or form other shared-living arrangements. A substantial increase in cohabitation offers the benefits of companionship without compromising the individual's financial survival or reducing the children's inheritance. We may see some college campuses convert into retirement communities, with dorm-style living.

The Effects of Population Changes on Values

Changes in values in the United States will depend to some extent on demographic change. Social institutions will continue to be stressed when population groups such as the aging baby boomers pass through society.

The baby boomers' children, the echo generation, now number more than 80 million people; they will be an even larger generation and a bigger social force than the baby boom was. They may be expected to stress and reshape education, justice, and work in turn, beginning now and accelerating through 2005, when they reach 20 and are ready to go to work.

Through the 1990s, the young echo boomers will increase school enrollment, then college enrollment. As they reach their late teens and move into their violence-prone years, the United States could experience an increase in violent crimes after the

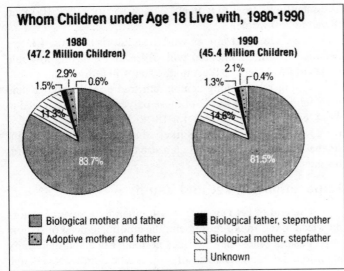

Whom Children under Age 18 Live with, 1980-1990

1980
(47.2 Million Children)

2.9%
1.5%
0.6%
11.3%
83.7%

1990
(45.4 Million Children)

2.1%
1.3%
0.4%
14.6%
81.5%

■ Biological mother and father

⠿ Adoptive mother and father

■ Biological father, stepmother

▨ Biological mother, stepfather

☐ Unknown

Source: Statistical Abstract of the United States, 1992.

turn of the century. At around the same time there may be some risk of social unrest either in universities or in cities, as the echo boom goes through its years of youthful idealism and discontent.

The aging of the baby boom in the 1990s and 2000s may push the dominant values of U.S. society to be more conservative, more security conscious, and more mature and less driven by youthful expectations. In 2010, the first of the baby boomers turn 65. If the conservatism of their elders becomes repressive, the echo boomers could have more to rebel against.

As the U.S. population grows, if the economy affords only shrinking opportunities, this may promote more conservative views. At the same time, there may be an emerging social activism around worker rights, employment stability, and related issues.

Effects of Shifting Family Patterns

As a flexible institution, the family will continue to accommodate itself to the economy and the values of the Information Age. In many societies, this means an ongoing shift to dual-income partnerships.

It has also meant a shift in what work is available for the family to earn its income—away from agriculture and manufacturing and to information and services. This shift has brought millions of women into the work force because the work now

requires education rather than raw physical might—mind, not muscle.

In many societies, men are finding it more difficult to find work unless they, too, can shift to information-based work. It is possible that women will become the higher wage earners in millions of families. It is also possible that as a result child care and family responsibilities will be more equally distributed between men and women.

People will continue to want to be part of families, but for some the economic necessity to do so will be less. For example, young people will need to spend more time in acquiring their education, and they will form their families later. Women with substantial careers will have less economic need to remarry after divorce.

Education, prosperity, and a decline in regard for authority will continue to secularize U.S. society, but concern for the family and community will tend to promote ties with religion. The church will continue to be a source of support for those who feel in some way disadvantaged by current values and attitudes. The other attractions of religion are its rituals, its shared experiences, its mysteries, and its social events. These will continue to bring in and keep people in religious groups, unless urban society develops some alternatives.

Conclusion: Belief in the Family Remains High

Anticipations of family life have not diminished to a significant degree in the last decades. In general, Americans are committed to the family as the core of a successful life. It is particularly gratifying to see this view widely maintained by young people. The percentage of college freshmen saying that raising a family is "essential" or "very important" has been fairly constant in the past quarter century: 67.5% in 1970 and 69.5% in 1990.

Adults' commitment to the family has become somewhat tempered by the higher likelihood of divorce. But most people still agree that being happily married and having a happy family is an important goal.

About the Author
Joseph F. Coates is president of Coates & Jarratt, Inc., 3738 Kanawha Street, N.W., Washington, D.C. 20015. Telephone 202/966–9307; fax 202/966–8349. This article is based on the "Social and Value Trends" section of a major report by Coates & Jarratt for its clients, *American Business in the New Millennium: Trends Shaping American Business, 1993–2010*. The author acknowledges the assistance of Christine Keen of the Domani Group and the team support of Jennifer Jarratt, John Mahaffie, Andy Hines, Andrew Braunberg, Sean Ryan, and Nina Papadopoulos of Coates & Jarratt, Inc.

NEWS YOU CAN USE

Happiness Explained

New science shows how to inject real joy into your life

BY HOLLY J. MORRIS

There's an ancient tale of happiness that appears in many cultures, and it goes something like this: Once there was a prince who was terribly unhappy. The king dispatched messengers to find the shirt of a happy man, as his advisers told him that was the only cure. They finally encountered a poor farmer who was supremely content. Alas, the happy man owned no shirt.

Ahhh, happiness. Ineffable, elusive, and seemingly just out of reach. For most of the 20th century, happiness was largely viewed as denial or delusion. Psychologists were busy healing sick minds, not bettering healthy ones. Today, however, a growing body of psychologists is taking the mystery out of happiness and the search for the good life. Three years ago, psychologist Martin Seligman, then president of the American Psychological Association, rallied colleagues to what he dubbed "positive psychology." The movement focuses on humanity's strengths, rather than its weaknesses, and seeks to help people move up in the continuum of happiness and fulfillment. Now, with millions of dollars in funding and over 60 scientists involved, the movement is showing real results. Far from being the sole product of genes, luck, delusions, or ignorance, happiness can be learned and cultivated, researchers are finding.

CONTENTMENT

WHAT IT IS: Feeling safe and calm.

WAYS TO GET IT: A friendly, nonthreatening environment is key. If you're not so lucky, relaxation exercises may mimic the body's response to contentment. **Rebecca Shaw** finds it in marriage to Ray Shaw, and in her two children, Christian, 3, and Sierra, 2—and by not putting up with mean people.

Decades of studying depression have helped millions become less sad, but not necessarily more happy—a crucial distinction. When you alleviate depression (no mean task), "the best you can ever get to is zero," says Seligman, a professor at the University of Pennsylvania. But "when you've got a nation in surplus and at peace and not in social turmoil," he explains, "I think the body politic lies awake at night thinking about 'How do I go from plus 2 to plus 8 in my life?'"

Indeed, people in peaceful, prosperous nations aren't necessarily getting any happier. Though census data show that many measures of quality of life have risen since World War II, the number of people who consider themselves happy remains flat. And people are 10 times as likely to suffer depression as those born two generations ago. Researchers have scads of information on what isn't making people happy. For example, once income provides basic needs, it doesn't correlate to happiness. Nor does intelligence, prestige, or sunny weather. People grow used to new climates, higher salaries, and better cars. Not only does the novelty fade but such changes do nothing to alleviate real problems—like that niggling fear that nobody likes you.

Happiness helpers. Scientists also know what works. Strong marriages, family ties, and friendships predict happiness, as do spirituality and self-esteem. Hope is crucial, as is the feeling that life has meaning. Yes, happy people may be more likely to have all these things at the start. But causality, researchers find, goes both ways. Helping people be a little happier can jump-start a process that will lead to stronger relationships, renewed hope, and a general upward spiraling of happiness.

The average person has a head start. Decades of international survey research suggest that most people in developed nations are basically happy. This tendency toward mild cheerfulness may have evolved to keep peo-

CHANGE

WHAT IT IS: What you need when your goals aren't satisfying you.

WAYS TO GET IT: Figure out why what you're doing isn't working. **Allison Waxberg**, a scientist in the cosmetics industry, wanted more creativity in her life. She took art classes, realized she had talent, and now attends Brooklyn's Pratt Institute.

ple moving—glum ancestors would have moped, not mobilized.

Some have more of a head start than others. University studies of twins suggest that about half of one's potential for happiness is inherited. Researchers think happiness is influenced not by a single "happy gene," but by inborn predispositions toward qualities that help or hinder happiness, such as optimism or shyness. And personality doesn't fluctuate that much over an average life span. People seem to have "happiness set points"—base lines that mood drifts back to after good and bad events.

There's a lot of wiggle room on either side of that base line, though. Most positive psychologists refer to a set range. "If you're a more gloomy, pessimistic person, you're probably never going to be really deliriously happy, but you can get into the high end of your possible range and stay there," says psychologist Ken Sheldon of the University of Missouri.

Michael Lee, too, believes happiness can be learned. "You practice it day in and day out," says the 28-year-old marketing director from San Jose, Calif. He has always been pretty happy but has seen his joy grow. A Catholic, he started a faith-sharing group with childhood friends. Under guidance from Jesuit priests, they learned to take time each night to reflect on the positive in their everyday lives—"subtle things like meeting a new person… or kids sitting out in the yard playing." In cultivating his appreciation of the routine, and surrounding himself with other happy people, Lee grew happier. Boosting your happiness isn't always easy, though: Moving up within your range can mean working against your inborn personality traits, learned thinking habits, environment, or all three. But the latter two can change. "If you want to keep your happiness at the higher end of the set range," says Sonja Lyubomirsky, a psychologist at the University of California-Riverside, "you have to commit yourself every day to doing things to make you happy."

One way is to find the right goals and pursue them. Sheldon's research suggests that goals reflecting your interests and values can help you attain and maintain new levels of happiness, rather than returning to base line. By setting and achieving a progression of goals, you can boost your well-being. Even when you fail, you can better

MOOD MEASUREMENT
How happy are you? Find out

One way scientists measure happiness is by simply asking people to evaluate their overall satisfaction with their lives. This scale of life satisfaction was developed by psychologist Ed Diener of the University of Illinois-Urbana-Champaign and is used worldwide to gather data on happiness. The scoring at the bottom shows how you compare with other Americans.

Taking the test
For each of the five items below (A-E), select an answer from the 0-to-6 response scale. Place a number on the line next to each statement, indicating your agreement or disagreement with that statement.
6: Strongly agree
5: Agree
4: Slightly agree
3: Neither agree or disagree
2: Slightly disagree
1: Disagree
0: Strongly disagree

A _____ Your life is very close to your ideal.
B _____ The conditions of your life are excellent.
C _____ You are completely satisfied with your life.
D _____ So far you have obtained the important things you want in your life.
E _____ If you could live your life over, you would change nothing.
_____ TOTAL

26 to 30: Extremely satisfied, much above average
21 to 25: Very satisfied, above average
15 to 20: Somewhat satisfied, average for Americans
11 to 14: Slightly dissatisfied, a bit below average
6 to 10: Dissatisfied, clearly below average
0 to 5: Very dissatisfied, much below average

maintain that higher level next time you reach it, though you'll probably top out at the high end of your range.

Allison Waxberg, 30, wasn't miserable and wasn't depressed—but she wasn't especially happy, either. After six years as a skin scientist in the cosmetics industry, she longed for more-creative work. "I grew up drawing, but I always felt like I had to do something like be a doctor or a lawyer or something professional," she says. When people feel they have no choice in the goals they pursue, they're not going to be satisfied. Goals that derive from

GAGGLE OF GIGGLES

Laughter as its own punch line

Peals of laughter cut through the persistent early-morning drizzle at Seattle's Green Lake Park. As passers-by gape—and then grin—four men and women titter, giggle, chortle, and guffaw, in what looks like a yoga class gone goofy. Led by energetic Stephanie Roche, they alternate rhythmic chanting and clapping with penguinlike waddling and pretend sneezing—all while howling with laughter. There's no punch line; there's not even a joke. This is a laughing club, one of at least 20 begun in the United States this year. They are held in parks, churches, and often in nursing homes, where the gentle cheer is especially welcome.

Laughing clubs are an export from India, where they're familiar sights in hundreds of neighborhoods. Invented by physician Madan Kataria in 1995, the clubs don't rely on humor or jokes. Rather, they focus on the act of laughing, which releases stress and promotes deep, healthy breathing. At first, the ha-has and hee-hees can be forced. Eye contact is required, which helps break the ice. But few can resist breaking into spontaneous laughter during the "lion laugh"—

stick out your tongue, google your eyes, and use your hands as paws. "Sometimes people have to fake it," says psychologist Steve Wilson, 60, of Columbus, Ohio, whose World Laughter Tour trains laughter-club leaders. "And then it flips and it just becomes hysterical."

Roche's laughing club started a mere two weeks ago. After she saw a documentary, *The Laughing Club of India*, at a Seattle film festival (it airs August 28 on Cinemax), she became a "certified laughter leader" at one of Wilson's workshops. She patterned her club after the Indian versions, holding it in a neighborhood park three days a week at 7 a.m. Clubs are encouraged to create their own laughs: Wilson can reel off a long list of obscure ones, such as the "airline safety instruction laugh," in which you gesture at exits and don an imaginary oxygen mask. The Seattle group is already customizing. Karen Schneider-Chen, a 49-year-old jail outreach worker, mimics raindrops with fluttering fingers. "We're working on a Seattle rain laugh," she says.

—H.J.M., *with Bellamy Pailthorp in Seattle*

FLOW

WHAT IT IS: The state of intense concentration that occurs during challenging, goal-directed activities.

WAYS TO GET IT: Flow can arise from pastimes, like playing sports or music, but also from reading and good conversation. College sophomore **Jason Vincens** finds flow in competitive wrestling.

fear, guilt, or social pressure probably won't make you happier, even if you attain them. "Ask yourself, 'Is this intrinsically interesting and enjoyable?' If it isn't, do I at least believe in it strongly?" says Sheldon. "If I don't, why the hell am I doing it?"

Waxberg tried a series of jobs, including making prosthetic limbs, but had yet to combine her technical and creative sides. Finally, she took some art classes and proved to herself that she had talent. She's now earning an industrial design master's from Brooklyn's Pratt Institute, where she has won acclaim for her ceramics, and is doing her thesis on skin. She hopes to start a new career as a design consultant this year.

For Waxberg, finding the right goal was key—but first she had to figure out why the old ones weren't working. The trick is to know what kind of goals you have. Diffuse

goals, such as "be someone," are next to impossible to achieve. More-concrete goals ("get a job") that relate back to the abstract goal ("be a success") are more satisfying. That also goes for the goal of "being happy." "You'll be happier if you can get involved in things and do well at them, but don't be thinking too much about trying to get happier by doing them," says Sheldon. "It's really kind of Zen in a way."

Out with the bad. Another path to greater happiness is cultivating positive emotions. They're good for more than warm fuzzies: Good feelings broaden thinking and banish negative emotions, says Barbara Fredrickson, a psychologist at the University of Michigan. Negative emotions narrow thought, by necessity. Ancestors didn't have time to sift through creative escape options when fears loomed. But positive emotions open new routes for thinking. When researchers induce positive emotions, thinking becomes more expansive and resourceful.

Most people can't feel positive emotions at will. But you can approach events in a way that gets them going, then let momentum take over. Jay Van Houten made a decision to see the positive when faced with a potentially fatal brain tumor. The 54-year-old business manager from Boise, Idaho, listed the benefits, such as "a built-in excuse for not hearing things like 'Please take out the trash,' " as the surgery left him deaf in one ear.

Though laughing at yourself is fleeting, Fredrickson believes such moments have lasting consequences. "Pos-

HIGHS AND LOWS

Taking one's happy temp

Scientists also measure happiness with "experience sampling," in which mood is assessed on multiple occasions over time. With Palm devices that beeped at random intervals, two *U.S. News* writers answered questions such as "How pleasant are you feeling?" several times a day for a week. Researcher Christie Scollon of the University of Illinois analyzed the data. The red and orange lines combine positive and negative emotions to show overall mood. Person A is happier than the average American—she feels more positive than negative emotions. Person B is unhappier than most—and she's moody. She feels a log of bad along with the good. This illustrates an important notion: Feeling good is more than just not feeling bad.—H.J.M.

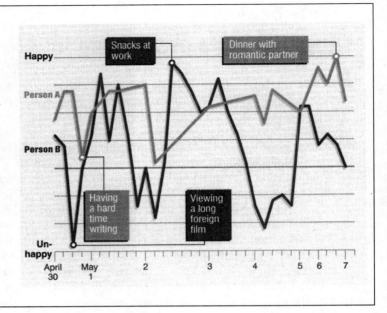

PERSPECTIVE

WHY GET IT: It helps peolple see the good in their lives when things are going badly.

WAYS TO GET IT: Comparing one's situation with a worst-case scenario really can make people feel better. After a potentially fatal brain tumor, not much fazes **Jay Van Houten** these days. ...he volunteers with the mentally and physically disabled.

itive emotions and broadened thinking are mutually building on one another, making people even more creative problem-solvers over time, and even better off emotionally," she says. Coping with one problem well—as Van Houten did with humor—may make people more resilient next time trouble comes along. Van Houten says he's much happier now, especially as nothing seems as bad as a potentially fatal brain tumor. After his surgery, he had to relearn balance. "I still drill into the ground if I turn too fast," he says. "You've got to approach it with a certain amount of humor to get you through the day."

Using humor to feel better works because thinking can't be both narrow and broad. To test this idea, Fredrickson had subjects prepare a speech, then let them off the hook. As they calmed, she showed them video clips that sparked various emotions: a puppy playing with a flower (joy), ocean waves (contentment), a scene from the 1979 tear-jerker *The Champ* (sadness), and a computer screen-saver (neutral). Those who felt joy and contentment calmed down faster. This doesn't mean you should think about puppies when you're down (though if it helps, go for it), but that when you've done all you can

about a problem, a positive distraction can banish lingering bad feelings.

One of the worst enemies of positive emotions is feeling threatened, says Fredrickson. A safe environment is key. Rebecca Shaw found that happiness just needed a chance to flourish. "The day I met my husband was the day my boyfriend broke up with me, and I was pregnant," says the 32-year-old of Ridge, Md. Miserable, lonely, and despairing, she had just moved back in with her parents to get her bearings. Then she ran into an old friend, Ray Shaw. As they spent time together in the following weeks, happiness "stole up" on her. "Suddenly I was just smiling and didn't even realize it—it was just such a subtle turn," she says. Now, four years after their marriage, the defense contractor, inventor, and stay-at-home mom doubts she could be happier. "My husband didn't replace any of the things that were missing," she says. "He just kind of gave me the sanctuary to go and find them myself."

Part of seeking positive emotions is being open to them in everyday life. Mindfully approaching sources of good feelings can be more lasting than seeking instant gratification. Distinctions can disappear. "Overeating ice cream and shopping get lumped in with spending time with your family or pursuing an interesting activity," says Fredrickson. People may choose shortcuts with little meaning over activities with positive consequences. A more nuanced appreciation of good feelings—"experiential wisdom," Fredrickson calls it—may help people benefit more from positive emotions. So think: Is ice cream really going to make me feel better for longer than the time it takes to eat it?

Some emotions simply aren't that hard to feel, if you take the time. Take gratitude. Robert Emmons of the University of California-Davis found that people who wrote down five things for which they were grateful in weekly or daily journals were not only more joyful; they were healthier, less stressed, more optimistic, and more likely to help others. You don't have to write things down to be grateful for them, of course, though it helps to make them concrete. During difficult times, "I just tend to focus on the things I'm grateful for and the parts of life that are good," says Sean David Griffiths, 38, a project officer at the Centers for Disease Control and Prevention in Atlanta. And gratitude could help ward off mindless materialism, says Emmons. "When you don't appreciate stuff is when you get rid of it and get something else."

Researchers are also finding more positive emotions than once were thought to exist. Anyone who has witnessed a touching good deed will recognize the heartwarming tingling in the chest that follows. Psychologist Jonathan Haidt of the University of Virginia dubbed this uplifting emotion "elevation," and finds that it makes people want to be kind. Such emotions break down mental barriers and help people see the world in new ways. Even mild feelings of elevation can change minds. Haidt found that students who watched a documentary about Mother Teresa were more interested in activities like volunteer work. (In contrast, the subjects who watched clips of *America's Funniest Home Videos* were interested in self-focused activities like watching TV and eating.)

The feeling of hope is one reason spirituality may correlate with well-being. Hope fosters optimism, and faith is, by definition, hope for the future. And the churchgoing form of faith can be a built-in social support network. This is not to say that atheists can't be happy, but it helps explain why so many do find happiness in faith, and why researchers continue to find connections between faith, optimism, and physical health.

Teaching positive. Nurturing optimism is a key way to help hope and happiness flourish. Optimism predisposes people toward positive emotions, whereas pessimism is a petri dish for depression. Over 20 years ago, Seligman and his colleagues developed a method to teach optimism by helping people recognize and dispute inaccurate thoughts. Called "learned optimism" (and outlined in the book of the same name), they found it could inoculate against depression as well. Teaching optimistic thinking styles to middle schoolers lowered the occurrence of depression as the children aged. Even optimistic children grew happier. "These are sticky skills," says Karen Reivich, codirector of the Penn Resiliency Project. "Once you start using them, you feel better, and you keep using them."

The skills of learned optimism are based on findings that pessimists blame themselves for problems, figure they will last forever, and let them invade every corner of their lives. Good events are freak occurrences. Optimists look for outside causes of bad events and assume they will be fleeting—but take credit for good events and bet they'll keep happening. (Because optimism tends to act as a self-fulfilling prophecy, they often do.) By learning new ways to explain events, pessimists can become more optimistic and more resilient, leaving them better equipped to appreciate the good and cope with the bad. Today, these skills are taught in Pennsylvania schools by teachers trained through Adaptiv Learning Systems, which also offers a more grown-up version to the corporate world.

One of the most positive states of all is easy enough to come by—if you're willing to concentrate. Dubbed "flow" by psychologist Mihaly Csikszentmihalyi, director of the Quality of Life Research Center in Claremont, Calif., it's the single-minded focus of athletes and artists, scientists and writers, or anyone doing anything that poses a challenge and demands full attention. People in flow are too busy to think about happiness, but afterward they think of the experience as incredibly positive. And it's followed by well-earned contentment.

People find flow in myriad ways—any hobbyist or athlete can tell you that. "The secret to my happiness isn't a secret at all," says 19-year-old Jason Vincens, a sophomore at the University of Illinois. "I found something I love and I'm doing it." He has been wrestling competitively since sixth grade. When he wrestles, he doesn't worry about anything else. Afterward, he doesn't have the energy. But you don't have to take up tennis or the violin to find flow: A discussion with good friends can do the trick.

The paradox of flow is that many people have it, but don't appreciate it. Csikszentmihalyi is endlessly puzzled that adults and teenagers feel more creative and excited while working but would rather be doing something else. "I think it's basically a set of assumptions for many people, that work is something that we do simply for our paycheck," he says. So rather than enjoy it, people tend to rush home and watch TV, which rarely provides much pleasure. It's the same principle that causes people to put off activities they enjoy, but which require effort, such as swimming laps.

With age, serenity. Wait around if you must, as some research suggests that people grow happier with age. You don't have to the high highs of youth, but neither do you have the low lows. Older people often pursue goals less out of guilt or social pressure and more for their own satisfaction. Also, age often brings wisdom, which adds depth to happiness. You could think of happiness growing out, rather than up.

And yet the stereotype that happy people are shallow persists. "Me being a chronically happy person doesn't mean that I haven't had some real down spells," says Lars Thorn, 24, who works in marketing in Manchester, Vt. During a difficult breakup, he told a friend he was feeling terrible. "And she said, 'Oh, no you're not—you're Lars!'" he recalls. "I was perceived as being a cardboard cutout of a person with no real emotion." But new research suggests happy people may be more realistic than unhappy folks. Psychologist Lisa Aspinwall of the University of Utah finds that optimists are more open to negative information about themselves than pessimists.

Positive mood gives them the resources to process bad news. Optimists are also more likely to accept what they cannot change and move on, says Aspinwall. Indeed, she says, they have an intuitive grasp of the Serenity Prayer, which asks for the wisdom to know the difference between what one can and cannot change.

There's no disputing that positive psychology's findings echo the exhortations of ancient wisdom, and let's face it—Oprah. Be grateful and kind and true to yourself. Find meaning in life. Seek silver linings. But then, what did you expect—be mean to children and animals?

So are people just not listening to their grandmothers and gurus? Psychologist Laura King of the University of Missouri has found that people at least say they know these things and consistently rate meaning and happiness above money. But in a study with colleague Christie Scollon, she found that people were all for meaning, yet most said they didn't want to work for it. Other evidence echoes her findings: People *say* one thing but do another. "One of the problems," says King, "might be that people don't understand that lives of happiness and meaning probably involve some hard work."

Will people work to learn happiness? Positive psychologists think that if they can tease out the best in people, happiness will follow. To Seligman, happiness is "the emotion that arises when we do something that stems from our strengths and virtues." And those, anyone can cultivate. "There's no set point for honesty," he says. The idea that happiness is the sum of what's best in people may sound suspiciously simple, but it's a whole lot easier than finding that happy man's shirt.

SPIRITUALITY

WHAT IT DOES: People with some form of spirtual belief (not just religion) are often happier and more optimistic.
WHY IT WORKS: Possibly because it can promote hope and social support. **Michael Lee** started Lighthouse, a faith-sharing group. ...he prays with his wife, **Agatha Chung**, at a meeting.

Article 47

Examining Family Rituals

Grace M. Viere
James Madison University

In this column, the notion of rituals from a historical perspective is provided. The definitions and classifications of family rituals as well as empirical studies are examined.

Family rituals, originating as a belief in mystical powers, have evolved into a vital component of family life that transcends race, culture, and socioeconomic levels. Researchers and practitioners have begun to incorporate family rituals into a variety of studies and therapeutic practices. This article reviews the definition and meaning of rituals and implications of family rituals for the health and well-being of families.

Rituals Defined

Anthropologist Victor Turner (1967) originally defined *ritual* as a "prescribed formal behavior for occasions not given over to technological routine, having reference to beliefs in mystical beings or powers" (p. 19). Turner's definition emphasizes symbols as the building blocks of rituals. The significance of symbols is explained in the following three areas: the ability to carry multiple meanings and thus contribute to the open parts of rituals, the ways symbols can link several disparate phenomena that could not be joined as complexly through words, and the ability of symbols to work with both the sensory and cognitive poles of meaning simultaneously.

Moore and Myerhoff (1977) suggested that the anthropological study of ritual has often been limited to religious and magical aspects of a culture partly because anthropologists have often worked in societies "in which everything has a religious significance" (p. 3). As societies become more secular, they continue to carry within them beliefs that have a similar role in society as religion. Moore and Myerhoff stressed the impor-

tance of recognizing the sacredness of these beliefs and the rituals carried out around them. Their definition of *sacred* reaches beyond the traditional religious definition to focus on "specialness" or "something colored with meaning beyond the ordinary."

Rappaport (1971) also suggested that the term *ritual* is not limited to religious practices. He described the following six key aspects to ritual of which family rituals are a part:

1. repetition: not necessarily just in action but also of content and form,
2. acting: not just saying or thinking something but also doing something,
3. special behavior or stylization: where behaviors and symbols are set apart from their usual common uses,
4. order: some beginning and end and containment for spontaneity.
5. evocative presentational style: where through staging and focus an "attentive state of mind" is created,
6. collective dimension: where there is social meaning.

Van Gennep (1960) developed three stages of rituals. In the first stage, separation, special preparations are made and new knowledge is passed on as the frame is set for marking a particular event. This time of preparing for the ritual is as important a part of the ritual process as the actual event itself. The second stage is transitional, in which people actually partake of the ritual and experience themselves in new ways and take on new roles. The third stage is reintegration, in which people are reconnected to their community with their new status. Ritual is not just the ceremony or actual performance but the whole process of preparing for it, experiencing it, and reintegration back into everyday life.

RITUALS IN FAMILIES

Wolin and Bennett (1984) viewed family ritual as a "a symbolic form of communication that, owing to the satisfaction that family members experience through its repetition, is acted out in a systematic fashion over time". They identified six typologies of ritual use in families. First is underritualized, in which families neither celebrate nor mark family changes nor join much in larger societal rituals. This underutilization leaves the family with little access to some of the benefits of ritual such as group cohesion, support for role shifts, and the ability to hold two dualities in place at the same time. Second is rigidly ritualized, in which there are very prescribed behaviors, a sense of "we must always do these things together in this way at this time." There are few open parts in the rituals, and rituals tend to stay the same over time rather than evolving. Third is skewed ritualization, in which one particular ethnic tradition in the family, or religious tradition, or even one particular side of the family has been emphasized at the expense of other aspects of the family. Fourth is hollow ritual as event, not process. This takes place when people celebrate events out of a sense of obligation, with little meaning found in either the process or the event. This may happen because rituals have become too closed or end up creating undue stress for family members. Fifth is ritual process interrupted or unable to be openly experienced. This occurs after sudden changes (e.g., death, moving, and illness) or traumatic events in the family or larger culture (e.g., war oppression and migration). Families may be unable to fully experience the whole ritual process. And finally, flexibility to adapt to rituals is the ability to change rituals over the life cycle, keeping the rituals meaningful for families and reworking roles, rules, and relationships.

Despite differences among families in terms of factors such as socioeconomic status, ethnic background, and religious orientation, the following four types of rituals are universal to nearly all families: family celebrations, family traditions, family life cycle rituals, and day-to-day life events that have become ritualized (Wolin & Bennett, 1984).

Family celebrations are defined as rituals that are widely practiced around events that are celebrated in the larger culture. Through larger cultural expectations, the society to some extent organizes the time, space, and symbols of these rituals. Examples include Passover and Christmas. Family traditions are less anchored in the culture and are more idiosyncratic to the family, based on what might be called an inside instead of an outside calendar. Anniversaries, birthdays, family reunions, vacations, and so on all fall into this category. Although the practice of traditions is influenced to some extent by the culture, the individual family determines which occasions it will adopt as traditions and how these activities will be enacted. Family life cycle rituals include weddings, showers, christenings, graduations, and retirement parties. These are events that mark the progression of the family through the life cycle. Rituals of daily family life, such as dinnertime, bedtime, and recreation, are those events that are infused with meaning as the family creates its roles, rules, and norms. Day-to-day rituals are the least deliberate and consciously planned of the family rituals as well as the

least standardized across families, the most variable over time, and the most frequently enacted.

Family rituals provide the family and individual members with a sense of identity by creating feelings of belonging (Bennett, Wolin, & McAvity, 1988; Fiese, 1992). Rituals are the occasions during which family members transmit family values and beliefs (Steinglass, Bennett, Wolin, & Reiss, 1987), reinforce the family's heritage (Troll, 1988), and recognize change in the family (Wolin & Bennett, 1984).

All families experience crisis or stress, and rituals have the capacity to provide families stability during these time (Cheal, 1988). For example, with a funeral wake or sitting Shiva, there are certain prescribed times for mourning. Groups of people meet to support and comfort each other in their sorrow, foods are shared, specific clothes may be worn, and certain words are said. Families draw comfort from knowing they can experience strong feelings of grief with some circumscribed limits and group support (Scheff, 1979).

Rituals can hold both sides of a contradiction at the same time. All individuals live with the ultimate paradoxes of life/death, connection/distance, ideal/real, and good/evil, and rituals can incorporate both sides of contradictions so that they can be managed simultaneously. For example, a wedding ceremony has included within it both loss and mourning and happiness and celebration. Parents give their child away at the same time they welcome another member into their extended family.

Ritual Versus Routine

Steinglass et al. (1987) described the following five types of family rituals that clearly distinguish between family rituals and daily routines: (a) bounded rituals, which are prepared with anticipation and have a clear beginning, middle, and end; (b) identifiable rituals, in which families are aware of their rituals and can clearly describe the organization and patterning of these behaviors; (c) compelling rituals, which families make rigorous efforts to maintain; (d) symbolic rituals, which are associated with meanings and strong emotions; and (e) organizing rituals, which are major regulators of stability for family life.

Although routines are observable and repetitious family behaviors that are important in structuring family life, they lack the symbolic content and the compelling, anticipatory nature that rituals possess (Keltner, Keltner, & Farren, 1990). Routines are activities that family members have to do rather than want to do. Routines have the potential to acquire ritual status if they exceed their functional purpose and become filled with psychological intensity and symbolic meaning (Boyce, Jensen, James, & Peacock, 1983). Conversely, rituals that lose meaning or become mundane may take on routine status for families. Sometimes family members simply outgrow a ritual. Another distinction that can be made between ritual and routine is the capacity of rituals to serve several distinct functions for the family that are symbolically important for the psychological well-being of the family system. Rituals are powerful organizers of behavior within the family system that provide the family with a sense of stability, a unique identity, and a means for socializing children within their cultural context.

Empirical Studies on Family Rituals

Systematic research on family rituals has focused on family risk conditions such as alcoholism and points of family transition such as becoming parents. Beginning in the 1970s, Wolin and Bennett began a series of studies examining the relationship between family rituals and alcoholism. In the first study, the relationship between ritual disruption and alcohol transmission was examined. The researchers hypothesized that families with more intact rituals would be less likely to transmit alcoholism in the next generation. Ritual disruption was assessed using the family ritual interview, focusing on the effect of the alcoholic parent's drinking behavior on family rituals. *Subsumptive* families, in which alcohol use had overridden and effectively controlled the practice of family rituals, were identified, as were *distinctive* families, in which the practice of family rituals remained distinct from alcohol use. The families in which alcohol had subsumed family ritual practice were more likely to have children who developed problematic drinking or married individuals with alcohol problems (Wolin, Bennett, Noonan, & Teitelbaum, 1987). Furthermore, protective factors were identified in the study of individuals raised in alcoholic households. When children of alcoholics chose spouses with highly developed nonalcoholic family rituals, there was less likelihood of developing an alcoholic family identity. The second protective factor was a distinctive dinner ritual in which children from alcoholic families whose parents preserved the dinner ritual had a higher likelihood of a nonalcoholic outcome (Bennett, Wolin, Reiss, & Teitelbaum, 1987).

Fiese (1992) found similar evidence for the role of family rituals in protecting children from the effects of family alcoholism. Using the Family Ritual Questionnaire and self-report measures of problematic drinking and health symptomatology, it was noted that the adolescents who reported meaningful family rituals in addition to parental problematic drinking were less likely to develop anxiety-related health symptoms than adolescents reporting parental problematic drinking and relatively hollow family rituals. The results from these studies suggest that under potentially stressful child-rearing conditions, such as parental alcoholism, family rituals may serve a protective function. In setting aside family gatherings as distinct from alcoholic behavior and in imbuing meaning and deliberateness in the practice of patterned family interactions such as dinnertime, the child may develop an identity of the family that is separate from the disruptions associated with alcoholism.

Family rituals may also serve a protective function during periods of normative family transitions. The transition to parenthood has been identified as a potentially stressful period for couples. A study of 115 married couples found that couples with preschoolers who were able to practice meaningful family rituals reported more marital satisfaction than those who reported relatively hollow family rituals (Fiese, Hooker, Kotrary, & Schwagler, 1993).

Two empirical studies investigated family rituals in families of children with disabilities. Gruszka (1988) examined families of children with mental retardation. She found that mothers of these children perceive that their families engage in fewer family celebrations than mothers of children who did not have any disabilities. Another study (Bucy, 1995) investigated rituals and parenting stress and their relationship to the disability characteristics of preschool children. Bucy (1995) found parents of preschool children with social skill deficits or motor impairments practice more religious and cultural family rituals than families of preschool children with cognitive delays. Furthermore, mothers of preschool children with disabilities that maintained meaningful participation in family rituals evidenced better abilities to cope with parenting stress than did mothers with less ritual participation.

SUMMARY

Rituals both reflect and shape the way people think about themselves and their world. Papp (1983) suggested rituals have a unique ability to "address themselves to the most primitive and profound level of experience" (p. vii)—the level where resistance lies and where real change often begins.

Family rituals provide the family and individual members with a sense of identity by creating feelings of belonging. Rituals are the occasions that serve to facilitate social interaction among family members so that families can transmit cultural and normative information as well as beliefs and values across generations. All families experience crisis or stress, and rituals have the capacity to provide families stability during these times. Rituals may provide a way for people to find support and containment for strong emotions. Families may be encouraged to examine their family rituals and continue those rituals that are working for them as well as to develop new rituals and adapt those that are no longer valued.

REFERENCES

Bennett, L. A., Wolin, S. J., & McAvity, K. J. (1988). Family identity, ritual and myth: A cultural perspective on life cycle transition. In C. J. Falicov (Ed.), *Family transitions* (pp. 211–234). New York: Guilford.

Bennett, L. A., Wolin, S. J., Reiss, D., & Teitelbaum, M. A. (1987). Couples at risk for transmission of alcoholism: Protective influences. *Family Process, 26,* 111–129.

Boyce, W., Jensen, E., James, S., & Peacock, J. (1983). The family routines inventory: Theoretical origins. *Social Science Medicine, 17,* 193–200.

Bucy, J. E. (1995). An exploratory study of family rituals, parenting stress, and developmental delay in early childhood. *Dissertation Abstracts International, 57*(2A), 575.

Cheal, D. (1988). The ritualization of family ties. *American Behavioral Scientist, 31,* 632–643.

Fiese, B. H. (1992). Dimensions of family rituals across two generations: Relations to adolescent identity. *Family Process, 31,* 151–162.

Fiese, B. H., Hooker, K. A., Kotrary, L., & Schwagler, J. (1993). Family rituals in the early stages of parenthood. *Journal of Marriage and Family, 55,* 633–642.

Gruszka, M. A. (1988). Family functioning and sibling adjustment in families with a handicapped child. *Dissertation Abstracts International, 50*(OB), 748.

Keltner, B., Keltner, N. L., & Farren, E. (1990). Family routines and conduct disorders in adolescent girls. *Western Journal of Nursing Research, 12,* 161–174.

Moore, S. F., & Myerhoff, B. G. (1977). (Eds.). *Secular ritual.* Amsterdam: Van Gorcum.

Papp, P. (1983). Preface. In O. Van der Hart (Ed.), *Rituals in psychotherapy: Transition and continuity* (pp. v–ix). New York: Irvington Publications.

Rappaport, R. A. (1971). Ritual sanctity and cybernetics. *American Anthropologist, 73,* 59–76.

Scheff, T. J. (1979). *Catharsis in healing, ritual, and drama.* Los Angeles: University of California Press.

Steinglass, P., Bennett, L. A., Wolin, S. J., & Reiss, D. (1987). *The alcoholic family.* New York: Basic Books.

Troll, L. E. (1988). Rituals and reunions. *American Behavioral Scientist, 31,* 621–631.

Turner, V. (1967). *The forest of symbols: Aspects of Ndembu ritual.* Ithaca, NY: Cornell University Press.

Van Gennep, A. (1960). *The rites of passage.* Chicago: University of Chicago Press.

Wolin, S. J., & Bennett, L. A. (1984). Family rituals. *Family Process, 23,* 401–420.

Wolin, S. J., Bennett, L. A., Noonan, D. L., & Teitelbaum, M. (1987). Disrupted family rituals: A factor in the intergenerational transmission of alcoholism. *Journal of Studies of A!coholism, 41,* 199–214.

Grace Viere, *Ph.D., is an assistant professor of counselor education at James Madison University in Harrisonburg, VA. Her current research interests include the examination of the relationship between family rituals and attachments and the use of family rituals by families with children who are adopted.*

From *The Family Journal: Counseling and Therapy for Couples and Families,* July 2001, pp. 285-288. © 2001 by Sage Publications, Inc. Reprinted by permission.

Our earliest relationships are irreplaceable, and we pay a steep price for severed ties. But if you value a person and the memories you share, says the author, you can...

RECONNECT WITH YOUR FAMILY

Resolve to change the patterns of personal hurt that lie at the heart of too many family gatherings.

BY DR. JOYCE BROTHERS

THANKSGIVING IS almost here, and Christmas and Chanukah are waiting in the wings. What could be better than planning to celebrate with our families?

But while the turkey may be perfect, your family's behavior may not be: Siblings snipe at one another, grandparents lose their patience, cousins drift off to watch TV, feuding relatives pout, and every single trait that ever annoyed you about a particular family member makes an appearance.

Even if you've had this experience, you may well be trying again this year, because hope springs eternal when it comes to holidays and families. You can be more effective if you understand why things sometimes go awry at holiday time and what you can do about it.

THE DEEPEST TIES

After the recent attacks on our country, all of us have been left with a heightened awareness of the preciousness of family ties: In its aftermath, fathers, mothers, sisters, brothers, uncles and aunts felt compelled to check on the well-being of relatives wherever they were and to reaffirm their love.

Thanksgiving dinner can be a time to cement relationships and foster warmth among young and old.

Indeed, even if families fail us in some ways, they're still the greatest influence on our lives. A decade ago, some therapists advised breaking away from families that were "toxic." Today, it's believed that it's best to stay connected, unless a family is very dysfunctional or abusive. There's a high emotional price for maintaining a "non-relationship," says family therapist Monica McGoldrick, author of *You Can Go Home Again.* Severed family ties cannot be replaced by lovers, children, friends or work, she maintains. A part of your spirit remains buried.

If you want to reconnect as a family, you first need to think about why problems arise.

GHOSTS AT THE HOLIDAY TABLE

Family get-togethers are crowded with ghosts—memories, relatives who are no longer alive and, particularly, old patterns of behavior. All strike at the way people relate to one another. Here are some unwelcome "guests" that can show up:

• *Sibling warfare.* There's no age limit on sibling rivalry. I was once at a Thanksgiving dinner where two elderly sisters were among the guests. The older sister passed around photos of her new grandchild. When they reached the younger sister, who had no grandchildren, some soup just happened to spill on them. Since childhood, the sisters had had a close but competitive relationship. The older sister thought her parents favored the younger one. The younger sister resented her sister's tendency to show off. Did the younger sister brush her hand against the soup plate? Who knows?

• *Childhood revisited.* "It doesn't matter how old I get," a friend said. "When I walk through my parents' door on Christmas Eve, I feel like a little girl again." She experiences the old anxiety of needing to please her parents. She becomes anxious and hypersensitive, interpreting a remark like "you've done something to your hair" as criticism.

• *Parental discontent.* A family gathering can provide the perfect opportunity for subtle propaganda from parents who haven't lost hope of getting an adult child to live up to their expectations. Any single daughter who's had to smile sweetly while a parent asks, "Are you dating anyone special?" knows what I mean.

• *Hidden hurt.* Years ago, Cousin Bob invited the family to a barbecue but neglected to invite Uncle Fred, whom he thought was out of town. Fred didn't ask the reason for the slight but, to this day, has carried a grievance against Bob. At some level, Fred enjoys nursing the grudge. He doesn't realize that his feelings put a damper on all family relationships.

• *Outsider syndrome.* Families don't always alter their traditions to accommodate newcomers. There may be family jokes that never get explained or a favorite dish that's always served. Even timing can be an issue. I know a family that enjoys a slow-paced Thanksgiving, but the daughter-in-law, who's used to a much faster celebration, feels impatient and left out.

MAKE A COMMITMENT TO RECONNECT

Personal hurt is at the heart of every family holiday gone wrong. But you can make things better. Here's how:

• *Ask, "Is it worth it?"* Think hard. If you value the individual with whom you're having difficulties, if there are happy mem-

TEN WAYS TO HEAL A FAMILY FEUD

A good mediator for family disputes can be a counselor, a spiritual advisor or a respected family member, such as yourself. If you're acting as a go-between, here are some steps you can take:

1 DON'T WAIT. If your family feud is like most, enough time has gone by.

2 MEET IN A NEUTRAL BUT COZY PLACE, such as your home. A restaurant or other public place is not a good idea.

3 MAKE IT CLEAR THAT YOU WON'T PLAY FAVORITES. Neither side should question your neutrality.

4 ESTABLISH A COMFORT LEVEL. Chat about the weather or a movie—anything to get the participants relaxed.

5 ASK HOW THE CONFLICT BEGAN. You'll often find that people don't remember, which means the issue has dissipated in some way. If so, you can say: "Well, I guess we can go on from here then."

6 REPHRASE THE QUARREL. If a feud no longer makes sense, rephrasing can drive home the point. For example, "Are you saying that at Thanksgiving 10 years ago she said you weren't entitled to Grandma's jewelry, and you've been angry ever since?"

7 ASK EACH TO SEE THE OTHER'S VIEWPOINT. Once the quarrel seems less serious, it's easier for the participants to do this.

8 SHARE HAPPY MEMORIES from a time when the relationship was positive. Ask each person to state at least one good quality about the other.

9 LOOK TO THE FUTURE. Point out that the clock is running. Why be alone at age 80? Time is short for all of us.

10 SETTLE FOR SATISFACTORY. Recognize that you won't attain a perfect level of reconciliation. Accept cordiality for starters. If the parties agree to talk to one another and attend the same family events, you've accomplished a lot.

ories and positive ties, it's probably worth working on the situation.

• *Analyze the problem* so that it does not sneak up and surprise you at the family gathering. Let's say you have a sister whose "helpful" advice somehow makes you feel terrible. She may suggest that you take the turkey out of the oven sooner than planned, so it doesn't get overdone the way it did last year. She might point out the lint on your jacket so you can brush it off. Ask yourself, "Why does she have the ability to push my buttons?" You may find that her ability to annoy is fueled by your own insecurities.

• *Evaluate whether it's possible for the person to change.* If so, take the initiative, particularly if you've been on the outs. Send a note, or phone and make an appointment to meet.

• *Sit down and talk.* The fundamental rule, says Monica McGoldrick, is: Don't attack and don't defend. Also, don't be judgmental. Instead, describe the situation from your perspective. For example, "I know you want to be helpful, but I feel hurt when you keep pointing out what I'm doing wrong." Limit your remarks to a few minutes and give the other person equal time to respond. Then try to recap what was said: "Are you saying that you'll try to give me less advice this year?" If the person is a sibling, you can point out that you don't have to compete for your parents' love anymore. And add an expression of affection: "We may have had our difficulties, but I'm so glad you're my sister. Let's keep on talking."

Get everyone involved in sharing old traditions and creating new ones.

TRANSFORM THE RELATIONSHIP

Reaching out is vital, but so is looking within. Altering your own point of view can free both of you from harmful patterns of behavior. Try to:

• *Change the interaction.* You can neutralize a problem simply by changing your response. Rather than becoming annoyed at an overbearing sister, for example, thank her for the advice but state firmly that you are in control of what needs to be done. Then move on to another subject. Before a family gathering, visualize the new interaction. Practice letting annoyances float away.

• *Walk in the other person's shoes.* It helps to see the situation as complex and not only aimed at you. Generally, troublesome family members don't feel too good about themselves. If you think about the factors contributing to their behavior, you may

be able to develop a sense of empathy. Empathy not only lowers your blood pressure, it also drains away anger.

• *Lower expectations.* Because feelings run so strong, we tend to be harder on family members than on others. Pretend that your family is a group of people you've never met before. You might find that you're less critical.

• *Value the payoffs.* Siblings grow closer through the years, no matter what their early relationship, according to Dr. Victor Cicirelli of Purdue University, who studied the sibling relationships of 300 older men and women.

• *Forgive, forgive, forgive.* Nothing brings families together faster than forgiveness. That should make it Step No. 1, but most of us find forgiving hard. We associate it with weakness and losing when, actually, the reverse is true. When you forgive, you gain strength and come out a winner. You break free of control by the other person's actions. You also free your body of the great stress that anger inflicts.

MAKE A FEAST OF RECONNECTION

Let's say you've resolved the differences between you and a family member. Now make your gathering a true feast of reconnection for the entire family.

If you're the host, you can ask for suggestions to make your time together easier and more fun. If you're talking to a family newcomer—a daughter-in-law, for example—you can say, "We have our ways of doing things, but I know you must have family traditions too. Is there something you'd like us to include?" Just posing the question creates a welcoming attitude.

Write down the ideas you receive. A common suggestion is that everyone shares in bringing food or cleaning up.

You may be surprised at the extent of the interest in the family's past. One friend of mine asked family members to bring along their favorite family pictures. After the Thanksgiving meal, the family had a grand time looking at previous celebrations, some dating back 30 years. Photos remind the family that they are, and always will be, connected.

Ask your family genealogists to distribute copies of the family tree and recount the family history. Or ask everyone to bring along items of family memorabilia—a great-grandparent's citizenship papers, for example. Even prosaic objects can testify to family history. I know a woman who always puts her grandmother's grater on the family Chanukah table, even though the grater has long since been replaced by a food processor for making potato pancakes. And remember, special crafts made by a child, such as a crepe-paper turkey centerpiece, are the makings of new "memorabilia."

Always emphasize the transition from the old to the new. The older generation can tell family stories as the young generation writes them down or records them with a tape recorder. By linking the two generations, you stress family continuity.

Welcome ideas for new rituals. They can be as simple as recounting the stories behind the ornaments on the Christmas tree, deciding to plant a flower each time a family member achieves something important or reading something inspirational at the holiday table.

Talk about ways to keep the family together after the holiday—even beyond telephone calls, e-mail and videotapes. A family newsletter, created with a computer-publishing program, can include photos, birth announcements and family history. Be sure to divide the cost of printing and mailing among family members, so that no one feels overly burdened and there are no hurt feelings.

Or create a family Web page at sites such as *www.myfamily.com* or *www.familybuzz.com*. They allow you to share photos, post news, chat online, exchange e-mail and even store the family tree.

Technology has made it easy for families to keep in touch, but the real connection begins in the heart. Joyful families send out vibrations that touch friends and neighbors and even reach across the globe. Pope John Paul II said it best: "As the family goes, so goes the nation and so goes the whole world in which we live." Happy holidays.

From *Parade*, November 4, 2001, pp. 4-7. © 2001 by Dr. Joyce Brothers. Reprinted by permission.

Index

Index

Test Your Knowledge Form

We encourage you to photocopy and use this page as a tool to assess how the articles in *Annual Editions* expand on the information in your textbook. By reflecting on the articles you will gain enhanced text information. You can also access this useful form on a product's book support Web site at *http://www.dushkin.com/online/*.

NAME: _____   DATE: _____

TITLE AND NUMBER OF ARTICLE: _____

BRIEFLY STATE THE MAIN IDEA OF THIS ARTICLE:

_____

LIST THREE IMPORTANT FACTS THAT THE AUTHOR USES TO SUPPORT THE MAIN IDEA:

_____

WHAT INFORMATION OR IDEAS DISCUSSED IN THIS ARTICLE ARE ALSO DISCUSSED IN YOUR TEXTBOOK OR OTHER READINGS THAT YOU HAVE DONE? LIST THE TEXTBOOK CHAPTERS AND PAGE NUMBERS:

_____

LIST ANY EXAMPLES OF BIAS OR FAULTY REASONING THAT YOU FOUND IN THE ARTICLE:

_____

LIST ANY NEW TERMS/CONCEPTS THAT WERE DISCUSSED IN THE ARTICLE, AND WRITE A SHORT DEFINITION:

We Want Your Advice

ANNUAL EDITIONS revisions depend on two major opinion sources: one is our Advisory Board, listed in the front of this volume, which works with us in scanning the thousands of articles published in the public press each year; the other is you—the person actually using the book. Please help us and the users of the next edition by completing the prepaid article rating form on this page and returning it to us. Thank you for your help!

ANNUAL EDITIONS: The Family 03/04

ARTICLE RATING FORM

Here is an opportunity for you to have direct input into the next revision of this volume.
We would like you to rate each of the articles listed below, using the following scale:

1. **Excellent: should definitely be retained**
2. **Above average: should probably be retained**
3. **Below average: should probably be deleted**
4. **Poor: should definitely be deleted**

Your ratings will play a vital part in the next revision.
Please mail this prepaid form to us as soon as possible.
Thanks for your help!

RATING	ARTICLE	RATING	ARTICLE
	1. The American Family		36. The Happy Divorce: How to Break Up and Make Up
	2. The Myth of the "Normal" Family		37. Divorced? Don't Even Think of Remarrying Until You Read This
	3. Weighing the Price of 'Perfect' in Family Life		38. When Strangers Become Family
	4. American Families Are Drifting Apart		39. Elder Care: Making the Right Choice
	5. Sex Differences in the Brain		40. Still Birth
	6. The New Woman: Daring to Be Less Than Perfect		41. After a Loss, Kids Need to Mourn—and Be Reassured
	7. The Feminization of American Culture		42. Breaking Free of the Family Tree
	8. Can Men and Women Be Friends?		43. Generation 9-11
	9. What's Your Love Story?		44. Getting the Word
	10. Love Is Not All You Need		45. What's Ahead for Families: Five Major Forces of Change
	11. Sex for Grown-Ups		46. Happiness Explained
	12. Making Time for a Baby		47. Examining Family Rituals
	13. Too Posh to Push?		48. Reconnect With Your Family
	14. Shaped by Life in the Womb		
	15. Our Babies, Ourselves		
	16. The Science of a Good Marriage		
	17. No Wedding? No Ring? No Problem		
	18. Welcome to the Love Lab		
	19. New Evidence for the Benefits of Never Spanking		
	20. Family Matters		
	21. Who's Raising Baby?		
	22. Father Nature: The Making of a Modern Dad		
	23. What About Black Fathers?		
	24. Unmarried, With Children		
	25. Adoption by Lesbian Couples		
	26. Why We Break Up With Our Siblings		
	27. The Importance of Partners to Lesbians' Intergenerational Relationships		
	28. Hitting Home		
	29. Sex & Marriage		
	30. Is Your Dog (Cat, Bird, Fish) More Faithful Than Your Spouse?		
	31. The Politics of Fatigue: The Gender War Has Been Replaced by the Exhaustion of Trying to Do It All		
	32. What Kids (Really) Need		
	33. The Binds That Tie—and Heal: How Families Cope With Mental Illness		
	34. Marriage and Divorce American Style		
	35. Is Divorce Too Easy?		

(Continued on next page)

ABOUT YOU

Name _____ Date _____

Are you a teacher? ☐ A student? ☐
Your school's name _____

Department _____

Address _____ City _____ State _____ Zip _____

School telephone # _____

YOUR COMMENTS ARE IMPORTANT TO US!

Please fill in the following information:
For which course did you use this book?
_____

Did you use a text with this ANNUAL EDITION? ☐ yes ☐ no
What was the title of the text?
_____

What are your general reactions to the *Annual Editions* concept?
_____

Have you read any pertinent articles recently that you think should be included in the next edition? Explain.
_____

Are there any articles that you feel should be replaced in the next edition? Why?
_____

Are there any World Wide Web sites that you feel should be included in the next edition? Please annotate.
_____

May we contact you for editorial input? ☐ yes ☐ no
May we quote your comments? ☐ yes ☐ no